The radical resurgence of Christianity in non-Western societies has continued to engender creative paradigms and models. Global Pentecostal movements remain one of the most enduring manifestations of this remarkable spiritual zeitgeist. This edited volume presents a robust account of Africa's indelible contributions to this remarkable phenomenon. It is historical, contextual, and theological. It is a welcome addition to the literature of African Christianity that continues to grow like a pole masquerade. This is a path-breaking and ambitious study of a topic that is germane to theological studies, missions, church history, and cross-cultural engagement.

—Akintunde E. Akinade
Professor of Theology, Georgetown University in Qatar,
Edmund A. Walsh School of Foreign Service

It is quite rare to find scholarly material that explores Christianity beyond the "dead," mechanical, cerebral, and ritualistic forms that had been accepted as orthodox in the world. It is even harder to read an extensively researched book that supplies an objective, balanced, and incredibly insightful look at the spirituality of original Christianity and God's plan to reach the world through indigenous Holy Spirit movements in Africa. I have not only learned from, but have also been challenged by, this book. *Global Renewal Christianity: Spirit-Empowered Movements Past, Present, and Future, Volume 3: Africa* is one of the most thorough works on African Pentecostalism I have ever read!

—Most Rev. Dr. Charles Agyinasare
Presiding Bishop, Perez Chapel International,
Chancellor, Pan African Christian University College, Ghana

This fine edited volume transports the reader to the various regions of Africa, introducing the Renewalist movements from Egypt to Ethiopia and Nigeria to Namibia and Malawi to Mozambique. In this multidisciplinary collection, the reader will encounter debates about the African origins and character of African Pentecostalism, expositions on the contextual theologies of African Pentecostalism, and explorations of the transnational currents within African Renewalist movements. For years to come, I believe that this book will be consulted in serious studies on Pentecostal, Charismatic, and neo-Charismatic movements in Africa.

—David D. Daniels III
Henry Winters Luce Professor of World Christianity,
McCormick Theological Seminary, Chicago, Illinois

This remarkable and insightful volume consists of a rich collection of essays on Pentecostalism on the African continent written by diverse scholars from a critical theological and historical perspective. Pentecostal/Charismatic Christianity has today become the new "mainline" church tradition in Africa. This is, therefore, essential reading for scholars and students in African Christianity and anyone interested in learning more about this fascinating Spirit-empowered phenomenon and Africa's fastest growing religious movement.

—Philomena Njeri Mwaura
Associate Professor and Director of the Centre for Gender
Equity and Empowerment,
Kenyatta University, Kenya

This book offers the reader a compelling account of the histories, theologies, and mission of Pentecostal/Charismatic movements in Africa. This comprehensive and sympathetically objective collection of essays by predominantly African scholars makes a significant contribution to the study of African Pentecostalism. Students of African Christianity will find it an indispensable resource.

—Cephas N. Omenyo
Professor of African Christianity and Mission, University of
Ghana, and Professor Extraordinary, Faculty of Theology,
University of Stellenbosch, South Africa

VOLUME THREE
AFRICA

GLOBAL RENEWAL Christianity

VINSON SYNAN, AMOS YONG,
and J. KWABENA ASAMOAH-GYADU

EDITORS

CHARISMA HOUSE

Most Charisma House Book Group products are available at special quantity discounts for bulk purchase for sales promotions, premiums, fund-raising, and educational needs. For details, write Charisma House Book Group, 600 Rinehart Road, Lake Mary, Florida 32746, or telephone (407) 333-0600.

Global Renewal Christianity: Spirit-Empowered Movements Past, Present, and Future, Volume 3: Africa by Vinson Synan, Amos Yong, and J. Kwabena Asamoah-Gyadu, Editors
Published by Charisma House
Charisma Media/Charisma House Book Group
600 Rinehart Road
Lake Mary, Florida 32746
www.charismahouse.com

Cover design by Lisa Rae McClure
Design Director: Justin Evans

Visit the Empowered21 website at http://empowered21.com/.

Library of Congress Cataloging-in-Publication Data:
An application to register this book for cataloging has been submitted to the Library of Congress.
International Standard Book Number: 978-1-62998-768-2
E-book ISBN: 978-1-62998-937-2

First edition

16 17 18 19 — 9 8 7 6 5 4 3 2 1
Printed in Canada

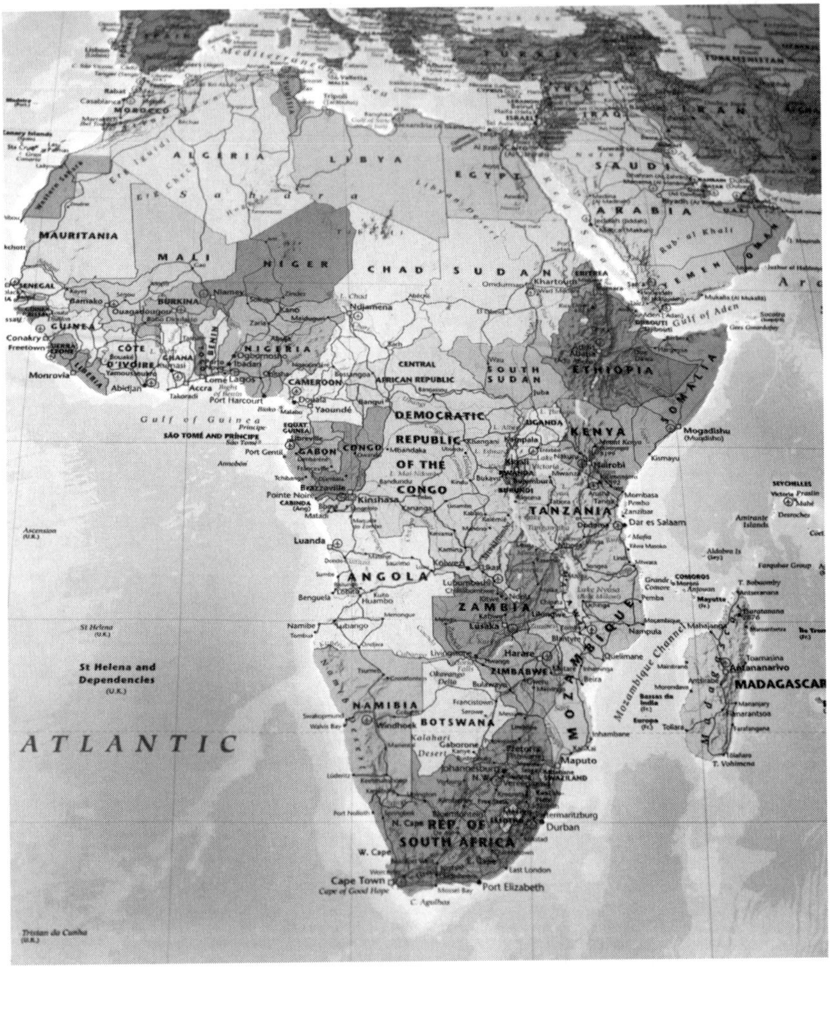

ALGERIA
LIBYA
EGYPT
MAURITANIA
MALI
NIGER
CHAD
SUDAN
SENEGAL
BURKINA
GUINEA
SIERRA LEONE
LIBERIA
CÔTE D'IVOIRE
GHANA
BENIN
NIGERIA
CAMEROON
CENTRAL AFRICAN REPUBLIC
SOUTH SUDAN
ETHIOPIA
SOMALIA
ERITREA
DJIBOUTI
UGANDA
KENYA
DEMOCRATIC REPUBLIC OF THE CONGO
CONGO
GABON
EQUAT. GUINEA
SÃO TOMÉ AND PRÍNCIPE
RWANDA
BURUNDI
TANZANIA
ANGOLA
ZAMBIA
MALAWI
MOZAMBIQUE
ZIMBABWE
NAMIBIA
BOTSWANA
SWAZILAND
LESOTHO
REP. OF SOUTH AFRICA
MADAGASCAR
SEYCHELLES
COMOROS
SAUDI ARABIA
YEMEN
OMAN
IRAQ
IRAN
TURKEY
SYRIA
ISRAEL
TURKMENISTAN
MOROCCO
SPAIN
Western Sahara
Sahara
Libyan Desert
Kalahari Desert
Mediterranean Sea
Red Sea
Gulf of Aden
Gulf of Guinea
Mozambique Channel
ATLANTIC
St Helena and Dependencies (U.K.)
St Helena (U.K.)
Ascension (U.K.)
Tristan da Cunha (U.K.)
Casablanca
Rabat
Dakar
Bamako
Ouagadougou
Niamey
Conakry
Freetown
Monrovia
Abidjan
Accra
Takoradi
Lomé
Lagos
Ibadan
Ogbomosho
Port Harcourt
Douala
Yaoundé
Malabo
Libreville
Port Gentil
Ndjamena
Bangui
Khartoum
Omdurman
Juba
Kampala
Nairobi
Mombasa
Mogadishu (Muqdisho)
Kismayu
Dar es Salaam
Dodoma
Kinshasa
Brazzaville
Pointe Noire
Luanda
Benguela
Huambo
Namibe
Lubumbashi
Lusaka
Harare
Blantyre
Beira
Nampula
Quelimane
Maputo
Windhoek
Walvis Bay
Gaborone
Francistown
Pretoria
Johannesburg
Durban
Pietermaritzburg
East London
Port Elizabeth
Cape Town
Cape of Good Hope
C. Agulhas
Antananarivo
Toamasina
Mahajanga
Victoria
Okavango Delta
Lake Victoria
Lake Nyasa (Lake Malawi)

Contents

Part III: Southern Africa

Part IV: Select Theological Themes

Foreword

THE WORK OF the Holy Spirit around the world in our lifetime is changing the face of global Christianity. The prayer movements from across Asia, to worship in Africa and Latin America, to church revitalization in Europe and North America and the masses being evangelized daily worldwide give evidence that a significant spiritual shift has taken place. At the heart of this shift are millions of Spirit-empowered believers. This volume of exceptional scholarly analysis, one of four on the global Spirit-empowered movement, helps bring definition, understanding, and depth to the dynamic work that God is doing today.

Spirit-empowered, or renewalist, Christianity continues to expand exponentially. As this growth takes place, the depth of the movement and a clear twenty-first-century hermeneutic must also grow. Isaiah 54:2 provides prophetic encouragement for this increased depth by stating, "Enlarge the place of your tent, and let them stretch out the curtains of your habitations; spare not, lengthen your cords, and strengthen your stakes" (MEV).

As the tent of Spirit-empowered Christianity grows, the stakes of theological understanding must also deepen. This will allow the movement to withstand the twenty-first-century storms that will rage against us while sheltering those believers in this ever-enlarging tent.

Empowered21 is committed to serving the broad spectrum of Spirit-empowered Christianity including Pentecostals, Charismatics, and every subsequent wave of Holy Spirit expression in the body of Christ. It is with deep gratitude to our editors, Dr. Vinson Synan, Dr. Amos Yong, and Dr. J. Kwabena Asamoah-Gyadu, that we publish this exciting volume of essays with the hope that God will use this work to indeed "deepen our stakes" for the exciting days ahead.

My prayer is that as you absorb this material, God's presence will overshadow you so you may personally experience the Holy Spirit, who is moving globally today.

Serving a movement, empowering a generation,

—Dr. William M. Wilson

President of Oral Roberts University

Global Cochair of Empowered21

Foreword

In his vision, John the Revelator saw "a great multitude which no one could count, from all nations and tribes and peoples and tongues, standing before the throne and before the Lamb, clothed with white robes, with palm branches in their hands. They cried out with a loud voice: 'Salvation belongs to our God who sits on the throne, and to the Lamb!'" (Rev. 7:9–10, MEV).

What was for John a revelation of the end times is increasingly for us a picture of the present. No longer is it possible—if, in fact, it ever was!—for Western Christians to speak of the faith of Jesus Christ as a European and North American faith. Instead, we must speak of global Christianity, for the faith has gone out from Jerusalem to the ends of the earth (Acts 1:8).

In the last one hundred years, global Pentecostalism has been used by God to advance the good news of the kingdom of God within every nation, tribe, people, and language. The volume you are reading is proof of that. It is one of four volumes assaying the past, present, and future of global Pentecostalism.

I said that John's end-times vision is "increasingly" a picture of the present for us, but that adverb reminds us that there is still work to do. May God use this scholarly volume to inform and inspire a new generation of Spirit-empowered leaders to take the good news about His Son into every global nook and cranny, so that today's unreached may become tomorrow's white-robed, palm-waving praisers of Jesus Christ! Then, and only then, will John's vision be realized in full.

—Dr. George O. Wood
General Superintendent of the Assemblies of God (USA)
Chairman of the World Assemblies of God Fellowship
Global Cochair of Empowered21

Series Preface

The Empowered21 movement had its origin in a vision given to Robert Fisher concerning a fitting celebration of the centennial of the Azusa Street revival that began in 1906. To plan for the event, Fisher organized the Center for Spiritual Renewal in 2000 in Cleveland, Tennessee. Unfortunately he passed away before the event took place, and his friend Billy Wilson was asked to complete the plans for the celebration and lead the conference. The celebration, which met in the Staples Center in Los Angeles in April of 2006, was a resounding success as more than fifty thousand persons attended the various events that were celebrated in several Los Angeles venues.

After the Azusa Street celebration in 2006, the center began a connection with Oral Roberts University (ORU) when Wilson and his friend Mart Green were chosen to lead the Board of Trustees of the university. From this association came a vision for another meeting on the campus of ORU. Although the meeting was under the auspices of ORU, the Center for Spiritual Renewal was chosen to administer the event. Called the "Global Congress on Holy Spirit Empowerment," the Tulsa meeting drew ten thousand persons to the campus in April 2010.

In preparing for the Tulsa meeting, Mart Green and his associates conducted a broad ranging survey of the young people of the next generation to find out what term best described the Pentecostal/Charismatic renewal in their minds. In the end the word *empowered* won out over the terms "Pentecostal,"

"Charismatic," or "full gospel." Also, since everyone wanted to look toward the future instead of the past, the numeral 21 was added, referring to the twenty-first century. Thus the term "Empowered21" (or E21) was born.

The vision statement of Empowered21 is powerful and pointed: "That every person on earth would have an authentic encounter with Jesus Christ through the Power and Presence of the Holy Spirit…by Pentecost 2033." Its mission statement proclaims that: "Empowered21 will help shape the future of the Global Spirit Empowered movement throughout the world by focusing on crucial issues facing the movement and connecting generations for intergenerational blessing and impartation." Thus the major focus is on what is called the "Nextgen" (next generation) in order to continue the "spiritual grace" of the Pentecostal/Charismatic renewal into future generations. Underlining all the efforts of this vision is a prayer for a "fresh outpouring of the Holy Spirit in the twenty-first century." These themes have permeated all the events and planning sessions of E21 from the beginning.

At the early years of the E21 movement Wilson led seventeen unique "conversations" with some five hundred church leaders and scholars from fifty-four nations and fifteen universities with the goal of answering the questions "What does it mean to be Spirit empowered in the twenty-first century?" and "What steps can be taken to engage new generations in the Spirit-filled experience?" Armed with the wealth of knowledge from these conversations, E21 conducted two major events on university campuses. The first was the aforementioned Global Congress on Holy Spirit Empowerment, which drew ten thousand persons to Oral Roberts University in April 2010 where 210 workshops produced a futuristic book edited by Vinson Synan titled *Spirit-Empowered Christianity in the 21st Century* (Charisma House, 2011). The second was a meeting at Regent University in 2012 in conjunction with the Society for Pentecostal Studies, which emphasized the "convergence" of Spirit-empowered generations and movements. More than five hundred leaders registered for this event.

During this time the E21 movement was organized on an international scale with a global cabinet and eleven regional cabinets around the world. Included in these groups were leaders from most of the Pentecostal and Charismatic movements in the world. The first global gathering after the American events at ORU and Regent University was the E21 Asia Congress held in Jakarta, Indonesia, in October 2011, which drew some fifteen thousand persons.

Other plans for the future include worldwide celebrations on Pentecost Sunday each year to celebrate the birthday of the church and the outpouring of the Holy Spirit in the Upper Room (Acts 2). On Pentecost Sunday 2012 many thousands gathered in local celebrations around the world. Totally ecumenical, the vision is to see Pentecost Sunday rise to the level of Easter and Christmas as great days to make a common witness to the world.

An important part of the E21 vision has been to gather scholars from around the world to study the past, present, and future of the Empowered movements on every continent and from as many nations as possible. To accomplish this goal, three meetings convened before the final one in Jerusalem in 2015. One was held in Oxford, England, in 2012 under the leadership of Dr. Harold Hunter. Another took place in Sydney, Australia, in 2013, where the focus was on Asia. Vinson Synan and Amos Yong directed this latter consultation and those that followed. The third meeting was in Quito, Ecuador, in 2014, where the focus was on Latin America. The last meeting of scholars was in Jerusalem in 2015 in the culminating congress where thousands of people gathered for one of the largest Christian meetings held in the Holy Land in modern times. Here the scholars read papers focusing on Africa, North America, and Europe.

In the end, four volumes of the papers read in these gatherings will be published and edited by Synan and Yong. They will be on Asia, Africa, Latin America, Europe, and North America, and will be published by Charisma House in Lake Mary, Florida. Many of the papers published in these volumes were initially presented in the above-mentioned conferences and consultations, but not all. Those who could not attend the conferences or consultations were invited to write specifically for the project. Most of the chapters across the volumes were intended thus to be read, although a few were written to be presented and heard and have retained their oral character (which will be easily identifiable as such in what follows). In all cases, scholars with a PhD or its equivalent and a recognized publication record were invited, although in a good number of cases our first choices were not able to participate because of other commitments or circumstances. In most cases, scholars are also personal participants in Pentecostal, Charismatic, or renewal movements, although again, not all. In any of the latter cases, of course, authors were invited because of their recognized capacity to present and discuss Pentecostal/Charismatic movements with sympathetic objectivity.

This mix of both confessional Pentecostal/Charismatic "insiders" and "outsiders" may result for some readers in a certain sense of unevenness as they move from chapter to chapter in each volume. Some writers write more from a first-person perspective, while others remain more distant. A few approached their task more pastorally, while many more academically, in overall orientation. Last but not least, many of the latter remain more descriptive in their approach while others are more normative with regard to the theology, practice, and mission of Spirit-empowered churches and communities. The editors hope that such a combination of voices, stances, and dispositions will introduce readers to the broad spectrum of Pentecostal/Charismatic scholarship. "Outsiders" might come to appreciate the animating concerns of Pentecostal/Charismatic scholars who are in touch with pastoral and ecclesial realities and challenges, while readers who are lay and ecclesial leaders, pastors, and bureaucrats (used here descriptively rather than pejoratively) in the Spirit-empowered renewal movement worldwide may perhaps also glean something useful from their academic colleagues.

The editors are hopeful that these volumes will be of wide-ranging benefit to readers from both of these domains in part because of the conceptual layout for the project. The task presented to each of the invitees was to write about the history and theology of Pentecostal/Charismatic or renewal movements in a specified region or country. With this, some assessment of theological orientation and development was expected, as well as analyses of opportunities and challenges lying ahead of these movements, especially on the theological front. Most chapters in these volumes follow this general format, although not all.

The Empowered21 movement, under the able leadership of Billy Wilson and the many worldwide leadership groups that he has gathered, seems poised to bring more coordination to all the Spirit-filled Pentecostal and Charismatic movements in the world to a level that has not been seen heretofore. In the long run, it is hoped that this set of books produced by these scholars will be a permanent and important milestone in the history and theology of the Empowered21 movement from the vantage point of the middle of the second decade of the twenty-first century.

Acknowledgments

Many friends contributed to making this book a reality. First, we thank the Empowered21 leadership team whose vision brought this and the other books in the series into being. They include Billy Wilson, Mart Green, Ossie Mills, Assif Reid, Robin Cole, and their colleagues. Also, special thanks are due to Tessie DeVore and Charisma House, publisher of the book; and to Mike Schatz, Adrienne Gaines, Debbie Marrie, and others for their help with the publication process.

This Africa volume owes much to the leaders of Empowered21, who provided facilities and support for the scholars to meet in the Pais Arena in Jerusalem as a track at the Jerusalem 2015 Empowered21 Global Congress. Special thanks go to Ossie Mills for site planning and Assif Reid for overseeing the scholars' track. Vinson Synan organized the African scholars' track at the congress, and Kwabena Asamoah-Gyadu cochaired its sessions. Above all, thanks to the authors of the following pages, whose excellent research and writing make this important book such a great contribution to the study of current Spirit-empowered movements across the globe.

Contributors

Allan Heaton Anderson (DTh, University of South Africa) is professor of mission and Pentecostal studies and director of the Centre for Pentecostal and Charismatic Studies at the University of Birmingham, Birmingham, United Kingdom.

J. Kwabena Asamoah-Gyadu (PhD, University of Birmingham) is dean of the faculty at Trinity Theological Seminary, Legon, Ghana.

Isaac Deji Ayegboyin (PhD, University of Ibadan) is professor of church history and African Christianity and current head of the Department of Religious Studies at the University of Ibadan, Ibadan, Nigeria.

Kudzai Biri (PhD, University of Zimbabwe) is an associate professor in the Department of Religious Studies, Classics, and Philosophy at the University of Zimbabwe, Harare, Zimbabwe.

Clifton Clarke (PhD, University of Birmingham) is associate professor of intercultural studies and world Christianity at Regent University's School of Divinity, Virginia Beach, Virginia.

Samson Adetunji Fatokun (PhD, University of Ibadan) is professor of church history, doctrinal theology, and Pentecostal studies in the Department of Religious Studies at the University of Ibadan, Ibadan, Nigeria.

Maria Frahm-Arp (PhD, University of Warwick) is lecturer in religion studies at the University of Johannesburg, Johannesburg, South Africa.

Jörg Haustein (PhD, University of Heidelberg) is senior lecturer in religions in Africa at the School of Oriental and African Studies, University of London, London, England.

Chammah J. Kaunda (PhD, University of KwaZulu-Natal) is a Zambian postdoctoral research fellow in Christian spirituality at the University of South Africa, Pretoria, South Africa.

Harvey C. Kwiyani (PhD, Luther Seminary) is lecturer in African Christianity, mission, and leadership at Church Mission Society, Oxford, United Kingdom.

E. Kingsley Larbi (PhD, University of Edinburgh) is founder and chancellor of Regent University College of Science and Technology, Accra, Ghana.

Madipoane Masenya (ngwan'a Mphahlele) (PhD, University of South Africa) is professor of Old Testament studies at the University of South Africa, Pretoria, South Africa.

Naar M'fundisi (PhD, University of Birmingham) teaches religious education, philosophy, and health/social care in Birmingham, United Kingdom.

Susan Murimi (PhD, Akrofi-Christaller Institute of Theology, Mission, and Culture) is an adjunct lecturer in theology at Daystar University, Nairobi, Kenya.

Tharwat Maher Nagib Adly Nagib (PhD student, Regent University) is lecturer in Wesleyan and Pentecostal studies at Faith Bible College, The First Pentecostal Seminary, and Veritas College International, Cairo, Egypt.

Trad Nogueira-Godsey (PhD, University of Cape Town) is a postdoctoral research fellow at the University of Cape Town, Cape Town, South Africa.

Alfred Olwa (PhD, Moore College) is senior lecturer and dean of Bishop Tucker School of Divinity and Theology, Mukono, Uganda.

Opoku Onyinah (PhD, University of Birmingham) is chairman of the Church of Pentecost, Accra, Ghana.

Joseph Quayesi-Amakye (PhD, Vrije Universiteit Amsterdam) is senior lecturer and acting dean of the School of Theology and Missions, Central University, Dansoman-Accra, Ghana.

Jean-Baptiste Roamba (PhD, Regent University) is senior pastor of Central Assembly of God in Ouagadougou, Burkina Faso, and member of the National Executive Board of the Assemblies of God, Burkina Faso.

Vinson Synan (PhD, University of Georgia) is emeritus professor of Christian history at Regent University's School of Divinity, Virginia Beach, Virginia.

Asonzeh Ukah (PhD and Dr. Habil., University of Bayreuth) is senior lecturer of African Christianity at the University of Cape Town, Cape Town, South Africa.

Donatus Pius Ukpong (PhD, Pontifical Urban University) is senior lecturer and acting head in the Department of Religious and Cultural Studies, University of Uyo, Uyo, Nigeria.

Nimi Wariboko (PhD, Princeton Theological Seminary) is the Walter G. Muelder Professor of Social Ethics at Boston University School of Theology, Boston, Massachusetts.

Amos Yong (PhD, Boston University) is professor of theology and mission at Fuller Theological Seminary, Pasadena, California.

Introduction

"From Every Nation Under Heaven": Africa in World Pentecostalism

J. Kwabena Asamoah-Gyadu

THE FOCUS OF this introductory essay is not to summarize points available from the works of the individual contributors. Rather, it reflects on the importance of Pentecostalism in Africa through the nonquantitative indices in the various write-ups. The histories of Pentecostalism from the different African contexts represented here are important for what they reveal about the experiences of ordinary people who were inspired to establish Spirit-empowered movements. Pentecostal growth and expansion has very often been a lay endeavor involving Christians from the margins of church life. Allan H. Anderson explains the impact of the laity on Pentecostalism as one of the main reasons for its success.[1] There was no need for a theologically articulate clergy, because cerebral and clerical Christianity had, in the minds of many people, already failed them.

In Africa, even in cases where the groundbreaking work is traceable to a visiting foreign Pentecostal preacher, a local Christian community has facilitated the eventual spread of the movement. Most importantly, in many cases, the movement starts from the periphery of more established church communities, showing how, by the workings of His Spirit, God has been consistent in using the foolish and weak things of the world to shame the wise and strong (1 Cor. 1:26–29).

This introduction is deliberately titled "From Every Nation Under Heaven" because of the firm theological conviction that the original, biblical Pentecost was meant to be an inclusive process for the nations. Pentecost was both an event and a process in which the promise of God held true for Jews, Gentiles, and those who were far off, as the Lord our God would call (Acts 2:39). In biblical terms, three key words underlie the self-definition of Pentecostal/Charismatic Christianity, and these may be identified as *promise*, *fulfillment*, and *experience*. The belief is that the *promise* of the Spirit that was *fulfilled* on the Day of Pentecost is what is now being *experienced* in the church, bringing together the different Spirit-empowered communities and movements that can be classified using the conjoined expression *Pentecostal/Charismatic Christianity*.

Here, in discussing the importance of Africa in world Pentecostalism, we begin with the Acts of Apostles, where Luke provides a list of the representative nations and peoples that were present:

> Parthians, Medes and Elamites, residents of Mesopotamia, Judea and Cappadocia, Pontus and Asia, Phrygia and Pamphylia, Egypt and the regions of Libya near Cyrene, and visitors from Rome, both Jews and proselytes, Cretans and Arabs—we hear them speaking in our own languages the mighty works of God.
>
> —Acts 2:9–11, mev

The presence of Egypt and Libya on the list means Pentecostalism has never been alien to the African experience. The encounter between Philip and the Ethiopian eunuch is further evidence of that fact (Acts 8:26–40). Perhaps except for North Africa, represented by Egypt, in almost every account of Pentecost we have in this volume, the types are clear and follow a certain order: first, indigenous, independent Spirit-empowered movements; second, classical Pentecostal denominations coming from the West; and third, new Pentecostal or Charismatic churches and movements of the late twentieth century. The typology constituting the third category, that is, the neo-Pentecostals, has three main groups in it: the new urban-centered Charismatic prosperity-oriented churches; transdenominational fellowships, like the Full Gospel Businessmen's Fellowship International; and renewal movements within historic mission denominations.

Itinerant Charismatic Prophets and Indigenous Pentecostalism

The essays in this volume clearly indicate that in spite of the common theme of the experience of the Spirit, we cannot talk about a monolithic type of Pentecostalism in Africa. In religious studies, quantitative data can be spurious and very deceptive, but even without specific numbers, statistical estimates clearly show that Pentecostal/Charismatic Christianity has become the new "mainline" church tradition in Christian Africa. Indeed, Harvey Cox, in *Fire From Heaven*, actually referred to the older African independent/initiated churches (AICs) as Africa's own version of the worldwide Pentecostal movement.[2] They pioneered the recovery of primal spirituality encapsulating primal speech in tongues-speaking, primal piety in trances, dreams and visions, and primal hope in the expectation of miracles, supernatural interventions from beyond, and the second coming of Christ. Close to a century after early-nineteenth-century mission work began with Portuguese Roman Catholic missions across the continent, African Christians, under the influence of indigenous Charismatic prophets, took their spiritual destiny into their own hands. Indigenous prophets, including William Wade Harris of Liberia, Garrick Sokari Braide of the Niger Delta, Isaiah Shembe of South Africa, and Simon Kimbangu of the Belgian Congo, "charismatized" the religious landscape, converting hundreds of thousands to Christianity. In the fashion of what we read in the Acts of the Apostles, prospective converts "traded in" their traditional gods, shrines, charms, and amulets in dramatic conversions to Christianity. One observer of the Harris phenomenon in the then Gold Coast (Ghana, since 1957) said of it, "This is not a revival; it is a Pentecost. Its orbit is worldwide.... It fills one with awe to hear some of these converts pray."[3]

A number of these early prophets were simply itinerant evangelists. It was their converts and followers who later constituted themselves into independent churches when their innovative pneumatic spirituality seemed to clash with the ordered and cerebral liturgies of the historic mission denominations. In the early 1920s, the Methodist Church of the Gold Coast, for example, described speaking in tongues, healings, visions, and trance experiences that characterized the prayer movement of one of its catechists in terms of "occult activities." The result was that the catechist, William Egyanka Appiah, was dismissed and subsequently led his sympathizers to form the Army of the Cross of Christ Church, where the so-called "occult activities" were fully integrated into Christian worship.[4] Those experiences were replicated throughout early-twentieth-century Africa. In spite of the importance of classical Pentecostal denominations from the United States and Europe in the evangelization of Africa, historically it has been extremely difficult for Western church historiography to accept the possibility that in both its indigenous and contemporary forms, Pentecostalism in Africa has mostly developed independently of developments in the West.

The ministries of the early-twentieth-century African prophets we have named above were characterized by the same pneumatic phenomena that are spoken about in euphoric terms as emanating from Azusa Street in 1906. In Western Pentecostal scholarship, unfortunately, non-Western expressions of Spirit-inspired Christianity do not usually qualify as Pentecostal. It has left a huge question mark on the faith of such movements as Africa's older independent churches, whose spirituality, although manifestly Spirit-inspired, has consistently been excluded from Pentecostal typologies. In much of the literature, they were marginalized in the historiography of world Pentecostalism for being unbiblical, irrational religious enthusiasts devoid of historical tradition and for wallowing in folk religiosity.[5] Except for southern Africa, the classical AICs, as they came to be called in the academic literature, are no longer paradigmatic of Christianity in Africa. Nevertheless, their main theological contributions of Spirit-inspired oral liturgical forms, existential soteriology, gender sensitivity, and the mainstreaming of Charismatic experiences in worship remain undeniable. Their use of sacramentals—anointing oils, holy water, blessed handkerchiefs for the mediation of spiritual power, and the perception of the Charismatic leader as the custodian of special anointing—has been reinvented within modern Pentecostal-Charismatic Christianity, creating theological and ecclesiological continuities between the two traditions.

Pneumatic Christianity/ Contemporary Pentecostalism

Precisely because scholars of Pentecostalism have often failed to recognize this fact—sometimes for good reason—I use the expression *pneumatic Christianity* in this introductory essay to refer to any form of Christianity that values, affirms, and consciously promotes the experiences of the Spirit as part of normal Christian life and worship. This allows me to bring into the discussion not only movements in Africa that scholars delineate as Pentecostal or Charismatic, but also the many indigenous expressions of Christianity from non-Western contexts that privilege the experiential presence of the Spirit in the faith. Many of these movements may not necessarily call themselves Pentecostal, but the vernacular expressions used to capture the theology of their experiences suggests a discernment that the Spirit was at work in these ministries. It means that in Africa, the history of what has come to be known as Pentecostalism within the different streams of world Christianity started with these older independent or spiritual churches. That they did not describe their initiatives as Pentecostal must not be taken to mean that they do not belong to that category, because there is really no vernacular translation for the biblical expression *Pentecost* from which the word *Pentecostalism* is derived.

Part of the significance of pneumatic Christianity may be seen in the fact that even in the secularizing West, it is the Christian communities that privilege the experiences of the Spirit in worship that are keeping the faith alive. Immigrant communities from Africa constitute many of these congregations.[6] Significantly, a number of these are of non-Western origins. In *Beyond Christendom*, Jehu Hanciles, writing on migration and African Christianity, noted that "the expansion and impact of Pentecostal/charismatic movements are most commonly shaped by individual or spontaneous initiatives that discountenance rigid institutional or denominational control mechanisms."[7] It is the lay participation through the experiences of the Holy Spirit that allows Pentecostalism to travel and spread without inhibitions. In Africa today, even churches that trace their roots to the work of German and English missions from London, Hamburg, Basel, and Bremen are all turning to Charismatic renewal in the search for contextual relevance. The argument of contemporary Charismatic movements has been that the absence of the dynamic presence of the Spirit from the church, particularly in its older Western forms, turns it into something other than a place to encounter God. In qualitative terms, the impact of Pentecostalism on the African religious landscape, according to the essays in this volume, has occurred through the following: the integration of Charismatic experiences into church life; exuberance and vitality; infectious, dynamic, and electronically driven worship; high public visibility through numbers and megasize "cathedroms"; innovative media programs; high-profile, charismatically gifted leadership; gender inclusivity based on spiritual experience; and, within the public and social spheres, politically active leaders and involvement in university education.[8]

African Pentecostalism has, in many respects, been very progressive. Today, Nigeria's Covenant University, owned by David O. Oyedepo's Living Faith Church Worldwide, also known as Winners Chapel, and the Central University College, owned by Mensa Otabil's International Central Gospel Church, are some of the best such private universities in Africa. The media programs of the new Pentecostal leaders are available and accessible worldwide through satellite television and the mass circulation of prerecorded sermons on various portable electronic devices. During a century of growth, speaking at international evangelistic healing crusades has ceased to be the preserve of North American televangelists. Bishop Charles Agyinasare of Ghana, whose ministry receives some more attention later, is now acknowledged as Ghana's "Morris Cerullo." Powerful and dramatic healings characterize his crusades, and he has ministered on every continent, including holding mass evangelistic meetings in Nigeria's Islamic regions, Pakistan, and Kiev in the Ukraine. We know quite a bit about African Pentecostal churches of the classical type, and so these reflections are deliberately giving disproportionate attention to the new Charismatic churches. Writing on the public significance of these contemporary Pentecostal movements, using Ghana as a representative sample, Paul Gifford notes:

> Nobody in Ghana is unaware of the shift. Everyone is aware of the charismatic prayer centers, their all-night prayer services, their crusades, conventions, and Bible Schools, their new buildings...their car bumper stickers and banners, and particularly the posters that everywhere advertise an enormous range of forthcoming activities. Everyone is aware of their media efforts. Above all everyone knows of the new religious superstars.[9]

The essays in this volume show that the African Pentecostal context is one in which the Bible has retained its authority and sanctity as the Word of God. Indeed, in some indigenous Pentecostal movements, the Bible is not simply text but also a sacred symbol that is potent for certain therapeutic rituals. The African context is also one in which things of the spirit and religious experience—defining factors in Pentecostal religions—have always been privileged over cerebral forms of piety. Additionally, in matters religious, that which is spiritual always has a certain resonance with African religio-cultural worldviews. It is thus not surprising that in essays covering the various African regions, the primal imagination has never been excluded from Pentecostal spirituality. Christianity of the historic Western mission kind tended to be a system of ideas, but religion in Africa, including much of indigenously initiated

Christianity, is pneumatic in orientation. If healing, prophecy, and prosperity within contemporary Christianity have therefore found a home in African Pentecostalism, it is not simply because they are biblical concepts, important as that may be. It is also because these phenomena strike response chords within the African primal or religio-cultural imagination.

Africa and the Changing Pentecostal Scape

These essays draw attention to Africa as an important geographical, religious, and cultural context in the development of Pentecostalism as a world religion. When at the Empowered21 world Pentecostal gathering in Jerusalem in May 2015 Pastor Enoch A. Adeboye, leader of Nigeria-based Redeemed Christian Church of God, mounted the podium as plenary speaker, it was a modest but an important recognition by organizers that African voices are no longer marginal to world Pentecostalism. It is impossible to talk about contemporary Pentecostalism in Africa without reference to the name of the late Benson Idahosa. Paul Emeka used a study of the "Benson Idahosa Factor in Nigerian Pentecostalism" to demonstrate how the linkage with twentieth-century North American televangelism enabled him to reshape contemporary Pentecostalism in Africa:

> He brought the prosperity gospel, the episcopal polity, televangelism, mega-church projects, and theological education that sponsored a large group of African students who spread the faith and deliverance theology throughout the continent. The watershed was the Fire Conference organized by Reinhard Bonnke in Harare, Zimbabwe in 1984 under the theme "Africa shall be saved." Four thousand evangelists from forty-four African countries participated in a tent

> supplied by Kenneth Copeland at a cost of one million dollars. Idahosa was the African among the keynote speakers.[10]

The influence of foreigners, especially North Americans on African Pentecostalism, is undeniable, as we see from the experience of Idahosa in the quotation above. In the past, the continent played host to a number of classical Pentecostal churches, but that sort of mission has seen a reversal with African-founded and African-led contemporary Pentecostal denominations making waves in virtually all of Europe and North America. Perhaps a more concrete indicator of this importance may be found in the numbers of academic publications that have been dedicated to the study of Spirit-empowered Christianity in Africa.[11] This attention could not have been otherwise when the skylines of South Africa, Nigeria, and Ghana have all been transformed by expensive, mega-sized Pentecostal "cathedroms" that were formerly associated with North America. In Ghana, the Church of Pentecost, an indigenous classical Pentecostal denomination, has just completed the building of a five-thousand-seat conference center named Jesus Town, with accompanying hostel and dining facilities all within a single geographical location. The largest Pentecostal gatherings anywhere in the world now take place in Nigeria under the leadership of Adeboye and David O. Oyedepo at Winners Chapel. Consider the following observation in John D. Y. Peel's foreword to Asonzeh Ukah's study on Adeboye's Redeemed Christian Church of God:

> The center of all RCCG's activities is the Redemption Camp, a 10 square kilometer site on the Lagos-Ibadan expressway…this has grown to the scale of a small town with all modern facilities, a high school and a university, its own drainage system, electricity and water supplies, banks

> and supermarkets, houses built by wealthy members...and at the center of it an auditorium that will seat half a million people. Here takes place every month the famous Holy Ghost Night, at which divine miracles and blessings are outpoured. A place where God reveals his dominion, a place where the *kingdom of heaven* is reproduced on earth.[12]

The important thing is that the resources were raised through local tithers, showing how indigenous and independent African Pentecostalism has become! When Ghana's Mensa Otabil holds his end-of-year Crossover services at the Accra sports stadium, he takes in more people than any visiting North American healing evangelist does today. Those who have followed the religious thought of Pastor Mensa Otabil of Ghana's International Central Gospel Church would also know that his work *Beyond the Rivers of Ethiopia* is written to affirm the important place that the black race occupies in God's economy of salvation and empowerment:

> I believe what we are seeing is the beginning of more fundamental and foundational changes. There is a shaking in the land! God is going to visit the black peoples of this world to bring them out [of] the state they are in, into their portion....There is the sense of urgency and a feeling of an appointment with destiny among black people. It is a feeling that makes you know that your time has come and God is bringing to fruition the days of intense intercessions, for his justice to prevail.[13]

God's "justice" in this context means the African would no longer be subservient to the West in matters physical and spiritual. It is a mind-set that informs the motivational messages of today's African Charismatic leaders. Mensa Otabil is only the most popular among a number of such contemporary Pentecostal pastors who have adopted a new way of preaching that uses the Bible to affirm the black race and to offer practical information for empowerment, development, and improvement. The other key voice here is Matthew Ashimolowo, whose slogan "Raising Champions and Taking Territories" summarizes what this new motivational gospel is about. This explains, in part, why contemporary Pentecostalism appeals a lot to the upwardly mobile youth, who may be looking for new sources of inspiration within the religious sphere.

As should be clear by now, African Pentecostalism, including the neo-Pentecostal or Charismatic movements, ought to be understood within the context of global developments. This is important because the contemporary Pentecostal movements that receive disproportionate attention here have never defined their efforts in purely local terms. That would be too limiting of their calling and transnational aspirations, as seen in the worldwide peregrinations of leaders and the choices of names and symbols. Each of these groups, as is evident in those cited in our African essays, has the words *global*, *international*, or *worldwide* as a prefix or suffix to their names.[14] Even where these terms and expressions are the transnational aspirations of the churches and their leaders, they are still discernible from the choice of religious symbols and logos, for as I have explained elsewhere, the eagle with its power of height, vision, longevity, and power of flight has eclipsed the humble dove as the preferred icon in this new form of prosperity-oriented Christianity.[15] The other symbol found among them is the globe. A global perspective of Pentecostal/Charismatic Christianity, Ogbu Kalu surmises:

> ...recognizes the integrity of the multiple contexts. It is beyond geography; it involves the enlargement of the

> religious space in the interior and at the surface levels. The global consists of the various ways in which charismatic spirituality is appropriated, expressed, articulated, and lived in response to the challenges from indigenous cultures and ecosystems and other competing religious forms. There is no center and there is no periphery.[16]

It is significant that a number of the essays on African neo-Pentecostalism point out that in its contemporary forms, the movement seemed to have some connection to the conservative Evangelical student associations of the 1960s and 1970s. What African indigenous Christian leaders did was to add a dynamic pneumatology to the emphasis on the born-again experience, the teaching on sanctification, and the recognition of the authority of the Bible that defined conservative Evangelicalism. In countries like Ghana, Nigeria, Kenya, Uganda, and the North African regions, meetings of the Scripture Union and International Fellowship of Evangelical Students turned completely Charismatic, much to the consternation of the leadership of the Evangelical movements of the time. The icons of twentieth-century Evangelicalism, Billy Graham and John Stott, accepted speaking in tongues as biblical but refused to concede that every Christian could have the benefit of that experience. African Evangelicals chose a slightly different path by blurring the lines between what is Evangelical and what is Charismatic, with the emphasis on speaking in tongues as a second confirmable experience after being born again.

African Pentecostalism and the "Enchanted" Worldview

If Pentecostalism in Africa shares the theological emphases of the global movements, then we ought to address the question of what makes a particular type of Pentecostalism African. African

Pentecostals defined themselves against the others by their emphasis on the Holy Spirit, saying that "I believe in the Holy Spirit," recited in the creeds of the church, is not the same as "I have experienced the Holy Spirit." What Pentecostals have sought to do, going by our definitions, is to bridge the gap between *belief* and *experience* in the encounter with the Holy Spirit. The classical Pentecostal traditions in Africa, such as the Assemblies of God and the various apostolic churches, share the theological emphases of their counterparts elsewhere, but there are still areas in which the African orientation is clear. Exuberant and expressive forms of worship are very constitutive of Pentecostal spirituality, but as most will attest, African Pentecostals bring into their informal liturgies a certain heightened vigor and the incorporation of supernatural worldviews that are usually not that discernible in Western forms of the movement. Based on his observations among the Spirit-empowered indigenous movements of the early twentieth century, Baëta describes the sort of Spirit-enchanted worship experiences I have in mind by saying that these churches

> engage in various activities which (by their own assertion) are either meant to invoke the Holy Spirit of God, or are to be interpreted as signs of his descent upon the worshippers.... These activities and "signs" include rhythmic swaying of the body, usually with stamping to repetitious music... hand-clappings, ejaculations, poignant cries and prayers, dancing, leaping, and various motor reactions expressive of intense religious emotion; prophesyings, "speaking with tongues," falling into trances, relating dreams and visions, and "witnessing," that is, recounting publicly one's own experience of miraculous redemption.[17]

The references to relating dreams and visions and recounting people's experiences of miraculous redemption in worship are important because it is during these moments that one sees the critical part that supernatural evil, especially witchcraft, plays in African lives and how Pentecostals create the ritual contexts to deal with the fears and insecurities associated with those beliefs.

Consider also the case of the Church of Pentecost that started as an Apostolic Church through the collaboration of a local leader from Ghana, Apostle Peter N. Anim, and a British Apostolic missionary, James McKeown, in the late 1920s. The Church of Pentecost considers itself a classical Pentecostal denomination, but it also operates within what Paul Gifford has described as an "enchanted worldview," in which the presence of traditional spirits, including witches, surviving as demons receive much attention. We see the same phenomenon, that is, the belief in demons as the principal cause of human affliction, in the Universal Church of the Kingdom of God originating in Brazil, which now has megasized churches in virtually all of urban Africa. This enchanted worldview is often extended to cover the personality of the Charismatic leader in the African Pentecostal church. In Zimbabwe, Archbishop Ezekiel Guti's "cultic leadership" and the name of his church—Zimbabwe Assemblies of God Africa (ZAOGA)—indicates both by the choice of name and spirituality that it has doctrinal beliefs and concerns that may be different from those of the Assemblies of God USA. For example, Guti's ZAOGA treats the "man of God" as one with a "sacred personality" and responds to him with the awe often associated with the traditional African medicine man/woman. His arrival at ZAOGA functions is heralded by proclamations that virtually merge his person with that of Christ. Thus, Guti is considered the custodian of special supernatural revelations, a phenomenon also familiar in traditional African religions. That this enchanted worldview is prevalent in virtually all African Pentecostal movements, such as Guti's ZAOGA, is indicative of the choices that

Africans have felt at liberty to make in the streams of Pentecostalism being practiced on the continent.[18] When Enoch A. Adeboye of the Redeemed Christian Church of God came to Ghana on an official visit some three years ago, younger African pastors coveting his level of anointing rubbed their palms over the seat on which he sat. They then passed the palms over their faces in an imaginary attempt to incorporate the same anointing that his personality is supposed to have into their own lives and ministries.

Gifford's explanation of this enchanted worldview associated with traditional philosophical thought that also pervades even the most contemporary of African Pentecostal movements is worth quoting in full:

> The physical realm and the realm of the spirit are not separate from each other.... This world is one of action and counteraction of potent forces, spirit acting upon spirit.... A stronger or higher spirit acting negatively upon the spirit of any human may affect the whole family, clan or state. It therefore becomes a central concern to avoid this or, where it is suspected to be imminent, ward it off quickly.... Religion is very largely the means of manipulating these forces. Deities are consulted to ward off negative influence in important matters, but consultations are also used for lesser evils like failure in business and education.... Consulting at shrines serves normally to discover why individual persons or communities are suffering particular afflictions. Causality is discerned primarily in the spirit realm, although natural causality is not entirely disregarded.[19]

This enchanted worldview is what has made spiritual warfare a nonnegotiable part of African Pentecostalism. This worldview is evident, for instance, in the preaching and ministry of Daniel

Olukoya of the Mountain of Fire and Miracles Ministries. As Gifford explains:

> Olukoya teaches that all Christians have a glorious destiny here in the world. "Every born again Christian is destined for an all-round success. Success is your kingdom right. It is your covenant and redemptive right." But we are all prey to spiritual forces determined to pollute, trap and destroy people's destiny. Most frequently mentioned is witchcraft, the exercise of supernatural powers by people who are in league with the devil, through manipulation, even with the use of satanic weapons.[20]

It is not being suggested that all contemporary Pentecostals preach about the power of supernatural evil in the same way pastors such as Olukoya specialize in so do, but the important thing is that you find these thoughts everywhere. Spiritual warfare is not necessarily an African or non-Western phenomenon. It has always been part of a global Charismatic culture and even in the West was repopularized from the late-twentieth century by scholars like C. Peter Wagner and Charles Kraft and practitioners like John Wimber and Derek Prince. However, the ways in which traditional spirits are "demonized" and considered agents of the devil and the means of exorcism and deliverance that have developed with that worldview is distinctively African. Pastor Abu Bako of Rhema Foundation in Ghana speaks about demonic strongholds as "altars." He defines an altar as any platform, launching pad, or operational base from which a spirit or deity operates:

> The implication then is that any platform erected for God or gods, angels or spirits to operate from, is an altar. This means humans and other creatures, lands, cities, organizations,

> communities, nations and even activities, can all serve as Altars once dedicated or offered for such purposes.[21]

My interest here is not the theological correctness of the altars. It is how he brings traditional deities into the equation and the thought expressed in his book that a Spirit-filled Christian can dominate physical spaces by erecting an alternative altar around himself or herself, making it impossible for unbelievers, especially people with negative alien spiritual influences, to fit into those spaces. In a context where land, in particular, could be a source of physical and spiritual violence or attacks, Pentecostal/Charismatic churches are known to "take control" over such spaces through "warfare prayers" meant to immobilize traditional spirits before even purchasing lands. Lands under litigation have been returned to churches following long periods of prayer and fasting aimed toward laying claim to those spaces in the spirit. Once they are secured, the spaces are appropriately anointed with oil and sealed with the blood of Christ to ward off the negative influences of those who have had interests in those lands. Abu Bako explains how this works in other cases:

> For many believers, the contact points for demonic visitation and activity could be attributed to the presence of seemingly innocent looking articles of decoration, like carvings, souvenirs, and religious pictures, which have been dedicated to particular spirits.... When altars are destroyed, the spirits and covenants that have kept the people bound are judged, their influence broken and their hold on the land, house or community is loosened. Those that are oppressed by the devil are set free.[22]

The main champions here are Spirit-empowered Christians with the ability to dislodge demons from territories where they are unwanted, including from human affairs and endeavors and physical spaces. This explains the continuing importance of healing and deliverance ministries in contemporary Pentecostalism.

Today the Church of Pentecost, for instance, operates prayer and healing camps throughout Ghana. They are led by prophets and prophetesses who specialize in traditional exorcisms but also cater for those needs that in a Western context may not even be placed within the arena of spiritual needs. At Church of Pentecost healing camps, people look for spiritual interventions for their homosexual orientations, visas to travel abroad (which are incredibly difficult to obtain if one carries an African passport), fruit of the womb, employment, marriages, promotion, and protection from enemies. If traditional religious shrines kept records of client needs, the registers would not reveal anything different from those ones that take people to Pentecostal healing camps. The phenomenon has developed as a subculture within African Christianity, with a new category of neo-Pentecostal prophetic figures popping up everywhere as specialists in diagnosing and praying for victims of demonic and other supernatural afflictions. In Ghana, Nigeria, Zimbabwe, Kenya, Uganda, and South Africa, there are Pentecostal/Charismatic prayer centers manned by people with the requisite charismatic anointing and devoted to fighting supernatural evil in the daily affairs of clients.

The relationship between this sort of religiosity and the prosperity gospel associated with contemporary Pentecostals is not hard to find. Fighting Africa's poverty through prosperity hermeneutics has become key to our understanding of the Charismatic Christian culture now prevalent across the continent. In the prosperity gospel, God is believed to supply every need of the believer, provided the right conditions are met, and this includes the faithful payments of tithes and offerings. Spiritual prosperity is important in the discourse, but overwhelmingly the emphasis is on material wealth and progress in this life. The mansions with swimming pools that prosperity-touting pastors have built, along with their luxurious automobiles, fashion-conscious appearances, expensive jewelry, and private businesses, are all meant to serve as concrete examples of prosperity to their hopeful following. In the African context in which witchcraft and other forms of supernatural evil are hyperactive, if the desired prosperity does not come, those who take the blame are the demons and evil spirits that work against people's destiny. The need to correct the imbalance has led to the rise of a new breed of Charismatic prophets who get invited from church to church and hold "breakthrough" services to release the desired prosperity into the atmosphere.

African Pentecostalism and World Evangelization

Another way to discern the importance of Africa in world Pentecostalism is to consider the fact that contemporary immigrant churches in Western and Eastern Europe and North America are overwhelmingly of the Pentecostal/Charismatic kind. Enoch A. Adeboye's Redeemed Christian Church of God, Daniel Olukoya's Mountain of Fire and Miracles Ministries, David O. Oyedepo's Living Faith Church Worldwide, and Ghana's Church of Pentecost have the most visible immigrant churches on the northern continents. With more than ten thousand worshippers attending its various weekly services in London alone, Pastor Ashimolowo's Kingsway International Christian Centre has taken over the territory of the Church of England as the church with the single-largest-active congregation in Western Europe. Pastor Ashimolowo, aided by a vibrant media ministry, addresses more people around the world than any Protestant leader in Western

Europe. These contemporary Pentecostals, together with their Africa-based compatriots—Ray McCauley, Enoch A. Adeboye, David O. Oyedepo, Ezekiel Guti, Chris Oyakhilome, Nicholas Duncan-Williams, Mensa Otabil, Charles Agyinasare, Dag Heward-Mills, and many others—have within a generation transformed the global Christian landscape with the Charismatic congregations helping to make Christianity a primarily non-Western religion.

On the qualitative significance of Africa in world Christianity, consider also the field of world healing evangelists that I mentioned at the beginning. It is interesting that many Western Pentecostal evangelists, as far as their miracle ministries are concerned, made their presence better felt in Africa than in their home regions. Through the experiences of the Spirit, majority-world Pentecostals have produced their own crop of world healing evangelists. In the history of mass evangelistic Pentecostal healing crusades, for example, the usual names mentioned would include Oral Roberts, T. L. Osborn, Reinhard Bonnke, Benny Hinn, and Morris Cerullo. The historical impact of their ministries on African Christianity and Pentecostalism in particular is not in doubt. Through powerful televangelism ministries and their extensive use of other media, Bishop T. D. Jakes and Joel Osteen may be considered the more contemporary names, in terms of influences on African Pentecostalism from North America. My point is that by raising awareness of international healing evangelists among African Pentecostals, we find a fulfillment of the promise of Pentecost, in terms of the democratization of graces or *charismata*. The inclusiveness of the Spirit, in terms of the experiences of Pentecostalism across the world, means that today Africa has its own traveling healing evangelists.

His Eminence, Bishop Charles Agyinasare—and here we have evidence of the Episcopal traditions on contemporary Pentecostals—founder and leader of the Perez Chapel International in Ghana, and Rev. Dr. Enoch A. Adeboye, leader of the Redeemed Christian Church of God based in Nigeria, both hold mass evangelistic public crusades. Their meetings attract crowds comparable, if not bigger, than those that were associated with visiting foreign, mainly North American televangelists. This was not the case even twenty years ago. The media ministry of South Africa–based Chris Oyakhilome is as important as some of those we have mentioned from North America. Prophet T. B. Joshua of The Synagogue, Church of All Nations in Nigeria has his critics for his unorthodox approach to the ministry of miracles, although I have no reason to believe that his methods belong to the occult as some allege. What is important for our purposes is that significant numbers of his clients fly in from Western countries for healing and deliverance. In the same vein, it is impossible to talk about the place of Africa in world Pentecostal missions today without reference to Ghana's Church of Pentecost and its international assemblies worldwide.

Bishop Charles Agyinasare has preached in more than sixty countries of the world, including the United States, Canada, the United Kingdom, Holland, Germany, France, Italy, Ukraine, Israel, India, the Islamic Republic of Pakistan, the Islamic Kingdom of Bahrain, Japan, and many other countries in Africa. His TV programs reach millions of people in Ghana, Nigeria, the Netherlands, and the United Kingdom. The impact of his crusades, stated in one of his publications, *Power in Prayer*, includes filling up large stadiums, healing the sick, and, in a few cases, causing the rain to stop so that open-air evangelistic crusades could proceed without interruption.[23]

The emergence of African Pentecostal ministries with worldwide significance shows that the Spirit brings into fellowship with

Christ those from the underside of history as equal participants in God's nonpartisan kingdom. In the economy of the Spirit, no one takes a privileged place in Christian mission. As an example, consider the ministry of Pastor Sunday Adelaja, who leads the Embassy of the Blessed Kingdom of God for all Nations in the Ukraine. At one point, his "God Embassy," as it is popularly called, had a worshipping community of more than twenty thousand white Eastern Europeans. Its history shows that the initial membership was made up of converted gangsters, drug addicts, and prostitutes and their grateful families who came to church because they had seen the wonders of God in the lives of their kith and kin.

Yet Pentecostal mission also bridges the public sphere and the spiritual world so that African pastors have been received within the political arena as custodians of spiritual power. To that end, many of them serve as the "spiritual advisors" of those in public office. Some, like Agyinasare, who work in the ministry of mass evangelistic crusades, serve as "exporters of spiritual power" through their healing-and-miracles ministries. These "exporters of spiritual power"—whether they travel simply to preach the gospel or as spiritual consultants for Diaspora problems—constitute an important means by which religion crosses the boundaries among denominations. Thus, they now function in the same way that T. L. Osborn, Oral Roberts, or Benny Hinn did, who visited Africa as born-again healing and crusading evangelists in the spread of the gospel. We have made the point that healing miracles have always been part of the African Pentecostal agenda not just because it is biblical but also because the African worldview itself is open to supernatural interventions in a way that one does not find in Western contexts. In the words of Keener:

> Even when trained in Western culture, Africans draw on a repertoire of experience and cultural interpretation that differs starkly from our inherited Western assumptions. Supernatural phenomena are compatible with most African worldviews and reports of miraculous healings are frequent in Africa especially where medical resources are difficult to come by. Healing and other miracles are important in the growth of religious movements in Africa, including most kinds of churches that are growing.[24]

The media play an important role in the way contemporary Pentecostal religion crosses boundaries because it is usually through media outlets that particular pastors or their ministries come to the attention of Diaspora communities.[25]

The Spirit, Christendom, and Its Dissolution

The emergence of gifted African televangelists and mass evangelistic crusades at the international level says something about both the past and future of the Christian enterprise. The making of Christianity into an empire in its early years and the creation of a Christendom with hegemonic tendencies from the Constantine era may have been required at the time, but it was not expedient when considered from the viewpoint of the workings of the Spirit of God. The ground for the democratization of the gospel was clearly articulated by John the Baptist as he sought to lay down the basic requirement for the reign of God in the lives of people. He told his Jewish audience, who presumably considered their race to be the custodians of an Abrahamic heritage that entitled them to a privileged place in God's kingdom:

> Therefore bear fruit worthy of repentance, and do not begin to say to yourselves, "We have Abraham as our father." For

> I say to you that God is able from these stones to raise up children for Abraham.
>
> —Luke 3:8, mev

As it turned out, the crowds wanted to know how to respond to the outpouring of the Holy Spirit in Acts and the wonders of God they had witnessed and heard through the disciples of Jesus. Peter explained that the way to benefit from the blessing of God was to repent and be baptized in the name of Jesus for the forgiveness of sin. "The promise," he noted, was for both present and future generations of believers in Jesus Christ. (See Acts 2:37–38.) Within a short period following Pentecost, the message traveled beyond its Jerusalem boundaries to Samaria and subsequently to Ethiopia through a eunuch yearning to understand a portion of the Scriptures that related to the mission of God's Suffering Servant (cf. Acts 8:34).

This good news of Jesus has traveled on the wings of the Spirit, in defiance of the logic of historical Christendom, to many parts of the world. African Christians in various parts of the continent have experienced their own Pentecosts and created the ecclesial spaces that allow them to worship God and experience the wonders of His power away from the control of church authority in the historic mission denominations that first evangelized the continent. The average international Pentecostal healing evangelist today is from one of these regions of the world: Africa, Asia, or Latin America. The experience of the Spirit of God makes possible a new ecclesiology defined by the democratization of *charismata*, the gifts of the Spirit enabling indigenous Charismatic figures to establish and lead various Pentecostal churches and movements. In twenty-first-century Africa, then, it is virtually impossible now to speak of the shift in the center of gravity of the Christian faith from the northern to the southern regions of Africa, Asia, and Latin America without reference to Pentecostal/Charismatic Christianity. In God's presence, no nations or peoples are anonymous, so it is not coincidental that in that list of nations in Acts 2, Rome and Spain, representing Europe, are named, but so are Libya and Egypt, representing Africa.

There is no doubt, Frank D. Macchia observes, that Pentecostalism worldwide has favored less rational forms of theological discourse.[26] In the thought of Eastwood Anaba of Ghana, the new Pentecostal churches were born to chart new paths in Christian mission:

> Whilst there is nothing new under the sun, these [new Pentecostals] are born for modification, alteration, revolution, modulation and variation. These latter ones are born to resurrect great things long abandoned and forgotten. This is a revival and restoration.... You may not have an example to follow but you can create your own path.[27]

Eastwood Anaba's use of the word *revolution* to describe the new Pentecostals is very instructive. They constitute, in his understanding, God's end-time militia, brought into being by the Holy Spirit as movements of revival and restoration. They have been called to chart a new path for Christianity by democratizing ministry, a process made possible by individual and corporate experiences of the Spirit. He suggests that the work of ministry must never be abandoned to professional clergy but that each person must function in the gifts and graces of the Spirit to the glory of God.[28] The veracity of Anaba's thoughts is seen not simply in the way the new Pentecostals have grown, but also in the influence that they now exercise in African religious and public life. What Latin American Pentecostal theologian Juan Sepúlveda says—that personal charismatic experiences have implications for the Christian community—is also relevant in Africa:

> The new person, who is incorporated into the Pentecostal community through conversion, receives, and is acknowl edged by the church to have received, a gift which will enable him or her to begin to participate in the carrying out of the evangelizing mission of the church. In this way, Pentecostalism carries into practice in a very radical way the idea of the "universal priesthood of the believers"![29]

That the Spirit democratizes charisma and provides access to the sacred thus redefines ecclesiology. This is how Eastwood Anaba, for example, interprets the cardinal text of the Pentecostal movement; the expression "all flesh" in the passage defies skin color, educational status, natural abilities, and social standing:

> "Professional believers," baptized, confirmed and complacent are being sidelined.... We are God's end-time militia being released in these end-times to replace, or augment the services of professional, regular and institutionalized Christendom. This militia is made up of Born-again believers who are not bound by rituals and religious limitations. We are the remnant of God's people.[30]

This democratization of charisma occurs through the outpouring and experiences of the Holy Spirit. It helps people to function in their gifts and graces, making the church charismatically functional. Our new task in the twenty first century, Allan Anderson proposes, "is to reflect on the role of Pentecostalism in the majority world in the transformation of Christianity."[31] In the new type of religious revolution, Mensa Otabil's International Central Gospel Church says it is "raising leaders, shaping vision, and influencing society through Christ." Sam Korankye Ankrah's Royalhouse Chapel International advertises itself as a church that is "touching our generation with the power of God." Charles Agyinasare's Perez Chapel International is "a place where Jesus makes everybody somebody." That these are not idle claims and empty catchphrases is seen in the profound testimonies of lives that have been turned around and in the different elevations in life that have come to people unfolded in the essays that follow this introduction.

Part I
West Africa

Chapter 1

West African Pentecostalism: A Survey of Everyday Theology

By Nimi Wariboko

I HAVE BEEN ASKED by the editors of this volume to write a theology of West African Pentecostalism. I am not sure if this is a good idea. The everyday language of West African Pentecostalism is characterized by theology-terminating clichés. The most complex and systematic theological treatises and understanding of Christian heritage are compressed, reduced, and transmuted into easily expressed Holy Ghost pronouncements and whispers. These and the movement leaders' unquestionable private interpretations, shortcuts, and "God's words" become the alpha and omega of any theological analysis. In this world of charismatic intensity and potent ideological brew, the term *theology* is used to summon and then flatly and disrespectfully dismiss any quest for alternative ideas, systematic exploration of notions and propositions, nuanced perspectives, or search for balanced intellectual judgment.

Yet this is not an environment of nonthought. There is an awful lot of thinking going on, reflections on practices, and fevered efforts to correlate questions of everyday existence with the resources of the Bible and thousands of years of Christian tradition. There is a theology—in spite of the contestations of the practitioners—to be squeezed out from the tubes of their connections to God's words or to be discerned from their practices and from all that is ordinary and prosaic. Indeed, the editors did not make a mistake when they asked me to construct a theology of West African Pentecostalism. Given the state of West African Pentecostalism—stretched by the majestic continental bulge, separated by nation states and linguistic polarities, soaked and smeared by popular TV images, and spurred by relentless growth—such a construction is no mean task. My point of departure is to find a veritable lens that can help us peer deeply into the discourses, practices, and aesthetics of West African Pentecostalism.

The central locus of divine-human encounter in the worship service and the primary theological activity of West African Pentecostals is not the Eucharist or preaching but prayer. More precisely, prayers as hedged, sustained, and driven by praise and worship anchor both beliefs and practices and characterize the Christian life. Prayers are objective, relational, and dispositional. The prayer spirituality has as its objective the attainment of human flourishing as empowered by the Holy Ghost, building and sustenance of better relationships with God and with human beings (relational), and living a life of Christlike holiness (dispositional). This chapter presents the theology of West African Pentecostalism through the lens of worship-fed prayers. The theology is discerned from the everyday beliefs, practices, and affections and from all that is ordinary and prosaic in the existence of West African Pentecostals.

I will use the metaphors of self-presentation and self-interpretation as a framework to analyze this prayer-infused worship. Each person in everyday social interaction produces for himself meanings, guides and controls his identities, and generates pleasures for himself within the interplay of meanings and identities. Thus, this chapter focuses on the ordinary believer's creative and interpretative capacities to rework materials from the clergy before they are consumed in the face of recalcitrant reality. Everyday theology is a second-order product of the correlation method. The method of correlation that Paul Tillich made famous charges theology to be relevant to the immediate context of its recipients by responding to the questions asked or obstacles confronting the people in a given social situation.[1] But this theology produced by the church, preacher, or theologian has to be reworked in daily social circumstances. Correlated theology undergoes another round of correlation in the hands of the people at the popular-cultural level in the West African Pentecostal community. The people make their own theology out of the resources and insights provided by the pulpit (armchair) system.

This does not mean that resources and insights for what can be called the popular-correlation method are only provided by the pulpit-correlation method. Believers do not passively consume the "products" of the pulpit. Their very consumption makes them into producers. The pulpit products produce a people who creatively produce their own *wearable* theology to further fit their "bodies," their lifestyles in the here and now or to circulate meanings and pleasures. The original sermon, preaching, or correlated theology is "a discursive structure of potential meanings and pleasures that constitutes a major resource of popular [correlation theology]."[2] This resource and others are employed by believers to produce meanings and pleasures and to resist or evade the containment or disciplinary efforts of the pulpit or social system. Their point is not to overturn or raid the existing social system or religious epistemic system but to nudge it to yield spaces for survival, the preservation of some sense of identity, and production of meaning and pleasure. Indeed, everyday theology is constructed and sustained by the interface of everyday life, the messages and teachings of the pulpit industry (church), and the social situation of the people as it currently bears on the pursuit of human flourishing.

We will limit our study of everyday theology to three areas pertaining to human flourishing: meaning, identities, and pleasure. John Fiske makes the triplex of meaning, pleasure, and identity and the relationship between them an important lens for the study of popular culture. He states that "culture is the constant process of producing meanings of and from our social experience, and such meanings necessarily produce a social identity for the people involved.... Within the production and circulation of these meanings lies pleasure."[3] Our task of constructing the theology of West African Pentecostals is to show how people live their spirituality to make meanings, construct identities, and find pleasures. The generation and regeneration of meanings, identities, and pleasures are not without constraints. They are always produced within the circumscriptions of the social system that envelops the believers and the boundaries patrolled by the clergy or the hierarchical authorities of the church. Contrary to the celebrated semiotic democracy and brotherhood of believers in Pentecostal churches, there is some panoptic power over the people. The disciplinary energy of the clergy is always quick to deploy its moral, aesthetic, suasive, and legal powers to control the meanings, pleasures, and social identities of the people.

Pleasures in Worship

In the study of everyday theology, it is vital to understand how the people use the products and services of the churches "to their own interest and find pleasures in using them to make their own meanings of their social identities and social relations."[4] Scholarly works on bodies of Pentecostals, however, have exclusively focused on the disciplining of the body, exerting control over the body to support their spiritual quest or sustenance of salvation and holiness. Pleasures of the body or participation in Pentecostal worship as motivated by pleasure, pleasure that centers on spiritual power to create new meanings in believers' lives, and the pleasure of evading the traps of Satan have not received adequate scholarly attention. There are also pleasures that certain believers derive from disciplining their bodies or internalizing the disciplinary regimes in themselves. The body and its pleasures are important in understanding the human nature and material form of the Pentecostal worship service.

Birgit Meyer has shown that Pentecostal worship is a fabric of material and sensory experiences, an aesthetics of persuasion: "One of the most salient features of Pentecostal/charismatic churches is their sensational appeal; they often operate via music and powerful oratory, through which born-again Christians are enabled to sense the presence of the Holy Spirit *with* and *in* their bodies."[5] Annalisa Butticci says that the Prayer City of the Mountain of Fire and Miracles Ministries in Nigeria "was purposely created to accommodate massive crowds of prayer warriors and to shape the emotional, sensory, physical and collective experience of prayer."[6] She describes a typical public collective prayer session with these words:

> Thousands of men and women fight their battle against demonic spirits and manifest miraculous touch of the Holy Spirit by throwing their bodies to the ground…shaking, trembling, rolling, and screaming at the top of their voices. The smell, sound, touch, and sight of so many people furiously praying is overpowering.…The massive movement and sound of the crowd and the multi-sensory experience of this spiritual and social catharsis are all overwhelming.[7]

A Pentecostal worship service is a means of release as much as recreation, devotion as much as display, piety as much as play. Praise and worship is often an intense pleasurable social experience in West African churches. Together, worship and worshippers' bodies become a site for the production of ecstasy, *jouissance*, and bliss. For some believers, the pleasures come from the excitement of the body and its senses; and for others, they are from pure contemplation of the divine or possible encounter with the Holy Spirit. The former pleasure, though it is given space in the worship, is also surveilled so that it does not exceed its limits. Pastors and their assistants are always equipped with clothes to cover exposed upper female thighs, or they quickly carry out women who appear to threaten the purity of the gathering when they are "slain" in the Spirit. Rules and unruliness are always watched so that the pleasures and excesses of the body (especially the female body) do not undo social control or pollute the anointing deemed to be circulating in the assembly.

During my visits to Pentecostal churches in West Africa, I have observed the power and supposed dangers of pleasures of worship services. The human body—in the intense moment of worship, especially in deliverance services—breaks down into its animal nature and, existing in that state of fracture, falls to the ground and displays serpentine movements. The believer's body eventually convulses in muscular spasms before collapsing into stillness, which signifies the end of the state of the fracture. The whole episode symbolizes orgasmic pleasure, just as any demonic possession can offer. Is this a manifestation of possession by demons or an extreme case of *jouissance* (erotic bliss) when the body breaks free of social control or the norms it had incarnated? The correct answer does not really matter. Whichever is the case, the members of the deliverance team will quickly move to cut off such a pleasure that threatens social control and corporate anointing. The human body in its animal realism, writhing on the ground with hands pressed to the sides, represents not only loss of behavioral control but also a disruption of semiotic, social categories. More importantly, the *spectacle* of the transformed, liminal, or grotesque body is a reminder of the fragility of the categorical boundaries of formal or official theology.

Use of Language: Creating New Meaning and Identity

It is not only the spectacle of bodies writhing on the ground that challenges categorical boundaries of formal theology. Common expressions of daily conversations convey theological interpretations that not only indict non-Pentecostal practices, but also celebrate Pentecostal sensibility. Take, for instance, the common expression used in Ghana to describe a well-received worship service: "The anointing was great." This phrase asserts both divine visitation and emotional energies given and received during the service. And this is only one dimension of the meaning. As Kwabena Asamoah-Gyadu argues, the expression is also a subtle "critique of the staid and over-formalized liturgical forms of worship found in historic mission denominations."[8] In West African Pentecostalism, language in the form of common expressions is often used to create new meanings, formulate dynamics of identity, stage a battleground between forms of aesthetics, and differentiate between inferior and superior or past and future.

The biblical language as a system is tactically appropriated and expressed as a "display" in the public to affirm community membership and identity. The quaint terminology of the old King James Bible, for instance, constitutes a cultural capital, which can be spent to acquire respectability in everyday life or deployed to extend the power of Spirit-filled words over personal and social existential spaces. The use of the language in this way serves to affirm or resist commonly accepted meanings in ways that acknowledge the transitory nature of most daily interpersonal encounters. Biblical language "is not [always] used to convey social, common meanings inherent in it as a system, but the unique transitory meanings of its speakers."[9]

There is more to language use in everyday West African Pentecostal theology. The everyday use of theological or religious language is often based on associative relation rather than logical connection, involving a great deal of parallel processing. A West African Pentecostal in prayer says, "Holy Ghost sword, shear, shear, shear; I cut the bars of iron asunder." *Holy Ghost sword* simultaneously means he has taken up the sword of the Holy Ghost in his hand or there is now an imaginary sword in his hand that is empowered by Jesus, and he is announcing that Jehovah Nissi is now fighting for him. Holy Ghost is not just the name of the Third Person of the Trinity; it is a cliché that articulates the dominant worldview and ideology of West African Pentecostalism. The name metaphorizes the power, invisibility, and adoration motifs of Pentecostals. The invisible Holy Spirit represents and performs the supernatural power of God as He is evoked by a spiritual warrior's adoration.

Shear, shear, shear is the whistling sound of the sword's blade as it slices through the defenses of the prayer warrior's enemies. The man's voice that makes the whistling sound is accompanied by his right hand furiously cutting the air like a blade. The punning meaning that arises as his hand becomes a physical sword as well as a spiritual sword of God—and his voice duplicating the killer sound of the sword hand—brings together many images, sounds, and words in associative freedom that is both liberating and threatening in its embodiedness.

I cut the bars of iron asunder is what the whole prayer exercise does as the Pentecostal warrior frees himself from spiritual cages or imagines himself being recreated as a new, triumphal person. In this particular prayer session and its use of language, three disparate but simultaneous bodies—the man, the Holy Ghost, and the implied new man—are in play and giving resources to each other. Understanding this prayer is not about *deciphering* the logic of the sentence or structure of theological discourse. Comprehension requires *reading*—the ability to bring "oral, vernacular culture to bear" upon the sentence, requiring "the parallel (not sequential) processing of words and image, of puns within words, of puns between words and image."[10] This ability to assess vernacular culture of the spiritual warrior opens up the deep structure of his prayer. At once he is calling on supreme power and exuding power, imaginatively re-creating himself through performative speech to give his life a new meaning and thus forging a new social identity. Pleasure is attached to this social identity. It is rooted in his new born-again identity and the joy of belonging to a vivifying body of Christ. The pleasures produced from this kind of spiritual exercise are of practical use, functional and relevant in the day-to-day negotiation of social experience on the micropolitical level.

Everyday theology brings to received (pulpit, official, scriptural) theology everyday oral culture that underlies, precedes, exceeds, subverts, contests, and affirms it. Everyday theology is full of contradictions: it contains the meanings of pulpit theology and those that insist that the people's theology is theirs to use and that they do not require pastoral or academic theologian approval. Resistance and affirmation are always present in it, and this ambiguity marks its creativity. Only those who bring an inappropriate set of criteria to judge it think this ambiguity or complexity undermines its creativity and aesthetic appeal. To avoid this, we at least need to pay attention to how pleasures are produced at the intersection of meanings and identities and how pleasures help to generate the people's theology.

Sweetness of Jesus's Blood: Meanings in Pleasures

> The clock strikes four on Saturday morning in Brooklyn, New York. The Nigerian Pentecostal church has just concluded its night vigil that began at ten o'clock the previous evening. Leftover wafers and small cups of juice rest on the Holy Communion table at the right corner of the sanctuary, in front of the altar space. An eleven-year-old boy named Emmanuel walks over to the pastor, who is clearing the table, and asks to drink from one of the cups. He has asked during past Communion services, which happens only on the first Friday night of the month, but the pastor has never obliged him. This time the pastor agrees. Emmanuel drinks the red juice and exclaims, "Jesus, Your blood is sweet!" He then licks his lips, rolling his tongue over them to suck in the remnants of the liquid. This is his first time drinking the Communion wine, because in this particular church, children under the age of thirteen and not yet baptized by immersion are not permitted to partake in the Holy Communion.

Why did this child literally characterize the juice as the sweet blood of Jesus? He clearly knew that the juice was not the blood of Jesus; he had seen the pastor pour the red juice from the Kedem grape juice bottle during preparations for the service. He was also not schooled in the niceties of the theology of transubstantiation. Adults spoke about the juice as the blood of Jesus but simultaneously regarded it as the juice from the Kedem bottle. The adults might have thought that the pastor's utterances in consecrating the cups of juice endued them with spiritual powers, but they did not believe they were actually drinking the physical blood of Jesus. The child was different. His acceptance of the liturgical truth places him outside the meanings and power of the dominant adult belief system.

Is there really a contradiction between the child's belief on the actual (transformed) nature of the juice and that of the adults? Not really. First, following Jacques Rancière, I will argue that the boy and the adults are caught up together in a particular distribution of the sensible, in one way of framing a sensory space and determining how the transcendental presents itself to sense experience.[11] In their shared sensorium, the thing-in-itself and its representation/symbol, the invisible and visible, can exchange their properties. This relation is both asserted and denied in everyday theology. Second, let us not forget that Emmanuel knew that the "blood" he drank after the service came from the Kedem bottle of juice. Before he drank, the adults had partaken of the consecrated juice, felt its materiality of life and supervening spiritual power coursing through their bodies, and believed the contact to heal them physically or spiritually. The adults and Emmanuel were not concerned with blood, not blood from wine or juice, but with the "blood principle," the materiality of sensuous (spiritual) encounter, bodily engagement that underlies and precedes Pentecostal spirituality and the vitality of life/existence. In West African Pentecostalism, religion is tasted, touched, smelled, seen, heard, and danced. In the committed engagement with the Spirit, the body becomes a *religious machine*. The Pentecostal body is an apparatus for seeing, hearing, tasting, dancing, incorporating, and feeling the numinous. I use the term *religious machine* not to say that Pentecostal religious experience is mechanistic, rule-governed, calculable, or linear. The term is used to gesture to the virtuosity of the Pentecostal body in divine-human interactions to both produce and consume religious goods (for example, semiotic commodities and emotional energies).

Let us press further our description of material and embodied sacraments with the example of anointing oil. Olive oil is used for cooking, and when it is consecrated it becomes anointing oil for rubbing on the body or head. As anointing oil, it is sacramental and used for religious purposes only. But in everyday Pentecostal practice in West Africa, anointing oil can also be poured into a boiling pot of food in a use that is neither religious nor sacrilegious. The believer in the kitchen frees the anointing oil from the binary opposition to use it to generate new meanings and pleasures for her. This behavior is a key part of everyday theology and social practices. Religious objects, ideas, or practices are often prized apart from their original uses and contexts and are combined in a new social and signifying context that reworks their original meaning or symbolic value. The assortment of anointing oil and food, derived from a transimmanent bricolage, could be termed *cooked sacrament*, a semiotic-numinous delicacy with a culinary edge.

Shopping as Spiritual Guerrilla Warfare

Just as religious objects can be prized apart from their original uses, Pentecostals "profane" the sacred aura and meaning that attend to window shopping in the "cathedrals of consumption," opening it up into new possible uses and meanings without demonizing it. There is a new kind of shopping that has emerged in West Africa as poor Pentecostals encounter the lure and forces of modern goods that late capitalism offers. I call this buying practice *born-again shopping*. This is a term that describes Pentecostals who visit marketplaces and malls, engage in window shopping, sensuously consume wares, and occasionally touch them or pray at or over them without spending money.[12]

The approach is a guerrilla tactic that invades the physical and "psychic" spaces of the goods in the market in the hopes that God will eventually provide the money to buy them or cause them to come to the person as a gift. In born-again shopping, the commodity is constructed as the object of the Pentecostal voyeuristic look, which places the believer in a position of special power over it and gives him possession of the commodity, or at least of its image. The pleasure of doing this translates the promises of wealth-and-health gospel, which is rooted in cargo-cult mentality, into everyday relevance in the period between their pronouncement and fulfillment. Born-again shopping is not only about pleasure, but also a tactic of the poor and weak to establish themselves in a controlling position over the market-commodity system that assiduously renders them powerless and dependent. It is important to understand that the shape of everyday theology is socially determined by (a) the weight of the world, excessive suffering, and the gravity of social existence; (b) the abrasive forces of information and meanings from the dominant, oppressive social system that assault them, which have to be reworked for personal and socially pertinent meanings; and (c) the fluidity of daily existence and their intransigent social experiences.

Prayer as the *Locus Classicus* of Everyday Theology

The everyday theology that we have set forth above is best exemplified by the deep structure of prayer. The everyday practices of believers live under the sign of *meaning structure of prayer*. Prayer gives rise to or anticipates thought that guides everyday practice. It anticipates thought because practices that give form to meaning are already an interpretation. Prayers in turn live under the logic and teleoaffectivity of everyday practices. We might say that everyday theology, for West African Pentecostals, is a sort of unity of prayer and practice. This is to say that it is crafted by prayers and the prayers are also forms of practice.

Together, everyday practices and prayer—constituent parts of everyday life—function under the sign of power, the projection of traditional and modern spiritual and nonspiritual forms of power into the daily, microsociological experiences of Pentecostals. The centrality of prayer and its imbrication in everyday practices derive from the sociohistorical significance of power in West Africa. As Matthews Ojo writes:

> I am convinced that nothing occupies the attention of Africans as much as power, particularly its manifestation, whether in the form of material wealth, political and social statuses, traditional privileges like chieftaincy titles, colonial heritage, etc.... Power is focal to social relations for most [Africans], amid a social milieu where "power" whether in terms of ethnic linkages, financial resources, filial relations, and business connections have been able to achieve. Crucial to the life and activities of Charismatic movements is the articulation and appropriation of new forms of power in very pragmatic terms to mediate and address [their] contemporary felt needs.[13]

In West African Pentecostal communities, power is primarily accessible through intimate relationship with the Holy Spirit and prayer. Prayer is the concrete analysis of a given social situation and theology in order to change social circumstances and their interpretation. Prayer analyzes the specific crisis of inherited theology, its particular cultural situation, and its present predicament. It does the same for personal or social predicaments. The Pentecostal prayer retrieves from practical existence the forms theology must take if it is to effectively translate Christianity into the African culture. The attentive eye that the prayer warrior brings to examining how various forms of theology touch the ground in real life enables her to discern the theological ideas that constitute meaning for her. In this way, prayer enables theology to both respond to the questions in a culture's creative self-interpretation and to challenge it.

Prayer does all these within the available modes of exchange in West Africa. Pentecostal prayer in West Africa pivots around four principles or modes of exchange, enabling it to socially determine the diverse orientations of everyday theology or practices. These modes of exchange also reflect communal norms about power or the intercourse between powers of being. An analysis of oral prayers and published prayers reveals that the intercourse between humans and the Holy Spirit is structured around pragmatic notions of *pure gift*, *reciprocity* (gift and countergift), *plunder and redistribution*, and *instrumental faith*.[14] In the mode of pure gift, God's response to human needs is taken to be a gratuitous act of benevolence. When God gives in this mode, the gift is complete and there is no need for reciprocal gift. God is expected to show God's superiority, and believers accept His gifts without making return gifts, positioning themselves as children, clients, and servants of an omnipotent chief. An example of such a divine gift is the pure pleasure that bodies experience during worship services.

In the mode of reciprocity, there is gift and countergift. Pentecostals believe that offering, fasting, and other disciplinary efforts can be directly exchanged for divine blessings and approval. The prayer language of the man who used his hand as a sword that we described earlier embeds this logic. He hopes to exchange time and energy expended in prayers for personal transformation.

Under the mode of plunder and distribution, the divine-human intercourse is solicited and sustained in order for the Pentecostal believer to acquire the necessary power to plunder the resources of enemies or nonbelievers and redistribute them for personal gains and the work of God's kingdom. Born-again shopping is an example of this principle of intercourse.

Finally, we have instrumental faith. Most West African Pentecostals perceive faith as the power of universal exchangeability in transactions of the spiritual realm or intercourse with the Holy Spirit. Faith is accumulated in order to acquire goods or translate "spiritual blessings that are hanging in the air" into physical goods and accomplishments. Here spiritual intercourse has taken the form of commodity exchange, and faith-as-money is the intermediary. It appears that with faith (as indexed by the name-it-and-claim-it gospel), believers can bypass the usual groveling and pleadings before a deity and move on to an exchange transaction that is presumably grounded on mutual consent between deity and human beings. At any rate, the consent of God might not even be solicited at all times, because, as the faith-drenched Pentecostals claim, "you shall decree a thing and it shall be established unto you." (See Job 22:28.) They believe that faith can produce wealth at will, and this partly explains the rise of born-again shopping. The prayer warrior swinging his hand as an imaginary sword and shouting, "Shear, shear, shear," is also drawing on instrumental faith to create the new man.

In any given prayer session or round of daily experience, these principles or modes of exchange operate simultaneously and in mutual interrelationship. So when I highlight one mode as characteristic of a prayer form or daily transaction, it is only to indicate that this form is dominant, while the others are subordinated to it. In the long-going, rapid-fire prayers or everyday practices of West African Pentecostals, the different modes of exchange turn over quickly.

It is germane to mention that the practices that constitute an everyday form of theology do not represent a domain of practices separate from these four principles or modes of exchange. Daily practices of Pentecostals are deeply connected to the modes of exchanges or a complex combination of them such that the principles can be used to shed light on them. But this should not be construed to mean that the organizing principles of daily practices derive from them. It is conceivable that the principles of divine-human intercourse may have originated from human-to-human exchanges or from everyday theology of African traditional religions, which subsequently transferred to a new register.

Conclusion: Everyday Theology as Source of Academic Theology

In a certain sense, academic theology is an interpretation and reinterpretation of texts of theologians, philosophers, and others. It is an exercise in textual reading, textual criticism, and the mining of meanings from texts. The texts are usually academic essays and books and not the tactics of everyday life, popular uses of theological language, or habits and thoughts of ordinary folks. Everyday theology, as we have shown above, can be an excellent source of theology for academic theologians or it can stand all by itself. My move here to accent everyday acts as sources of theology is not an attempt to reveal the subtle, subterranean movements of the divine life in quotidian human existence. It also does not express a desire to work out any notion of religious *a priori* in human life or social existence. For me, everyday theology is where we can discern the stirrings of West African Pentecostalism's Yes and No to the totality of Christianity's interpretation of life or existence. Everyday theology is also the principal source for microtheology, a minimally explored dimension of Pentecostal scholarship. Microtheology investigates what people actually do in social situations with their faith, what kind of interactions actually happen that are evidently marked and colored by beliefs, and what are the theological meanings of such interactions.

Pentecostal theology has made admirable strides in many areas, but it is still focused on global-level, large-scale constructive projects or the macro configuration of thoughts. The key thinkers of the Pentecostal movement are only grappling with the grand theories of spirituality, doctrines, the kingdom of God, the Pentecostal distinctive of baptism in the Holy Spirit, pneumatology, interreligious dialogue, the Pentecostal principle, and the formulation of global theology, to name just a few. These efforts give a short shrift to the local, face-to-face, ephemeral patterns of everyday life, small aspects of encounters, and the flux and variation of the social life of Pentecostals. Apart from a few exceptions, the major thinkers have so far ignored interactional situations and interactional rituals of the social world of Pentecostals. It need not be so. They need innovative ideas, tools, and frameworks to theorize and theologize about the everyday life of ordinary Pentecostals. The tools of their regular constructive/systematic theologies are too cumbersome, blunt, and ill-suited for this new task. We need a turn to what I have named above as *microtheology*, which is more suited for the task. Microtheology will complement and expand traditional macrotheological approaches to Pentecostal spirituality.

Microtheology is an interpretative analysis of everyday embodied theological interactions and agency at the individual, face-to-face level. It is a study of everyday social interactions of individuals or small groups that demonstrate the linkages between spirituality (practices and affections) and embodied theological ideas (beliefs). Theologies, beliefs, and doctrines play an important role in structuring the daily, microsociological experiences of Pentecostals, and theologians need to understand these influences.

Chapter 2

The New Face of African Christianity: David Oyedepo's Winners Chapel and the Pentecostal Message of Salvation

E. Kingsley Larbi

THIS CHAPTER FOCUSES on the ministry of David Oyedepo and his Winners Chapel as a case study of the neo-Pentecostal movement in Nigeria and Ghana. Its four sections provide the background of the neo-Pentecostal growth, describe the emerging identity of this movement, explicate Oyedepo's ministry and message, and provide an initial assessment.

The Pentecostal Explosion and the Quest for Salvation

In sub-Saharan Africa today, Christianity is the most potent social force and the Pentecostal movement the most vibrant. Nigeria, with a population of over 170 million, has the largest Pentecostal constituency, with approximately 30 percent identified as such.[1] Though it appears difficult to concede, the spirituality of this new group palpably defines the spirituality of other churches. The Pentecostals originally emerged from the margins of society but now occupy the center of the religious landscape. In spite of what appears to be a cacophony of voices, there is clear evidence that some leaders have emerged with a message of salvation understood in both material and spiritual terms. What is the message and aspiration of this group, compared with the primal aspirations and the message of salvation in the wider African historical context?

The Portuguese first introduced Christianity to Africa in the fifteenth century, but it wasn't until the eighteenth and nineteenth centuries that Christianity was firmly established on the continent. The colonial churches, however, were, in form and content, replicas of the missionaries' homeland churches. Informed by the eighteenth-century Enlightenment mind-set, the missionaries relegated to the realm of superstition the activities of the spirit force.[2]

This attitude undermined the Christianization process, as it failed to engage the people at the point of their worldview. It was from this background that the Pentecostals emerged with their distinctive message of salvation. The Pentecostals, while accepting the worldview of the people, placed Jesus Christ at the center of the cosmic warfare, presenting Him as the Almighty, the only true Savior.

Preceding the prophet-healing movement and the Pentecostal churches were some Pentecostal-type charismatic figures. The first and the most prominent among them was a Liberian evangelist, William Wade Harris. When he entered the Ivory Coast in 1913 and in the western parts of the Gold Coast (Ghana) in 1914, he left no doubt that he was indeed the prophet of God! Wade Harris was able to tread the path where the missionaries failed. He understood the cosmology of the people, demonstrated the reign and the power of God over the local deities, and set their captives free! This gave him a real advantage over the missionaries. He challenged hundreds of people, chiefs and subjects alike, to surrender their idols for destruction and to submit themselves for baptism. Where the locals had been quite untouched by the message of the missionaries, Harris is said to have moved thousands to faith, leading converts to join the mission churches.[3]

Following after Harris and other charismatic figures came what has now become known as the African Independent or Initiated Churches (AICs). They are known as *Aladura* in Nigeria, *Zionist* in South Africa, and *spiritual churches* in Ghana. The activities of the AICs center primarily on healing, exorcism, prophecies, and visions. Because of certain theological differences, the AICs in Ghana and Nigeria belong to different ecumenical groupings.

The Christ Apostolic Church, the Apostolic Church, the Church of Pentecost, the Assemblies of God, and the Foursquare Gospel Church constitute the main Evangelical, classical Pentecostal churches in Ghana and Nigeria. The first three were originally inspired by indigenous initiatives of D. O. Odubanjo in Nigeria[4] and Peter Anim from Ghana.[5] The last two had roots in Western missionary activities. Although members of the two groups once belonged to the mission churches, they had a common passion: a search for a deeper religious experience.

The prominent neo-Pentecostal churches emerged between the 1970s and 1980s, and the proliferation has continued. One of the movement's leading ministers of the last century, Benson Andrew Idahosa (1938–1998) was and remains an influential African Pentecostal preacher.[6] He established the Church of God Mission in Nigeria with several branches. He is known as the father of Nigerian Pentecostalism. He led in the establishment of the Pentecostal Fellowship of Nigeria and mentored some of the key leaders of the movement in Nigeria and Ghana.[7]

Apart from the "born again" message, the core of the Pentecostal message is "salvation today," which deals with the concrete realities of life. The understanding of "salvation today," for most African Christians, exhibits similarities with the primal understanding of "salvation today"; however, the way salvation is sought in the two realms differs. Whereas in the primal milieu salvation is sought through the traditional forms of supernatural succour, the Pentecostals look to the Christian God as the *sole* source of relief. The position of the born-again Pentecostals therefore contrasts sharply with the assertion that "in Africa generally, one form of religion does not necessarily negate another. In their search for answers people easily accumulate in their personal world as many religious resources as they deem appropriate for their salvific needs."[8]

The Identity of the Pentecostals: Bible, Sacraments, and Mission

One scholar, in his recent book, presents African Pentecostalism in this light:

> The pervasiveness of the success or victory motif makes it difficult to equate African Pentecostals with evangelicalism, for even basic ideas of British/American evangelicalism (...biblicentrism, the cross, personal conversion, mission) have been transformed out of all recognition, even when the words are preserved. The cross is not frequently mentioned, but when it is, it is more in the following vein: Jesus hung on the cross so you can experience sweet things in your life.[9]

Is this scholar right? What is the identity of African Pentecostals?

The most significant marker of African Pentecostals is reverence for the Bible. It is the source of authority for faith, conduct, and affirmation of identity. Pentecostals believe in both the Old and New Testament as the Word of God. Anim's group, the Christ Apostolic Church, maintains:

> The Bible is our all-sufficient rule for faith and practice. It is the inspired Word of God, a revelation from GOD to man,

> the INFALLIBLE guide of conduct and faith. The Bible is SUPERIOR to conscience and reason, but not contrary to wisdom (2 Tim. 3:15, 16; I Pet. 1:21). The Bible—both OLD and NEW TESTAMENTS is the pure Word of God that cannot be changed, added to, nor taken away from its words, without terrific consequences.[10]

Oyedepo's organization also believes:

> The Bible, made up of the Old and New Testaments is the inspired Word of God, the product of holy men of old who spoke and wrote, as the Holy Spirit moved them. In these, we find the complete revelation of God's will for the salvation of mankind, and the divine and final authority for the Christian faith and life (1 Tim. 2:5; Luke 1:27–35; 1 Tim 3:16; Rom. 8:34).[11]

It is part of the African Pentecostals' spirituality to own and carry personal Bibles. What is more, the Bible is to be taken along to all major church gatherings. They are instructed to read and meditate upon it and, above all, obey its contents. Out of Pentecostals' understanding of the Bible flows the emphasis on patterns of behavior pleasing to God (Rom. 12:1–2). Though salvation is by grace (Eph. 2:8–9), for them true conversion enjoins believers to produce good works (2 Tim. 2:19–26; James 2:20).[12]

Pentecostals further maintain that one can only understand the Bible through the agency of the Holy Spirit, which only happens after conversion. For conversion to take place, the individual is required to consciously follow certain defined steps: a recognition of the consequences of the lost state of humankind (Rom. 3:23; 6:23); an understanding of God's provision for salvation; and an appropriating of this salvation by faith (John 1:12; 3:16; cf. 1 John 5.10–13), through the acceptance of Jesus Christ as Savior and Lord (Rom. 10:9–11).[13] Water baptism then follows.

Whereas mainline Pentecostals recognize water baptism and the Eucharist as the two main ordinances, some of the neo-Pentecostals have more than two. It needs, however, to be stated that the movement as a whole sees water baptism and Holy Communion as the key sacraments instituted by Christ.

Water baptism by immersion for Pentecostals means identifying with Jesus in His life, death, and resurrection. This is an affirmation that the convert has died to the old sinful nature and has made a commitment to live a new life (2 Cor. 5:17). Regarding water baptism, the following is representative of the position: "Water baptism is administered to those who hear and believe the gospel and accept and confess Jesus Christ as...personal savior....Water baptism by immersion in the Name of JESUS is an outward testimony that we are dead to our old sins, but rise to walk in newness of life with Jesus Christ."[14] Oyedepo and the Winners Chapel are emphatic along the same perspective in stating that "Water Baptism is a Biblical ordinance instituted by God. It is the commandment of Jesus Christ for every believer after repentance....Water Baptism, as a spiritual exercise, is an act of obedience that follows inward repentance. It is by immersion in water. At Baptism, we are buried with him."[15]

The theological significance to the Eucharist, representatively speaking again, is: "The cup represents the shed Blood of Christ on the cross for our redemption; the bread represents the broken body of Jesus Christ for our healing...and is a living prophecy of the SECOND COMING OF CHRIST."[16] The Eucharist, or Communion, is regarded as an institution of Christ to remind believers of His life, death, resurrection, and Second Advent. For African Pentecostals, the atonement also makes full provision for the healing and personal well-being of believers (Isa. 53:5; cf. 1 Pet. 2:25).

Apart from the two main sacraments mentioned above, which classical and neo-Pentecostals consider as timeless ordinances established by Christ, there are other practices within the movement, especially the neo-Pentecostal segment, which have been institutionalized as ordinances. I refer to these ones as the *enigmatic sacraments* because of their uncertain nature. These include practices such as the application of the anointing oil, the blood of sprinkling, the mantle, and feet washing.[17] These practices, in most cases, have come into being in particular churches through a revelation or what is believed to be a directive from God to certain individuals, especially the founders of churches. Their demonstrable efficacy in the original context sometimes influences other churches to follow suit simply by copying, believing that the same efficacy will be recorded in the new context.

The anointing oil has been identified by some as a sacrament or ordinance in African Pentecostal Christianity.[18] Inasmuch as this may be the case within the neo-Pentecostal movement, it will be inaccurate to suggest that it is so for the African movement as a whole. The classical Pentecostals—for example, the Church of Pentecost, the largest Pentecostal denomination in Ghana—will have nothing to do with it. The same could be said of other classical Pentecostal churches. Within the neo-Pentecostal movement in Ghana, we may identify two different arrangements regarding the use of the anointing oil. There is a group that uses it occasionally during major gatherings, like the 31st December Watch Night service. Mensa Otabil's International Central Gospel Church, Accra-Ghana, belongs to this group. There is another group that has it as a prominent and regular feature.

The African Pentecostal ethos is replete with evangelistic zeal.[19] The love of Christ and their commitment to Him compel them to "go and tell" others.[20] To this end, Oyedepo's emphasis on

Winners Chapel's yearly Missions Week is instructive. During this period, every church member is expected to win at least one soul and work with that person till "Christ is formed in him or her."[21] For them, "soul winning" and the equipping of the saints (Eph. 4:12–16) are their passion and at the core of their business. The contemporary mission strategy of the Pentecostals stands on three pillars: 1) the ecumenical paradigm of *presence*, or *being*; the evangelical paradigm of *proclamation*; and the New Testament, apostolic paradigm of *power* demonstration, following after the Mark 16:15–18 mandate and Jesus's own manifesto (Luke 4:18; cf. Isa. 61:1–7).[22] African Pentecostals see the power factor as critical because they believe it is the New Testament pattern of evangelism (Luke 10:18–19; Mark 16:15–18; Matt. 9:35–38).

The Bible is more than a yardstick for measuring faith and conduct. Equally critical to African Pentecostals is that the Bible affirms who they are and defines their identity (Gen. 1:26–28; Ps. 8:5–8; 139:14; Acts 17:26). The Scriptures assume fresh meaning in light of their own history. As God's vice-regents, in the midst of filth, disease, poverty, and illiteracy, believers on the continent are commanded to assume responsibility and turn things around (Gen. 1:26–28). The imperatives of Genesis 1:28—"God blessed them and said to them, 'Be fruitful and multiply, and replenish the earth and subdue it. Rule over the fish of the sea and over the birds of the air and over every living thing that moves on the earth'" (MEV)—challenges the African Pentecostal to contribute to the development of the continent because this is where God, by providence, has located them (Acts 17:26). They are therefore not just here on the earth as mere strangers passing through, but as God's agents for change. And until their labors on the earth are done, their work is not yet finished.

The foregoing are markers that identify African Pentecostals as followers of Christ. How does Oyedepo's and Winners Chapel's ministry illuminate this general description?

Oyedepo, the Winners Chapel, and the Message of Hope and Salvation

David Olaniyi Oyedepo was born on September 27, 1954. He was raised most of the time by his godly grandmother, an Anglican, who instilled in him the importance of hard work and integrity, the dangers of debt, and the snares of bad companionship.[23] He accepted Jesus as his personal Savior—was born again, according to contemporary West African Pentecostal-Evangelical parlance—on February 19, 1969, and was healed of tuberculosis the same year. At age sixteen, God used him to raise his seven-year-old dead brother.[24] His life and ministry have been profoundly influenced by Pentecostals like T. L. Osborn, Kenneth Hagin, J. Oswald Smith, Smith Wigglesworth, and Benson Idahosa, among others. The following discusses Oyedepo's message, presents his notions of prosperity and seed faith, and highlights lessons to be learned.

Mandate, ministry, and message

Oyedepo's entry into the full-time ministry was influenced by an eighteen-hour vision in 1981:

> I saw a lineup of the afflicted and the oppressed, rows of the blind, the lame, the wretched, and the battered and beaten.... I saw their groaning as they filed past me. I could not help it.... "Lord what is this?" I asked. I heard God say to me, "But from the beginning it was not so." I broke down the more in tears.... I heard God say distinctly to me: "And now, the hour has come to liberate the world from all oppressions

> of the devil, through the preaching of the Word of faith; and I am sending you to undertake this task."[25]

This is what the ministry refers to as the liberation mandate that propelled Oyedepo into full-time ministry.[26] The prosperity and signs-and-wonders mandates were received in 1987 and 1992, respectively. The prosperity mandate came with specific command—"Arise, and get back home and make My People Rich"—received while on a ministry trip to the United States.[27]

A vision-sharing meeting was held on May 8, 1981, that gave birth to the Power House group, which engaged in a "chain of prayer and fasting for 28 months for the fulfillment of the Liberation Mandate."[28] The Faith Liberation Hour, a weekly teaching program, came into being on May 22, 1981. Oyedepo was later commissioned into full-time ministry on September 17, 1983, at a service conducted by E. A. Adeboye. The Living Faith Church was subsequently established in Kaduna on December 11, 1983.[29] The administrative office was later relocated from Illorin to Kaduna on September 30, 1984.

In 1989, Oyedepo recalls that God directed him by saying, "Arise, get down to Lagos and raise me a People."[30] He was obedient. The name Winners Chapel was subsequently adopted. Though the maiden Sunday service in Lagos attracted 250 attendants, the church has since seen a phenomenal growth. The ministry's headquarters is now located on a 530-acre facility named Canaanland. This is the home of the fifty-thousand-seat capacity Faith Tabernacle auditorium, one of the biggest single church auditoriums in the world, constructed in twelve months and fully funded by Winners Chapel. There are many other innovations at Canaanland. The Covenant University and other educational institutions are also located here. The facility also includes the publishing house, the Hebron bottled water processing plant, four banks, and several residential estates that provide housing for thousands of the ministry's employees and Covenant University students.

Every message preached has an element of the liberation mandate. It is important also to observe that every message, irrespective of the topic, is delivered with the same passion and energy. Oyedepo's own statement on the subject matter is significant:

> Ever since the *Liberation Mandate* was given, I have consistently done exactly what God has asked me to do. I have decided not to turn to the right or to the left, but have steadfastly and in the fullness of his grace pursued the task as raw as He gave me. I have kept to his calling upon my life...to liberate the world from all oppressions of the devil through...the Word of Faith....I am privileged to be a messenger of the Most High God....God sent me to bring heaven down to the earth. He sent me to tell the devil, "Enough is enough!" I was sent to silence the harassment of the forces of darkness.[31]

Prosperity and "seed faith"

Though Oyedepo believes he is today holding the baton of the "Word of Faith" message,[32] we need to examine the essential elements of his teachings on prosperity and "seed faith."[33] One scholar, Paul Gifford, speaks of the *faith gospel* as "the belief that faith is what you need to share in the victory of Christ over sin, sickness and poverty. In faith you simply claim what is already yours. This swiftly became linked to the idea of 'seed faith,' that by planting seed you determine your harvest."[34] Further examination of Oyedepo's message reveals the following two major elements.

First is emphasis on taking responsibility and working hard. Oyedepo believes one does not just become prosperous simply by believing, confessing, sowing a seed, claiming, or releasing the prophet's anointing. He unwaveringly insists that only hard work is consistent with God's covenant of prosperity and posits that unless one commits oneself to honest labor and pursues that diligently, one will end up a beggar. For Oyedepo, work is critical because one cannot operate within the "covenant of prosperity" without being a worker, since all the patriarchs were workers: Abraham, he says, was a "worker" (Gen. 13:2; 24:35), Isaac a "tireless worker" (Gen. 26:1–14), and Jacob a "creative worker" (Gen. 30:27, 33).[35] Oyedepo insists that it is the "quality of our input that defines the limits of the returns on our giving." Apart from the patriarchs, he cites examples of Jesus Himself (John 5:17) and the Apostle Paul (1 Cor. 15:10). He believes God never blesses the idle and insists Christians must work because that is the platform on which God's blessings flow (Prov. 12:24; 13:7; 20:4). Oyedepo himself puts in about eighteen hours of work daily.

The second major element of Oyedepo's prosperity message is the avoidance of sloth and wastefulness. Oyedepo identifies sloth and wastefulness as some of the major causes of poverty. He is particularly critical of frivolous use of telephones, careless use of time, and reckless spending. He resolutely states that both the idle and the waster will equally end up in want. Oyedepo's brand of the prosperity message calls for thrift, investment, savings, avoidance of waste, adherence to budgetary controls, and austerity measures. For him, this is what will make the believer's giving profitable. In line with his own philosophy, Oyedepo mentions that it is a policy in his organization that only 30 percent of financial receipts be spent on overhead. The remaining 70 percent is invested. All capital projects are funded from the investment account.

Oyedepo's "seed faith" theology is anchored in the following theological self-understanding. First, he believes wealth is an entrustment by God and must be seen as an instrument of service to God and humanity. He thinks one cannot be blessed beyond the level that one is committed to be a blessing. Second, he asserts wealth must be acquired honestly; otherwise, it becomes cancerous. Third, he believes it is love for God and the desire to be of service to humanity that qualifies one for "covenant blessings." Fourth, Oyedepo thinks one reason why some have not achieved financial dominion is that outlets for distribution have not been created.

The key passage to Oyedepo's "seed faith" theology is 2 Corinthians 9:6–11. He asserts that the "seed faith" is a covenant between God and the believer; it holds the key to financial dominion. He believes believers are "connected to the Abrahamic blessings by covenant through the blood of Jesus Christ" (Gal. 3:13–14; Gen. 12:1–3) and that "all the seed of Abraham are by covenant, lenders and not borrowers" (Deut. 28:11–12).[36] He outlines the various forms of giving in Scripture as tithing; offering; sacrifice; kingdom investments; and giving to parents, the poor, and God's servants as He Himself directs. He calls these outlets "spiritual transactions" that provoke divine investment or "launching pads" by which one attains financial dominion. The organization, however, thinks tithing is the "one and the only financial obligation; and that every other form of giving is as each one purposes in his heart."[37]

Oyedepo thinks the experience of financial dominion is for all believers and that this is God's financial agenda for the redeemed (Rev. 5:9–12). Though he insists every believer has an inheritance of riches in Christ (2 Cor. 8:9), he believes those who do not know will be poor and that those who know but are unwilling to fulfill the foregoing instructions will also remain poor.

Oyedepo has numerous verifiable outlets for his giving. He funds several public-spirited institutions. Accident victims on the Ota-Canaanland-Benin Republic road are treated at the Ota medical complex at his cost. He has demonstrated concern for the poor and the needy within his church since its incipient stages. Oyedepo encourages everyone to be a giver; he believes there will not be needy members in the body of Christ if people share his attitude of giving. The evidence available provides a contrasting perspective to critics who say that "perhaps in response to criticisms made against prosperity preachers, Oyedepo has introduced the idea of giving to others."[38]

Lessons to Learn from Oyedepo and the Winners Chapel

We will now look at other distinctives that are central to Oyedepo's ministry and teachings.

Possibility spirit

Oyedepo has demonstrated that well-resourced institutions can be established in Africa with local funding. The Canaanland model is also a demonstration that it is possible for systems to run efficiently throughout the continent if the same philosophy and leadership spirit and principles are adopted. He confidently teaches that the believer's prosperity is linked to his or her own country of origin (Acts 17:26).

Emphasis on quality education

Oyedepo has demonstrated that establishing a top-class university is not incompatible with "soul winning." He has made it abundantly clear that denominations can purposefully establish institutions of higher learning as evangelistic tools for the transformation of Africa. Oyedepo's vision for establishing his universities is to bring about a revolution, particularly in Nigeria, by raising the required ethically minded human capital.

Low-profile fund-raising methods

At Winners Chapel, people give according to conviction; there is nothing like "pressure giving." Oyedepo thinks giving under pressure is not in line with Scripture. He is convinced that his ministry operates "under open heaven covenant through the obedience to scriptural demand of tithing (Mal. 3:6–18)," and, because of this, the ministry, he indicates, has never come under pressure for funds.[39] As soon as the need arises, God provides! As large denominations in Ghana, for instance, are struggling to fund their educational institutions, with some of them seriously saddled with bank loans, the message of Oyedepo is that this shouldn't be the case, because "our God is El-Shaddai, the all sufficient God (Gen. 22:14, 2 Cor. 9:8–11)" and, furthermore, "Borrowing is contrary to the faith that we preach (Ps. 34:9–10)."[40] Oyedepo's fund-raising methods will put to shame the various unorthodox methods adopted for fund-raising in various parts of the church world.

An advocate of cultural, social, and economic renaissance

One of the cultural issues working against Africa's speedy development is disinterest in forward planning. The current struggle with Ghana's energy sector is basically due to this canker: the failure of leadership to project into the future.[41] The other cultural challenges impeding Africa's progress are the obvious lack of a sense of urgency with respect to time management; undue stress on position, power, and pedigrees (titles and qualifications) at the expense of the performance of specific tasks, and the absence of the "can do" spirit among leadership and the educated elite. Whereas the lower-class masses of Africa today are surviving precisely because of their "can do" spirit, leadership has made a poor show here. Oyedepo is championing a renaissance in these areas. He is successfully doing this through his teachings, preaching, leadership seminars, and workshops. Most importantly, he is demonstrating it through his personal lifestyle, even as he demands such of the ministers at Winners Chapel. The leadership of Winners Chapel offers the following statement on punctuality:

> Pastors are required to observe the blessedness of keeping to time as scheduled for our services. This allows them to raise a responsible congregation, which can plan their lives as a requirement for excellent pursuit of purpose. Therefore, all pastors are to observe that timeliness is an asset when applied with discipline.[42]

Viable institutional structures and constitutional order

Church constitutions have traditionally not been an ally of Pentecostals. In West Africa, even churches that are considered to be the leading ones are either unwilling to show their constitutions to outsiders or will tell you, "We are still working on it." Even the churches that have them publish them in the form of booklets, lacking the required details. Oyedepo has broken the jinx through the publication of *The Mandate,* a 504-page book containing the constitution, statutes, and administrative manual of the organization. It is publicly on sale. Oyedepo's organization has been able to do this because he believes "efficient structure is what sustains the impact and continuity and relevance of any organisation."[43]

Impactful missions presence

One of the fascinating things about the external missions efforts of Winners Chapel on the continent of Africa is their phenomenal growth. Somehow, they are able to attract the cream of the crop of the host country. When others are struggling both financially and numerically to make any meaningful impact in the host country, Winners Chapel does not seem to have such challenges. In the Democratic Republic of the Congo, for instance, Winners

Kinshasha congregation has over forty thousand worshippers, among which are some very influential people.[44] The story is virtually the same in Kenya and elsewhere.

Oyedepo's place in history

By all standards, among the "Pentecostal generals" of Africa today, Oyedepo stands as one of the tallest; and indeed, he stands as one of the giants of the global church. Oyedepo's life and ministry have inspired so many people, challenging them to take their call and ministries to greater heights. He believes his obedience to God has brought him this far. In his own words, "Obedience may be costly, but the end result is priceless," and, "Every challenge on the path of life is a test and only those who pass it become champions."[45] Winners Chapel adherents and many African Pentecostals feel that Oyedepo has become the champion he is today because he obeyed the heavenly vision.

Conclusions: Modernity, African Renaissance, and an Agenda for Change

Africa's developmental agenda undoubtedly has taken a slow pace; indeed, many citizens have become impatient with leadership across the continent. In spite of this low rate of African development, it is simplistic to suggest that nothing positive is taking place on the continent. Such people will fall into the camp of "agnostic-pessimists." These are people who have taken the position that nothing good can happen to a particular group of people, and even when good things are happening, they simply ignore that reality because they don't want to admit any such change. It is in this regard that some observers of African Pentecostalism could ignore the achievements at Canaanland and concentrate only on a partial picture of Oyedepo and his church.[46]

Does the movement in Africa have certain challenges to address? Certainly. In spite of these challenges, African Pentecostalism is poised to bring Africa into the modern world. In April 2015, the Church of Pentecost (Ghana) introduced the first-ever affordable in-vitro fertilization treatment at its medical center with specialist doctors drawn from the same church.

Oyedepo's Covenant University is one of the well-endowed and fast-growing universities in Africa. In January 2015, Webometrics ranked it as the best university in Nigeria, the best in West Africa, and fifteenth in sub-Saharan Africa. In May 2014, Covenant University organized its first international conference on African development. Another conference was held in 2015, which focused on the theme "Biotechnology, ICT, Materials, and Renewable Energy: Potential Catalyst for African Development." Landmark University, Oyedepo's second university, was established to help in the revitalization of agriculture in Nigeria. Students whose main concentration is in agriculture are on scholarship from Oyedepo's foundation, David Oyedepo Ministries. All these efforts are undoubtedly geared toward the development of Nigeria, which, by extension, affects the continent of Africa. It also needs to be mentioned that all these Pentecostal faith-based institutions of higher learning are not-for-profit entities.

To enable the movement to preserve her gains, the Pentecostal leadership must, *inter alia*, consider the following: Pentecostal leaders must work toward the empowerment of the educated elites among them to take seriously academic research on the movement; academics from the various branches of the theological discipline must help the movement to preserve and articulate its gains at the apologetic level; and leadership must work toward a more responsible membership. Sometimes an impression is created that prayers alone will automatically solve every problem.

But "economic salvation" doesn't just come by praying, confessing, hoping, and wishing; neither does it come only by the anointing or prayers of the man of God or the touch of the mantle and use of the anointing oil. Important as some or all of these might or might not be, Oyedepo has shown the way that they must not be seen as ends in themselves. On this, John Mahama, a Pentecostal himself, has this New Year message for all:

> Our bishops and the men of God can pray for us, they can pray divine favor on us, but we need to have that sense of optimism to claim the favor that they prayed for us.... And so when bishop says that, 2015 will be a fruitful year, it doesn't mean that, if you sit in your bedroom for 365 days, that fruit will reach you in your bedroom. *You have to get out and claim it and work for it and take it with both hands.*[47]

Oyedepo well echoes the above sentiments. To this end, we are confident that African Pentecostals must and will play a leading role toward Africa's total salvation: economic, social, political, spiritual.

Pentecostalism, like any other religion, is about salvation. Whether understood in spiritual or material terms, or a combination of both, it is the search of mortal humans for a merciful and an all-powerful God to answer to the challenges of existence. Human experience has amply demonstrated that scientific and technological developments alone cannot fill the void in the human soul. Saint Augustine had it right when he said, "Thou hast made us for Thyself, O Lord, and our heart is restless until it finds its rest in Thee." This restlessness will continue in spite of humanity's greatest and loftiest scientific advancements until human creatures discover their true and ultimate source. Oyedepo shows one way in which African Pentecostals are experiencing the *Nkwa* (shalom) of God.

Chapter 3

Indigenous Classical Pentecostalism: The Church of Pentecost in Ghana

Opoku Onyinah

THE EMERGENCE, GROWTH, and development of Pentecostal churches in Ghana signal a new era of African Christianity. In their introduction to *Pentecostal Mission and Global Christianity*, Wonsuk Ma et al. point out, "Today in Africa, as in other non-western contexts, the force of Pentecostalism has led to the Pentecostalization of historic mission churches to the point where in many countries the expressions Pentecostal, charismatic and evangelical are becoming indistinguishable from each other."[1] Pentecostalism in Ghana can be classified under three broad headings: first, what is normally referred to as *spiritual churches*, which originated primarily from African prophets within the historical churches; second, the classical Pentecostal churches that derived from or were remotely linked with the Azusa Street revival in North America; and third, neo-Pentecostal churches, commonly referred to in Ghana as *Charismatic churches*, which are the newly independent Pentecostal churches.[2] This chapter, however, focuses on the emergence, challenges, growth, and development of classical Pentecostalism in Ghana, with special reference to the Church of Pentecost (CoP). This analysis of the CoP focuses on the theological factors and practices thought to be responsible for the church's remarkable growth.

Origin of Pentecostalism

Before the establishment of the Pentecostal churches in Ghana, the initial attempt to evangelize Ghana was made by the Portuguese Roman Catholic Mission at the end of the fifteenth century and had not been very successful. However, by the mid-1800s, Christianity had firmly been established through the enterprising missionary activities of the Basel Mission (1828), the Bremen Mission (1847), the Wesleyan Methodist mission (1835), and the second Catholic mission (1880).[3] For various reasons, including a desire for freedom to worship in culturally relevant ways, religious changes, socioeconomic and spiritual hunger (prophetism), from 1922 onward, some Ghanaians established their own independent churches. These churches are commonly referred to in Ghana as *sunsum söre* (spiritual churches), and they have grown effectively. The attraction to these churches stemmed from the fact that they sought to incorporate charismatic experiences, especially healing and prophecy, into Christian worship. In doing so, they provided forms of worship that satisfied the holistic religious needs of Ghanaians. Yet scholars point out that the absence of administrative structures, promotion of personality cults, failure to test revelations, lack of accountability, unsubstantiated miracles, sexual promiscuity, and exploitation of people for personal gain—all of this negatively affected their popularity and gave rise to the growth of classical Pentecostalism in the country.[4] The following focuses on three classical Pentecostal churches: the Assemblies of God Church and the Apostolic and Christ Apostolic churches.

The Assemblies of God Church

The first Pentecostal mission agency to serve in Ghana was the Assemblies of God (AG) from the United States. They arrived in 1931, setting up their mission station in the northern territories. Irrespective of health challenges faced by the early AG missionaries, leading to the death of some of them, such as Guy Hickok and Beulah Buchwalter, the mission was established firmly in the north and subsequently expanded to the south. Some of the contributions of the AG church in Ghana include the provision of social services, such as medical care and literature development. The AG mission is also credited with the translation of the Dagomba version of the New Testament and the establishment of Bible institutes.[5] Some of the early missionaries of the AG attempted to be culturally meaningful to the local communities in which they served. Hans Debrunner reports that "the Shirers [referring to Lloyd and Margaret Shirer] really 'got under the skin' of the northern peoples more than missionaries ordinarily will do."[6] As a result of this, Mr. Shirer became so popular that he was ordained as a chief by the people. However, it looks like other AG missionaries did not follow the example of the Shirers, and, as a result, these others were accused of not identifying themselves with the local people among whom they served.[7]

Darkwa Jones Amanor observes that "being a missionary-sponsored mission, the AG depended very heavily on financial and other assistance from America"[8] and, as a result, could not achieve rapid numerical growth at these initial stages. This slow growth persisted until the late 1980s, when it became less dependent upon American missionaries. Kingsley Larbi also notes:

> Unlike the other Pentecostal denominations, the work of the Assemblies of God was heavily dependent upon a western

> financial and personnel support system. Between 1931 and 1970, about 99 missionaries worked with the mission in various capacities: Typists, clerks, cooks, and building contractors were all included in the list along side medical personnel, teachers and church planters.[9]

Nevertheless, the AG has grown in recent times to become one of the most prominent classical Pentecostal churches in the country. The AG played a prominent role in the formation of the Ghana Pentecostal and Charismatic Council. It was one of the AG senior pastors, Gyan Ofosu, who became its first president.

The Apostolic and Christ Apostolic Churches

Before the arrival of the AG church, Peter Anim, a former member of the Presbyterian Church, had already organized an independent group after reading a magazine called *The Sword of the Spirit* from the Faith Tabernacle Ministry based in Philadelphia, Pennsylvania, USA, in 1917. Anim's movement developed into a church and had affiliations with three different churches within a period of thirteen years: first with Faith Tabernacle church in 1922, second with the Apostolic Faith in 1930, and, subsequently, with the Apostolic Church in the United Kingdom in 1935. Anim's affiliation with the Apostolic Church led to the sending of the first Bradford Apostolic missionary to Ghana (then Gold Coast) in the person of Pastor James McKeown, in 1937.

The Apostolic Church that sent McKeown to Ghana had its birth in the Welsh revival. It was a church that displayed all the features of classical Pentecostalism. The doyen of Pentecostal studies Walter Hollenweger describes the Apostolic Church as a church that "gives greater play to the gifts of the Spirit."[10] In the church, men are called through prophecy to be apostles, prophets, evangelists, pastors, and teachers. Others were called to the offices of elder and deacon. Even though women were not ordained into full-time ministry as pastors, they were called and ordained as deaconesses. Consequently, the Apostolic Church developed a strict hierarchical structure.[11] Besides, the church held to an ethical rigorism, prohibiting activities such as drinking alcohol and smoking. Members who were found going to questionable places or falling into such "sins" were disciplined.[12]

Anim was pleased to have a missionary from the Apostolic Church to assist him. However, as a result of some differences on the doctrine of divine healing, Anim broke relations with the Apostolic Church to form the Christ Apostolic Church (CAC). The CAC under the leadership of Anim initially lacked internal cohesion, which led to quite a number of schisms and secessions from the organization. The attempts by the CAC to establish schools were also not very successful due to political and financial challenges.[13] In spite of all these, the CAC has grown to become a strong classical Pentecostal denomination in Ghana. It is one of the founding members of the Ghana Pentecostal and Charismatic Council.

Alongside the Christ Apostolic Church, the Apostolic Church also continued to expand under the leadership of different Apostolic missionaries sent from Britain within the period of 1953 to 1982, when the last missionary, E. H. Williams, left. Similar to the AG, government and mission activities within the Apostolic Churches were controlled from the mission office in the United Kingdom. Larbi indicates:

> All pastoral appointments and promotions were ratified in UK before ordination in Ghana. Minutes in Ghana were sent to UK for ratification before their adoption. Salaries of missionaries were paid by the UK office, whereas car maintenance allowances and travelling expenses were borne by the local church.[14]

Like the Christ Apostolic Church, the numerical growth of the Apostolic Church within recent years has been faster than previously.

As of 1993, when the second survey of the Ghana Evangelism Committee was published, the AG had the second-highest attendance among the classical Pentecostal churches (60,298). This was followed by the Apostolic Church (55,100) and Christ Apostolic Church (36,270). This means that as of the time of the survey, these churches had already outgrown some of the earlier mainline churches, such as the Anglican Church (29,354), the Baptist Convention (26,259), and A. M. E. Zion (11,070). Meanwhile, at the same period, attendance in the Church of Pentecost stood at 259,920, which was more than total attendance of the three other classical Pentecostal churches put together. Note that the AG, the Christ Apostolic Church, the Apostolic Church, and the Church of Pentecost remained the primary Pentecostal churches until the 1970s, when neo-Pentecostalism (charismatic ministries) emerged, with the latter movement resembling their counterparts in Nigeria and America.

The Church of Pentecost

McKeown continued to work as a missionary of the UK Apostolic Church till 1953, when he was dismissed over church practices and constitutional disputes. Following McKeown's departure from his parent church in the United Kingdom, he was invited to lead an indigenous group that defected from the UK Apostolic Church and had taken on a new name, the Gold Coast Apostolic Church. In 1957, when Ghana attained independence, the name was changed to the Ghana Apostolic Church. Thus, for some time, the two Apostolic churches were operating side by side in Ghana: the Apostolic Church, Ghana (the original one from the UK), and the Ghana Apostolic Church. This situation prevailed until 1962, when the president of Ghana, Kwame Nkrumah, intervened in a legal battle between the two churches. As part of the outcome of Nkrumah's ruling, the Ghana Apostolic Church (McKeown's group) was asked to change its name, and a new name, the Church of Pentecost, was then adopted.

The Church of Pentecost (CoP) experienced phenomenal growth after the end of the internal squabbles between the two Apostolic churches, which attracted the attention of researchers. For instance, both Larbi and Asamoah-Gyadu assess the context of the collective historical, religious, and theological orientation of Ghanaian indigenous Pentecostal movements. Asamoah-Gyadu, for example, cites the emergence of CoP as one of the factors that has contributed to the decline of the older African initiated, or spiritual, churches in Ghana. For him and against the backdrop of the difficulties faced by the spiritual churches cited earlier, CoP has become a "more respectable option in indigenous Pentecostalism."[15]

At the end of 2014, the State of the Church address by the chairman indicated that the CoP had a total membership of 2,626,902. The church has branches on all continents, with 1,868 districts and 17,963 assemblies (congregations). The total membership of the church in Ghana was 2,251,109, representing 8 percent of the Ghanaian population. It is important at this point to discuss the factors that have led to the growth and respectability of the CoP.

Factors Responsible for the Growth of the CoP

Allan Anderson rightly states that there are many reasons for the emergence and growth of Pentecostalism in the majority world.[16] For him, the Pentecostals' constant effort to expand is underpinned by their firm belief in the Bible as an independent authority and their experience of the Holy Spirit, who empowers the believers' mission to the world. He identified other reasons such as:

> ...the practice of "indigenous church" principles, the ability to adapt to different cultures, the widespread use of mass media, the breakdown of the dichotomy between clergy and laity, its claim on the experience of the supernatural for healing and deliverance, as well as its offer of the power of the Spirit to all, regardless of education, language, race, class, or gender.[17]

The main theology of the Church of Pentecost can be found in what is generally referred to by Pentecostals as the *fourfold gospel.* This is enumerated as Jesus the Savior, Jesus the baptizer in the Holy Spirit, Jesus the healer, and Jesus the soon-coming King. It can therefore be argued that the theology of the CoP is Christocentric in character. The Holy Spirit, however, represents Jesus in all the activities of the church, and this makes the church's expression pneumatic in outlook, just as with all other Pentecostals.

For the purpose of this paper, two main factors are discussed below as spurring the phenomenal growth of the CoP. First is the emphasis on Holy Spirit baptism, and second is the conscious effort to adapt the gospel in culturally relevant ways. While the former leads to vibrant evangelism by all church members at all levels, the latter accounts for the respectability and acceptability of the church within the Ghanaian community. Both vibrant evangelism and acceptability within community give rise to growth.

Emphasis on Holy Spirit Baptism for All Believers

The Church of Pentecost places strong emphasis on Spirit baptism. All pastors report on the number of converts baptized in the Spirit in their annual reports. Thus, the work of the Holy Spirit in the lives of believers is prioritized in the church. The Holy Spirit is thought of as the One who guides the church and also enables Christians to effectively perform the tasks assigned to believers in Christian ministry. The Holy Spirit gives supernatural ability to Christians to witness, preach, cast out evil spirits, heal the sick, and be protected from evil forces. It is believed that once people experience the baptism of the Holy Spirit with the initial evidence of speaking in tongues, they are expected to testify of Christ to others. Though this has been the stand of many classical Pentecostals,[18] CoP has been practicing and even reporting on members baptized in the Holy Spirit annually. Thus, people baptized in the Holy Spirit are evangelists and missionaries wherever they are.

Russell Spittler, the North American Pentecostal theologian, writes, "Pentecostal success in mission can be laid to their drive for personal religious experience…the experiential particularism involved in every Pentecostal baptism in the Holy Spirit."[19] Paul Pomerville, the Pentecostal missiologist, observes that church-growth specialists assign many causes for Pentecostal church growth and missions, including the mobilization of the laity, praying for the sick, and aggressive evangelism. Nevertheless, he rightly shows that "the Pentecostal experience of individual believers has always been and still is the primary cause of growth of Pentecostal churches."[20] The CoP emphasizes this theological rationale for its growth, as opposed to sociological or other immanent explanations.[21]

A natural outflow of the baptism of the Holy Spirit is evangelistic passion and church planting. The strategy of the CoP is to encourage local churches and pastors to plant churches in unreached towns and within every community. Against this backdrop, the Witness Movement, now Evangelism Ministry, was formed to take up evangelistic activities. The Witness Movement usually identifies "new grounds" where the gospel has not been preached, gathers a team, and sends them to the area to reside there for about a week. The team prays during the period, preaches the gospel, and subsequently establishes a local church with the converts won.

Potential leaders are then identified, nurtured, and trained. Support is given to this new church from the mother church. After a period ranging from six months to one year, the church will be recognized to be able to grow without external support. It will be left in the hands of the locally trained leaders, with occasional visits from leaders of the mother church. The new churches will also be encouraged to open other churches in unreached communities. As the number of members increases, a new pastor will be sent to nurture the churches. This cycle then continues over and over again. In this way, the CoP is able to provide a church for ordinary people within their own communities.

It has been a regular feature within the CoP's fellowship meetings for people to hear reports of signs and wonders wrought in the power of the Holy Spirit, including cripples walking, the blind seeing, and demons being cast out, during evangelistic activities. Gerrie ter Haar observes that Pentecostals "detect the hand of God" in their daily affairs.[22] For Steve Land, Pentecostalism is the "unseen recovery of the universal call to witness in the power and demonstration of the Spirit in order to carry out the universal mission of the church."[23] Thus the emphasis on signs and wonders by the church, which is also part of the Pentecostal evangelistic strategy throughout the world, has contributed to the growth of the church in Ghana. The performing of signs and wonders is believed to follow those who are baptized in the Spirit, as Pentecostals believe, following the longer ending of St. Mark, among other scriptural warrants.

It is also obvious that even though the CoP does not ordain women into full-time ministry, once a woman is baptized in the Holy Spirit, she performs prominent roles that have aided the rapid growth of the church. It is also on record that the first organized group formed in the CoP was the women's movement. Women were the first interpreters for McKeown, the first missionary. Women financed the early years of the church, and they opened assemblies (congregations) and "pastored" some of these assemblies. McKeown himself knew this and gave full credit to the Ghanaian women.

Pentecostals' emphasis on the Holy Spirit baptism, especially regarding *glossolalia*, has not gone unchallenged.[24] Gary McGee's observation sums up critics' remarks against speaking in tongues: "Critics branded *glossolalia* as nonsense."[25] Nonetheless, Pentecostals and Charismatics involved in the renewal in Africa and other parts of the world believe that their churches are growing because of the work of the Holy Spirit. Undoubtedly, the Pentecostal experience and success has prompted the larger church world to reassess the work of the Holy Spirit in its activities,[26] and in that sense, Pentecostalism has contributed positively to Ghanaian Christianity just as it has to African and world Christianity.

The emphasis placed on the need for each person to receive the Holy Spirit enables participation in the life of the church, including its liturgy. This direct experience of God through the indwelling Holy Spirit thus empowers the contribution of all members. The result of this is indigenous assimilation.

Indigenous Assimilation

Right from the beginning of his ministry in Ghana, McKeown, as if he was aware of the indigenous policy of self-supporting, self-propagating, and self-governing churches,[27] wanted the church to be indigenous with Ghanaian culture, ministry, and finance. He realized that "it would be difficult to grow an 'English oak' in Ghana. A local 'species', at home in its culture, should grow, reproduce and spread: a church with foreign roots was more likely to struggle."[28] His concern was to sow what he called the "local species" to produce an indigenous church. He stressed the fact that the church must be self-reliant in finance, government, and propagation of the gospel.

This indigenous church policy influenced church planting, governance, and the finances of the church. For example, in terms of governance, the church uses a centralized structure that is similar to that of the Apostolic Church in the United Kingdom, where the highest decision making body of the church is the General Council.[29] This structure is replicated at the area, district, and local levels of the church, making it impossible for any one person to assume supremacy in decision-making. The structure may have its weaknesses, but on the whole, it fits in with the Ghanaian culture, especially that of the Akan, with its various military organs.[30] Hence, the members feel secure in its formality, accountability, and disciplinary measures. On finance, the church uses whatever local resources are available for its administration and projects, such as putting up of church buildings, schools, and health centers. The church also takes care of the welfare and social needs of its members and the Ghanaian community as a whole by offering scholarships to needy students and providing various supports to nongovernmental organizations and parachurch organizations. By insisting on being self-supporting, the church has stood on its feet right from the start.

It is not clear if McKeown had knowledge of the three-self policy before he began his work in Ghana. Some Pentecostal scholars, including Hollenweger and Spittler, point out that Pentecostals had been influenced by Roland Allen's missionary methods.[31] Pentecostal historian of missions Gary McGee has shown that Allen's books were already circulating in Pentecostal circles as early as 1921.[32] Nevertheless, Leonard thinks that McKeown was not aware of these ideas,[33] although McKeown's stress on self-supporting districts might imply that he had read about them elsewhere. Undoubtedly, it can be assumed that McKeown, like many Pentecostals,[34] believed he was implementing New Testament methods through the leading of the Holy Spirit. For Larbi, "These principles helped to place the organization on a sound footing morally, financially, and in terms of its strong and uncompromising evangelistic drive. These principles have since defined the ethos of the Church. McKeown played the role of a facilitator par excellence."[35]

Beyond the idea of the "three-self policy," the attempt to indigenize the gospel in culturally relevant ways permeated the worship or liturgy of the church. The result of this can be likened to what Paul Hiebert calls "self-theologizing."[36] Even though worship in the CoP is similar to that of other classical Pentecostals, some cultural distinctives are identifiable, manifest in activities such as preaching, the giving of testimonies, locally "received" or written Pentecostal songs, praises (accompanied by clapping of hands and dancing), and special times of prayer called "worship." These are opportunities to express oneself before God in diverse ways. The CoP has appealed to ordinary Ghanaians because worship takes place in the local languages and through local expressions.

As McKeown felt that other missionaries were westernizing their churches in Ghana, he sought to indigenize his mission and has been credited for using the Ghanaian people to achieve this aim.[37] For example, apart from allowing the Ghanaians to use their local drums and dances to praise the Lord during worship,

McKeown is also reported to have allowed Afua Kuma to use primal religious and poetic forms in praise and worship.[38] For the Ghanaian and probably most Africans, Afua Kuma's praise and poems connect and invoke a clear understanding of God, just as the psalms did for the ancient Hebrews. Afua Kuma's poems have since become a classical example of local theologizing within Africa.[39] Allan Anderson's concluding remarks about the Church of Pentecost is, "To all intents and purposes this was an autochthonous Ghanaian church."[40]

Also, indigenous CoP songs are believed to be "received" by the people or congregation, rather than written by individuals. Most often during prayer sessions after preaching or worship, a member receives, through the inspiration of the Holy Spirit, a song that would be sung spontaneously, without first being written down. These songs also reveal the theology and spirituality of the ordinary Church of Pentecost member. For example, in describing how Eunice Johnson[41] receives Pentecostal songs, David Nyansah Hayfron notes:

> And then suddenly, she heard in her ears a very loud sound of instruments playing in heaven. She saw in a vision above the clouds people playing the instruments. Those instruments were nothing she had ever seen on this earth before. Then, she tried to sing along with them.[42]

The church's forms of worship, especially its songs, have had an impact on the entire Ghanaian society.

Larbi thus observes that the Church of Pentecost "has bequeathed to Ghanaian Christianity more locally brewed Christian songs than any other church in the country."[43] Similarly, Asamoah-Gyadu indicates that "the greatest advantage of such informal theology is that it is born out of real encounters with Jesus Christ, how African Christians understand their walk with him, and how they as ordinary people express the faith."[44] Thus, although the CoP has not yet intellectually systematized its faith theologically, these are echoed in its normal church activities, such as worship, songs, preaching, conventions, and meetings of ministries, with the members carrying these along orally.

During the early part of 1990, the leadership of the church realized that the strong emphasis on local assimilation was having a negative impact on expatriates and a new generation of Ghanaians who preferred to worship in the English language or in a multicultural environment. To address this challenge, the Pentecost International Worship Centers were formed. These are churches that use the English language in their worship and conduct the liturgy to suit multicultural environments.

Mission Activities

In some respects, the beginning of the spread of the CoP to other countries was not an organized one. As CoP members migrated along the coast of West Africa, they shared their faith with others, and small groups of new converts were quickly formed. The immigrants sent information home about the existence of these new churches that they had established, and in response, pastors (usually without formal training) were then sent out as "missionaries" to support these groups. Note that the establishment of these branches of the church outside Ghana shows the effectiveness of oral culture. Hollenweger observes that "all the elements of oral theology function as a logic system for passing on theological and social value information in oral society."[45] Thus, the CoP members carry their theology orally along wherever they go.

In a similar way, when Ghanaian immigrants went to the West, they began to worship and to contribute to the growth of Western churches, including those with Caucasian majorities. Yet many did not feel at home. What Roswith Gerloff writes about the African American experience applies also to that of Ghanaian immigrants: "The religion of the slaves [African Americans and, by extension, Africans] and the religion of the slave master [whites] were never identical, even when both referred to the same Bible."[46] Thus, in the efforts to establish themselves, CoP immigrants founded their own communities, religious networks, and places of worship. As of December 2014, the CoP has congregations in ninety-one countries on all continents.

In order to coordinate the activities of the branches overseas, the CoP established an International Missions Office. This department is under the International Missions Director (IMD), who reports directly to the chairman of the church on the same basis as the church's general secretary. One of the functions of the IMD is to advise missionaries and, where appropriate, organize with them into evangelistic outreaches, rallies, and conventions for effective evangelism of the nations.

Conclusion

The emergence, development, and growth of the Church of Pentecost can be placed within the broader context of the twentieth-century Pentecostal renewal. Drawing especially on the Pentecostal experience of the baptism of the Holy Spirit and adapting this to suit the Ghanaian cultural milieu, the Church of Pentecost has progressively developed to become an example of a successful African indigenous Pentecostal church. Its form of Pentecostal worship has impacted the modes of worship in other churches in Ghana. The structure, administration, and financial policies that have undergirded the church's growth could be a pattern for other African Pentecostal churches to emulate.

Chapter 4

The Growth and Expansion of Pentecostalism in Francophone West Africa: The Assemblies of God of Burkina Faso

Jean-Baptiste Roamba

THE PURPOSE OF this paper is to survey the history of Christianity in Burkina Faso, especially the Assemblies of God Church and how it has affected Burkina Faso and its neighboring countries. I will show that the Burkina Faso Assemblies of God Church has been a missionary church from its inception, reaching out to neighboring countries despite the lack of national natural resources as one of the poorest in the world. Because of this economic context, young people have migrated to the surrounding countries, such as Ghana and Ivory Coast, in search of better lives but have brought the gospel with them along the way.

The Country

Burkina Faso, formerly Upper Volta, is a landlocked country in West Africa. It is surrounded by Ghana and Ivory Coast on the south, Benin and Togo on the southeast, and Mali and Niger on the north. With an area of 105,900 square miles, Burkina Faso has a tropical Sudano-Sahelean climate characterized by a long dry season from October to April and a short rainy season from May to September. The rainy season does not offer many opportunities to the inhabitants. Because of its geographical situation, Burkina Faso has no seaport. For its importation and exportation, it depends heavily on the coast.

The last census estimated the population at seventeen million, not counting the estimated four million living in the surrounding countries—especially in Ivory Coast, where at least three million Burkina Bé live and work in coffee and cocoa plantations.

For twenty-seven years, President Blaise Compaoré led the country. In October 2014, because of his dictatorial leadership, the population forced him to resign. Since then, Burkina Faso has been in a period of transition, led by a civilian president and a prime minister.

The nation's multiethnic groups live in relative peace, and the Moose are the largest group, making up more than half the population. The Moose live in a hierarchical society in which the emperor is the supreme chief while other chiefs serve under his authority. When the colonizers conquered the country at the end of the nineteenth century, they found the Moose to be well organized and ready to fight. But as their weapons were ineffective, the French submitted the Moose to their rule. This was not without difficulties, as people were resistant. The country became a French colony until its independence in 1960.

During the colonization of the late-1800s, West Africa was a fertile ground for new religions. Islam was already there and making converts. Elliot Skinner reported about the failed attempt by the Muslims to convert the emperor of the Moose to Islam.[1] But as ancestor worshippers, the Moose did not accept easily other religious groups. When Muslim traders invited the Moose ruler to convert, he consulted with the ancestors, whom he believed would not allow him to accept the new religion. It was clear that the Moose monarch would not embrace Islam, but the Muslims attacked the northern part of the country and took control, forcing their subjects to convert to Islam. According to Dim Delobsom, the first mosque was built in Burkina Faso in the middle of the eighteenth century in Ouagadougou.[2] Today, Islam is the largest religious group in the country, claiming more than half of the population. Despite the presence of Islam, other religious groups have entered.

How Christianity Came to Burkina Faso

At the end of the nineteenth century, West Africa was a center of intense religious activity. The British missionary societies were already present on the coast, but Burkina Faso had yet to be evangelized. The first missionary group to enter the country was the *Pères Blancs* (White Fathers) of the Roman Catholic Church in about 1900.

The Moose people were evangelized from Koupela, a town located in the east. From the beginning, the French administration competed with Catholic priests because their work tended to elude the colonizers. The locals seemed to love Catholic priests while they showed overt resistance to the French administrators. Later, the Catholic priests moved their headquarters to Ouagadougou. They became active in education, health care, and other forms of social work. They established primary and secondary schools to train the children. They also opened clinics to meet the physical needs of the population. The girls who had been banned from their families were welcomed in the mission and were prepared to be good wives for their husbands. One of their strategies was also to liberate young girls from undesired weddings. The Moose parents at that time were giving their daughters to be wed without their agreement.

During this period of intense spiritual activity, revival broke out in the United States. In 1906, William Joseph Seymour arrived in Los Angeles to lead a small church. In his sermons he emphasized the baptism of the Holy Spirit with the evidence of speaking in tongues. This mission, known as the Azusa Street revival, sent missionaries all over the world. Cecil Mel Robeck states, "If pastor William J. Seymour and the people of Azusa Street Mission wanted to spread the message of salvation, holiness, and spiritual empowerment across North America, they wanted even more to carry it around the world. They believed that God was restoring something to the church that has been missing for centuries."[3]

Many received their missionary call from this revival and began sailing toward the places to which they had been called. While the revival was spreading in the United States, many people who had been newly baptized in the Holy Spirit were rejected by their churches. In order to keep the fire they received through the baptism of the Holy Spirit, believers organized themselves. The Assemblies of God USA was formed in April 1914 as a cooperative effort partly in order to send missionaries. Missionary zeal and work was and is still a top priority for the Assemblies of God.

While the Catholic Church was occupying the ground, Assemblies of God USA missionaries received a prophetic word to go to the Moose Land that was unknown to them. Wilbur Taylor was a missionary working out of the Stone Church (Assemblies of God) in Chicago, Illinois. In 1918, he contacted the Stone Church when he received a burden for the Moose, the largest tribal group of West Africa, and the church supported his mission to the Moose in the French Sudan. Although he had been stationed in Sierra Leone under the Christian and Missionary Alliance for a number of years previously, in 1919, Taylor set sail for Sierra Leone with Brother Harry Wright and his wife. Almost immediately upon arrival, Taylor and Wright set out for the interior, a thousand-mile trip.[4] One important aspect of this missionary trip is that they did not consult their home-based missions board. They decided independently to reach out to this largest tribal group of West Africa.

Wilbur Taylor and Harry Wright, accompanied by their wives and two single women, were the first Pentecostal missionaries who arrived in Mossi Land on January 1, 1921. Because they did not know anything concerning this tribe, they had to question people on their journey. The emperor of the Moose sent them to one of his ministers so that he could take care of them. They were well received. He gave them a piece of land that is still today the site of the headquarters of the General Council of the Assemblies of God of Burkina Faso. They built mud houses as their residences and began to settle in the country. Upon their arrival, the missionaries soon began to learn Mooré, the language of the Moose tribe. Entering the land had not been an easy task, but they felt they had been led by the Holy Spirit for this task.

Foundation of an Indigenous Church

Some Moose people were open to the gospel. In order to reach them, the missionaries began to socialize with the local people and learn their language. They recruited some of them as housekeepers, night guards, and so on. The American missionaries were the first to write the Mooré alphabet. As the language barrier delayed the evangelization of the people, the missionaries began learning Mooré and French. Despite the challenges, the work started by faith.

Tapsoba Tennoaga M'Ba Zapa was the first native to accept Christ among the Moose people. Others followed, and the first converts were among those who worked for the missionaries, plus their families and the young children who came to play on the mission station. In a report to the mission headquarters, Harry Wright stated:

> We have many victories to report for the Lord has wonderfully blessed us and His own Word to the hearts of those that have been in our midst as workmen. Some twenty-two have made a confession and accepted the Lord as their Savior. We can truly say that the Lord has spoken and we trust He will carry them through to His soon coming. The situation is somewhat perplexing as over half of these converts are men who were forced here by the government.[5]

Many of the new converts suffered persecution, and some of them were banned from their own families. Entire families came under pressure because one of their members got saved. The parents of the young boys and girls were not happy that they had accepted Christ. Not only did the young converts suffer bitter persecution from their families, the missionaries also endured persecution from other religious leaders in the country. They faced further adversity, such as sickness and even death. Many missionaries at that time packed their belongings in their coffins when they left their home countries for the mission field. Vinson Synan calls these pioneers "the missionaries of the one-way ticket."[6]

The first Assemblies of God missionary to lay down his life for the sake of the gospel in Burkina Faso was John Eric Booth-Clibborn, grandson of the Salvation Army founder, William Booth. In her account of John Eric's call to the Mossi Land, his wife, Lucille, said that as a seventeen year-old in 1913, John Eric first heard the call of God to go to the "dark continent of Africa."[7] John Eric was one of the most qualified to meet the challenges on the field. His father had moved to France to start a Salvation Army work there. There, he learned the French language and culture. This enabled him to communicate effectively with the French governor on behalf of the other missionaries. John Eric suffered from dysentery and malaria on his way to his calling field. He died on July 2, 1924. This was considered a great loss for the field, but because of his death, other missionaries would rise up to meet the needs on the Mossi Land field.

Other Assemblies of God missionaries, both American and French, laid down their lives for the gospel in Burkina Faso, and their bodies are buried in different parts of the country. Not only did missionaries die, but their children also lost their lives because they followed their parents to fulfill the mission. One of these missionary children, Paul Weidman Jr., who was translating the Mooré language for his father, died when he was six years old and is buried in the city of Tenkodogo. Other children who died include Michel Dupret, baby Florence Chastagner, baby Bill Hall, the daughter of Raymond Sanders, and a little girl named Litta Ann Kitch. Bernadine Kitch, an Assemblies of God missionary's wife, sent a letter to the Division of Foreign Missions of the Assemblies of God that arrived two days after her death. She wrote:

> We are aware of the great difficulties you are facing in getting reinforcements to our field, and to be assured that we are sticking at the post as long as health will permit. Our sorrows and our sicknesses have not turned our eyes homeward, instead, we feel thrust onward to greater service in this needy land. The waters have been deep this past year, but His grace has proven sufficient every time.[8]

One may ask why God would allow these tragic losses in such a desperate, needy mission field. These Pentecostal missionaries believed that God allowed these losses so that the church could be built in this country. Indeed, the death of these saints has not been in vain. Death did not extinguish the call of young men and women who were willing to sacrifice their lives for this cause. Many young people responded to the call to serve in the country despite dangers and sorrows. Their sacrifices became the seeds of the gospel in Mossi Land.[9]

THE DEVELOPMENT OF MISSIONS STRATEGIES[10]

The missionaries made their first converts among those who came to work with them. The church started among the poor and the uneducated. The members were initially on the margins of society, but the growth and expansion of the movement brought it to the forefront. It was known in the region as the religion of the sick or possessed because the majority of the converts were either sick or demon-possessed.[11] The beginning was difficult due to the traditional religions and the presence of other religious groups.

Today, the church is experiencing major growth to the point that it is sending missionaries to other countries. The Assemblies of God of Burkina Faso is influencing the rest of West Africa's francophone countries and beyond. Even though, at the beginning, the country was divided between the different Evangelical churches, the Assemblies of God—which was and remains the largest Evangelical denomination in the country—decided early to go beyond the country's borders. Yet in order to avoid conflicts with other denominations, the governor divided the country into different zones of evangelization and confined the Assemblies of God to work solely among the Moose tribe (unfortunately, the northern part was left without the presence of the Evangelicals under this partition, even as the Assemblies was forbidden to reach out to the rest of some sixty tribal groups). As the church settled in Mossi Land, missionaries and native church leaders began to venture into new territories.

The first mission station opened outside the capital city was Kaya in 1926, which was established by missionary Arthur Wilson and his wife. Though the overall strategy of the Assemblies of God of Burkina Faso was to reach the capital city with the gospel, the rest of the country was also part of the vision.

After opening the Kaya station, Lloyd Shirer opened Yako in 1928 with the help of the first convert, Mba Zapa. Other missionary stations were opened, such as Tenkodogo, Koudougou, Ouahigouya, and Boulsa. After many stations were opened through the initiatives of the American missionaries, the national pastors opened other mission stations. Among these pastors who opened new stations were Bingassida Zida and Zabré Poutêryalma.

The first native pastors were ordained on November 30, 1934. According to the statistics, by the year 1935, the largest towns of Mossi Land had been presented with the gospel message. Despite the colonial restriction on venturing outside the Moose tribe, missionaries and national pastors went to the south to reach out to the Kasena, a large tribe near the Ghanaian border.

Reaching Beyond the Borders

Early on, the missionaries and national pastors had a vision of reaching out to the surrounding countries. Often missionaries would send reports to the headquarters about what God was doing through them on the field, sometimes ignoring their helpers who were their African brothers. The history of the Assemblies of God of Burkina Faso has shown that, in their vision of reaching to other countries, local pastors went along with the missionaries to establish the church.

The Assemblies of God has been formed as a global organization to reach the world. For this reason, missionaries were sent out. Those on the field followed the same vision. Without waiting to reach the entire Mossi Land, the missionaries crossed borders to start new mission stations in the neighboring countries. The first country to be reached was the Gold Coast, now Ghana. In 1931, pastors like Yembila Sawadogo from Kaya, Tiga Ouedraogo, and Yemdaogo Tapsoba from Ouagadougou joined the missionary team led by Lloyd Shirer to start the work in the northern part of Ghana. Other pastors followed to continue the work. Kingsley Larbi stated, "The Assemblies of God was the first foreign Pentecostal body to work in Ghana. The Rev Lloyd and Margaret Shirer, Assemblies of God missionaries in Mosiland (Wagadugu) crossed over to the northern region of the then Gold Coast in 1931."[12] Under the leadership of these exemplars, mission stations were opened in Yendi, Tamale, Bawku, and Kumbugu, where the first Bible school was started. Speaking about the important role the pastors played in the organization of the Assemblies of God of Ghana, the first general superintendent was Tiga Ouedraogo from Burkina Faso.

The next country to be reached was Togo. In 1936, Rev. Murray Brown left Mossi Land to start the work in Dapaong, which is in northern Togo. He went along with Pastor Nizemba Dentoumda. Daniel Pasgo and Soukba Kere later joined the team. Rev. Daniel Pasgo served as the general superintendent of the Assemblies of God of Togo and Benin when the two countries were considered to be one missionary field. When each country became able to organize its own fellowship, Reverend Pasgo remained the general superintendent of the Assemblies of God of Togo until his retirement. Under his leadership, the Assemblies of God has grown to become the largest Pentecostal denomination in the country.

Benin also began to receive missionaries. In this country, the strategy was different. Even though trained pastors went with the missionaries, others were trained on-site in the Bible institute with the hope that they would stay and serve. Among those who went and stayed for a while were the following pastors: Somebkieta Ouédraogo from Kaya, Médo Ouédraogo from Ouahigouya, Gomtanga Yanogo, Kienga Zongo, Bila Ouédraogo, Azaria Sorgho, Etienne Minoungou, and Joel Zabsonré. For some time, they labored in the country. Unfortunately, none of them remained as pastors as others did in Ghana and Togo.

The missionary effort toward Ivory Coast was different from the rest of these countries. In 1958, a handful of believers in Abidjan came to Ouagadougou to ask the French Mission of the Assemblies of God—which had already been present in Burkina Faso since 1948, when they arrived to help out the American in this francophone context—to send a missionary who would care for the young flock. The French missionaries were much involved in health and education systems, and the country needed these services. Since Ivory Coast was a French colony, the governor did not see with a good eye that other nationalities were offering these services. André and Josette Brisset responded to the call, and they took with them Rev. Gedeon Kere as their helper. In an effort to establish the Assemblies of God in the Ivory Coast, young people from Burkina Faso were sent to enroll in the Bible institute founded in 1958 by André and Josette Brisset. Among these young people were Jérémie Bayala, Sondo Pouraogo, and Gombila Ouédraogo. The second cohort of the school included two others from Burkina Faso: Pawêntaoré Ouédraogo and Kabré Gomtibo.

Rev. Adama Ouédraogo, a young Burkina Bé who went to Abidjan to work, felt called and went to the Bible institute in Katadji to be trained as a pastor. He later became the general superintendant of the Assemblies of God of the Ivory Coast. He has had a long tenure of ministry and is regarded as one of the outstanding leaders of the Ivorian church.

The contribution of the pastors from Burkina Faso has been crucial. Until recently, they worked closely with their Ivorian colleagues. Unfortunately, some of them left the Assemblies of God Church to form the *Mission Evangélique Internationale de Côte d'Ivoire* (International Evangelical Mission of Ivory Coast). Their leader claims to have more than three hundred pastors in his constituency. Rev. Koumbem Lazare was the leader of that movement until his health would not allow him to continue overseeing the movement. Rev. Georges Compaoré was elected in 2014 as the general superintendent of the movement. At the heart of the problem that caused so many to leave, according to their leaders, was the lack of consideration of the needs of the pastors from Burkina Faso. Because of this, Lazare and his followers decided to start a new movement, which is now flourishing among the Burkina Bé.

Despite these difficulties, the contribution of the pastors from Burkina Faso is visible. Other pioneers from Burkina Faso include Pierre Yaméogo and Lévi Kaboré. Yaméogo converted in 1938 in his hometown of Koudougou, but his family persecuted him. As the story goes, he decided to go to Ivory Coast, as did many young men of his age. After walking for thirty-one days, he reached the town of Bouake, where he stayed for a short period of time.[13] From there, he went southwest of Bouake to the city of Zuenoula, where he found some brothers from his hometown who were members of an Assemblies of God church back in their country. Having not found an Assemblies of God church, they started attending a World Evangelical Crusade church. Yaméogo became a key person in the founding of the Assemblies of God Church in that region.

Missionaries from Burkina Faso have also reached other countries with the gospel, such as Senegal. Rev. Kienga Zongo and Etienne Minoungou labored in Senegal to start the Assemblies of God. The Assemblies of God of Burkina Faso needed an organized structure to coordinate the missionary effort.

Missionary Vision of the Assemblies of God of Burkina Faso

According to Pierre-Joseph Laurent, the Assemblies of God of Burkina Faso has played an important role in the expansion of the movement on the African continent.[14] One frequently encounters Moose pastors responsible for missions in neighboring countries. At the same time, its influence on sister churches throughout Africa is renowned.

None of the pastors from Burkina Faso who accompanied the Western missionaries to the neighboring countries to start the work received any financial support. They had to work on their farms and use the missionary method of Saint Paul. They showed their determination and courage by staying faithful to their call despite the difficulties.

In 1984, three pastors shared the vision of starting a mission program with a small budget. Five years later, the mission department was able to send three missionary couples to Benin, Senegal, and Niger. The need to organize the mission department became necessary, as many were being called into the mission field.

The Assemblies of God of Burkina Faso has both home missionaries and foreign missionaries. Rev. Jean Sawadogo, who headed the mission department since 1984, retired in 2013. Rev. Abel Ouédraogo, who was a missionary to Senegal, was called to replace him. Under the leadership of Reverend Sawadogo, the mission department grew, and new mission stations have been opened in Mali, Niger, Guinea Conakry, Chad, and Belgium. The needs to support these missionaries are great, and new ways of collecting the funds need to be developed.

While missionaries were sent to surrounding countries, the missionary vision of the Assemblies of God has focused on unreached groups where no churches were present. In order to be more efficient in their plans, the Assemblies of God of Burkina Faso started Bible institutes in the areas where they were most needed. In 2012, they opened a new Bible school among the Gulmacema tribe to not only serve the country, but also to train the tribal leaders who live in neighboring Benin, Niger, and Togo. They also have a few students from Niger. The first cohort is graduating in 2015. East of Burkina Faso, there are tens of churches without pastors, and hundreds of couples have been sent as home and foreign missionaries from VIMAB (*Vision Missionnaire des Assemblées de Dieu du Burkina*, or, in English, Missionary Vision of the Assemblies of God of Burkina). While there is a real need to train pastors, the VIMAB needs to develop better ways to support the home missionaries working among the unreached groups.

Because of the dynamics of the Assemblies of God missions department, many African countries have also started their own missions departments. Reverend Sawadogo has been invited by many Assemblies of God church leaders to partner in his vision for missions in Nigeria, Gabon, Equatorial Guinea, South Africa, Malawi, and Kenya.[15] Despite these opportunities in missions, the Assemblies of God of Burkina Faso is still facing challenges.

Future Challenges

Many observers of the history of the church have noted the shift in missions. There is remarkable church growth in non-Western countries. Over the past century, the center of gravity in the Christian world has shifted inexorably southward to Africa, Asia, and Latin America.[16] Though there is remarkable growth in these regions, there is still a great need to unite missionary efforts. Partnership becomes necessary if the church desires to fulfill the Great Commission.

A growing church always faces challenges, and the Assemblies of God of Burkina Faso is no exception. The history of the church in Africa clearly shows that despite human tragedies such as civil wars, poverty, genocides, AIDS, hunger, and drought, the church persists. In Burkina Faso, the church is now regarded as a model of stability. It is no longer viewed as being only for the poor. Government personalities and high-ranking members of the society are becoming members of the church. If the church wants to make an impact on society, it must be the salt and light of the world.

The growing Pentecostal church in Burkina Faso is also in need of sound theology. There is a need for a contextualized theology that will be properly Christological and pneumatological. This contextualized approach must be without compromise in letting indigenous Christianity find its way into the culture through writing local hymnody and using local dialects, idioms, and concepts to express its own faith. The pneumatological experiences of the Pentecostal churches of Africa are shaping the face of Christianity.

The growth of the Assemblies of God of Burkina Faso is rich in lessons, but it also brings some concerns. The capital city, Ouagadougou, has more than seven hundred Assemblies of God churches for a population of two million people. The reason for the great number of churches is that many pastors do not want to leave the city.

Concluding Thoughts

As the center of gravity of Christianity is moving south, this shift will facilitate southern influence and impact on the rest of the Christian world. The Assemblies of God of Burkina Faso has played and continues to play an important role in reaching the francophone countries of West Africa and beyond. The church has influence on society through many primary schools, clinics, and orphanages. People who travel in the country can see the Assemblies of God Church's logo on their buildings. The church is well respected, and the leaders have a place of choice in the nation. The politicians often consult them for advice. Recently, with the overthrow of President Compaoré's regime, the Assemblies of God leaders have been invited to help set the course for the nation's future. This situation has elevated the social status of the Assemblies of God Church in Burkina Faso, but there is still a lot to do if the church wants to remain faithful to its missionary commitments.

Even though the Assemblies of God of Burkina Faso is the first and largest Pentecostal denomination in the country, the leaders still need to give the right hand of association to other denominations. The Assemblies of God is a founding member of the Federation of the Evangelical Churches and Missions (FEME), and the current president is one of its pastors, Rev. Samuel Yaméogo. From the Assemblies of God, other Pentecostal denominations have been formed, such as the Apostolic Mission, which resulted in a split of Central Assembly of God of Ouagadougou on October 25, 1959. At that time, some of the leaders of the Apostolic Mission protested against the nomination of the pastor because they wanted to install their own. The national security incarcerated eleven members of the group, but they were freed two days later. Because of this, the security asked them not to return to the church. They started prayer meetings in their homes not far from the Assemblies of God headquarters. They later founded the Apostolic Mission based in Ghana. Another group of people left the Apostolic Mission to found the Apostolic Church for the same reasons. Both denominations are growing and planting churches all over the country.

The International Center of Evangelization, founded by Dr. Mamadou Philippe Karambiri, a former member of the Assemblies of God, is a case in point. He was converted in an Assemblies of God church during his studies in Toulouse, France. When he returned to Burkina Faso in the late '70s, he started a cell group with ten or fifteen people. Actually, the denomination is growing, and he is leading one of the largest local churches in the capital city. He launched his private digital satellite television station to spread the message. He has opened churches in Africa, Europe, and America.

There are Pentecostal churches, such as Church of Pentecost and Deeper Life, and independent churches, like the International Center for Mission, Intercession, and Deliverance, founded by Emmanuel Sawadogo, that are planting churches in many parts of the country. Non-Pentecostal movements, including the Christian and Missionary Alliance and the Association of Evangelical Churches, are also working alongside the churches as members of the FEME.

As other national Assemblies of God church leaders of Africa are engaged in the so-called "Decade of Pentecost," the Assemblies of God of Burkina Faso needs to review its strategy to plant a church in every village. There are around four thousand churches in the country, serving more than eight thousand villages. The vision is to have at least four thousand more churches by the year 2020.

As the Assemblies of God of Burkina Faso is preparing for the centennial celebration, new ways of spreading the gospel are needed. Churches around the continent are asking for more missionaries, but in these times, a united effort is more than necessary. Elijah Kim was right when he said that the greatest need for the global church is to unite and follow the Great Commission without being limited to one's native country or church denomination.[17] The Assemblies of God of Burkina Faso has an opportunity to expand its influence to other countries through missions, social action, evangelism, and discipleship. Challenges but also new opportunities remain.

Chapter 5

Pentecostalism in Cameroon and Nigeria's Cross-Border Pentecostal Influence

Samson Adetunji Fatokun and Isaac Deji Ayegboyin

GLOBAL PENTECOSTALISM, WITH its emphasis on the end-time move of the Holy Spirit, has revitalized Cameroonian Christianity. Pentecostalism is so synonymous with revivalism in Cameroon that its churches are commonly referred to as "revivalist churches."[1]

Cameroon is constitutionally a secular state with a plurality of religions, of which Christianity is the most dominant. Approximately 70 percent of the population is at least nominally Christian, 20 percent is nominally Muslim, and 6 percent practice traditional indigenous religious beliefs, while other religious groups (like Orthodox Judaism and Baha'i Faith) constitute less than 5 percent of the population. The Christian population in Cameroon is historically shared between the Catholics (mostly the French-speaking population of southern and western parts) and the Protestants (mostly the English-speaking population of the western region). While the Catholic population outnumbers the Protestants, Pentecostalism is bridging the two traditions, as its ideas and practices are increasingly absorbed by the older churches in their efforts to check the loss of members to the Pentecostals.

Pentecostalism is proliferating in Cameroon, and many independent Pentecostal churches are springing up virtually daily. There are presently hundreds of Pentecostal congregations and groups of churches in Cameroon (mostly pioneered by cross-border evangelists from Nigeria). The thrust of this chapter is to examine the historical origins of some of these churches in connection with their Nigerian transborder roots and to assess their "marketing strategies,"[2] especially from a theological perspective, and the implications of such on the spiritual, socioeconomic, and political life of Cameroon.

Historical Roots of Pentecostalism in Cameroon and Nigerian Transborder Missions

Cameroonian Pentecostalism has much historical connection with Nigerian Pentecostalism and, in fact, shares many of the features of Nigerian Pentecostalism. The socioeconomic situation of Cameroon in recent years made it a more fertile ground for the reception of the Pentecostal gospel message of material and financial prosperity, deliverance, miracles, and signs and wonders. Thus, a good number of the Nigerian Pentecostal denominations and independent founders have taken advantage of this situation for cross-border Pentecostalization of Cameroon.[3]

The oldest transborder Pentecostal denomination in Cameroon from Nigerian soil is The Apostolic Church, a classical Pentecostal mission founded in 1916, with general headquarters in Penygroes, South Wales, United Kingdom, and then established in Nigeria in 1931.[4] This church arrived in Cameroon in 1949 through the missionary activities of one Evangelist Oyoyo from the Old Eastern Region of Nigeria.[5] Between 1949 and 1960, the church opened several branches in different places in Cameroon. Until 1960, all these branches were administratively controlled by The Apostolic Church, Cross River Field, in the Old Eastern Region of Nigeria.[6] However, in 1960, the Nigerian church, which was then still led by the general headquarters in Great Britain, handed oversight of the church in Cameroon to The Apostolic Church in Switzerland as a practical way of solving some administrative challenges arising from the bilingual nature of Cameroon.

In 1977, The Apostolic Church Cameroon received her autonomy from the church in Switzerland, with Rev. Apostle Adolf Ntungwen emerging as the first indigenous national president. Since 1977, the church has been led by six national presidents, with Rev. Apostle Dr. Tengi Victor Ndih currently in this role. The highest administrative body of the church is the National Council, which is made up of sixteen indigenous Cameroonian ministers and presided over by the national president. This is followed by the Field Councils, District Meetings, and Assembly Presbytery Meetings at the lower ebb.

The ecclesiology of The Apostolic Church Cameroon includes a doctrine of "divine church government" operationalized through the fivefold ascended gifts of Christ: apostles, prophets, evangelists, pastors, and teachers (cf. Eph. 4:11).[7] Thus, the church has living apostles and ranks the office of apostle as the highest level of ordination.

The Apostolic Church Cameroon presently has about seven hundred eighty local assemblies, with about four hundred pastors and well over a thousand elders who jointly administer the branches. The church is organizationally divided into nine administrative fields, each headed by a superintendent who is, in most cases, either an ordained apostle or prophet. The church equally has one international mission field in the Niger Republic, headed by Rev. Keminfe Theodore as superintendent. The nine administrative fields are further subdivided into thirty-two groups, each headed by a supervisor. The thirty-two groups are further divided into districts, subdistricts, and centers, with the last consisting of a number of local assemblies. Local assemblies, or congregations, are headed by pastors and assisted by a presbytery of elders, deacons, and deaconesses.

To tackle the challenges of theological education and ministerial training in Cameroon, The Apostolic Church Cameroon has opened theological colleges and a seminary. In all, the church has a total number of six Bible institutes and one bilingual seminary (The Apostolic Church Bilingual Seminary at Kumba) that caters to the bilingual nature of Cameroon. The national coordinator of the Apostolic Bible Institute is Rev. Dr. Okposin David.

The church also attempts to meet social needs. In her response to the prevailing maternal mortality challenges in Cameroon, the church has opened eight medical institutions—three hospital units and five health centers—with Pastor Nicholas Alobwede as the national hospital administrator. To provide quality education in Cameroon at primary, secondary, and nursery levels, the church has opened fourteen private schools that include Western curriculum and Christian religious education.

The Apostolic Church Cameroon continues to grow, with many assemblies in almost all the regions of the country. In an interview with a Cameroonian Pentecostal pastor of another denomination (Winners Chapel), he affirmed that The Apostolic Church is currently one of the strongest Pentecostal denominations in the whole of Cameroon.[8]

The Apostolic Church Nigeria was the world's largest church auditorium when originally erected.

Another Cameroonian classical Pentecostal denomination of Nigerian origin is the Assemblies of God, founded in Nigeria in 1939.[9] A branch of this church began in Cameroon in June 1996 at Yaoundé, with Rev. and Rev. Dr. (Mrs.) P. Oganya from Nigeria as pioneer missionaries. According to Rev. Oganya,[10] the church presently has over one hundred branches, with five regional headquarters, each headed by a regional overseer. The national headquarters of the church is at Yaoundé, with Rev. Benice as the indigenous general superintendent. The church established in March 2000 an indigenous theological institution called the Assemblies of God Theological College, which is currently headed by Rev. A. Tawo as principal.

There are also other African independent and indigenous Pentecostal churches in Cameroon that have their historical roots in their mother Nigerian churches that date from the 1920s to the 1950s. Notable among these are Christ Apostolic Church; the Church of the Lord (Aladura), founded by Primate Josiah Oshitelu;[11] the Cherubim and Seraphim Church, founded by Saint Moses Orimolade Tunlase;[12] and the Celestial Church of Christ, founded by Samuel Bilewu Osoffa.[13] Quite a number of these churches freely incorporated African indigenous religious elements into their Pentecostalism in their efforts to make Christianity more relevant to Africans.[14] Some Cameroonian Pentecostals have said these are syncretic churches, owing to their incorporation of African traditional religious elements such as ritual sacrifices, spirit invocation, and other practices. Some would not even accept these as Pentecostals and would simply call them African indigenous churches, Aladura churches, or spirit churches.[15] But the fact remains that these churches manifest spiritual gifts, such as speaking in tongues, prophecy, healing, and miracles, all of which are cardinal elements of Pentecostalism.

Apart from the above, there are also other African independent denominations of Nigerian origin from the 1950s that occupy Cameroonian Pentecostal space. Notable among these are the Redeemed Christian Church of God and the Gospel Faith Mission International. The Redeemed Christian Church of God was founded in Nigeria in 1952 by Rev. Akindayomi, a former member of the Cherubim and Seraphim Church.[16] Through the missionary expansion drive of the present general overseer of the church, Pastor Enoch Adeboye, the Redeemed Christian Church of God was able to establish the church in Cameroon in 1996. The church spread rapidly so that by 2011, there were sixty parishes spread across different regions in Cameroon.[17] The rapid growth of this Nigerian church (with others) contributed, allegedly, to President Biya's clampdown on Nigerian churches on the basis of illegality. The closing down of Pentecostal churches seriously affected the growth of Redeemed Christian Church of God in Cameroon.[18] The Gospel Faith Mission International, founded in Nigeria in 1955 by the late Pastor Reuben George, was established in Cameroon on July 26, 2007, and presently has two assemblies.[19]

Another group of Pentecostal denominational churches in Cameroon are the Neo-Pentecostal and Charismatic churches. A number of these, with their characteristic prosperity gospel, arrived from Nigeria in direct response to the Cameroonian socioeconomic hardship. Most notable here are Winners Chapel (Living Faith Church) of Bishop David Oyedepo, Mountain of Fire and Miracles of Dr. Daniel Olukoya, Christ Embassy of Chris Oyakhilome, Christ Chapel International Churches of Dr. Tunde Joda, and Deeper Life Bible Church of Pastor W. F. Kumuyi.

Winners Chapel Cameroon was established in 1996, first at Akwa Douala. As the church increased in membership, it moved to Bonakwana and later to Ndobong Douala, where property was secured as the permanent headquarters for Cameroon. The pioneer pastors are Pastor Steve and Pastor Olajide, both Nigerians. Within a short time, Winners Chapel spread through Cameroon, with branches in many cities, towns, and villages. The current administrative head of the church in Cameroon is Pastor Dominion Anso, a Nigerian.[20] The church has a ministerial training arm, the Word of Faith Bible Institute, in Douala, but its general coordinating center is still in Nigeria.

The Deeper Life Bible Church, on the other hand, is a Holiness Charismatic denomination. Deeper Life Christian Ministry had been in Cameroon as early as 1981, operating as a house-caring fellowship, with Pastor Adaramodu as the pioneer minister. It metamorphosized into a full-fledged church around 1991 under Pastor John Atoyebi. Currently, the church has been successively planted in the ten regions of Cameroon, with an average of fourteen thousand members. The national overseer of the church in Cameroon is presently Pastor Martin Benue, significantly the first indigenous national leader.[21]

Independent Pentecostal churches are springing up almost on a daily basis across the country. These compete for space and identity with their Nigerian counterparts, making use of every available venue, including private homes,[22] and implementing sophisticated marketing strategies for gaining adherents. Notable among these are Faith Bible Church, founded by the late Pastor Zachariah, now one of the leading Cameroonian independent Pentecostal churches, with branches in many districts in Cameroon. Others include Full Gospel Church and Kingship International Church, founded by Pastor Frank, with headquarters in Douala,[23] and the Rhema Christian Center of Pastor Warah Solomon at Bamenda, with about five thousand worshippers.[24] Expectedly, a number of Cameroonian indigenous independent Pentecostal church founders pulled out from under their Nigerian founders in their quest for autonomy.

The large number of Nigerian Pentecostal churches has been identified as a threat to the economy by the Cameroonian government. According to an April 24, 2007, BBC report cited by News Express, as far back as 2007, Cameroonian authorities had been "seeking to control the surging number of Pentecostal churches in the country being set up by Nigerian pastors crossing over the border."[25]

Cameroonian Pentecostal Features and Marketing Strategies

In part because of its extensive Nigerian provenance, Cameroonian Pentecostalism shares many features with its Nigerian counterpart. Here we describe and assess these "marketing strategies" of Cameroonian Pentecostals in order to understand them as tools intended to expand and grow their churches.

Attractive environment

Unlike many older churches, the Cameroonian Pentecostals emphasize both the outward and inward beauty of the church auditoria. A number of them have constructed imposing architectural spaces that draw outsiders in to behold the "goodness of the Lord," as some pastors emphasize. Often new Pentecostal church-planters prioritize the development of attractive places of worship. Ironically, this has degenerated into a competitive struggle for stature among some Pentecostal leaders.

Nomenclature and branding

As a way of appearing different from the traditional churches, some of these Pentecostal churches avoid using the conventional word *church* in their name and prefer such words as *ministries*, *assembly*, *center*, *embassy*, *royal court*, *royal pavilion*, and other substitutes. Close to this is the use of catchy phrases, commonly put below the real name of some of these churches as a kind of aka (also known as) that reflects the vision and mission of the church and that serves as a branding technique. Take, for example, the Living Faith Church in Cameroon, which is commonly known as Winners Chapel. Thus, Winners is a brand name in Cameroonian Pentecostalism that easily identifies members and ministers of Living Faith Church.

Use of ushers and protocols

Another distinguishing feature of Cameroonian Pentecostalism is the posture and mannerism of ushers and protocols. Ushers and protocols are given special consideration in Pentecostal settings, especially the neo-Pentecostal and Charismatic churches. Their dress is often quite conspicuous, as in the corporate suits and ties of bank and company officials. In some places, ushers and protocols are strategically stationed to communicate to first-time visitors that the God of material prosperity and success is here. Part of the goal is to impress visitors so they will consider returning.

Enthusiastic and flexible worship

Worship in most Pentecostal churches in Cameroon is characteristically lively and less formal, in contrast to what they describe as the "cemetery-like worship" in the mainline churches. Worship is spontaneous, lengthy, and participatory.[26] Some do not even follow an order of service but unfold "as led by the Spirit." The goal is to foster maximum participation and meaningful involvement of all present. Worship sessions generally involve responses to the Spirit expressed in excessive emotional displays (such as shaking, jerking, sighing, quaking, and even a form of "laughing in the Spirit")[27] and sporadic interjections as worshippers are sublimed into divine presence and become filled or possessed by the Spirit.

More problematic is that Pentecostal services are often too noisy, arguably in some instances abusing the constitutional freedom of worship as, in the name of "liberty of the Spirit," congregations produce excessive noise that violate the rights of neighbors to a peaceful coexistence. Cameroonian Christians who have felt overwhelmed by the worship of Pentecostals were jubilant when the government clamped down on this noise pollution.[28] There may be a need for legislation regarding soundproofing these churches, as has been implemented in Western nations.

Radical/warfare-like prayers

Another distinctive feature of Cameroonian Pentecostalism that has increased its renown in the religious marketplace is its radical and warfare-like prayers that stand at variance with prayer patterns in the mainline church traditions. Pentecostal prayers are often dynamic and full of emotional displays. Emphasis is laid on aggressiveness of spirit in prayer, as it is believed to be more effective in reaching the throne of God. The Cameroonian Pentecostal prayer language is generally "violent." It is believed that African demons and demonic agents wreak destructive violence, so the only language they understand and respect are the equally violent prayers of the saints. Often quoted is the biblical passage that says, "From the days of John the Baptist until now the kingdom of heaven suffereth violence, and the violent take it by force" (Matt. 11:12, KJV). Hence, Cameroonian Pentecostals not only pray energetically, but they also shout at the top of their voices, as if engaged in a face-to-face battle with the devil, demons, and their human agents. Prayer sessions are often rowdy and at times chaotic, with people sweating profusely.

Outsiders are drawn into the Pentecostal churches by this powerful Christianity that purports to overcome challenges by witches and wizards, demonic oppression, and various life ills, like barrenness, ill luck, sickness, and disease. To some extent, Pentecostal prayers are a practical Christian response to the African worldview and its spiritual realities and a reflection of an indigenous religious temperament.[29]

Aggressive evangelism

Compared to the older churches, the Cameroonian Pentecostal churches have engaged in aggressive evangelism, making use of every possible media form and available space to disseminate the gospel of salvation in cities, towns, and even villages. The use of print and electronic media, including radio and television, play a leading role in the promotion of Cameroonian Pentecostalism. Otherwise, evangelism can be conducted variously, during the morning cry, on buses, and at motor parks and marketplaces. Tracts, handbills, and other materials are distributed. Some use megaphones in open public places to disseminate their message, not minding the environmental noise produced. Recently, Reinhard Bonnke and Daniel Kolenda staged an open-air interdenominational gospel campaign in Douala that attracted some three hundred seventy thousand people. Thousands of souls were reportedly saved, with many testimonies of healing miracles.[30] There is no denying that Pentecostal evangelism is more intense and passionate in spreading the Christian gospel than the mainline churches.

Yet Pentecostal evangelism is a mixed bag. Here the spirit of competition and rivalry sets in, with some Pentecostal evangelists openly condemning, directly or indirectly, other church denominations (Pentecostals inclusive) in a bid to promote their churches.[31] Perhaps more problematically, critical examination shows that evangelism and conversion are more intrareligious than interreligious in character. Pentecostal evangelistic outreach results more in cross-denominational conversion that attracts converts from the Roman Catholic and other churches, and even other Pentecostal churches, rather than the unchurched. Cameroonian Pentecostal churches have thus been accused of "sheep stealing."

Material prosperity gospel campaigns

Another attractive feature of Cameroonian Pentecostalism is the proclamation of a gospel of liberation from material, financial, and economic hardship. The origin of the prosperity gospel in Cameroon can be traced to the activities of Nigerian preachers like Bishop David Oyedepo and others allied with the American faith movement. This group recognized in the socioeconomic crisis in Cameroon the opportunity to introduce the message of material prosperity and social well-being as a formula for socioeconomic recovery. Robert Mbe Akoko correlates the recent wave of Pentecostal groups in Cameroon with the growing popularity of prosperity teaching.[32] And in contrast to their previous ascetic positions, even mainline and classical Pentecostal churches are shifting their attention to the prosperity doctrine as a survival strategy.

These prosperity preachers present a God of prosperity who is equally interested in and even rejoices in the prosperity of His people. Consequently, through their teachings, seminars, and conferences, people are educated on how to exercise financial and economic dominion in the midst of economic hardship. Partnership with God and investment in the kingdom through massive seed-sowing are the keys to material breakthrough. A number of Nigerian prosperity preachers who established churches in Cameroon were directly or indirectly groomed by the late Nigerian protagonist of the material prosperity gospel, the Archbishop Benson Idahosa, whose catchy slogans include "You are made for successes and not for failure!" and "God is going to send Holy Ghost riches to put miracles in your hands!"[33] In the words of the founder of Winners Chapel, "You don't resemble God by being poor."[34] Dr. Tunde Joda, the founder of Christ Chapel International Churches, even predicted, "A revival of prosperity is coming into the body of Christ in the millennium such that God's people are going to break loose from the spirit of poverty."[35]

By claiming to liberate Christians from the "demon called poverty" (as is often used by some Pentecostal preachers), these churches periodically organize business seminars and symposia at which stakeholders from companies and industries are invited to teach or train people on entrepreneurship. Some larger churches assist in getting time off for trusted members. Anointing programs are held for divine impartation for prosperity. These have served as successful recruitment tools, as invitees often end up becoming active members of these churches.

To some extent, the prosperity campaign of the Pentecostals has gone a long way to reconnect the spiritual and material dimensions of life and liberate Christians from the idea that poverty is a sign of godliness. That Christian spirituality does not entail poverty, as some have perceived, has been practically demonstrated by the display of wealth in these Pentecostal churches.

On the other hand, the prosperity gospel has been bastardized in some quarters, as some pastors, instead of financially empowering their members, have impoverished them through their overemphasis on seed offerings, often manipulating parishioners to sow bountifully (not minding their financial situation) with assurance they will receive back an abundant harvest. Similarly, some of these churches fail to strike a balance by overemphasizing material prosperity at the expense of spiritual well-being, here in contrast to the Apostle John's admonition to Gaius in 3 John 2 (a popular but often wrongly quoted passage by prosperity gospelers).

Emphasis on deliverance miracles, signs, and wonders

Deliverance campaigns form yet another ministry strategy in Cameroonian Pentecostal churches. Liberation from demonic yokes (obsession, oppression, and possession) through the powerful name of Jesus is a direct response to the African worldview and its spiritual consciousness. Cameroonian Pentecostal pastors often believe that unseen wicked spirits and demonic human agents lie behind every life misfortune, and they claim to possess a higher spiritual power to vanquish these forces. This Pentecostal emphasis on the spiritual forces behind events in the material world parallels traditional cosmologies.[36] Rather than sidelining these issues, as mainline denominations appear to do, Pentecostal churches confront them directly and make the vanquishing of witches, evil spirits, and other agents of Satan central elements of church practice. Thus, Pentecostal churches in Cameroon provide a place of refuge from fears and activities of witches and wizards (who are perceived palpably in Africa)[37] through their practical demonstration of the power of God in delivering people from spiritual bondages, sicknesses, troubles, harms, and other problems.

Similarly, emphasis on miracles, signs, and wonders is a dominating feature in Cameroonian Pentecostalism. These churches stress the availability of the miracle-working power of the Holy Spirit in the church to liberate believers from all life's problems. Sundry testimonies of signs and wonders abound in these churches.[38]

On the other hand, there is a commercialization of the gospel in some Pentecostal churches, as ministers, in the name of deliverance and miracles, offer for sale during and after services sacred objects for special miracles, such as breakthrough handkerchiefs (technically styled "mantles"), consecrated water and oil, and success perfumes. Some ministers even charge fees for consultations, healing prayers, and deliverance rituals.

There is also in some quarters the error of antimedicinal theology. Some of these Cameroonian faith healers go as far as sharing the view of faith preachers that no remedy or cure exists outside the blood of Jesus Christ.[39] Deplorably, as research has shown, this antimedicinal theology has resulted in the premature death of some in Cameroonian "faith clinics."[40]

Enhanced position of women

The elevated position accorded to the female gender in active ministry is another striking feature of Cameroonian Pentecostalism that has contributed to its expansion. Apart from the female gender being freely given equal opportunities with their male counterparts to serve and head departments in the lay ministries of the Pentecostal churches, females hold equal positions with the males in the ordained ministries, as they serve as pastors, evangelists, prophetesses, and even bishops. This stands in contrast to the place of women in the mainline church traditions. As pointed out by Ayeboyin and Ishola, in spite of the fact that the mission churches preach the principle of equality of sexes, men usually hold the principal positions of authority.[41] Thus, one can say that Cameroonian Pentecostalism has successfully transformed the role of women in churches from that of marginality to equality. The elevated positions of women in Cameroonian Pentecostalism has drawn gifted women with divine callings who felt caged in by the mainline constraints.[42]

Theological education and ministerial training

With little to no emphasis on qualified ministerial training and sound theological education, many laypeople find it very easy to set up independent churches without any check. Apart from the few classical Pentecostals who have received some education in theological institutions established mostly by their churches and compared further to the leadership of older mainline churches in Cameroon, there is evidence that indicates that most Cameroonian independent Pentecostal church founders and leaders do not possess quality theological education and ministerial training.[43] The general attitude of Cameroonian Pentecostal leaders to formal theological education is antipathy at best. Thus, these Pentecostal leaders often read Scripture one-dimensionally for its practical benefits.[44] This may render such churches vulnerable to questionable beliefs and practices.

Yet this is not to say that Cameroonian Pentecostals do not study the Bible. As a church-growth strategy, some congregations advertise Bible study programs with promises of life transformation. For instance, the Redeemed Christian Church of God

Cameroon's weekly study is "Digging Deep," which signals that here we do more of an in-depth study of the Word of God than elsewhere.

Social networks

In spite of financial extortion in some quarters, some of these Cameroonian Pentecostal churches provide supporting social networks for their members. Apart from serving as solution centers to the spiritually oppressed, some provide succor to the socially deprived, the jobless, orphans, the aged, the barren, and other societal outcasts. A number of these churches care for the poor and the oppressed and take up special collections for such during their services. Others provide free humanitarian services, such as food distribution, medical tests and counseling, and drug distribution.

These churches have also organized "health talks," ranging from free medical diagnosis and treatments on one end of the spectrum to academic seminars and symposia on the other end. Churches also work to develop their members through vocational training. For membership retention and to foster camaraderie, special classes are offered especially to beginners. Worker-training sessions are designed to integrate newcomers into the church workforce, and people are always encouraged to join groups and units in the church.

Pentecostal churches in Cameroon thus ought to be understood both as a social and religious movement,[45] particularly to the extent they have played a functional and discernible role in alleviating the fears and sufferings of the spiritually oppressed and socially deprived. Like in Nigeria,[46] Pentecostals have responded practically to the pressing needs of Cameroonian society as much as if not more than other Christian groups.

Administrative structure

In terms of leadership style, some Pentecostals who are founders of ministries appear to be autocratic in the way they run the affairs of their churches. Research reveals that some leaders are not accountable to any board, executive committee, or church-in-conference.[47] A number of the independent Pentecostal churches in Cameroon do not keep proper records, while in some places there are no records at all, as the founder is the "alpha and omega" in every affair of the church ministry and runs it like a family business.[48]

A related aspect of these family-business enterprises are the "Pastor and Pastor (Mrs.)" phenomenon, whereby an average Cameroonian independent Pentecostal church founder's wife automatically becomes either a pastor or reverend without indication of divine calling or ministerial training. On the billboards, posters, and other media, the photographs of the couple (at times in a romantic form) are conspicuous, with such titles as "Bishop and Bishop (Mrs.)," "Rev. (Dr.) and Rev. (Dr.) Mrs.," "Rev./Prophet and Lady Evangelist/Prophetess," and the like. While the Pentecostal idea of according ministers' wives an active role in the ministry is a welcomed development, critical questions are unavoidable: Should ministers' wives be ordained as co-ministers before they assist their husbands in the ministry? How is calling and anointing transferred from the husband to the wife? What about the automatic appointment of the spouse as the deputy leader and successor of the founding pastor? To be sure, these "family churches" have aided the spread of Pentecostalism, as those discontented under a leader easily break away to start their own churches, thus making the Pentecostal gospel available to the yet unreached in different locations in the country.

Evaluation, Recommendations, and Conclusion

Like most other Pentecostals,[49] Cameroonian Pentecostalism emphasizes the new-birth or born-again experience, speaking in tongues as the outward proof of Spirit baptism, and manifestation of the *charismata* (spiritual gifts). If classical groups like The Apostolic Church mostly focus on the nine gifts listed in 1 Corinthians 12:4–10, Charismatics and neo-Pentecostals include the other gifts in 1 Corinthians 12:27–31, Romans 12:6, and Ephesians 4:11. While the classical Pentecostal denominations and a few Charismatic groups, like Deeper Life Bible Church, stress sanctification and holiness, modesty in dress, and strict moral ethics, the majority of the movement allows for and encourages contemporary fashions on the grounds that the heart of people is what matters more to God than the physical appearance. Against this broader perspective, objective observers can acknowledge that despite questionable developments in Cameroonian Pentecostalism, the movement has significantly transformed Cameroonian Christianity, like in Nigeria, from a cold, formalistic religion into a dynamic and experiential spirituality. Pentecostalism in Cameroon is such a potent force that it has challenged the older churches to embrace Pentecostal features as the only way to avoid losing members.

Arguably from a theological perspective, as Christianity without the raw manifestations of the Holy Spirit of Christ is empty, so also a church without the living power of the Holy Spirit is nothing less than a social club. In this vein, one can say that Pentecostalism, with its wave of the move of the Spirit, has revitalized Christianity in this country. It is not an overstatement to suggest that the movement's holistic message of salvation, sanctification, baptism in the Holy Spirit, healing, deliverance, and divine success has marked Cameroonian Christianity. Arguably, Cameroonian Pentecostalism, with its "marketing strategies" and evangelization initiatives, has responded more positively to the existential needs of the African worldview than the historic churches and even other religious options in that country. Thus, one can conclude that the Pentecostal gospel, as developed in Cameroon, is meeting the spiritual, social, and psychological yearnings of an increasingly secular society.

To be sure, Cameroonian Pentecostalism is not free from problems. The competitive spirit that characterizes the posture of some of these churches needs to be checked, and unity in diversity must be emphasized. Similarly, Cameroonian Pentecostals will need to develop and emphasize theological education at all levels. This will go a long way toward enabling Cameroonians to fully realize the spiritual and social benefits of the gospel in the church and the society at large.

Part II
Northeast and East Africa

Chapter 6

"Blessed Be Egypt My People": The Neo-Charismatic Movement in Egypt

Tharwat Maher Nagib Adly Nagib

In 1991, for the first and only time hitherto, thousands of Egyptian Christians gathered in the main hall of the Cairo International Conference Center (CICC) to praise and worship the Lord for three days. In this exceptional event, loud Christian singing and thunderous praise filled the famous official Egyptian conference center. Coming from a Methodist church, it was unfamiliar to me at that time to see people weeping, shouting, raising hands, and falling under the power of the Holy Spirit. Nearly ten thousand Egyptian Christians participated in a very lively charismatic worship during these days and listened to Father Daniel El Baramosy's sermons.[1] For reasons to be discussed below, at that time, Father Daniel, a former Coptic monk, had just been excommunicated from the Coptic Church by the Coptic pope, Shenouda III.[2] Through the financial support of rich Egyptian families from Upper Egypt, Father Daniel rented the CICC and held this three-day conference. This conference represented a starting point of a new phase in Father Daniel's ministry and a springboard for spreading a new wave of Egyptian Pentecostalism named the *neo-Charismatic movement.*

Pentecostalism has rapidly spread from Upper Egypt across the country in three waves: classical Pentecostal, Charismatic, and neo-Charismatic movements.[3] The classical Pentecostal movement in Egypt, or the first wave, emerged in Upper Egypt in the first quarter of the twentieth century as a direct result of the work of the Western Pentecostal missionaries who came from North America to Egypt. Pentecostal congregations were formed and churches were established within this wave based on the theology of the Azusa Street movement. The Charismatic renewal movement, or the second wave, emerged in the 1970s due to the spread of Pentecostalism into the mainline denominations in Egypt.

The third wave of Pentecostalism in Egypt, or the neo-Charismatic movement, began as a strong indigenous revival in the 1980s in Upper Egypt through Father Daniel's meetings and expanded to the north through internal migration due to socio-economic reasons. Coinciding with Father Daniel's meetings, a house-church movement emerged in Cairo and strengthened the neo-Charismatic wave. As mentioned above, Father Daniel's CICC conference in 1991 was a pivotal factor in spreading this third wave of Pentecostalism. The neo-Charismatic movement includes many independent spiritual ministries, nondenominational groups, and parachurch organizations.

According to estimates at the turn of the third millennium, the numbers of Pentecostals, Charismatics, and neo-Charismatics in Egypt were 165,338, 422,795, and 164,868, respectively.[4] Although the three waves are flourishing, there is a general (anecdotal) sense that in the last decade plus, the third wave's growth is outpacing the other two due to a skillful usage of satellite TV channels and social media by the neo-Charismatics, in addition to the departure of many of the Charismatics from the mainstream denominations to neo-Charismatic congregations and ministries.

This chapter studies the third, or neo-Charismatic, wave in Egypt and situates its various permutations within the broader historical context of the preceding developments. Surely, this study does not cover all the details of the third wave, but rather it gives an overview of the varieties and complexities of the movement, aiming to open future trajectories for further studies on Pentecostalism in Egypt. Furthermore, this chapter, based on field research and drawing from original Arabic Charismatic resources, focuses on the theological developments within the movement and highlights some of the challenges and opportunities that neo-Charismatic ministries face in the Egyptian context in the second decade of the twenty-first century.

The Pre-Pentecostal Era in Egypt

In April 1899, Herbert Edward Randall came to Egypt as a Holiness Movement Church's missionary.[5] The Holiness Movement Church (HMC) was established by Ralph Cecil Horner in Ottawa, Canada, in 1895. Horner, a Canadian Holiness evangelist, was among those pioneer "radical" Holiness groups who taught a distinct "third blessing," or a definite "third work" of grace, that follows salvation and sanctification, and they called this experience "baptism with fire."[6] Four years after establishing the Canadian HMC, Horner sent Randall as the first Holiness missionary to Egypt. Randall came to Assiut (southern Egypt) and founded the Egyptian Holiness Movement Church (EHMC), or *Kānīsāt Nhḍet al-Kdāsā*, in 1899, based on the "third blessing" theology. The sanctifying fire of the Holy Spirit took over the lives of many Egyptians, and the meetings were full of anointed dancing and hallelujah shouting. Randall's belief in the supernatural and his desire to experience signs and wonders most probably enhanced his acceptance among the Copts, who believe in miracles.[7] Furthermore,

Randall's theology of sanctification and baptism with fire, which was rooted in Wesleyan theology, strongly attracted Egyptians who had experienced the fire of the Holy Spirit. Revivals broke out in villages and towns nearby, and many lively Wesleyan churches were rapidly formed. The Canadian HMC sent three women missionaries to help Randall: Cora Van Camp, Edith Burke, and Carrie Reynolds.[8] The nascent enthusiastic churches attracted more Egyptians, and a Pentecostal-like movement emerged in Upper Egypt before the 1906 Azusa Street revival.[9]

In 1907, Randall visited the Hebden Mission in Toronto, where he received his Pentecostal baptism in the Holy Spirit, with speaking in tongues as the initial evidence. Randall returned to Egypt in 1912 as an independent Pentecostal missionary and participated with other missionaries from the Azusa Street Mission in establishing the classical Pentecostal Church in Egypt.[10]

The First Wave of Pentecostalism in Egypt: The Classical Pentecostal Movements

J. Booze's "Africa, North, and the Middle East (Survey)" and John T. Nichol's *The Pentecostals* connect the establishment of the first Pentecostal church in Egypt directly to G. S. Brelsford, a missionary from the Azusa Street Mission, who came to Assiut in 1909.[11] The following year, Ansel H. Post, another Pentecostal missionary, came to Alexandria (northern Egypt) and worked to spread the Pentecostal beliefs and experience.[12] Herbert E. Randall, as mentioned before, came back to Egypt in 1912 and established a Pentecostal church. The efforts of Brelsford, Post, and Randall were formative for the classical Pentecostal community in Egypt.

In contrast to Booze and Nichol, Allan Anderson argues for another historiography. He highlights Pentecostalism as an indigenous movement that received support and accelerated through the

Western Pentecostal missionary work.[13] Anderson attributes the first spark of Pentecostalism in Egypt to an Egyptian from Assiut called Ghali Hanna, who had received the baptism of the Holy Spirit in a conference held in Jerusalem by Lucy Leatherman, a missionary from the Azusa Street Mission. Hanna came back to Assiut and started a "great revival there... multitudes had been saved, sanctified, and baptized with the Holy Ghost and fire."[14] According to Anderson, Hanna and other Egyptian Pentecostals were the initiators who invited the American Pentecostal missionaries to come to Egypt.[15] Anderson illustrates the work of the Western Pentecostal missionaries in supporting the Egyptian Pentecostals, agreeing in this sense with Booze on the centrality of Brelsford, Post, and Randall in establishing the Pentecostal Church in Egypt.

Pentecostal women missionaries played a significant role in spreading and shaping classical Pentecostalism in Egypt during its first stages. Lillian Trasher established a huge orphanage in Assiut, which "became the centerpiece of the Pentecostal mission in Egypt, producing many of its converts, preachers, and leaders."[16] Mabel Dean, who lived thirty-seven years in Upper Egypt, "left 45 active Pentecostal congregations with leaders she had trained."[17] Today, the classical Pentecostal churches in Egypt include many different denominations, such as the Church of God (Cleveland, Tennessee), the Church of God of Prophecy, the Pentecost Faith Mission, and the Assemblies of God USA. The Assemblies of God is the largest Egyptian Pentecostal denomination, which includes 160 churches with almost two hundred thousand members.[18]

The Second Wave of Pentecostalism: The Charismatic Movements in Egypt

The Charismatic movements in Egypt, or the second wave of Pentecostalism, emerged in the 1970s due to the spread of

Pentecostalism into some Catholic and Orthodox communities in Egypt as a result of the Egyptian Catholics' openness toward the Charismatic Renewal, especially in North America.[19] In 1982, Good News Ministry was established as an official renewal movement inside the Coptic Catholic Church.[20] The Egyptian Catholic movement has formed a contextual Catholic Charismatic theology similar to the "organic view," wherein Pentecostal baptism with the Holy Spirit is seen as an essential part of the rites of initiation, such as water baptism and confirmation, while the later experience of tongues and other gifts are seen as a revitalization of the grace that had already been accepted in water baptism[21]—which was adopted by some streams of the Western Charismatic movements. Today, Good News Ministry includes fifteen congregations in Egypt, Jordan, and Sudan.[22]

In the early 1970s, a Charismatic Catholic group from Ann Arbor, Michigan, came to Cairo and was received by the Catholic Society of Jesus in Egypt.[23] This group held charismatic meetings in Cairo where some Coptic Orthodox leaders unofficially attended. During these meetings and through Francis MacNutt's writings, the Charismatic Renewal began to penetrate into the Coptic community.[24] The Charismatic Copts "emphasized the power of the Holy Spirit to mobilize spiritual activism; sought 'ecstatic spirituality,' including faith healing."[25] They also organized at-home Bible studies and engaged in lively worship services with charismatic singing and praise. Orthodox Christians have never been cessationists (who think the spiritual gifts belong only in the apostolic age) but have always believed in miracles, signs and wonders, healing, and prophecies.[26] Some Orthodox scholars say that "charismatic renewal has always been a primary goal in the Orthodox Church."[27] This innate charismatic identity of the Orthodox Church bridges the gap between the ancient church and contemporary charismatic practice and renewal. Two of the most famous contemporary renewal movements in the Coptic Orthodox Church, led by Father Makary Younan and Father Samaan Ibrahim, thus feature exorcism, divine healing, and lively praise and worship.[28]

It is also worth mentioning that by the mid-1980s, charismatic influences had entered into some of the mainline Protestant churches, especially in the big cities. Cell-group models and Paul Cho's paradigm of church growth influenced some Presbyterian and Methodist churches in Cairo, and the Alpha course penetrated many mainline Protestant churches.[29]

The Third Wave of Pentecostalism: The Neo-Charismatic Movements in Egypt

By the early 1980s, the complexities of the movement heavily increased with the emergence of the neo-Charismatic wave. The neo-Charismatics in Egypt are independent nondenominational groups with Pentecostal-like experiences and have no traditional denominational historical roots. The new wave produced various indigenous Pentecostal theologies and reshaped Pentecostalism in Egypt in a very significant way. It might be beneficial to survey the main streams of the neo-Charismatic movements in order to discover the uniqueness of each strand.

House-church movements

In 1984, Mohsen Nazem, an Egyptian physician, began a spiritual movement called "Faith and Love Ministry." The ministry's slogan was taken from the New Testament: "that he might present it to himself a glorious church" (Eph. 5:27, KJV). Nazem, with other local leaders, emphasized the centrality of the house-church model in the life of the early church and began to establish many independent Charismatic house churches, which rapidly spread all over the country. After Nazem's immigration to Canada in 1988, a national board assumed full responsibility for the ministerial work. By the end of the 1980s, there were over two thousand Charismatic house churches in Egypt, and the movement adopted a new name, the Call of the Kingdom Movement.[30] The churches were growing and producing new churches. Healing, speaking in tongues, intercession, Eucharistic gatherings, charismatic worship and praise, and dancing with flags in the presence of the Lord were widespread practices of this indigenous neo-Charismatic movement.

The years of 1990 to 1995 were the golden era of the Call of the Kingdom Movement. There were two general conferences in Cairo that annually gathered all the members of the movement, in addition to many other local conferences, which were frequently held in different places in Egypt. The movement's large conferences started to draw more attention among the mainline Protestant churches, and many today recall concerns and discussion at that time in mainline pastoral circles about Charismatic teachings of blessings and curses, the practice of the Eucharist in house-church environments, and the (perceived) radical lifestyle of the movement's members. In spite of the criticism, the movement continued to grow not only in Egypt, but also in many countries around the Arab world and in Europe. In 1999, because of many complicated internal and external problems, the movement's leadership board decided to stop the ministry in Egypt and around the world. The leaders of the ministry proclaimed at that time that although the movement was an effective tool in God's hand for a time, it had now run its course. After this sudden end of the ministry, many house churches merged with Charismatic mainline Protestant churches, some of them stumbled and vanished, and a few house churches continued to grow independently. Although the house-church movement did not continue as a whole, its significance during the 1980s as a pioneering indigenous independent movement that prepared the way for many other neo-Charismatic independent movements is undeniable.

Independent classical spiritual ministries

Since the beginning of the last decade of the twentieth century, independent spiritual ministries began to emerge in Egypt. Unlike the house-church movement, these independent spiritual ministries began, continued, and have become one of the most important spiritual streams in Egypt. Most of these contemporary ministries owe their theologies to the teachings of Father Daniel El Baramosy. What distinguishes these ministries is the centrality of spiritual warfare, laying on of hands for healing and deliverance with different physical manifestations, classical discipleship through cell groups, and focus on the baptism of the Holy Spirit as a second work of grace. The starting point of the independent spiritual ministries could be traced to the discipleship groups that emerged within the Coptic Orthodox Church in Upper Egypt in the late 1980s under the supervision of Father Daniel.[31]

In the 1980s, Father Daniel, who was ordained as a Coptic monk in 1978, led a spiritual movement within the Orthodox Church. Through his weekly meetings, powerful sermons, and anointed writings, he had a large-scale impact on the Orthodox Church. Father Daniel was a pioneer in Egypt, teaching about the manifested presence of the Holy Spirit, inner healing, physical healing, deliverance, and laying on of hands. Over the years, the gap increased between the traditional Orthodox Church and Father Daniel's teachings. Two books by Father Daniel, *Wā Hūm Ghālābūh* (And they overcame him) (1987) and *Al-Fūkh Īnkūsūr* (The snare is broken) (1988), which focused on spiritual warfare, caused a storm in the Coptic

Church.[32] The debates between Father Daniel and the Coptic pope, Shenouda III, reached a peak when Pope Shenouda published two articles in the official magazine of the Orthodox Church, *al-Kīrāzā al-Qbtīā*, in which he assailed Father Daniel's writings.[33] In 1991, Pope Shenouda excommunicated Father Daniel from the Coptic Orthodox Church, and the excommunication's formal resolution was published in *al-Kīrāzā al-Qbtīā*.[34]

Accordingly, Father Daniel, with many of his disciples, left Upper Egypt and went to Cairo, where he founded the Rivers of Life Ministry as the first independent spiritual ministry in Egypt. In 1992, Youhanna Reda, a disciple of Father Daniel, founded The Way of Life Ministry as the second independent spiritual ministry in Egypt. Rivers of Life and The Way of Life ministries have played significant roles in revitalizing the spiritual life in Egypt. Over the years, other independent ministries have come and gone. Although the number of independent neo-Charismatic ministries in Egypt is not large, their impact is quite significant. Father Daniel's teachings have penetrated many of the mainline Protestant churches through his books, booklets, conferences, and daily TV programs. While Father Daniel's ministry is based in Cairo, its influence also reaches Arab communities worldwide through international conferences and satellite programs. Currently, Rivers of Life Canada, a church founded in 1995 by one of Father Daniel's Egyptian disciples, Guirguis Halim, and affiliated with Rivers of Life Egypt, is considered one of the biggest Arabic Charismatic congregations in Canada. Rivers of Life Canada includes many believers from the Middle East, North Africa, sub-Saharan Africa, and North America. There are other congregations affiliated with Rivers of Life Egypt in the United States, France, and the Gulf area.[35]

Ecumenical ministries

During the last two decades, many Egyptian mainline churches, in addition to Charismatic and neo-Charismatic groups, have called for an Egyptian ecumenical movement. Most of these attempts have lacked a methodology to achieve such ecumenical relationships. A promising ecumenical methodology that focuses on corporate worship as a means to unite the various Egyptian Christian communities began to appear with the emergence of the neo-Charismatic ecumenical ministries. Various patterns of neo-Charismatic ecumenical ministries emerged in Egypt during the last decade, including parachurch organizations and sacramental congregations.

The *Al-Kārouz* movement, literally translated as the Evangelist's Movement, is an example of an effective neo-Charismatic ecumenical ministry in Egypt. Brother Maher Fayez, a prominent Christian singer, musician, and theological thinker, established the *Al-Kārouz* ensemble of over one hundred worshippers, musicians, and technicians in 2004, after fifteen-plus years of an intensive itinerant ministry among different Egyptian Christian communities. From the beginning of the ensemble, Maher Fayez, as a spiritual father, focused on offering theological training for his spiritual daughters and sons that blended the mysticism of Eastern Orthodox theology and Pentecostal emphases on the centrality of the second work of grace in the Christian life and the importance of the spiritual gifts, including speaking in tongues and prophecy.[36]

After seven years of *Al-Kārouz*'s success as a music and worship ensemble, Maher Fayez announced the establishment of *Al-Kārouz* as an Egyptian ecumenical movement in order to develop and distribute ecumenical materials for devotional and worship studies.[37] The movement was launched through its first conference in 2011, where thousands gathered to worship and listen to three

African guest speakers from the Global Apostolic and Prophetic Network.[38] This "new beginning" was effectively a reformulation and expansion of the ecumenical meetings of *Al-Kāroūz* that already had gathered over a thousand believers from all denominational and nondenominational Christian groups on a weekly basis. The movement has influenced millions of Egyptian and Arab Christians all around the world through many conferences and a plethora of satellite programs and video clips on the Internet. *Al-Kāroūz* emphasizes the Coptic Eastern Orthodox roots of the Christian community in Egypt and enhances this aspect through producing different patterns of Egyptian Christian music that focus on highlighting the Eastern theology in the spiritual songs.

Another example of neo-Charismatic ecumenical ministry in Egypt is the Holy Synod of Saint Athanasius Congregation (HSSAC) founded by Archbishop Maximus the First in 2006. Archbishop Maximus was one of these Coptic lay leaders who attended the Charismatic meetings that were held in the early 1970s by a Catholic Charismatic group from Ann Arbor. As a lay leader in the 1970s, Archbishop Maximus was later denied ecclesiastical service in the Orthodox Church (in May 1976) due to his Pentecostal beliefs and practices.[39] In 1982, Maximus began an early Charismatic ecumenical congregation in Cairo, and during the following years, many other congregations were added in different cities in Egypt. Divine healing, prophecies, and Eucharistic meetings were the most significant practices of these congregations.[40] The Eastern Orthodox mystical theology that focuses on union with God, or deification, was and is the essential source of teaching in these Charismatic ecumenical groups. In 2006, Archbishop Maximus, who was consecrated by the Metropolitans of the Holy Synod of the American Diaspora in 2005, founded the HSSAC for Egyptian and Middle Eastern Orthodox Christians as an ecumenical church. At present,

HSSAC includes seven churches in Egypt that accept the membership of all Christians who recognize the Nicene Creed and believe in the real presence of Christ in the Eucharist.

Neo-Charismatic megaconferences

By the beginning of the twenty-first century, the third wave of Pentecostalism in Egypt entered a new phase of proliferation through the emergence of the annual neo-Charismatic megaconferences. Since the conference that was held by Father Daniel in 1991 in the CICC, there had not been any large conferences for more than ten years. In 2004, influenced by the Ugandan prayer movement, many parachurch organizations, Charismatic mainline churches, and neo-Charismatic independent ministries participated in the first Egyptian mega prayer conference of the new century.[41] Five thousand Egyptian Christians from all over the country came to Alexandria, northern Egypt, and gathered to pray for Egypt. The following years, the number of people attending these prayer conferences grew to an average of ten thousand annually. John Mulinde and Michael Kimuli, two revivalists from Uganda, played a significant role in the early stages of the emergence of these mega prayer conferences in Egypt. Their teachings on intercessory prayer and spiritual warfare have inspired many Egyptian believers and spiritual leaders.[42] The distribution of tens of thousands of translated books written by international Charismatic teachers and revivalists such as Derek Prince, Reinhard Bonnke, Carlos Annacondia, and Ed Silvoso, also catalyzed these megaconferences, which resulted in the growth of Charismatic renewal in Egypt during the last decade.

In 2009, the Onething conference, an annual gathering of thousands of young adults, emerged as another type of megaconference. *Kasr El-Dobara* Evangelical Church (KDEC), in cooperation with many Egyptian Charismatic mainline churches and neo-Charismatic ministries, inspired by the ministry of the International House of Prayer of Kansas City (IHOPKC) and supported by Mike Bickle, called for the first Onething conference in October 2009 in Wadi Al-Natrun, ninety kilometers northwest of Cairo. Five thousand young adults gathered to worship and listen to spiritual sermons during this three-day event.[43] The number of youth multiplied over the following years and reached twenty-five thousand attendants in 2014, when Mike Bickle and Misty Edwards came to Egypt to participate in the conference. Since 2009, Onething has impacted millions of Egyptian and Arab youth through the live broadcast of the conference on the satellite Arabic Christian TV channel SAT-7 and live online streaming. Prophecies, deliverance, shouting, and dancing before the Lord are common at Onething conferences. The influence of these annual mega youth conferences includes the establishment of four hundred houses of prayer using IHOPKC's 24/7 model in different Egyptian cities during the last five years.[44]

Fivefold ministries

The fivefold ministries—apostle, prophet, evangelist, pastor, and teacher—represent another type of independent neo-Charismatic movement. These fivefold ministries, in general, minimize classical discipleship practices, such as the formation of cell groups, and emphasize the centrality of the prophetic apostolic anointing with signs and wonders following. A typical example is New Life Ministry (NLM). Nader Yassa founded NLM in the late 1990s, and over the years the ministry's focus has crystallized in the fivefold direction. NLM has prompted the spread of divine healing in Egypt. Many documented cases of physical healing have been announced in NLM meetings during the last five years. The centrality of the manifested presence of the Lord for healing, deliverance, sanctification, filling of the Holy Spirit, and discipleship is the essential foundation of Nader Yassa's teaching, and these have penetrated many Charismatic and non-Charismatic mainline churches. NLM's weekly meetings usually gather nearly fifteen thousand believers from many places around Egypt. Its influence has spread to thirteen Arab countries, four African states, and several Western nations.[45] Its teachings have also impacted multitudes of people through satellite TV programs and social media. Many international speakers have visited NLM, such as John Arnott, the founding pastor and president of the Toronto Airport Christian Fellowship; Steve Thompson, who was the associate director of Morning Star Fellowship Church for twenty-two years (based in North Carolina, USA); and Ché Ahn, the head pastor of Harvest Rock Church in Pasadena, California, USA.

Conclusion: Challenges and Opportunities

This research provides a perspective on Pentecostalism in Egypt, especially from the vantage point of the neo-Charismatic movements that emerged in the 1980s. Our survey of these different movements shows that Egyptian Pentecostalism has significant challenges and expansive opportunities. At the scholarly level, there is a need for further historical and ecumenical study to advance the discussion. Academic historical studies of Pentecostalism in Egypt are still rare and lag behind for a movement that has now existed for more than a hundred years. While the few academic sources that are available offer glimpses on the subject, most focus only on the first wave of Pentecostalism in Egypt and do not even provide sufficient coverage concerning this aspect of the topic. The lack of sources represents a real challenge to any academic research on the topic but, at the same time, offers opportunities for future studies of Pentecostalism in Egypt. Further studies on the classical Pentecostal movement in Egypt with respect to its historical and theological roots are needed. There is also a need for academic biographical studies on the Egyptian Pentecostal and Charismatic pioneers. Further, there is no doubt that future trajectories of the study of Pentecostalism in Egypt should focus on the details of the Charismatic and neo-Charismatic movements. For instance, each type of the neo-Charismatic movements mentioned in this research needs a detailed study. The multiplicity and divergence of the Charismatic movements in Egypt, similar to Pentecostalism all over the globe, increases the difficulty of the historiographical process but, on the other hand, also urges exploration of these complexities.

These historical and theological studies of Pentecostalism could positively influence ecumenical relationships in Egypt. As shown above, the neo-Charismatic ministries and parachurch organizations already play a significant role in the Egyptian ecumenical movement. In spite of this important role and the intensive efforts, many major Christian congregations in Egypt do not have an integrated knowledge about the other major Egyptian Christian congregations due to the lack of written sources. The development of a mature Pentecostal-Charismatic academy could help present the movement to its adherents and others all over the country, and this will begin to overcome misunderstandings and also stimulate ecumenical relationships among the different renewal congregations in Egypt. Finally, the importance of such scholarship will also connect Egyptian Pentecostalism with the global Pentecostal-Charismatic and ecumenical movements.

Chapter 7

Kenyan Pentecostalism: An Epitome of Theological Shifts Within Pentecostal Christianity

Susan Murimi

PENTECOSTAL CHRISTIANITY IN Kenya is of various forms and of multiple origins and is woven together by various strands and influences. A precise taxonomy of these varieties is difficult to formulate, as they exceedingly overlap. However, they range from the classical Pentecostals to the African Independent Pentecostal churches, variously referred to as the *Roho* (Spirit) churches to the Charismatics to the neo-Pentecostals. This chapter overviews historical developments among these churches. From the planting of the first mission station at Nyang'ori in 1910, Pentecostalism has witnessed demographic, theological, and practical shifts. Whereas theological shifts abound, this work focuses primarily, although not exclusively, on eschatology, which has been the cutting edge of many Pentecostal practices.

Historical Developments

The beginning of Pentecostalism in Kenya may be described as accidental. It was not premeditated by any one missionary group, as was the case with other historic mission denominations that were established at the same period. The earliest protagonists were independent missionaries and Africans from different backgrounds and experiences. These formed the various tributaries that converged into the contemporary Pentecostal expressions in Kenya. Clyde Toliver Miller and his wife, Lila Sturges, set in motion the first trajectory in 1910, when the land they had purchased at Nyang'ori in 1908 was officially transferred to them. It was here that they planted the first Pentecostal mission station in Kenya. Though they were associated with a Pentecostal mission in Iowa in the United States, they came to Kenya as independent missionaries. They initially helped at the Nilotic Independent Mission (NIM) at Oganda before moving to Nyang'ori. Lila had had a Pentecostal experience while still a student at Topeka Bible College in Kansas.[1] It was this experience that they sought to popularize at Nyang'ori. The first conversion was recorded in 1910, which was Andrea Waudi. He was the first Kenyan Pentecostal believer to be baptized, in 1911.

The second trajectory developed as tragedies and world politics came into play. This happened when two of the three Pentecostal missionaries, Karl Wittick, Marian Wittick, and Clarence Grothaus, who had arrived in Tanganyika in 1913, died because of sudden illness caused by contaminated water within the first three months of their arrival. They were of the New Bremen Pentecostal Mission in Ohio. Grothaus and Wittick were Americans, while Marian was from Parry Sound, Canada.[2] Marian recovered and continued with the work for three more years.[3] Otto Keller, a close friend of Wittick, decided to go to Tanganyika to continue what the deceased had barely started. Due to world politics, Keller was not allowed to enter Tanganyika, then a German colony while Kenya was a British colony. By default, therefore, he settled in Kenya. Meanwhile, after four years of service in Tanganyika, Marian decided to go on furlough. Providentially, there was no transport to the coast; hence, she sailed across Lake Victoria to Kisumu. At Kisumu, she met Keller, to whom she got engaged and later married.[4] After working with Miller for some time, the Kellers purchased the Nyang'ori Pentecostal mission from him; Miller eventually returned to America in 1925.[5] Though they were independent missionaries, there was need for the Kellers to get affiliated with a chartered mission organization to qualify for grants from the government.[6] On August 30, 1923, the Kellers were received into the cooperative fellowship of the Pentecostal Assemblies of Canada (PAOC), and Nyang'ori Mission became part of its worldwide fellowship.[7]

The brand of Pentecostalism that was planted at Nyang'ori continued to grow numerically and in practice. In December 1926, the Kellers conducted the first baptismal service, where eighteen people were baptized. The numbers gradually increased in subsequent years, and by April 1942, there were 1,000 candidates.[8] The number of churches was also rising steadily. By the end of 1938, there were 88 under the Nyang'ori mission; by 1941, it had reached 120, and by February 1942, a record high of 140.[9] Expansion of the mission's activities to its peripheries and the increase of churches necessitated the opening of other mission stations. By October 1942, three mission stations (Nyang'ori, Goibei, and Awasi) had been established, with about 200 churches under African pastors.[10] By 1960, there were 420 places of worship, 20,000 members, 51,616 adherents, a three-year-course Bible school at Nyang'ori, and ten regional training schools.[11]

Pentecostalism and Secessionism

The growth indicated earlier paralleled secessions and developments of other variants of Pentecostalism. A major contributing factor was development of confidence by Africans in their leadership abilities and their pursuit of self-determination.

A group commonly known as the *Vokoyani*, or the *Roho*, was the first to detach itself from the Pentecostal mission at Nyang'ori in 1933. The group alleged that the Holy Spirit had revealed to them that the white people were animals. Hence, to them, the Nyang'ori mission was defective, as it was led by white people.[12] In addition, the *Vokoyani* were against formal education. Education to them was a hindrance to receiving direct revelations from the Holy Spirit. They regarded themselves as "holy people" and hence could not greet or eat with sinners. They also adopted Saturday as their day of worship, and spouses were to abstain from sexual intimacy on the eve of the Sabbath. Interestingly, the changing of the Sabbath day was based on their reading and interpretation of the Old Testament.

Another major breakaway from Nyang'ori mission happened on January 26, 1942. The secessionists formed African Israel Church Nineveh, an important indigenous church in the religious panorama of Western Kenya.[13] Its leader, Zakayo Kivuli, had been a devout member at the Nyang'ori mission and is said to have "received the spirit" on February 12, 1932, after a serious bout of illness. After the experience, he started moving from village to village, amassing followers.[14] He turned the Pentecostal congregation that held meetings in his home into his own church.

In 1948, the PAOC went through another secession. Those who separated formed the African Divine Church (ADC), led by Jacob Ananda and later taken up by Saul Chabuga.[15] The ADC still has visibility in Kenya's major towns.

Other early breakaways include the Pentecostal Evangelistic Fellowship of Africa and the Pentecostal Assemblies of God (PAG) Nyanza. By default, the breakaways greatly aided in the growth of Pentecostal Christianity. This they did, first, by starting other Pentecostal congregations; second, by carrying over the Pentecostal practices and beliefs that they had learned from Nyang'ori; and third, by developing their own theologies and praxis. In addition to African leadership, some of the breakaways grew by incorporating African values and worldviews in their practices, such as spirit possession, dreams, and visions.

Apart from the secessionists, other Spirit movements emerged independently among Africans. Among them was a group in Western Kenya popularly known as the *Jo Roho.* The movement was credited to Alfayo Odongo Mango, a former priest with the Church Missionary Society (CMS).[16] It is claimed that the Spirit made "its" initial appearance in 1912 in a place called Ruwe in former Nyanza. Allegedly, the spirit would "come" in the form of a voice hovering over people's homes. The first public manifestation is when "it" came over a group of CMS converts who were gathered under a tree. The Spirit eventually "fell" on Ibrahim Osodo, who had built a prayer house in his homestead. From then on, the Spirit started talking to the people through Osodo. But with the outbreak of World War I, the band that had gathered around Osodo dispersed. Many, including Osodo, were conscripted in the army. With Osodo's exit, the activity of the Spirit in Ruwe ebbed away, only to reappear in 1916. This time, "it" fell on Mango, who was based at Musanda.[17]

The movement seemingly subsided soon after it began, as both administrative and missionary records have little to say about it. It found new momentum in 1933, when it fell again upon Silvano Nyamogo and Lawi Obonyo.[18] Two adherents who joined the *Jo Roho* reported that they left CMS because:

> ...in the CMS, we were taught to worship Christ, but the influence was not strong enough to prevent people from sinning. We prayed for guidance and the visitations advised us

> to worship the spirit which would be a stronger influence. We believe in God and his son Christ but we worship the spirit.[19]

The characteristics of the *Jo Roho* were, however, markedly different from the *Roho* Christianity at Nyang'ori. They prohibited use of medicine, as the Spirit could cure all sickness; they were not to shake hands to deter transmission of sin; and neither could they take food prepared by nonadherents.[20]

Institutionalization, Independence, and Growth of Pentecostal Christianity

The 1940s brought a turning point to the Pentecostal work at Nyang'ori in its structure and administration. From May 10–15, 1948, a conference was held, and a Kenya district of the PAOC work was formed. This developed into the Pentecostal Assembly of East Africa and later into the Pentecostal Assembly of God, giving a new impetus to Pentecostalism. There was a surge to open new Pentecostal churches beyond the precincts of Nyang'ori. Churches were founded in towns such as Busia, Kakamega, Kisii, and Nakuru.[21] Of greater significance was its entry into the city of Nairobi. Other mission groups of a Pentecostal background, such as the Elim Missionary Assembly, the Apostolic Faith Mission from South Africa, and the Full Gospel Churches of Kenya, had also started gaining more ground in Kenya from the mid-1940s. Consequently, by the 1950s, Pentecostalism had not only crossed the immediate ethnic boundaries of Western Kenya, but also geographical and administrative boundaries across the nation.

The eve and dawn of independence in Kenya (1963) witnessed a concerted growth and spread of African Independent Churches (AICs) as the spirit of nationalism gained momentum. Apart from the AICs, other homegrown Pentecostal churches and ministries, variously referred to as the neo-Pentecostals, started to emerge. One that deserves mention is the Deliverance Church that has had a growing national presence and influence in the last three decades. It was started in 1970 by Joe Kayo, a former PAG pastor who had attended Bible school at Nyang'ori. Its current bishop, Mark Kariuki, is the chairman of the Evangelical Alliance of Kenya that was established in 1975.[22] From the 1980s, Kenya has witnessed a proliferation of Pentecostal Christianity of various expressions. Among other factors, globalization has greatly contributed to the emergence of these new churches.[23]

Cross-Cultural and Interdenominational Influences in Pentecostal Development

The contemporary Pentecostal expression in Kenya has been shaped by various influences and interactions across historical space and contexts. Two that require special mention are the Spirit revival witnessed in Western Kenya between 1926 and 1928 and the East African revival movement (the *Balokole* revival) that began in the early 1930s. The Spirit revival, whose cradle was the Friends African Mission, emphasized baptism in the Spirit, speaking in tongues, and frenzied prayers and singing. This gave birth to and popularized the practice of *amavugano gokulinda* (tarrying meetings). Sessions would be organized whereby seekers would wait for hours and days to be filled with the Spirit.[24]

The East African revival was characterized by public confession of sins and emphasis on personal conversion that led to being "born again." At the center of their beliefs were the crucifixion of Jesus and the work of His blood in effecting salvation. Other features included indifference toward organizational structure, which was perceived as a hindrance to spiritual renewal; spontaneity and the giving of testimonies during meetings; puritanical lifestyles;

noninvolvement in politics; and disdain for secularism and materialism, among others.[25] The beliefs and practices of the *Balokole* had a direct impact on the expression of Kenyan Christianity in general and Pentecostalism in particular. Of major import was the Christocentric nature of the revival that acted as a balance to the pneumacentric character of Pentecostal Christianity.[26] The present Pentecostal Christianity in Kenya is characterized by carryovers of these two revivals.

Andrew Walls's observation that "a leading characteristic of historic Christianity is that though it crosses cultural frontiers, it rapidly acculturates and takes new forms dictated by the culture in which it becomes rooted"[27] is true in the Kenyan context. The Pentecostal Christianity that emerged within the confines of Western Kenya has taken a new form, practice, and identity, dictated by various cultural interactions and its interface with other denominations.

Eschatology: The Intersecting Theology

The theology and doctrine perpetuated by Kenyan Pentecostals have had a direct bearing on their expression of Christianity, in terms of spirituality, practices, demography, and social action. They subscribe to the theology of "being saved," baptism in the Holy Spirit, divine healing, and the second coming of Christ. Of these, conviction and obsession with the imminent return of Christ based on their reading of various texts (1 Thess. 4:16–18; Jude 14–15; Rev. 1:7) by far influenced the theological articulation and practices of the first generations of Pentecostals in Kenya. It pervaded their daily conversations, sermons, teachings, evangelism, spirituality, and lifestyles. For instance, in early 1927, Keller reported that he planned to add more outstations in the following year. He was, however, quick to add that this would only be possible "if Jesus tarries; His coming seems so near."[28] In May 1927, Marian concluded her report on Sunday school work with almost similar sentiments: "Our Lord is coming soon. May we be ready and occupy until he comes."[29] Similarly, in 1941, Keller predicted that "it will not be long now and we shall see the king whom we love and serve. May we keep the upward gaze."[30] These were sentiments of a people who were convinced that they were living on the edge of time. This conviction influenced their evangelism and mission, ethos and morality, and sociopolitical attitudes, as analyzed in the following.

Eschatology: evangelism and mission

The earlier decades' Pentecostal missiological model was considerably shaped by their eschatological tenets. To them, one of the fundamental conditions for the second coming of Christ was preaching the gospel to all nations (Matt. 24:14; 28:19; Mark 16:15). They were categorical that "we are a missionary people because we believe in the second coming of Jesus, and because we desire to fulfil his great commission."[31] As such, apart from the above texts providing scriptural justification and motivation for their involvement in evangelism, they also validated their enthusiasm of evangelizing the lost in order to speed up Christ's return. Admonitions such as, "Do you love his appearing? What will you do to help bring back the king?" were therefore commonplace.[32] In his 1940 report, Keller confirmed most adherents' stance on the imminent *parousia* and the resultant need to win souls. He stated, "The Spirit of God is impressing many of our people with the nearness of the coming of the Lord, the necessity of being prepared to meet God, and how essential that all who can should be giving out the word of God to those who are still outside the Ark of safety."[33] John Kitts, one of the Pentecostal workers, dubbed the work of evangelism as "speeding the light." He maintained, "We are all very conscious that Jesus is coming very soon…our prayer and objective is to evangelize as many souls as possible before Jesus comes."[34] In 1958, a group of students from Pentecostal Bible College at Nyang'ori who were on an evangelistic mission for one month carried a placard that read, *"Ujiweke tayari kuonana na Mungu wako"* ["Be prepared to meet with your God"].[35] Evidently, the perception of living in the last days and the imminent return of Christ provided heightened momentum to the work of evangelism. To this end, many became itinerant evangelists in order to prepare people and speed up Christ's return, as depicted in the Gospel of Matthew (Matt. 24:14).

As part of evangelism, the Pentecostals took to the practice of processions. They moved from village to village and marketplaces, singing and drumming in order to attract crowds. After crowds gathered, they would preach the message of repentance. The songs sung during the processions would have an evangelistic message. Notably, other Christian expressions, such as the Salvation Army and the Quakers, would also have processions. To distinguish themselves from other groups, the Pentecostals started putting on white gowns to symbolize their inner purity. They also designed a flag that had red and white colors to accompany them during the processions. The colors represented the blood of Jesus and its cleansing work. The flag was later redesigned to incorporate black and green colors, symbolizing a life of sin and God's provisions, respectively. The cross and Scripture references were embroidered at the center of the flag to underscore the significance of Christ's death on the cross and that of the Bible in a believer's life.[36]

Eschatology, ethos, and morality

The earlier generations of Pentecostals adhered to an unwritten holiness and moral code based on their eschatological perspective.

Adherents were expected to live beyond reproach as they prepared for the coming of Christ. Correspondences from the early decades affirm this. A letter written to Keller on September 1931 stressed that "the coming of Christ cannot be far distant; the long-looked for day may soon be ushered in. Oh, how the blessed hope inspires one to a nobler and holier service."[37] This was echoed by Keller in 1934 in the face of conflict between Pentecostals and members of the Friends' church. He distanced himself from the hostility by maintaining, "In the face of present world conditions and the soon coming of the Lord Jesus Christ I want to be right with God and men."[38] This reveals emphasis on personal holiness and unquestionable public character.

The fervor of Christ's return and the need to be holy was still evident in the 1950s and 1960s. Some of the earliest publications of *Ushahidi wa Pentekoste* (The Pentecostal testimony) affirm this. Issue number 8, in October 1950, carried an article based on Matthew 24:48–50 that stressed:

> *Siku hizi ni siku za kurudi kwa bwana yesu Kristo. Je, sisi tumejitayarisha? Tusifanye dhambi, kwa sababu Mungu anachukia hizi. . . . Kumbukeni kurudi kwa Yesu. Atakuja upesi.* [These days are the days of the coming back of the Lord Jesus Christ. Are we ready? We should not commit sin, because the Lord hates it. . . . Remember the coming back of Jesus. He will come soon.][39]

The emphasis was one of shunning sin and its manifestations. These Pentecostals continually admonished one another, "We may not be here tomorrow. Jesus might come today."[40] The thrust of the admonitions was one of vigilance, a call for perpetual preparedness and unyielding holiness in lieu of Christ coming like a thief in the night.

A stringent moral code also led Pentecostals to a strict dress code. Women adorned long white dresses and white headgear when attending church and prayer meetings. This was based on the Pentecostals' interpretation of Paul's admonitions to the Corinthian women to have a covering for their heads (1 Cor. 11:13–15). It was also meant to distinguish them from women of other Christian expressions. In addition, based on their interpretation of 1 Timothy 2:9–10, they were prohibited from braiding their hair, dressing in expensive clothes, and adorning themselves with jewelry. These practices were assumedly worldly. The strict dress code was equally meant to buttress their quest for unquestionable public character. Observably, there was an overly literalistic approach to interpretation of scriptural texts.

Eschatology and sociopolitical engagement

The Pentecostals' upward gaze in their earlier days minimized their concern for earthly affairs and clamor for earthly possessions. They were preoccupied with not being of this world (John 8:23; 18:36). As a result, an ambivalent stance on social action and particularly educational matters was visible from their first decades. They harbored mixed feelings, attitudes, positions, and approaches to education. Whereas some felt that education was an indispensable tool in the propagation of Pentecostalism, to others it was a hindrance to that cause. These opposing fronts were mostly apparent among classical Pentecostals, whose leadership was answerable to their home office. A conversation held in 1929 between Keller and Walter McAlister, who represented the home office, illustrates this tension. McAlister stated:

> We have often wondered and it has been expressed from different angles if there was not a danger of you going ahead too far with the building and educational programmes to

> the neglect of bringing people into the experience of the baptism of the Holy spirit. This ought to be the ultimate object of all our work and building or education only as a means to that end.[41]

In response, Keller clarified that they had not deviated from the primary objective of bringing people into the experience of baptism in the Holy Spirit. He disclosed:

> We dislike the word "education" and we should call it Christian training for that is what we are doing and all to this end alone that men and women may know God, be filled with the Holy spirit and ready for his coming. Please do not think that we are trying to educate unconverted men or women to prepare them for better positions in life. We are simply training men and women to become useful Christian workers.[42]

This displays an apologetic attitude when involved in education work.

A write-up in *Plenteous Harvest,* a booklet of the PAOC, categorically stated:

> Our missionaries have not gone to Kenya or to any of the other fields to civilize a backward people nor to raise their standards of living, nor to conduct social services, nor to train political leaders. They have gone to take Christ to them, for indeed Christ is the only answer.[43]

Accordingly, Christ was the only answer to all human concerns, thereby downplaying the role of social and political institutions to that end.

Education was thus neither an end in itself, nor primarily a social service to the society. Rather, it was a conduit for expansion of Christianity in general and Pentecostalism in particular. It is not surprising, then, that even among the African independent Pentecostals, there was a general disdain for education. For instance, the *Vokoyani* group earlier described was against formal education, as this was presumably worldly and hindered the flow of the Spirit.

For the most part of their first century of existence, Pentecostals in Kenya have held on to a policy of noninvolvement in politics. Engaging politics in the earlier decades was regarded as sinful, as politics was worldly and therefore evil.[44] To them, political involvement was incompatible with being of the Spirit. The general rule was that if an adherent vied for or was elected into a political position, they were to relinquish leadership positions in the church. Such a stance was intrinsically tied to their eschatological interpretations of political institutions as human creations with limited ability to bring social transformation. Politics had the power to contaminate anyone and thus compromise the Pentecostal principles of personal holiness and strict morality. It was only prudent to avoid politics altogether. A case in point: during the tenure of the third African general superintendent of the PAG church, Shem Irangi (1976–1992), his treasurer, Mr. Yakundi, contested for a position of a councilor. When Irangi learned of it, he sacked Yakundi on the spot, without warning.[45]

TOWARD A HOLISTIC THEOLOGY

The last few decades have witnessed a radical shift from the overly eschatologically woven theology to a more holistic approach. A survey carried out on some Pentecostal churches in Nairobi between the years 2011 and 2013 reveals a gaping decline of sermons, songs, and conversations on Jesus's second coming.[46] Consequently, other areas of Christian life have received more attention. Some of the factors causing these changes are higher levels of formal and theological education that expose participants to new ways of thinking. Theological education has also aided in moving from a purely literalistic approach to interpretation of Scripture to the use of other hermeneutical tools.

An area that has witnessed significant shifts is Pentecostals' socioeconomic and political engagement. There is a palpable heightened awareness of and activities in sociopolitical matters. Inasmuch as their involvement was visible in 2005 during the agitation for a new constitution in Kenya,[47] their new political thinking became obvious to the public eye during the 2007 general elections. Unlike in earlier elections, Pentecostals contested for political positions in an unprecedented manner. Pastor Pius Muiru of Maximum Miracle Centre ran for the presidential position and also sought to be elected as the Kamukunji member of Parliament. Bishop Margaret Wanjiru of Jesus Is Alive Ministries (JIAM) vied for a parliamentary position and was elected as the member of Parliament representing the *Starehe* constituency in Nairobi. She was later nominated as the assistant minister for housing.[48] This was a major break from the initial position of noninvolvement and noninterference in politics. For the majority of Pentecostals, there had been a clear divide between religious and political matters.

This political enthusiasm did not abate, and by the 2013 general elections, the tempo had increased. Key personalities within Pentecostal circles delved into politics. For instance, Rev. Moses Akaranga and George Munyasa Khaniri, both of the PAG Church, were elected as the Vihiga governor and senator, respectively.[49] Bonifes Adoyo, the retired bishop of Christ Is the Answer Ministries (CITAM, formerly Nairobi Pentecostal Church), contested for the Nairobi gubernatorial position. The crux of this new political involvement was witnessed when the current CITAM bishop, David Oginde, made the inaugural prayers for the fourth president of Kenya, Uhuru Kenyatta, and his deputy president, William Ruto, on April 9, 2013.[50]

There are also notable shifts in Pentecostals' attitudes toward, objectives regarding, and emphases in formal and theological education. As noted, earlier generations of Pentecostals were averse to education and accentuated the place of charisma, founded on 1 Corinthians 12:8–10. To them, the Holy Spirit gives various gifts to different people for ministry, even without training. There is a notable growing awareness of the need to balance charisma and training. For instance, the current PAG constitution states that for one to qualify to be a pastor, he or she must "have successfully completed Bible College training and possess an appropriate credential given by the PAG-Kenya Credentials Committee."[51] CITAM, one of the leading Pentecostal churches in Kenya, is notable for its formally and theologically educated pastoral team. Its first bishop, Bonifes Adoyo (now retired), is a degree-holder in design and has a master's degree in divinity. David Oginde, the present bishop, holds a bachelor's degree in architecture, a master's degree in leadership, and a PhD in organizational leadership.[52]

Inversely, the holistic approach to Christian faith and life has led to a growing emphasis on an ethics of success. In 2000, Kirk Kauffeldt, the academic dean of Pan Africa Christian College (a Pentecostal college), registered his concern on the infiltration of the "wealth and health" gospel, which he said was "spreading like wildfire" in Kenya.[53] Proponents of this prosperity teaching argue that all human needs have been met through the suffering and death of Christ and that this truth grants Christians victory over sin, sickness, and lack. Consequently, a believer should be wealthy, forever in good health, and free from pain and suffering. This victorious life can be effected by a simple confession of faith.[54] From their interpretation of the third epistle of John, material blessings and good health are indicators of the condition of the soul (3 John 2).

In like manner, *panda mbegu* (plant a seed) theology, which is essentially a North American innovation, has pervaded Kenyan Pentecostalism. Teachings and sermons on the necessity of tithing, giving, and planting a "faith seed" in order to be rewarded with material success are increasingly taking dominance not only among the newer Pentecostals, but even among the classical ones. To buttress these messages, testimonies of people who attribute their success and prosperity to their giving are commonplace during church services and through the media (radio and TV stations). There is also a growing consumption of literature and messages on self-actualization, business success, strategic management, and investments, a trend that has been aptly captured by Paul Gifford in his analysis of Pentecostalism in Kenya.[55]

What this trend portends is a materialist understanding of blessings, God's favor, victorious living, and success. The explosion of this success-and-prosperity craze based on sowing and reaping drove Pentecostals in their masses into pyramid investment schemes that proliferated in Kenya between 2006 and 2009. The most popular ones among Christians were the Developing Entrepreneurship and Community Initiative[56] and Christian Leaders in Publishing. Some Pentecostal pastors were at the fore in encouraging their members to join these ventures, claiming it was reaping time for Christians. Inasmuch as Kenyans from all backgrounds were culprits, Pentecostals were the most affected by the collapse of these schemes.

Whereas affluence was disdained by the earlier generations of Pentecostals, it is now sought after, with ministries and individuals flaunting their wealth. There is a corresponding lack of emphasis on moral issues, resulting with outright extortion and fraud in some cases. This has become common on Kenyan television channels and radio stations, where some of the preachers appeal to viewers and listeners to remit money through their cell phones (popularly known as *Mpesa*) so as to receive a miracle in return. A case in point is Pastor James Kanyari of the Salvation Healing Ministry Church, who in the earlier months of 2013 was asking viewers to send a "seed" of Ksh 310. In July 2013, he claimed that God had told him to tell the viewers to increase the seed from Ksh 310 to Ksh 477 for a miracle to take place.[57]

Challenges and Opportunities in the Face of a Waning Eschatology

With the declining emphasis on eschatology on one hand and a growing holistic approach to Christian life on the other, new theologies and practices have emerged. As in the earlier decades, these theologies are fairly oral and experiential. From a general perspective, all religious experiences demand theological interpretations. It is therefore needful for Kenyan Pentecostals to come up with theological formulations in regard to their heightened political involvement and their success ethics. These formulations, however, should be subjected to the authority of Scripture, based on the understanding that theology is a "critical reflection on Christian practice in the light of the word."[58] Hence, all experiences, practices, actions, convictions, and claims must be tested against Scripture. It is unfortunate that in most cases, scriptural references have been used as proof texts to justify questionable practices.

In agreement with Andrew Walls, theology "springs out of practical situations [and] it is therefore occasional and local in character."[59] Walls further comments that theology "arises out of situations that actually happen, not from broad general principles."[60] As such, theological formulations must be true to the

Kenyan context. As the Kenyan society surges through the myriad sociopolitical challenges in the twenty-first century, Pentecostals should not only settle for contesting for elective political positions but are obliged to come up with a constructive theology that addresses itself to all dimensions of society. Issues of social injustices, corruption, ethics, governance, tribalism, nepotism, health, gender disparities, terrorism, and others must be attended to as part of the full gospel of Christ. In formulation of these theologies, a fitting approach would be Kwame Bediako's construct of using Scripture as the hermeneutic of culture and tradition.[61] He points out that the gospel should engage the cultural, socioeconomic, and political realities of a people. Scripture should be the road map with which to navigate human concerns and interpret humanity's essence in their specific cultural and sociopolitical contexts. This calls for deep research and understanding of the Kenyan socioeconomic and political issues by Pentecostals in order to engage these with the person of Christ.

Conclusion

From the foregoing, Pentecostalism in Kenya has undergone various shifts in theology and praxis. As it enters its second century of existence, it is expected that more shifts will be witnessed as contexts change. It is the responsibility of Pentecostal scholars to develop theologies that are local in character in response to local concerns. Nonetheless, as much as a holistic approach is imperative, the eschatological fervor that shaped the ethos and morals, mission and evangelism, social action and spirituality of the first generations of Pentecostals should not be relegated to the past. There is need for balance between a heavenly and an earthly gaze.

Chapter 8

Pentecostalism in Ethiopia: A Unique Case in Africa

Jörg Haustein

ETHIOPIA HAS OFTEN escaped the attention of global scholarship on Pentecostalism, yet the country offers a unique and highly interesting case in Africa. This is all the more the case as an unprecedented shift is taking place in the country's religious landscape. Over the past three decades, the population share of Protestantism has risen from a little over 5 percent to 21 percent, which has significant implications for this traditionally Orthodox and Muslim country.[1] Ethiopia is now one of the African states with the highest numbers of Evangelicals in absolute terms, next to countries more often associated with Evangelical or born-again Christianity, like Nigeria or Kenya.[2] Moreover, this rise of Protestantism coincides with, or arguably is fueled by, the indisputable Pentecostal or Charismatic character of most Protestant churches, not just in vernacular practice, but also in theological declaration. Almost all of the classical Protestant churches have accommodated Charismatic doctrine in their statements of faith and liturgies, and—notwithstanding some regional variation—services in these churches often do not differ significantly from Pentecostal ones.

These developments have a considerable impact on Ethiopian public spheres, which scholarship is only just beginning to address.[3] Ethiopian towns and villages now host a plurality of small and large churches, competing with the established religious traditions. On Sunday mornings, their amplifiers, keyboards, singing, and ululations join the street medley of religious sounds alongside the publicly broadcast Orthodox liturgy and the Muslim call to prayer. Stickers with their token slogan "*Iyesus geta näw!*" ("Jesus is Lord") have become as much a public presence as Orthodox icons or *shahāda* calligraphy. Tensions occasionally occur, such as when Pentecostal missions disrespect traditional religious boundaries between Christianity and Islam or when Orthodox preachers warn against "renewal movements" and their alleged detrimental effects on Ethiopian culture and identity. Finally, the rise of Pentecostalism is also leaving its mark in Ethiopian politics and economic development, most visibly in the ascent of Hailemariam Desalegn to the office of prime minister, who is not only the first non-Orthodox leader of Ethiopia since the fourth century but belongs to the sizable—and ostracized—Oneness Pentecostal Church, adding a peculiar political twist to Pentecostal politics.[4]

These introductory remarks invoke three major themes to be explored in this chapter. First, the rise of Pentecostalism and the presently almost-complete conflation between Pentecostal and Protestant identities beckon for an explanation, which has to be rooted in the vicissitudes of Ethiopian history since the 1960s. Second, the plural religious configuration of Ethiopia brings to the fore aspects of religious boundaries and their contestation, especially in the form of Orthodox Charismatic movements and Pentecostal attempts at an "insider mission" among Muslims. Last, but certainly not least, the emergence of Pentecostalism in the public sphere has a significant political and economic impact, highlighting questions of political allegiance, prosperity theology, and moral challenges of development. The chapter will address these themes in turn, concluding with a brief outlook that summarizes the main current challenges of the movement.

History and Identity[5]

In comparison to other African countries, Pentecostalism arrived fairly late in Ethiopia, dating to Finnish and Swedish Pentecostal mission initiatives in the 1950s. The most influential ones were the Finnish mission station in Addis Ababa and the Swedish Philadelphia Church Mission in Awasa, which provided a hub for Pentecostal youths from all over the country via its annual summer conferences.

Ethiopian histories of the Pentecostal revival tend to give little weight to missionary input, however. Even their "initial outpouring" event—though placed at the Swedish mission in Awasa in 1963—is typically linked to a Kenyan evangelist who was present there.[6] While this narrative downplays the significant and lasting involvement of missionaries in the movement, it adequately places the emphasis on the Ethiopian initiatives that rose up all over the country in the 1960s. A number of these initiatives converged in Addis Ababa and led to the foundation of the Full Gospel Believers' Church (also called Mulu Wongel Church) in 1967. Significantly, this movement was established and led by university students. The international connections and contemporary style of Pentecostalism matched their modernizing ambitions, and their considerable mobility aided the quick spread of their faith all over the country.

A few months after its foundation, the Full Gospel Believers' Church applied for government registration as a religious association. This was a bold reflection of the modernizing impulse of the Pentecostal youths, because in public sentiment and political reality, the Ethiopian Orthodox Church was the only legitimate representative of Ethiopian Christianity. All other Christian groups and churches were still operating under the "Regulations Governing the Activities of Missions" from 1944, and legal provisions for the registration of other faith groups had only been introduced in the immediate years prior. When the Pentecostal youths became the first ones to test this new legislation without any favorable reputation or missionary umbrella, the government denied their request, which entailed the immediate closure of Pentecostal meeting places.

The Full Gospel Believers at first complied with this ruling and relied on smaller meetings in private homes, accepting at times the help of the Swedish Philadelphia Church Mission for meeting premises or governmental negotiations. During this time, the movement encountered its first doctrinal division when one of its evangelists joined recently arrived Oneness Pentecostal missionaries from the United States (the United Pentecostal Mission) and founded the Apostolic Church of Ethiopia, which later became one of the largest branches of Pentecostalism in the country.[7] From the end of 1971 onward, the government increased its pressure on religious groups without a permit, and when all negotiations led to no results, the Ethiopian youths decided to insist on their constitutional rights and resumed public meetings. This attempt failed and led to the arrest of approximately two hundred fifty worshippers in the summer of 1972 in a government crackdown that also targeted Jehovah's Witnesses. The arrested were charged with illegal assembly and sentenced to a fine or prison, and a Pentecostal appeal to the high court was unsuccessful. Through some Protestant allies, the youths also managed to bring international attention to their case through magazines like *Christianity*

Today and *Newsweek* (international edition), which reported on the arrests, and the World Council of Churches investigated the matter. However, none of these efforts bore any fruit, and the Pentecostals again resorted to congregating in secret groups until Haile Selassie's government came to an end in 1974.[8]

The revolution of that year at first brought some degree of religious freedom. The Full Gospel Believers' Church resumed public meetings and set up a new national structure. The establishment of central leadership structures also entailed a second doctrinal division in the church when some began to subscribe to Derek Prince's deliverance theology and contended that born-again and Spirit-filled believers may also be possessed by demons. They were forced out of the church and established the Gospel Deliverance Church.[9]

As the revolution turned into the violent Socialist regime of the Derg, the pressure on Pentecostals increased again, while the Orthodox Church was co-opted by the state.[10] The Full Gospel Believers' Church in Addis Ababa still managed to acquire land and completed its first building in 1978. However, it was closed and confiscated by the government a few months later. By this time, many rural Full Gospel churches had already been shut down, and the church as a whole relied on secret home meetings once more until almost the end of the Derg regime in 1991. The Pentecostal missions also turned their work over to Ethiopian nationals during this time, but in both cases the churches were closed almost immediately after gaining missionary independence, and their property was confiscated. Both churches set up underground structures as well.

Pentecostals were an obvious target of the regime, due to their public religiosity and open defiance of certain aspects of the revolution, such as the shouting of certain Socialist slogans or attending Sunday youth meetings. Some of the mainline churches already had Charismatic groups operating in their midst at this time, which now were in a somewhat precarious position, especially as the government began to extend the derogatory term *Pente* to all Protestants. In a number of instances, this caused the mainline churches to draw a clear distinction between them and Pentecostals by not allowing Pentecostals to participate in their services or by exiling their own Charismatic groups. However, many Protestant mainline churches were soon subject to closures as well, and in some instances the Charismatic elements led the way in establishing underground meetings. Altogether, it appears that the Derg regime indirectly furthered the spread of Pentecostalism within Protestantism. The strong repression of Pentecostals and their relatively defiant attitude toward government power resulted in the creation of stable underground structures that effected significant church growth. On account of these developments, Pentecostal and Charismatic Christians began to be seen as a political alternative to the more accommodating attitudes of some established churches. Moreover, government propaganda increasingly identified all Protestants as Pentecostals, and their ubiquitous application of the term *Pente* became widespread, even as self-identification. Finally, the early attempts by mainline churches to exclude Charismatic groups gave the latter the moral upper hand after the Derg had come to an end in 1991.

Protestants in Ethiopia now began to see an unprecedented level of religious liberties. The present constitution includes robust provisions for religious freedom and the separation of church and state. The old imperial process for registering religious associations remained in place but was put into practice for the first time. Pentecostals immediately took advantage of the changes and reemerged in public spaces, discovering that their numbers had risen substantially in the underground. In the past two decades,

Pentecostal growth continued alongside denominational fragmentation. Numerous new churches emerged, and the number of registered religious associations rose sharply.[11] The "charismatization" of mainline Protestant churches continued at an accelerated rate, reflecting an increased influence of Charismatic groups and local competition with the Pentecostal attractiveness to youths.[12] These fairly porous borders between Pentecostals and mainline Protestantism have an organizational correlate in the Evangelical Churches Fellowship of Ethiopia. It is the only significant ecumenical body on the Protestant side, and almost all the major (Trinitarian) Pentecostal denominations are among its members, alongside the older mainline churches. The fellowship facilitates theological discussions, as well as cooperation in evangelism, development projects, or other practical matters, and to some extent it seeks a common political representation of Protestants. In these collaborations, Pentecostal/Charismatic theological positions often appear to be less contentious than other issues, such as adult versus infant baptism or proselytism.

A number of key points emerge from this historical exposition regarding the identity of the Pentecostal movement in Ethiopia today. First, and most importantly, it has become analytically impossible to clearly separate Pentecostalism from mainline Protestantism, as there is a confluence between Protestant and Pentecostal identities in terms of worship practice, theology, interdenominational collaboration and transfer, and even in terminology (*Pente*). This does not preclude considerable theological or liturgical variations, but these often run through denominations as much as in between them. The (Lutheran) Mekane Yesus Church, for example, may exhibit generational conflicts over charismatic practices in its traditional regions, but where the church arrived later than Pentecostals, its worship may appear more vibrant and charismatic than that of the Full Gospel Believers' Church. Pentecostal and charismatic practices may not be evenly distributed, but they form a sort of discourse running through all Protestant churches, as all the large churches have adopted doctrinal and liturgical regulations in this regard.[13]

Second, this Protestant confluence also spans a considerable variety of doctrine and churches. Alongside the more classical issues, such as water baptism and ecclesiology, there is a considerable variety of Pentecostal doctrine. While most churches may be counted as classical Pentecostals, the Gospel Deliverance Church and a few smaller ones advocate spiritual warfare, and some newly founded churches preach faith or prosperity theology, albeit with only measured success. The Oneness doctrine of the Apostolic Church adds to this variety, but the church is seen as heretical by all other denominations.

A third important aspect of Pentecostal identity is the past experience of government oppression or persecution. With Pentecostals already being unable to freely operate under Haile Selassie, government oppression became a shared experience during the Derg. It is important to note that in both instances, attempts at political negotiations or accommodation failed to yield lasting results, whereas a silent defiance of government orders carried the underground movement. This political legacy still very much informs many churches, since many are still led by elders from the first generation, who were merely students in the 1960s.

Finally, while the opposition against Pentecostals was usually based on allegations of their foreignness or an alleged American or CIA influence, Pentecostals have always insisted that they are an indigenous movement. For the first student movement, the assertion of mission independence became an important part of its historical narrative, and later even the mission-founded Pentecostal churches followed suit. Largely cut off from outside contacts during the Derg, Pentecostals learned to utilize missionary support where available, but stayed independent otherwise. While it has been easier to receive outside support in recent years, this contribution has remained minimal. External influence and financial support do exist, but in almost all Pentecostal churches this is either negligible or raised by Ethiopians living abroad. The indigenous character of the Pentecostal movement is also evident in its worship forms. The Pentecostal combination of Ethiopian pop styles and Amharic lyrics has created a vibrant music scene from the beginning of the movement,[14] and only very few churches in the capital conduct English-speaking services, while all others use Amharic or other Ethiopian languages.

Ecumenical and Interreligious Relations

The Pentecostal claims to an Ethiopian identity have often been contested by the Orthodox Church. Due to its century-long alliance with the Ethiopian state, the Orthodox Church continues to view itself as the only guarantor of Ethiopian culture and national integrity, whereas all other churches are seen to represent foreign incursions. In recent years, the Orthodox youth movement *Mahibere Kidusan* has emphasized this sentiment and accused Pentecostals and Protestants of contributing to the country's moral decay and social disintegration by their insistence on salvation by grace.[15] Even stronger warnings have been published in Ethiopian Orthodox quarters abroad, detecting a Protestant "jihad" on the country, which aims to spread an alleged white and Western version of Christianity.[16]

This opposition against Protestantism has to be understood in its demographic and historical context. The above-mentioned rise of Protestantism in many ways presents a direct challenge to the traditional hegemony of the Orthodox Church. Its overall population share decreased from 54 to 43.5 percent between the 1984 and 2007 censuses, roughly mirroring the Protestant increase.[17] Moreover, there is a significant regional variance to the presence of both Christian confessions. The traditional heartlands of Ethiopia, the Tigray and Amhara regions, are still predominantly Orthodox, with Protestantism forming a minority of less than a half percent. Even in Addis Ababa, the share of Protestants was only 7.7 percent in the 2007 census, well below the country average.[18] On the other hand, Protestantism is the majority religion in some southern, western, and southwestern regions, all of which were annexed by the Ethiopian Empire in the nineteenth century. So Ethiopia is still religiously divided along the old lines of power, and arguably Pentecostalism has accentuated but not altered this traditional divide.

Even though their numbers are small in the Orthodox heartlands, Protestants have used the opportunities afforded by the government to establish churches and cemeteries in areas they hitherto had no access to. This new Protestant presence can seem disruptive to Orthodox Christians and has occasionally led to tensions. In some northern towns, like Bahir Dar, Pentecostal buildings appear to visually compete with Orthodox churches, being larger and more opulent than their counterparts in the south.[19] In addition, Pentecostal open-air events have incited riots in the past, such as in Mekele in 2002, which Pentecostals have integrated into their persecution narrative despite the government protection afforded to them.[20] Tensions not only exist in the public sphere, but also pervade within families. Pentecostal and Charismatic Ethiopians do not drink alcohol, they abstain from (secular) dancing, and they do not participate in many Orthodox customs. The social gap between both Christian confessions is therefore especially visible at weddings, during fasting days, or on Orthodox holidays, thereby contributing to the Orthodox notion of "*Pentes*" being a disruptive social force. It is still not uncommon for Protestant converts to be disowned by their families, and this often takes the form of a generational conflict as youths turn away from Orthodoxy. Finally, Pentecostals have also contributed their share in polemical statements and publications against Orthodox customs and traditions.[21]

In this climate of mutual alienation, it is hardly surprising that Charismatic movements have not been very successful within the Orthodox Church. Where such movements exist, they often run into conflict with the hierarchy or certain parts of Orthodox theology, especially with regard to the veneration of saints or Mary. A number of groups therefore operate as secret fellowships without official recognition. Other groups have managed to maintain a semiofficial status by avoiding conflict; however, these also tend to facilitate members' transitions to Pentecostal forms of worship, despite the opposite intent of their leaders.

A very prominent example of the difficulty of maintaining a place "in between" is the Amanuel United Church.[22] Its origins date to the early 1990s, when Orthodox Charismatic groups in Nazaret and in Addis Ababa ran into conflict with the Orthodox Church over the exorcism of demons, modern music and preaching styles, female leadership, and other issues. Both groups were exiled by their parishes and formed the Amanuel Fellowship in 1994, seeking to establish themselves as an explicitly Orthodox renewal movement in distinction to Protestant Pentecostalism. Quite paradoxically, this profile made them even more interesting to Ethiopian Pentecostals, many of whom are of Orthodox background and have retained the impetus to reform their national church. In addition, the distinctive music style of the Amanuel Fellowship, making use of traditional Orthodox instruments and melodies, was very attractive to many Pentecostals. Gradually, various contacts, invitations to church services, and the warm Pentecostal reception led to a "Protestantization" of the Amanuel Fellowship. Mary and the saints lost their role as intermediaries in 1995; later on, adult baptism was introduced and infant baptism no longer recognized; and finally, the Protestant form of Communion was adopted. The fellowship then turned into a denomination with the name Amanuel Fellowship Church and organized branches in other parts of the country. The transformation to Protestantism was complete when the Amanuel Fellowship Church joined the Evangelical Churches Fellowship of Ethiopia in 2004. Given the lack of a middle ground between Orthodoxy and Pentecostals, this development is perhaps not surprising, but it also contributed to the rift, since the Amanuel Fellowship only confirmed Orthodox suspicions about the "real ends" of renewal groups in their midst.

Ecumenical relations therefore remain tense, and the only forum of mutual collaboration between most Protestants, the Orthodox Church, and the (quite small) Catholic Church is the Ethiopian Bible Society. With the exception of the Mekane Yesus Church, no other Protestant church accepts Orthodox baptism, and there still is no theological forum for dialogue between both sides.

There is even less dialogue when it comes to other religions. Ethiopian Pentecostals, as everywhere in Africa, tend to draw clear borders between themselves and traditional religions or Islam. Interestingly, however, these borders are somewhat fluid upon closer examination. As detailed elsewhere,[23] Ethiopian Pentecostals integrate traditional spirit names and concepts by translating them into the Christian concept of demon possession, but this is not always a straightforward exercise. On the one hand, it may be difficult to account for certain phenomenological parallels between traditional and Pentecostal practices (such as glossolalic or prophetic utterances); and on the other hand, there is the issue of recurring spirit possessions, something quite common in traditional spirit management but normally not acceptable for born-again, Spirit-filled believers. Deliverance Pentecostalism offers a theological way out of these dilemmas by allowing for certain degrees of possession or oppression, which have to be treated but do not call into question the soteriological status of a believer. However, as mentioned above, this theological orientation led to conflict very early on and was split off into a separate denomination. So although deliverance practices certainly feature strongly in other Pentecostal churches as well, including the problem of recurring spirit possessions, the theological articulation of these issues was left to the Gospel Deliverance Church—a rather small denomination on the fringe of the Evangelical Churches Fellowship.

Pentecostal attention to Islam has been growing in recent years in a situation of rising tension between the Ethiopian government and the Muslim community. Unlike Protestantism, Islam has been subject to considerable government regimentation and interference, especially in the aftermath of Ethiopia's involvement in Somalia from 2006 to 2009. Citing a threat of terrorism, the government has placed stricter controls on Muslim communities, has sought to impose an Ethiopian version of Islam, and has reacted quite harshly to Muslim protests against these measures. Despite its historical presence in the country, Islam has often been treated as a foreign religion in Ethiopia's past, so these recent measures amplified long-standing tensions. However, unlike the 1974 revolution, when Pentecostals joined Muslims in their demonstrations for greater religious freedom, today they tend to echo the government narrative about the "dangers of Islam." In some cases, this is combined with sustained efforts at missions among Muslims, linking up Ethiopia with 10/40-window mission strategies. While the Evangelical Churches Fellowship is a member of the established Christian-Muslim dialogue initiative PROCUMURA (formerly the Islam in Africa Project), a number of its Pentecostal member churches engage in strategic mission efforts in Muslim areas, disregarding established boundaries in religiously fragmented areas, such as the Rift Valley. This has led to conflicts in the past, but the fellowship seems to have little control over such grassroots efforts. In recent years, some churches have begun to pursue a somewhat covert and highly adaptive approach to their missions, claiming that while they convert Muslims, they keep "cultural aspects" of Islam intact, such as not requiring women to lay down the *ḥijāb*, calling the pastor *imam*, and not putting up crosses when converting a village mosque.[24] These claims are contested by some and need more research, but these and similar efforts, like a planned Bible translation taking into account Muslim terminology and sensibilities, have recently prompted an Evangelical magazine to compile a critical dossier of what it understood to be syncretistic efforts at establishing "Chrislam" in Ethiopia.[25] As with traditional religions, the Pentecostal efforts at drawing a clear boundary with Islam therefore appear to be more of a hybrid and fluid contact zone, which might provide a way forward for understanding Christian-Muslim relations beyond the classical dialogue initiatives.

Pentecostals and the Ethiopian State: Politics and Development

As has become evident, Pentecostalism has benefited majorly from the now almost twenty-five-year rule of the Ethiopian People's Revolutionary Democratic Front (EPRDF), especially in comparison to other religious groups. Their numbers have increased constantly, their mode of organization fits well with the government's registration requirements, and they have not seen major government interference; instead, local authorities have respected their right to property leases and public gatherings. Perhaps the only major exception to this considerable compatibility is the Ethiopian legislation concerning nongovernmental organizations (NGOs), which has forced churches to separate their development efforts into separate NGOs and, more recently, has stipulated that organizations advancing humanitarian or advocacy causes cannot receive more than 10 percent of their income from abroad.

So how do Pentecostals interact with the Ethiopian state, especially given its somewhat mixed record with regard to political freedom, human rights, and economic development? Constitutionally, the state is a federal democracy, but in practice, only one party, the EPRDF, is organized countrywide and capable of winning national elections. Intimidation of opposition candidates and parties is common; cases of fraud have been reported in past elections; and when faced with public demonstrations or unrest, police forces have routinely responded with a heavy hand, including live ammunition. The press has also been severely curtailed in recent years, with prominent opposition journalists being put in jail or charged with terrorism. Economically, Ethiopia has been boasting double-digit growth rates for over a decade, and the impact of this is highly visible, especially in the larger towns. There have been considerable investments in infrastructure, a boom of export-oriented agriculture (coffee, flowers, grain, khat), a significant increase of higher education, and a growing wealthy class. Inequality is rising, however, and especially in recent years, the staggering inflation rates have taken a toll on the middle class.

Moreover, while Ethiopia officially subscribes to liberal economic policies, the central industries, resources, and infrastructure are in the hands of the government, encouraging nepotism and corruption.

Overall, it seems that Pentecostals have neither embraced the Ethiopian government, nor do they critically interact with its failures. Rather, the overarching understanding is that a sustainable regeneration of Ethiopia's society, economy, and politics must begin with the rejuvenation of the church and individual conversions to the Pentecostal faith. The most prominent proponent of this idea is Tamrat Layne, the former prime minister of the transitional government (1991–1995) and first deputy prime minister under Meles Zenawi. In 1996, he fell out with Meles and was imprisoned and sentenced for corruption. He converted to Evangelical Christianity while in prison, and since his release, he has been preaching a message of forgiveness and reconciliation for the improvement of the country while refraining from direct political comment.[26] His message has resonated quite strongly with fellow Pentecostals,[27] since it mirrors their previous experience in the Ethiopian Empire and the Derg: political attempts at securing the movement's future had failed, but focusing on spiritual matters in defiance of political powers had sustained the churches in the underground.[28] While this view is fairly common, it is worth noting that it is not universal. Especially, new Pentecostal groups have argued that their fellow churches have not done enough to secure a positive political influence. However, since they, in effect, seek a similar spiritual transformation and face various obstacles when interacting with the government, they have not altered the Pentecostal political discourse overall.[29]

Interestingly, the ascension of Hailemariam Desalegn to the Office of the Prime Minister has also not changed these dynamics in a noticeable way. Hailemariam has tried to cast himself as a prime minister for all religions while not denying his (Oneness) Pentecostal faith. An interview about his faith shortly after his inauguration shows that this is a thin line to walk. On the one hand, he affirmed the importance of the government's philosophy of a strict separation of church and state, noting that religion is a private matter. On the other hand, he asserted that God had led him to his political office, that he seeks God's guidance in leading the country, and that he had to "repent" of almost deifying the late Meles Zenawi in a tribute to him when taking the oath of office.[30] Furthermore, he sought to bridge the gap between the doctrines of his church and the rest of Christianity with an affirmation of Father, Son, and Holy Ghost, which somewhat stunned the interviewer, who was unfamiliar with the Modalist reasoning of Oneness theology. However, the Pentecostal community has remained cautious. In interviews a few months after his ascent, informants tended to praise Hailemariam but also stated his ascent would not substantially alter their nonrelations with his church. More significantly, the old and experienced founder and leader of the Apostolic Church, Teklemariam Gezahegne, did not comment on the political developments and has been seen going out of his way to greet opposition leaders and government figures alike. As someone who has successfully steered his church through the turmoils of the last four and a half decades, he seems quite aware of the dangers of close political affiliations. No Pentecostal church therefore seems likely to capitalize on the first Pentecostal prime minister of the country.

On the economic front, Pentecostals have engaged with the development state in a positive and active manner but with varying results. Dena Freeman recently presented a stunning case study from the Gamo highlands, where Pentecostals were on the forefront of the apple-growing business.[31] Having left the faith and traditions of their forefathers, they initially lived in the socioeconomic periphery of their communities, being largely unsuccessful small traders and weavers and unable to win converts. When World Vision piloted apple farming in the region, Pentecostals were the first to come aboard, and since they refused to participate in the traditional redistributive feasts, they were able to reinvest their profit. Seeing their example, others became interested in their business and religion, and within a few years the majority of some communities had turned into Pentecostal apple farmers. While many of these initial conversions led to longer processes of spiritual transformation, Freeman's work shows how a certain compatibility of the Pentecostal ethos with market forces formed an essential catalyst to their breakthrough. With rising inequality, however, it is also clear that this Pentecostal ethos does not offer systemic answers to the socioeconomic challenges of the country.

Emanuele Fantini has also observed an energetic and positive engagement with the Ethiopian development economy among urban Pentecostals, but he also points to a significant hiatus between aspirations and achievements.[32] Studying a business fellowship of the neo-Pentecostal Unique 7,000 Church, Fantini shows how especially a younger generation of Pentecostals has embraced narratives of modernity, development, and prosperity that mirror the promises of the developmental state. Preaching spiritual warfare and the necessity for Christians to seek prosperity, the church and its business fellowship aim to make a difference in the Ethiopian economy and the attitudes of the Protestant community. However, they are outsiders on two fronts. First, as a new and fairly small church, their message is seen as a fringe doctrine and is not accepted in the wider community of Christians. Second, given the overarching nature of the patrimonial Ethiopian state, they lack access to essential resources and connections, as well as the economic liberty to carry out their plans successfully. Fantini diagnoses a direct impact of the Ethiopian development policies here: while the state has introduced elements of religious and economic liberalization, it seeks to "retain full control of these processes,"[33] which severely limits the impact of religious actors, such as Pentecostal business networks.

Conclusion

The strong emergence of Pentecostals in the Ethiopian public sphere points to a unique story of religious, social, and political transformation in Africa. Rising in the old empire among the vanguards of modernization, the transformational potential of the Pentecostal faith was long hidden from sight due to the oppressive measures it encountered in its first two decades. Yet the movement did not lie dormant, and in many ways its recent successes are still informed by its troubled past: the times of suppression have laid the foundation for the *Pente* conflation with Protestantism, they still inform the movement's political outlook, and they provide a nostalgic vision of the "pure church" in contrast to present church fragmentation and politics.

This story of transformation is still in the making. Pentecostal growth has not yet plateaued, but its inability to transcend the regional confines of Protestantism foreshadows a likely horizon. Moreover, it is not yet clear whether the tremendous rise of Pentecostalism in Ethiopia provides answers to the country's challenges or is to be counted among them. The various changes and tensions the movement has brought seem to suggest that it is both, which will make the Ethiopian story fascinating to watch in years to come.

Chapter 9

Coming of Age: Pentecostalism and *Umunthu* in Malawi

Harvey C. Kwiyani

THIS ESSAY EXPLORES the rise and coming of age of Pentecostalism in Malawi. It also explores how Pentecostalism has contextualized Christianity for the Malawian people, a process in which Pentecostalism has had to engage with Malawi's spiritual and cultural philosophy of *umunthu*.[1] To achieve this goal, the essay will first make a historical inquiry into the emergence of Pentecostalism in Malawi. This will involve a cursory look at the political and social histories of the country, especially where such histories connect with that of Pentecostalism in Malawi. Second, the essay wonders how Pentecostal Christianity contextualizes itself for Malawi, where religion and spirituality form the bedrock of the culture. It argues that even though Pentecostalism connects with the spirit-centered worldview of many Africans—which makes it easier for Africans to embrace its forms of Christianity—its failure to effectively wrestle with the social implications of the African worldview, *umunthu* in this instance, highlights difficulties in contextualization, which may potentially undermine the long-term impact of Pentecostalism in Malawi. Finally, it will try to imagine how Malawian Pentecostals shaped by *umunthu* might live out their faith.

Religion and Christianity in Malawi: A Brief History

Like most of the African peoples, Malawians have a strong religious culture—a pneumatocentric culture—whose history predates the advent of Christianity in the country. Before the arrival of the missionaries, every ethnic group in the land that became Malawi had its own religious ways of connecting with the deity and the spirit world. A few of these religions—now generally referred to as *traditional religions*—have survived into the twenty-first century, but a majority of them have disappeared. The Nyau cult of the Chewa people in the central region of Malawi, for instance, continues to be a significant cultural and religious force that frustrates the growth of Christianity in some areas. In addition, among the Mang'anja of the Lower Shire in southern Malawi, Mbona's shrine at Khulubvi is a long-standing spiritual center where the spirit of Mbona, the rainmaker, is worshipped, as has been for centuries. Thus, for most Malawians, a conversion to Christianity meant a change from one of these traditional religions. Consequently, as Christianity has gained ground in the past century, most of these religions disappeared.

Christianity first appeared in Malawi with the coming of the Universities' Mission to Central Africa (UMCA) missionaries in 1861. This was a result of David Livingstone's appeal at Oxford and Cambridge Universities in 1857, where he urged his listeners to do everything in their power to stop the slave trade in Central Africa that was still being perpetrated by the Arabs and Portuguese. At Cambridge University, he pleaded, "I go back to Africa to try to make an open path for commerce and Christianity. Do you carry on the work I have begun? I leave it with you."[2] The response of his hearers was to form the Oxford and Cambridge Universities'

Mission to Central Africa. Soon, Durham and Dublin universities joined and the whole adventure became known as the Universities' Mission to Central Africa.[3]

In the same speaking campaign, and in an effort to strengthen his persuasion, Livingstone began to make an argument for the development of a British colony in Central Africa—a colony in which the Arabic and Portuguese slave traders would be prohibited, the people would be trained in agriculture and thus would not need to trade in slavery, and where Christianity would be propagated. He believed that "it is the mission of England to colonize and to plant her Christianity with her sons on the broad earth which the Lord has given to the children of men."[4] Of course, he would later add:

> I am becoming everyday more convinced that we must have an English colony in the cotton-producing districts of Africa...colonization from a country such as ours ought to be one of hope, and not despair...the performance of an imperative duty to our blood, our country, our religion, and to humankind.[5]

The outworking of this conviction—Livingstone's concept of the Three Cs—Christianity, commerce, and civilization—has had ramifications that still shape life in Central Africa in significant ways. In 1861, Livingstone brought Bishop Charles McKenzie and the first Universities' Mission to Central Africa sent a group of missionaries to Magomero in the Shire Highlands of southern Malawi. Thus entered Christianity into Malawi. Yet in this single event also entered the seeds of British colonialism in Malawi, if not in all of Central Africa.

Any telling of the development of Christianity in Malawi—in all its types and flavors—must bear this landmark in mind, for it continues to shape the story of not only Christianity in the country, but also that of the country itself. Of course, the history of Pentecostal Christianity in Malawi cannot be faithfully told without mentioning that the only two Pentecostal denominations that had connections with white missionaries—the Apostolic Faith Mission (AFM) and the Assemblies of God (AG)—were recognized by the colonial government. Writing in the shadows of the one-hundred-fifty-year commemoration of the UMCA's entry into Malawi that took place in 2011, we see Malawi's Christianity coming of age with over 80 percent of Malawi's sixteen million people identifying themselves as Christian.[6] However, we see a Malawian Christianity in which Pentecostals and Charismatic Christians, who could not have been imagined by the early missionaries, have taken the lead.[7]

Pentecostalism, Charismatics, Neo-Pentecostals and Neo-Charismatics

In his book on the history of Pentecostalism in Malawi, entitled *Pentecostalism in Malawi: A History of the Apostolic Faith Mission in Malawi, 1931–1994*, Ulf Strohbehn suggests that Pentecostalism came to Malawi in the late 1920s or early 1930s through the work of the Apostolic Faith Mission.[8] While Strohbehn suggests that Malawian Pentecostalism descended from the Azusa Street revival of 1906 through the ministry of John G. Lake in South Africa, many Malawian theologians, like Harvey Sindima and Augustine Musopole, believe that characteristics of Pentecostal Christianity were present in Malawi before the AFM arrived.[9] If this is true, then what the AFM did was to provide a formal label for these types of Christianity that could be recognized around the world. Thus, Strohbehn's history is best understood to be the history of the Apostolic Faith Mission in Malawi and not of Pentecostalism in Malawi.

Nevertheless, this history of the AFM suggests that Pentecostalism did not start in Malawi through the work of Western missionaries, as is the case in other African countries, but that of Malawians who had migrated to Zimbabwe and South Africa for work. Thousands of Malawian men worked in Zimbabwe and South Africa starting in the early 1900s. While away at work, many of them converted to Christianity, and many others found new types of Christianity like Pentecostalism. When they returned to Malawi, they brought their newly found faith to their communities, and Pentecostal communities emerged. The history of the first thirty years of the AFM is filled with such men who had joined the AFM in Zimbabwe and South Africa and brought it with them to Malawi. By 1940, there were more than a handful of the AFM's formal Pentecostal gatherings across the country, and all of them were started by or connected to a returning migrant from Zimbabwe and South Africa.

The most important figure in this history is Robert Chinguwo, whom Strohbehn credits as the father and founder of the Apostolic Faith Mission in Malawi.[10] He might as well be recognized as the father of Pentecostalism in Malawi. Chinguwo migrated from Zomba in southern Malawi to work in the mines in Zimbabwe in the mid-1920s. He had been raised in the Church of Christ in Malawi, but when he found the AFM in Harare, Zimbabwe, he was attracted by the supernatural miracles and prophecies. Consequently, he was baptized in 1928 and was subsequently ordained an elder. According to Strohbehn, Chinguwo attributed his conversion to Pentecostalism to prophetic insight that told him of his sins and the miraculous healing of sicknesses.[11] Chinguwo returned to Malawi in 1933 and immediately became a Pentecostal pioneer among his own people. His ministry stretched from Zomba to most of southern and central Malawi and would continue for the following thirty years. Soon after his return, a network of returning migrant AFM converts emerged and set up their own churches, but they would all identify Chinguwo as their leader. The key pastors included Robert Frederic Masi, Kakhobwe, Graham Muhulere, Lighton Kalambule, and Chitakata.

The colonial government did not look favorably on independent African churches. Earlier, in 1915, a Malawian Baptist minister called John Chilembwe led an uprising against colonial rule in which several colonial agents and white farmers were killed.[12] As a result, the government disallowed any form of independent Christianity—be it African instituted churches or Pentecostalism—for they were regarded as nesting grounds for nationalism and anti-European politics.[13] This meant that only those denominations that were deemed safe by the colonial government—*those that had white leadership*—could operate in the country. As far as history can tell, only the AFM and the Assemblies of God were safe, and that is because the AFM had white connections in South Africa that gave them a "white sect" status, while the AG had white missionaries resident in Malawi from 1948.[14] This meant that both the AFM and the AG could operate somewhat freely in the country, even though they were still closely monitored to make sure no anti-European sentiments would develop.

Malawi gained her independence from Britain in 1964. Like in many other African countries, the process of political decolonization in Malawi was long and tedious. By the time self-governance was given, it had also become clear that Malawian Christianity needed to be decolonized as well. Several factors led to this. On the one hand, a generation of capable young Malawian Christians who—just like their counterparts in the political arena—believed they could lead the church had emerged and were starting to push for leadership positions. On the other hand, many African leaders in neighboring countries had begun to demand a moratorium on Western missionary work in Africa. They wanted African Christianity to be free from Western hegemony and thus argued that stopping Western missionary work in Africa could "teach the short man to hang his knapsack within reach."[15] While the moratorium was never formally effected, many Western missionaries returned home, leaving the churches under the leadership of local Africans. Most of them had become so identified with and sympathetic to the colonial project that it was impossible to stay after independence. Thus, on a regional scale, the collapse of political colonialism not only led to political independence but also set in motion the forces that would liberate African Christianity.

Consequently, the decade following 1964 is critical in the development of Malawian Christianity. First, for the mainline denominational churches (those established and run by Western missionaries—for instance, the Presbyterian Church), Malawian leadership took over from the missionaries. Even though most financial resources continued to come from the West, Malawian leaders were responsible for the running of the church in Malawi. Second, the government control of independent African churches was loosened. The limitations placed upon Pentecostal churches in the country by the colonial government no longer existed. Malawian Pentecostalism was thus free from the shackles of colonialism even though it had to deal with the politics of Kamuzu Banda, the first president of Malawi, who was a Presbyterian Church elder as well as a ruthless dictator.[16] It would take another decade for Pentecostalism to spread across the country, but at least the foundations were laid in the early 1970s, when both the AFM and the AG experienced great growth. The late 1970s saw the start of a revival in Malawi, a revival that would reach its crescendo with a Reinhard Bonnke crusade in Blantyre in 1986. It was in the 1980s that many independent Pentecostal churches were born. By the turn of the century, both the AFM and the AG would be overshadowed by these younger independent churches, two major ones being Living Waters Outreach Ministries and Calvary Family Church.

Third, the Charismatic movement also emerged in Malawi in the 1970s.[17] Several scholars of Malawian Christianity have connected the emergence of Charismatic Christianity in the country to the Western Charismatic movement that started in North America in the 1960s. Both Klaus Fiedler and Rhodian Munyenyembe, for instance, discuss Malawian Charismatic churches in the light of the Dennis Bennett movement.[18] However, it is likely that the movement emerged because Malawians were free to live their own Christianity without the supervision of the missionaries, and that Malawian Christianity would be influenced by Malawian culture that is inherently spirit-oriented. To connect the Malawian Charismatic movement to the United States is to overlook the propensity of African Christianity to gravitate toward a spirit type of Christianity when left to itself.[19] If anything, the most recognized Charismatic church in Malawi was Blantyre Christian Centre, which started in 1980.

African church history is replete with stories of enthusiastic movements, largely because these types of Christianity are close to African spirit-centered cultures and worldviews. Many spiritist independent churches existed in Africa before the Western Charismatic movement came into existence. Many of them would be labeled African Independent Churches simply because, theologically, they did not follow Western standards of orthodoxy. It is because of this natural tendency toward enthusiastic Christianity in Malawi that it is generally difficult to separate Charismatic Christians, Pentecostals, and mainline Christians. For instance, as part of his doctoral studies on the subject of apostleship in

Malawian Pentecostalism, Felix Nyika tried to clarify the differences between Pentecostals, Charismatics, and neo-Charismatics in Malawi.[20] The exercise was unsuccessful simply because the gap between these groups is very permeable and Pentecostals and Charismatics now influence most of Malawi's Christianity. Every denomination in the country now has a significant presence of Charismatic members. The Church of Central Africa Presbyterian, for instance, lost a good portion of its younger-generation members when the latter left the church to form the Presbyterian Church of Malawi in 1998, where they would be free to follow their charismatic inclinations, like singing choruses and speaking in tongues. Even in the Roman Catholic Church, the charismatic ministry of Father Mark Kambalazaza was forced to break away to start the Charismatic Catholic Church in Malawi in 2006.

Evangelists, Apostle-Doctors, and Prophets

The development of Pentecostal and Charismatic Christianity in Malawi is reflected in this unique story of forty years of leadership, honor, and titles. During the revivals of the 1980s, the leaders were mostly evangelists travelling up and down the country to preach the gospel of salvation. Rijk van Dijk explored the impact of these "young preachers" in his article of 1992 entitled "Young Puritan Preachers."[21] They were young evangelists who preached for people to be born again from the claws of dead Christianity of the mainline churches in Malawi. In the 1990s, these young evangelists were establishing their own Pentecostal churches and thus were transitioning to become pastors. As the churches became bigger, the founding pastors became apostles, leading large networks of churches. These networks developed a second tier of leaders known as bishops. Toward the turn of the century, Malawian Pentecostals became aware of the importance of theological education. Each one of the apostles received honorary doctorate degrees, and they all became apostle-doctors. However, since the apostles and bishops were not so generous with leadership positions, an emerging younger generation of leaders formed their own ministries and chose to be identified as prophets. This is the second wave of Pentecostal and Charismatic leadership in the country. These prophets are generally young—most of them in their twenties—and their ministries are more spirit-focused than those of the older generation. Their ministries have developed in a free-market spiritual economy, and they style their ministries after other international prophets. They are very effective in their usage of media technology. They are taking advantage of, or probably abusing, the spiritual hunger of Malawians, a hunger that may be explained as an obsession with the spirit world.[22]

The coming of this second wave of Charismatic and anointed prophets in Malawi signifies the rise of second-generation Pentecostals in the country. The movement has produced a second generation of leaders. However, while we celebrate this development, there is need for caution; the rise of this second generation of Pentecostals in Malawi also makes visible the vulnerabilities of the movement. Greed—disguised as the gospel of blessings, also known as the prosperity gospel—seems to be the driving energy of the movement. The move of the Spirit of God seems so manipulable and predictable that it does not look like the God of the Bible. Dubious prophecies and suspicious miracles that cannot be verified seem rampant, raising concerns of manufactured and staged wonders. The power of the Spirit seems to be on sale to the highest bidder. All these concerns, in my opinion, show problems that the movement has experienced in contextualizing itself for Africa, especially in Malawi, where *umunthu* provides a time-tested philosophy that balances spirituality and humanity. Because

Pentecostalism in Malawi has not engaged *umunthu*, it runs the risk of turning into a spiritual-power vending movement like that of the other mediums.

Malawian Pentecostalism: An *Umunthu* Critique

The story of Malawian Christianity from its inception in 1861 to the twenty-first century—currently with millions of adherents across the country—is one that shows a constant need to contextualize the Christian message. Contextualizing Pentecostal Christianity for Malawi means that a Malawian Pentecostalism has to emerge—one that engages local cultural philosophies, like *umunthu*, to shape itself and to spread its gospel. In Malawi, therefore, Pentecostalism needs to embrace *umunthu* spirituality to connect Malawi's religious culture and its theology. Of course, the same can be said of the majority of sub-Saharan Africa, where Bantu peoples reside.

Umunthu is an expansive philosophical, theological, and spiritual concept that is rooted in the spirituality of the human being. According to Harvey Sindima (who explored the concept of *umunthu* in his PhD dissertation), to have *umunthu*, the person must have certain moral qualities that make him or her a person that the community can trust and depend upon.[23] The person must be kind, sociable, caring, self-giving, plus many other such qualities. When a person has that, in Malawi, that person is said to have a spirit. To have *umunthu* is therefore, in literal translation, to have a spirit. However, to have a spirit, when used in this sense, does not mean to *have* spirit. It means to *be* spirit. This, then, puts the individual in a spiritual communion with the deity, ancestors, community at large, and nature. Such an individual is in harmony with the universe. To lack the moral qualities of *umunthu* is to lack *umunthu* and, therefore, to not be *munthu* (person/human being) or to be *chirombo* (a beast). This is said of those people who terrorize their communities, such as thugs, murderers, and the like. *Umunthu* believes that the real person is the spirit, as Malawians usually say *munthu ndi mzimu* (a person is a spirit) because it is the spirit that makes a person to have the moral qualities needed. Above all, to be the spiritual being that *umunthu* is means that one is communal, always there for others, and always working for the good of the community. Consequently, *umunthu* is a spirit-centered philosophy that could greatly invigorate the spirit-centered movement that Pentecostalism is.

The religious world of the African is spiritually vibrant. For most Africans, the spiritual realm is real, so real that life is not imaginable without it. Africans usually say that the spiritual realm is more real than the physical one—it is only invisible—and even though the two worlds are distinguished, they cannot be separated. They are interconnected, and they work together. Such a worldview was propagated by the first group of Africanist scholars and novelists that published their works on African life in the wake of postcolonialism. The most popular among them is John Mbiti, who in 1968 published *African Religions and Philosophy.*[24] In this masterful work, Mbiti explored the central place that spirits take in the African's world. The spirits cover everything. They are a living part of the community even after the death of the persons. In his other work, *Introduction to African Religion*,[25] Mbiti dedicated an entire chapter to exploring the types of spirits in Africa. Mbiti's works are in agreement with other authors from all over sub-Saharan Africa. For instance, the works of John Gwengwe (*Kukula Ndi Mwambo,* Malawi), Chinua Achebe (*Things Fall Apart,* Nigeria), Camara Laye (*The Dark Child,* Senegal), Ngugi Wa Thiong'o (*The River Between,* Kenya), Alex Kagame (*La Philosophie*

Bantu Comparée, Rwanda), Gwinyai Muzorewa (*The Origins and Development of African Theology,* Zimbabwe), Osadolor Imasogie (*Guidelines for Christian Theology in Africa,* Nigeria), and many others reclaimed the spiritual nature of African culture that had been suppressed by the colonialists and the Western missionaries. Writing in the 1990s, Harvey Sindima managed to synthesize most of the philosophies from the earlier generation in order to move the conversation forward by providing grounding in the concept of *umunthu* theology.[26]

With a worldview that has a close connection between human beings and the spirits, it would be fair to expect a well-articulated theology of the Holy Spirit among African Christians. However, this is not the case. One would be hard-pressed to find an authentically African treatment of the subject of the Holy Spirit.[27] A great deal has been written about African traditional religions and the role of the spirits in these. Even a greater deal has been written on the impact of this spirit-centered worldview on the spread of Christianity on the continent. Many of these works have "African Spirituality" in their titles. However, they do not attend to the theology of the Holy Spirit at all. The works of Peter Paris,[28] Inus Daneel,[29] Bengt Sundkler,[30] Alwyn Shorter,[31] Gerrie ter Haar,[32] and many others have attempted to attend to the implications of such a worldview on Christianity, but they are more focused on the spirits than on the Holy Spirit in African Christianity. *Umunthu* allows us to think about the Holy Spirit in ways that resonate with most Africans.

Certainly, *umunthu* has some serious implications for Pentecostal theology. For instance, it makes possible a rather rich Trinitarian theology in which (1) God is truly understood to be Spirit; (2) this Spirit is communal and relational—both intra-Trinitarian among God the Father, the Son, and the Spirit, and extra-Trinitarian in the fellowship of the Spirit into which human beings have been adopted; and (3) this Spirit is omnipotent. *Umunthu* theology leads to the understanding of the ubiquitousness of the spirit—even the Spirit of God—in whom we live and move and have our being (Acts 17:28). It helps Paul's argument that the Galatians ought to walk by the Spirit (Gal. 5:16). In addition, since Africans understand the spirit to be immortal, persons live forever even after their physical bodies have died. In this state of eternity, the deceased who had *umunthu* become ancestors and continue to be part of the community of the living. They maintain their personalities, which makes it possible for them to be remembered and venerated—but not worshipped—long after death. Thus, it appears that *umunthu* spirituality is only possible because of the spiritual nature of human beings.

Of course, Africans generally avoid impersonal notions of the spirit as a vital force, life force, or a force field.[33] Defining the spirit in such abstract terms is almost offensive to some Africans, who would rather think of their ancestors as persons and not forces. Therefore, most Africans do not always go to the Spirit because of the need for power, as most scholars have believed.[34] Of course, many Africans understand that spirits have power—spiritual power—but access to this power is only a small part of the benefits of paying attention to the spiritual realm. A well-established reason for spirituality among the Lhomwe of Malawi is the sense of community that they want to feel with the ancestors, nature, and the spirit world. Most Africans go to the Spirit because of fellowship and communion. For them, the Holy Spirit is a Being—an ontological Being—and a person whose nearness brings comfort.

The observation of the "personhood" of the spirits has two strong implications for African theology. In the first place, it makes possible a strong claim in African theology for the personhood of the Holy Spirit. It is the third person of the Trinity. By saying that, African Christians are able to relate with the Holy Spirit in the same way that they relate with the other spirits that fill their world. Living in a world where spirits and human beings interact on a constant basis, it becomes easier for Africans to imagine what Jesus means when He says, "The Spirit of the Lord is upon Me" (Luke 4:18, MEV, citing Isaiah 61:1). Any truly African theology will, thus, be rich in pneumatology and thus should be at home in Pentecostalism.

Second, the concept of the "personhood" of the spirits helps us get rid of the spirit-material dichotomy. The reality of the spirit realm and the proximity between the spirits and human beings imply a very close relationship between the body and the spirit. In the African understanding, human beings and spirits interact on a constant basis. For instance, the beating of the drum in religious ceremonies is usually a spiritual act carried out to invoke the spiritual world. As the spirits respond to the drum, the spirits that the human beings are respond along with them, and their bodies begin to respond too. Usually, the bodies are fully engaged, both in reverence to the powerful spirits that are "in action" among them, but also simply as acts of worship. It is also common for the bodies to be overwhelmed—possessed—by the spirits, causing them to behave in unusual manners or to speak in unknown languages, or even gain otherwise inaccessible knowledge. Be it in trances and spirit possessions or in lifting up holy hands or dancing in the church, the spirit and the body are constantly influencing one another. The body is not an enemy to the spirit.[35] Among Malawians, the body is home and temple to the spirit, and both the spirit and the body make up the human being. As a result, there is no distinction between the secular and the sacred.

Ecclesiological Implications

A truly Malawian Pentecostalism—one that contextualizes itself for *umunthu*—will bear several marks of the Malawian culture. Here, I will outline only three aspects where I believe that this would make a difference: generosity, communality, and empowerment.

Generosity in a greedy world

In everyday life in Malawi, *umunthu* means "generosity." Among the Lhomwe of southern Malawi—a people indigenous to this writer—children are taught from infancy that generosity is what *umunthu* looks like in real life. To be a self-giving person for the good of the community is what comes to most people's minds when someone is said to have *umunthu*. The Chewas have a proverb that says *patse patse nkulanda, mwana mfulu adziwa yekha*, which translates "Forcing someone to give to you equals extortion; the free know to give without being asked." Theologically, this kind of generosity is in line with God's sacrificial gift of God's only Son for the salvation of humanity. It is in this sense that God is actually known as the Great *Munthu* from whom we all get our *umunthu*. Of course, generosity is a virtue that seems to be the baseline of the biblical story. God's love for the world is directly connected to God's generosity—a generosity that we see throughout the Bible.

However, we live in a world that exalts receiving higher than giving. Our financial systems encourage people to accumulate as much as they can for fear of the day in the future when circumstances will be unfriendly. The gospel of faith and giving—or the prosperity gospel—encourages the masses to be generous with their resources for the enrichment of their leaders. Many Pentecostal leaders, even in Malawi, are known for their money-grabbing tactics, preying on the spiritual hunger of the poor.

Umunthu would demand that even leaders live up to the same measures of generosity.

Communal incarnational spirituality in a dividing world

The African understanding of the spirit world demands a communal understanding of spirituality. Another popular Malawian proverb, *chala chimodzi sichiswa nsabwe,* reminds us that "a single thumb does not kill a louse." *Umunthu* spirituality is a communal event; it is best done in company. Be it in ancestral veneration or a simple pouring of libation, there is a way in which the community is represented. In most cases, the community will be present and actively involved. Just like *umunthu* says that one's personhood is constituted through other persons, in this communal spirituality, one's spirituality is also constituted through the spirituality of others. While *umunthu* says, "I am because we are," Pentecostal Christians and their churches would also believe that we belong together. There would be no need for competition and strife. Most of the breakaways that characterize the movement in Malawi would disappear. Any Pentecostal person with *umunthu* will selflessly pay attention to the spirituality of others as well as that of the community in an incarnational way. Individual spirituality is never consummated if it does not lead to communal spirituality. Together with the community, one worships the God of the community. The entire spiritual experience is a public and communal phenomenon. For instance, when a soothsayer enters a village, life stops for the whole village in order that the community is able to hear what the spirits have to say. In those cultures where trances are a means of spiritual communication, when someone falls into a trance, the elders of the village are brought together to listen and mediate with the entire community. Individual spirituality has its *telos* purpose and goal in communal spirituality. Religion and the matters of faith still reign greatly in the public arena. The gifts of the Spirit are not for the separation of the church from the world. They are for the incarnational ministry of God's people in the world to serve the needy and the marginalized.

Empowering in a colonizing world

Umunthu is ultimately about humanizing others—and this is only possible through the gift of empowerment. Leaders with *umunthu* get their job done by empowering those they lead. Generally, this will make communal leadership possible, such that the leader is only effective as the community of followers works along with him. *Umunthu* leaders equip and empower others in order to sustain and improve their community's life. Because of this, in the context of *umunthu,* power is almost never concentrated in one individual or in one special group. Under normal circumstances, power dwells in the relationships between leaders and their followers. Thus, the society falls or thrives—together—on the negotiated spaces between the leaders and the community. In the context of Malawian Pentecostalism, *umunthu* would make leaders pay more attention to discipleship as a way of equipping and empowering followers to recognize and take advantage of the spiritual power also available to them. Leadership ought not to grab and hoard power but must follow the Spirit, who may anoint and empower those at the margins.

Conclusion

This essay has argued that Pentecostal Christianity in Malawi has been able to connect with the spirit-centered Malawian culture but has overlooked the communal responsibility that comes with the spiritual power. This is a result of failed contextualization. *Umunthu* spirituality is not only about the charismatic gifts.

It is primarily for the helping and empowering of the community, and it uses the gifts for this purpose. If *umunthu* is embraced, Pentecostalism will have the ability to reach peoples of all classes and contexts. It may even be able to silence some of its critics. More importantly, I believe that it will help change the nation for the better.

Chapter 10

Pentecostalism in Tanzania and Uganda: A Historical and Theological Perspective

Alfred Olwa

PENTECOSTALISM IN TANZANIA and Uganda did not emerge from a vacuum. Our historical investigation reveals its gradual growth and provides a broader context to understand the theological developments of Pentecostalism and their significance in the social and daily life of both countries. No attempts to appreciate Pentecostalism in sub-Saharan Africa today should ignore how Pentecostal spirituality is empowering engagement with the broader society, so we will expend some effort to understand these connections. We proceed in three parts: a historical overview of Pentecostalism and social change in Tanzania first and then Uganda, and then some theological analysis of Pentecostalism in the two nations.

A word here is needed about our reliance on interview materials in much of this chapter, particularly in the third part of theological assessment. Two main reasons warrant our use and reliance on such sources in this work. First, the pastors—Pentecostal as well as Anglican priests—I interviewed are actively engaged in church ministry and are knowledgeable about these contexts. Their insights into the historical and theological understanding of Pentecostalism complement what is otherwise missing in the still scant English literature on Pentecostalism in Tanzania and

Uganda. In a limited scholarly field, there is the danger of reducing the story of Pentecostalism in Tanzania and Uganda to incomplete and biased strands. Second, my informants have given me express permission to represent their views in this work. I have attempted to judiciously represent their perspectives, although at times such has been paraphrased for the purpose of clarity, especially as I have had to translate into English from Swahili, the official language of Tanzania, through which our interviews were conducted.

Tanzania: Pentecostal Diversity and Social Change

There are many Pentecostal groups in Tanzania. The following more historic groups are included in my discussion: the Holiness Movement, Elim Pentecostal Church, Free Pentecostal Evangelical Fellowship, Pentecostal Assemblies of God, Mountain of the Fire of God, the Free Pentecostal Churches of Tanzania, and the Council of Churches of Tanzania.[1] There are also mission agencies that have had links with the Pentecostal churches in Tanzania: Church Mission Society, Africa Inland Mission, and the Swedish Free Mission. Many of the main Protestant Churches in Tanzania also have had links with the Pentecostal churches: the Anglican Church of Tanzania, the Evangelical Lutheran Church of Tanzania, the Africa Inland Church, and the Mennonite and Monrovian Churches. Within the Catholic Church in Tanzania, the Pentecostal link is with its arm Caritas.

In 1897, Catholic and Anglican missionaries passing through Sukumaland, northwestern Tanzania (formerly Tanganyika), planted churches on their way to Uganda.[2] By 1909, the Anglicans had established about one hundred fifty churches that the African Inland Church (AICT) took over. Two Pentecostal missionaries of AICT, Emil and Marie Sywalka, working under Africa Inland

Mission, took over from Church Missionary Society, whose mission work focused on the Sukuma people: they used the Sukuma language and identified with the Sukuma people.

Close to two decades later, in 1927, Pentecostals who were part of the Holiness Movement reached the Mbeya region in southwestern Tanzania. While this stream of the Pentecostal movement was spreading in the southwestern region, the East African revival and Charismatic forms of Pentecostalism originating from Rwanda were also growing in the northwestern region of Tanzania. These movements were characterized by confession of sins, practice of forgiveness, and radically changed lives centered in Jesus Christ.

More may be said about the marks of the revival. The *Balokole* (saved ones) of the East African revival rejected African customs, considering them to be a threat to their newfound faith.[3] Some revivalists took their Pentecostalism with them: Moses Kulola moved from the Anglican Church to the AICT in Mwanza, and Emmanuel Lazaro moved to the Lutheran Church in Moshi. In their new movements, they became Charismatic leaders. Of course, their building new churches created tensions with their former denominations that have lasted to the present.

In 1932, the Swedish Free Mission arrived in Tanzania, evangelizing the Tabora region, and in 1946, the Elim Pentecostal Church arrived in the Morogoro area.[4] In 1949, the field of Mbeya region that had been reached by the Holiness Movement was taken over by the Assemblies of God. By the 1950s, early Pentecostal missionaries in Tanzania evangelized only in specific areas, in part because comity agreements still remained. For example, the Scandinavian missionaries focused on areas such as Tabora and Kigoma, in the center and west of the country. The Scandinavian Pentecostals have had a long history of practicing holistic missions, integrating spiritual as well as social work.[5]

The early Pentecostal churches created clinics, hospitals, schools, and other social services across Tanzania.[6] Today the objectives of the Free Pentecostal Churches of Tanzania include providing social welfare and community activities as well as facilitating hand in hand with the government relief services, education, health programs, orphanage care, and service care for destitute and disabled persons.[7]

As Pentecostalism expanded in the country, a significant thing happened. In 1953, a split occurred when the revival movement considered the mission churches not to be radical enough in their witness. So the Church of the Holy Spirit split from the Evangelical Lutheran Church. However, this independent African church did not go far in its influence. Ten years later, by 1963, half of its members had already returned to the mother church.[8]

In the 1960s, the government of Tanzania took control of the development activities in the local communities with the goal of improving the life of its citizens. Protestant and Catholic churches were among those that fully supported government activities and in this sense played key roles in the development of the local communities.[9]

By the middle of the 1960s, the Christian Council of Tanzania had formed itself into a central authority that also represented the main Protestant churches—Anglican, Lutheran, Mennonite, and Monravian—with regard to development projects. Then, in the early 1970s, the Catholic Church in Tanzania, through its arm the Tanzania Episcopal Conference, formed Caritas with the specific responsibility for the social development initiatives of the Catholic Church.[10]

While we may consider that by the 1960s to 1970s the Pentecostal churches had already been in Tanzania for a reasonable time, their influence was marginal. Nevertheless, in the 1970s, the picture changed: the Pentecostal churches, especially the Assemblies of God (PAG), become the fastest-growing churches not only in Tanzania, but also in the whole region of East Africa. The PAG developed into a well-organized institution, with an archbishop as its head and a General Council as its executive branch.[11] The fast growth spurred the social development of the Tanzanian communities as well so that social impact was no longer attributable only to the mainline Protestant churches or the Catholic Church.

By the 1980s, Pentecostalism had become noted in contemporary Tanzanian Christianity for its public confession of sins, rapturous singing and hand clapping, prayers for healing, and its miraculous signs. These were observable also in mainline church environments—for instance, at the Lutheran Theological College, Makumira. In the Evangelical Lutheran Church of Tanzania, healing became important under Bishop J. B. Kiwovele, from the University of Heidelberg. This was noteworthy because as a bishop belonging to a mainline church, he was expected to defend the faith and not be involved with these Pentecostal churches and their so-called prophetic ministries. Consequently, for working as a prophet, he was removed from office as a bishop.[12]

In the present time, the apparent success of the Pentecostal churches has posed new challenges to the mainline Protestant and Catholic churches along two main fronts. The first relates to the attitude of Pentecostals to the established churches. The comment of the general secretary of the Anglican Diocese of Mara, who doubles as the general secretary of Christian fellowships in the region, is telling: "Pentecostals in Tanzania did not like joining the established Protestant church groups. They say that there is no Holy Spirit with us. Is this not pride? Where is humility in their attitude to us?"[13] Second, the mainline Protestant churches have made more room in their churches for more charismatics elements: confessions, visions, prophecies, and healing.[14] For example, the

Anglican Church of Tanzania's Diocese of Mara built the Edmond John healing center, which is providing the ministry of healing and deliverance to all people; however, the Pentecostals in Mara do not see this center as important because for them healing may be received anywhere and anytime when prayer is released for healing.

With the growing influence of the Pentecostal and Charismatic churches in Tanzania, since the 1980s, there is a clear recognition by members of the Protestant churches and the Catholic Church that something is missing in their experience. Have the politics of African socialism in Tanzania challenged different aspects of Christian practice in the established churches? Or how has African socialism contributed, if at all, to the expansion of Christianity in the Pentecostal churches? Hilikiah Omindo, a senior Anglican bishop of Mara Diocese reputed for his acceptance by the Pentecostal as well as Protestant churches and the Catholic Church in Tanzania, gives us a helpful perspective on these questions:

> *Ujamaa* [socialist] policy, with its focus in part on village programs, helped to make our churches—Pentecostal churches, in particular—to grow. Preachers of the gospel could now reach many villages easily. On the part of the mainline churches, some had found it difficult to leave behind their old buildings. To their advantage, Pentecostals quickly adapted with ease to the new circumstances.[15]

To clearly follow Omindo's comment on the growth of Pentecostalism, we need to understand something of the new prevailing situation in Tanzania. The social and economic life of the people since the 1980s is very different from the 1960s. The Protestant churches and the Catholic Church in the 1960s taught people to work hard to overcome their economic problems.

Contemporary Pentecostals put emphasis on signs and miraculous interventions from God. This focus contrasted with traditional Protestant and Catholic doctrine, which taught that nation building is a gradual, deliberative, and intentional process of hard work.

Yet how to understand this shift in Pentecostal rhetoric is disputed. On the one hand, scholars argue that the teaching of Pentecostal churches accentuating divine miracles and interventions offers no motivation or agenda for social and political reform.[16] On the other hand, other scholars in this recent period have interpreted the Pentecostal teachings as a means of enabling their adherents to make the best of rapid social change, since Pentecostal teachings have been correlated to spiritual practices such as prayer and faithfulness with meritoriousness in relationship to social mobility. Such correlation, it is argued, actually does offer a way of escaping from extreme poverty and destitution.[17]

It is perhaps helpful to make some observations on aspects of the recent teachings of Pentecostal churches in light of their earlier emphases. The recent focus is on prosperity. This has set a standard that makes appealing promises to believers. The Pentecostal churches that I interacted with taught that sickness and poverty are caused by lack of faith or demonic influence.[18] According to them, there is a battle between the Holy Spirit and satanic power.[19] Yet beyond such diagnosis of the problems confronting believers, there is a constructive and more attractive element to their teaching: they encourage accumulation of wealth, individualism, entrepreneurship, and displays of affluence (in a way quite different from the rural Pentecostals). Linked to these practices is the sense of spiritual striving to get ahead in life.[20]

My observations on Pentecostalism in Tanzania have persuaded me that there is a definite shift from the early Pentecostal missionary focus on individual salvation to a present emphasis on economic gain. This new state of teaching promises to encourage accumulation of wealth at the expense of the moral obligation of kinship presumed in traditional African societies. In fact, we may ask, Is there a sin of accumulation of wealth in this recent teaching of Pentecostal churches? Of course, the time has changed from the days of the older Pentecostal doctrine of the Protestant work ethic. However, is not the goal of salvation a changed life rather than entirely economic gain?[21]

In summary, contemporary Pentecostalism in Tanzania exists as a movement of healing and deliverance from various aspects of poverty and sickness. Arguably, there are within this movement dynamics conducive toward social and spiritual transformation, such as their radically equalizing ethos drawn from the ongoing healing, delivering, and transforming power of the Holy Spirit that challenges traditional barriers related to social status and hierarchies. Pentecostal experience and spirituality nurtures such free spaces that serve as a powerful platform upon which personal and communal transformation is fostered. Yet there are questions and concerns, and such ambiguities are found also in the Ugandan context.

Pentecostalism in Uganda

We now turn to Pentecostalism and social change in Uganda. The first known Pentecostal church in modern Uganda began with the Pentecostal Assemblies of God that came from neighboring Kenya to eastern Uganda in the 1930s.[22] The main focus of the PAG was preaching the gospel of salvation, consequently bringing about particularly spiritual transformation. The Pentecostal Assemblies of Canada arrived via Kenya in Mbale, also in the same eastern region of Uganda, in 1950. These missionaries did not follow the path of the historic religions in Uganda, Islam and Christianity, namely, and settled first the strategic location of the commercial city (and now capital) of Uganda: Kampala.

In 1960, when these Pentecostal churches realized what they were missing by operating in the eastern region, far away from the commercial center of Uganda, the Full Gospel Church and the Elim Church established congregations in Kampala. From here on, Kampala was considered to be the point of entry for Pentecostal groups seeking to evangelize in Uganda. By the middle of the decade, the first indigenous Pentecostal church in Uganda, the Deliverance Church Uganda, was now well on its way to being established in the capital city. Joe Kayo, a Kenyan evangelist, had founded the Young Christian Ambassadors Fellowship, and by 1970 this had become the Deliverance Church Uganda.

Within five years of the planting of the Deliverance Church Uganda, another indigenous Pentecostal church, the Redeemed Church, was established in Kibuye, Kampala, by a Ghanaian, John Obiri Yeboah. His followers considered him a prophet because of the miracles that he performed. Following Yeboah's lead, many other Pentecostal churches have since originated in Kampala through individual initiatives.

Amidst what was a steady growth expansion of the Pentecostal churches in Uganda at this time, some "dark days" were on the horizon. On January 25, 1971, Idi Amin Dada, in a military coup, overthrew the democratically elected government of President Apolo Milton Obote I.[23] Amin's rule was to last for about nine years (January 1971–April 1979). In 1973, Amin barred eleven Pentecostal groups as "Unlawful Societies,"[24] thus prohibiting their meeting and worshipping together.

Some of the Pentecostal leaders of these groups fled into exile for fear of their lives while those that remained in the country sought refuge in the Catholic Church and, especially, in the Church of Uganda. The latter affiliation was perfectly understandable, given that there was in the Church of Uganda the *Balokole* of the East African revival, whose message and ethics were similar to those of the Pentecostals.[25] The *Balokole* also taught that church leaders should not be involved in politics, and the same was true also of the Charismatics in the Catholic Church.

In 1979, the ban was extended to cover twenty-seven churches and religious organizations, most of which were Pentecostal. Why did President Amin ban these churches? According to Paddy Musana, "Amin claimed that these religious organizations were of foreign origins," adding that "therefore they posed national security concern since 'instead of preaching the word of God, they have been preaching politics.'"[26] Most Pentecostal leaders of the time resisted Amin's claim that they were a security threat. Rather, as Musana further observes, "Most of them having a pacifist view of the events, their only hope lay in God who 'knows the times and seasons, who sets up leaders and brings down others'"; for such pacifists, "Amin was in God's divine plan, appointed by God to execute His judgment at the time. To such, Romans 13 stands supreme: all leadership is God-ordained."[27]

But if we fast-forward to 1986, we note that the ban slowed rather than stopped Pentecostal growth. In reflecting on the public role of African Christianity, Paul Gifford observes, "Since about 1986 when [President Yoweri Kaguata] Museveni restored order, enabling Uganda to rejoin the international community, and most Ugandans to resume their lives, new churches have appeared with an enormous increase in the numbers of Christians."[28]

By the time of this writing, there are more than six thousand Pentecostal churches and faith-based organizations, with the former including those both registered and unregistered with the government of Uganda.[29] This highlights the fast growth of Pentecostalism in Uganda and is testimony to the present government's promotion of the freedom of religious worship enshrined in the constitution more than any of the previous governments. Currently, there is no district in Uganda without a significant number of Pentecostal churches, and there is widespread acknowledgment of the Pentecostal movement as the leading evangelizing arm of contemporary Christian church growth, mission, and social involvement.

In 2010, the different Pentecostal denominations in Uganda came together in Kampala and celebrated fifty years of Pentecostalism in the country. This event gathered different older and newer Pentecostal organizations, including the Evangelical Fellowship of Uganda, Miracle Center Churches, the National Fellowship of Born Again Pentecostal Churches, Christian Life Ministries, and the Born Again Faith Federation of Uganda, among others. In reflecting on this event, an insider of the Pentecostal churches in Uganda, Pastor Fred Wantaate, said, "Pentecostalism is one of the most influential and fastest-growing 'movements' in the world. However, the Pentecostal movement in Uganda had humble beginnings"; to this, he added remarks that register the social-political shift in the life of Ugandan society:

> In the early 1960s, Spirit-filled believers were stereotyped as poor, ignorant, fanatical, and semiliterate people. At first they were marginalized, ridiculed, and greatly despised by traditional churches. Now the *Abalokole Ab'omwoyo*, or Spirit-filled believers, by and large, have become part of mainstream Christianity in Uganda. It would be foolhardy to ignore them. Pentecostals, by virtue of their strong evangelistic stance, style of worship and music, plus their great appeal to young people, have influence that goes beyond their numbers.[30]

Graham Sewanyana, another leader in the inner circle of Pentecostal leadership in the Miracle Church, Mukono branch, recalls the mood at the Pentecostal jubilee celebrations: "During the celebrations, it was evident that many of the 'homegrown' Pentecostal churches were not interested in the 'old, missionary-focused' Pentecostal churches." He added that the reason for this lack of enthusiasm was plain: "Seriously, we have no shared Pentecostal experience, not even speaking in tongues."[31]

The Pentecostal churches are variously and actively engaging the Ugandan society. In secondary schools, through the Scripture Union, they are impacting the students greatly. They demonstrate the power of God through their biblical teaching and prayer; this is appealing and attractive to the young students in schools. Politically, they are working hard to wield wider influence. Their activities in the nation are quite telling. In the 2011 presidential elections, the Pentecostals filed a candidate, even if the candidate did not gather enough votes. In Kampala city, they filed a candidate, a pastor of a Pentecostal church, for the post of mayor of Kampala, although the candidate did not succeed. Yet beyond these political efforts, Pentecostals have excelled in the field of Christian education and have built the Pentecostal University of Uganda. They have many private FM radio stations that are used to broadcast news for business but also, importantly, for preaching the gospel. The appointing authority of Uganda has, on individual merit, installed some top civil servants who are "born again," with the hope that these can bring sanity to governmental positions that have been rocked by corruption.[32]

In summary, a clear progression of change seems evident. Following the shift within the earlier Pentecostal missionary churches, whose main focus was on preaching the gospel and not actively being involved in politics, the new Pentecostal leaders that started after 1986 have argued that Pentecostals are the salt and light of the world (Matt. 5:13–16) and that they should not stay away from active politics. The last two-plus decades thus have seen the rise of pastors who doubled as members of Parliament.

The Pentecostal churches are therefore out of the closet. Their leaders are working to change the social and moral ethos of a corrupt nation. The major breakthrough for the Pentecostal churches across the different denominations in Uganda covers a wide range of areas in national development including the fields of business, education, and governance. The Pentecostal denominations have successful businesses, such as FM radio stations used for both spiritual and commercial purposes. Educationally, they are offering some of the best Christian education in the country through their schools, including private Christian universities. And in the area of governance, they are occupying top offices by merit—but behind their successful performance lies their Christian commitment and motivation. These developments mean that the former religious fear of being corrupted by politics can be laid to rest, at least in theory.

The Pentecostal jubilee celebration in 2010 raised awareness of the movement's fast-growing influence. Is there a majority group in Uganda that is currently opposed to Pentecostalism in Uganda? Our brief survey indicates that Ugandans have not only become more accepting of Pentecostalism but are, if anything, more accepting of it than Tanzanians.

Pentecostal Theology in Tanzania and Uganda

The question of theological perspectives of Pentecostalism can now be raised. Where does Pentecostal theology in Tanzania and Uganda fit in relationship to changes on the social front? As a whole, and especially in Tanzania and Uganda, Pentecostals have not formulated a systematic set of theological beliefs; even the intention to produce such a systematic set of theological beliefs has not surfaced. Pentecostal theology in the two countries is simply what a Pentecostal does. It is an ongoing exercise in praxis, inasmuch as reflection arises out of experience, is put into dialogue with Scripture and the witness of the community, and then flows back into concerted action. Given this background, we attempt to define Pentecostal theology in Tanzania and Uganda in the following five ways: (1) the person and work of Jesus Christ, (2) personal experience of God through the witness of the Word of God, (3) the revelation of God as found in the Bible, (4) personal encounter with God, and (5) theology as not abstract but real.

The person and work of Jesus Christ

One way of identifying Pentecostal theology in Tanzania and Uganda is to clarify how Pentecostals look at the person and work of Jesus Christ and what they make of this. None of the Pentecostal groups I have engaged with in the two countries would deny that Jesus Christ is the chief healer, the Savior and Son of God, and the coming King. Attention to Pentecostal prayers in the two countries reveals these representations of the person and work of Jesus Christ as central to how they perceive God. Additionally, some of the recent Pentecostals, like those in the Miracle Centre, add to these Christological motifs emphasis that Christ gives the fullness of the Spirit and abundant blessings from God. They teach that believers ought to name and claim what they need and they will receive their blessing from God. Not all Pentecostals aggressively pursue this understanding of the person and work of God.

Personal experience of God through the witness of the Word of God

In a conversation with the academic dean at the PAG Pentecostal Bible College in Mwanza, it was reiterated that Pentecostals in Tanzania do not have an organized or written-out theology.[33] However, he was quick to attempt to describe a short form of what he considered Pentecostal theology in Tanzania:

> Pentecostal theology in Tanzania has primarily a character of "witness," accompanied with purity of doctrine that is preserved by checking to see that the new "witness" has experienced all that was experienced by the first "witness"; and that both conform to the primary witness of the Bible.

It is this view of "witness" that most Pentecostals in Tanzania and Uganda seem to heed in their preaching. I come to this above observation with a keen interest, as one who is actively involved in teaching homiletics and biblical theology at our theological college. Our students are largely coming from the two countries, and a significant number are Pentecostals.

The revelation of God as found in the Bible

After I addressed twenty-seven pastors from the Pentecostal Evangelistic Fellowship of Africa (PEFA) on the lack of theological education among Pentecostal pastors in Uganda and Tanzania, one pastor from the floor put his finger on the issue at stake: "Most of us [Pentecostal pastors] are known for our bad interpretation of the revelation of God in the Bible." His reference is to their reputation among the Protestant churches and the Catholic Church for disregarding formal theological education regarding the Bible and related matters. Although this comment was primarily about Pentecostals in Tanzania, in Uganda, I have seen Pentecostals across sub-Saharan Africa employing a kind of down-to-earth interpretation of the Bible: "You just obey what would be taken literally as found in the Bible"; "Just spiritualize and allegorize the hard passages that present the revelation of God in the Bible."

Yet it should be said that for Pentecostals, the revelation of God is not merely understood as affecting the mind. It is broader, affecting the personal emotions of believers. To put it differently, theology for the Pentecostals embraces both the intellectual as well as the daily experience of God. This real-life experience in turn connects the believer to God, His Word, and the community of believers. If Pentecostals in Tanzania and Uganda do not find experiencing God relevant to daily life, surely then believing in God is unhelpful.

But there is more to experiencing God. Not all Pentecostal preachers who have experienced God are well schooled in their interpretation of how God has revealed Himself through the Bible, and few pastors have a good understanding of the Bible. However, the majority of pastors are in dire need of theological training to be able to interpret clearly and faithfully the revelation of God as found in Scripture.

Personal encounter with God

Bishop Tom Ibrahim Okello of Elim Pentecostals in Africa, based in Lira, Uganda, makes a helpful observation that is common to most Pentecostals: "For Pentecostals, encounter with God takes precedence over a systematic way of explaining meaning in the Bible."[34] This statement on the Pentecostal way of encountering God stops short of a call for the development of a more articulate Pentecostal theological understanding and interpretation of the Bible. This might be expected when, upon review of the library and curriculum of the Pentecostal Bible College in Mwanza, few solid theological books or resources are observable, even of older foundational texts.

Other Pentecostals, however, are not bothered by the Pentecostal style of interpreting the Bible. Pastor Eustace Obadiah, lecturer at Kagera Bible College, Ngara, observes that for most Pentecostals in the Kagera region, "Our pastors do not bother with deep understanding of the Bible."[35] For that matter, he adds, "Trying to rationalize the theological meaning of biblical passages is not a worry to them." Pastor Eustace Obadiah adds, "To them it is not difficult to understand why experiential, relational, emotional, and living faith does not go by a set of rules cast in hard stone." In the process, he adds, "To be frank with you, it is hard to explain any mystical experiences in the Bible, were it not for the working of the Holy Spirit in the pastors." But even more, Rev. Naris Sebukwekwe, a lecturer at Ngara Bible College and a PhD candidate, notes:

> It is hard to interpret metaphors in the Bible even for those pastors with reasonable theological grounding, but how much harder is it for those without any form of basic theological education? And so in most cases the Pentecostal experiences cannot be explained systematically; in their view, it is only the working of the Holy Spirit that gives the real meaning behind the metaphors in the Bible.[36]

Bishop Jacton Lugumira of the Anglican Diocese of Luwero, a doctor of ministry candidate at Uganda Christian University who himself is sympathetic to the Pentecostals, observes:

> Pentecostals within the academy in Tanzania seem to have tended to align themselves with Evangelicals in their move toward adopting the method of interpreting the Bible; and they are doing this coupled with maintaining a

> commitment to the reliability of telling the biblical story in their preaching.[37]

Lugumira further notes that the Pentecostal preachers in Tanzania have continued the traditional modes of communicating the gospel, "with their emphasis on the immediacy of the biblical text." He claims that Pentecostals' emphasis upon the role of the Holy Spirit in appropriating the multiple meanings of the biblical text is an important contribution to the transformation of individual lives and societies where Pentecostal churches are operating. How can this be explained?

Through the working of the Holy Spirit, those who sit under the ministry of Pentecostal pastors recognize a spiritual kinship between them and the ancient authors of the biblical text through the Holy Spirit. This connection between present-day congregants and the biblical text overcomes the historical and cultural gaps between them and is where the Pentecostal emphasis on experience and the New Testament church come together. Hence, the Bible is not merely a historical record of God's actions in the past; it is the primary sourcebook for the present life. For that matter, personal and corporate experience is not to be divorced from the interpretive task. In this interpretative task, personal encounter with God is in view.

Theology is not abstract but real

In Pentecostalism in Tanzania and Uganda, emphasis on historical storytelling gives authority to the narrative sections of the biblical text, which allows for the text to be part of the total person. This way of understanding has implications for theological reflection on the social and political life in Uganda and Tanzania Pentecostals have come to believe that reality in the African setting is not unconnected with the Bible. Society issues, like poverty, health, education, and politics, are not separated from the truth of the Bible. Instead, experience is engaged in dialogue with God's Word. So there is an ongoing interpretation of experience by the norm of the Bible. Speaking as a Pentecostal pastor-scholar (a PhD candidate) from Kenya who lives and works in Uganda, Lawrence Oseje observes:

> The theological task of the church ought never to be approached as a mere intellectual exercise. The only kind of theological experience that can lead to purposeful and spiritual ends is that which is done in an atmosphere of prayer, worship, and openness of the Holy Spirit.[38]

Pastor Oseje's observation above is compelling. There are great similarities in Pentecostalism in Tanzania and Uganda. For Pentecostals in Uganda, Bishop Martin Ogwal of Faith Mission, Lira, Uganda, observes, "For us in Faith Mission Church, teaching the Scripture is a matter of not merely ideas, but a way of living."[39] Martin's statement correctly indicates that Pentecostal preachers should relate the Bible text to the testimonies of daily life.

In sum, we have shown that in Tanzania and Uganda, Pentecostal theology is praxis-oriented, with experience and Scripture being maintained in a dialectical relationship. The Holy Spirit is the one, Pentecostals believe, who maintains this ongoing relationship. Scripture is the final theological authority of truth proclaimed and lived, but most Pentecostals insist that even biblical truth is neither abstract nor merely philosophical. The truth must be manifest and confirmed in life experience. Lived faith is inspired by the theological knowledge of Scripture. Such a dynamic is conducive for bringing about transformation in the light of the norms of the Bible.

Conclusion

We have revealed in this essay that, to a large extent, in the second half of the twentieth century, Pentecostal history and theology in Tanzania and Uganda began to change and that these changes followed sociological factors. These rapid changes in society as well as in the way the new Pentecostal churches did theology at the grassroots level have accelerated to the point where, currently, grassroots Pentecostal theology is a significant force shaping the basic values and structures of Tanzanian and Ugandan society. We have traced the history of the churches and shown the shift in the sociopolitical arena. Clearly, the changing attitudes within the churches have both moved in step with society in general and specifically shaped explicit reaction to social and political developments. But who is to say that this may not be the calling of God on the Pentecostals in Tanzania and Uganda in this season? And if it is, then the future is bright.

Part III
Southern Africa

Chapter 11

Pentecostal and Charismatic Christianity in Zambia: Historical and Theological Developments and Civic Engagement

Naar M'fundisi

CHRISTIANITY AND ITS spirituality and practices permeate every part of daily life in Zambia. The emergence of Christianity in Zambia initially is linked to the arrival of Dr. David Livingstone, a missionary who arrived in the late nineteenth century. He preceded other missionary activities, leading to the formation of Christian mission stations and churches. This then resulted, at least in part, in the rise of African Initiated Churches (AICs).[1] The leaders of these AICs did not shun the Christianity of the missionaries but rather endeavored to retain the African traditional flavor and idiom within the ecclesiology and liturgy of their movements. The arrival of Pentecostalism in the early 1940s helped restore a spiritual connection (a worldview that is innately African) that was neglected, if not rejected, by missionaries.[2] A connection was inevitable between experiences in the AICs and Pentecostalism due to the classical Pentecostals' emphasis on the indwelling and experience of the Spirit of God in one's Christian walk.

Following the death of Dr. David Livingstone, a succession of missionary stations were planted throughout the country. Rotberg records that over one hundred mission stations were opened in Zambia between 1882 and 1924.[3] Since the late nineteenth century, Zambia has enjoyed a plurality of mission-led churches even as AICs have enjoyed enormous growth across the country. Pentecostal growth benefited greatly from this religious plurality, as some of its members had prior links to mainline churches and AICs. Many young people left their churches, converted, and joined this seemingly vibrant movement with new religious sensibilities.[4] This also led to the development of Charismatic churches in the 1980s.[5]

At the outset, it is important to make a clear distinction regarding my use of the terms *Pentecostal* and *Charismatic* (PC). In order to remain within the confines of the Zambian context, I will define *Pentecostal* and *Charismatic* in the following ways. *Pentecostal* will refer to those churches that emphasize the baptism in the Holy Spirit as demonstrated by the believer through the evidence of speaking in tongues (glossolalia).[6] The early Pentecostal churches in Zambia, like the Assemblies of God, had roots in North America. The term *Charismatic* will refer to churches that are independent of mainline or classical Pentecostal churches, emphasize the empowerment of the Spirit, and yet "do not insist on initial evidence of tongues but encourage the practice of the gifts of the [Spirit] within [one's] Christian church life."[7]

As the Pentecostal movement in Zambia continued to gain momentum in the 1990s, mainline churches began to experience splits (also known as *breakaway churches*) as people who were discontented with the beliefs and practices of the mainline churches broke away and formed their own independent churches. These breakaway churches largely adopted PC forms of spirituality.

After a comment on the methodology that was used to collect as well as analyze the data, a brief history of the PC movement will provide the foundation upon which the theological developments are then examined, especially in the area of civic engagement as well as the characteristics of the PC movement, both in the twentieth and twenty-first centuries. This will shed light on the ways in which the movement has been shaped and reshaped by experiences within Zambian society and the religious plurality therein, as well as help to draw conclusions.

This research was interdisciplinary in nature, and the data oriented was collected by employing methods drawn from the social sciences, history, and theological research. Quantitative congregational survey data was collected through the administration of questionnaires. The questionnaire survey, which was mainly distributed among church members, was used to supplement interviews that were carried out among church leaders. The aim was to secure balanced responses and a basis for generalizations about Christians from the grassroots of the church as well as their leaders.[8] Andre Droogers's three-dimensional anthropological model was used to explain PC civic engagement. The model was used to assess how the sacred/transcendental dimension (Pentecostal experiences, altruistic sentiments, missionary zeal, prosperity gospel, healing) combined with the internal dimensions (leadership, organizational structures, gender) influences their external dimension (civic engagement, media use, ecumenical relations, transnational networks, support of certain politicians, interreligious relations, mission, evangelism).[9] Focus was placed on expressions and dimensions of PC spirituality and how these have influenced civic engagement and, conversely, how experiences of civic engagement have influenced the shape of PC spirituality.

The History of Pentecostal and Charismatic Christianity in Zambia

The Apostolic Faith Mission (AFM) in Zambia officially started between 1946 and 1947 and appears to be the oldest Pentecostal church in Zambia.[10] The AFM traces its roots to Rev. John G. Lake, who was sent from Indianapolis, Indiana, to South Africa, where an Azusa Street leader had established a congregation. The AFM spread to Zambia (then known as Northern Rhodesia) through Afrikaner expatriate workers from South Africa working in the mines on the Copperbelt. The Pentecostal Holiness Church has classical Pentecostal roots and was established in Zambia in 1948. Zambians working in the mines in South Africa were converted, and this inspired missionaries there to expand their mission efforts to Central Africa and Zambia.[11] The Pentecostal Assembly of God Canada (now Pentecostal Assemblies of God Zambia, or PAOGZ) followed and was first established at the Mwambashi Mission Station in 1955.[12] The Church of God found its home in Zambia in 1964 under the name Full Gospel Church of God, which had roots in South Africa.[13]

Charismatic churches followed thereafter. Bread of Life Church International is one of the biggest Charismatic churches in Zambia today and was started in 1992.[14] The Bible Gospel Church in Africa was established on March 6, 2001, under the leadership of Bishop Peter Ndhlovu.[15] There are many other smaller breakaway churches dotted across the country, especially in main towns.

Early Pentecostals faced a lot of opposition and marginalization from mainline churches. The pastors were very young, predominantly in their early twenties (like the pioneer group of PAOGZ). Furthermore, some of the earlier pastors had little or no formal pastoral training, in contrast to those in mainline churches. This is why some referred to PAOGZ as the "church of young children," and Bishop Sakala recalls Baptists saying, "We will pump doctrine into their empty heads!"[16] Reverend Mwale also recalls moments when some members of the mainline churches would plot to frame some of the Pentecostal leaders in order to discredit their moral stances. For example, all-night prayer meetings were portrayed as times when Pentecostal pastors would sleep with young girls. Consequently, representatives of these churches felt isolated even when they were established and were invited to join interdenominational meetings. This is because exclusive announcements were made, like, "We do not want any people making noises here because God also listens in the quiet place."[17]

Many did not think that Pentecostalism would survive in the religious marketplace because it took a while to develop solid organizational structures.[18] Despite this opposition, it is clear that the young people at that time provided the foundation on which the PC movement continues to build at present. To date, PC spirituality has continued to permeate and influence mainline churches so strongly that the latter also have incorporated some of its practices within their own liturgies.

Theological Developments: Civic Engagement

Civic engagement in this chapter will connote the way in which people "connect with the life of their community."[19] These connections can be developed in various ways and at different levels, depending on the capacity of the service provider as well as the severity of the needs of the community. It will also be understood as the influence that PC beliefs and practices have on personal and social transformation and on wider civic culture and economic growth in both civic and congregational settings. What is evident is that PC Christianity has had an impact on society, and, in turn, society has influenced PCs. This is because, while engaging with the public domain, they continue to encounter diverse socioeconomic problems that they may not have anticipated. This then helps them to rethink their understanding of the transcendent and reorganize themselves and their resources in order to diversify their levels of civic engagement. It is not only about the relationship between humankind and the transcendent, but also about how the experiences of humankind's altruistic behaviors shape their understanding of God.

The Pentecostal movement in Zambia has undergone a period of significant change. Initially it placed an overwhelming emphasis on holiness and winning souls in preparation for the Second Coming. It is now the case that the movement pays attention to practical concerns without neglecting the message of salvation and eternal life. An example of such a change includes the growth in emphasis on civic engagement. PCs in Zambia now participate in politics, and in some cases PCs have become political leaders, like former president Frederick Chiluba; brigadier general Godfrey Miyanda (vice president during the Chiluba era and a Pentecostal now), who has a political party called the Heritage Party (HP); and Dr. Nevers Mumba, who stepped down from his pastoral role and created his own political party, which he called the National Christian Coalition (later changed to National Citizens Coalition and then to the Reformed Party in 2006).[20] Mumba served as vice president during President Mwanawasa's era and is now the president of the Movement for Multiparty Democracy party. Rev. Steven Mwale also has a political party, called People's Redemption Party, and was one of those that filed an application as a presidential candidate for the 2011 general elections but failed to meet the requirements.[21]

Pentecostals have begun to build orphanages, schools that run from nursery to high school, universities, and colleges that offer a broad variety of courses besides biblical studies. They are also involved in the health-care sector, especially since the explosion of the HIV/AIDS pandemic. Chreso Clinic and Circle of Hope Clinic are examples of such centers owned by Pentecostal churches, providing professional services that diagnose, treat, and track HIV/AIDS. Being centers that are also involved in the distribution of free antiretroviral drugs, these clinics have become a part of the redemptive work that antiretroviral drugs have achieved through prolonging the lives of those living with HIV/AIDS. According to Rijk van Dijk, "Christianity is becoming one of the most influential factors in the engagement of AIDS in some African countries,"[22] including Zambia.

As Pentecostals in Zambia emphasized the idea of having a personal relationship with Christ and that Christ was soon to return, they ridiculed the mainline churches for their lack of attention to what they believed was critical in preparation for the Second Coming. The development of educational and social-welfare institutions was not a priority for early Pentecostals, despite the fact that they would have possibly been educated or would have accessed medical treatment in a mainline health-care center or academic institution. Civic engagement was seen as a secular diversion and carnality. The phrase *carnal Christian* referred to Christians that were involved in the cares of this world.[23]

This mind-set has changed, especially in the twenty-first century, as PCs in Zambia have become more socially and politically engaged. Bishop Ng'ambi of Praise Christian Centre was quick to say:

> It is us, the Pentecostals, who looked down upon mainline churches. God does not, because remember, a lot of educated

> people in Zambia went to a missionary school. That means that the exposure to knowing God came through the mainline churches as they learnt to read and hear the Word of God as a foundation God was building in them. In later days, He took Christianity to a higher level by bringing in Pentecostals and Charismatics. The Bible says God is not unrighteous that He should forget our works of righteousness. For the sake of the prayers they prayed and the seeds they planted, God cannot forget them, even though they may not have been where they were supposed to be spiritually at that time.[24]

Bishop Ng'ambi went on to argue that on many occasions, it is the senior leaders in the movement that have opposed change in the past. However, that has not prevented change because some of those churches that split from traditional Pentecostal churches have engaged in activities that would have been disallowed within their fellowships. Today, PCs can comfortably sit among leaders of other mainline churches and present their views on different issues relating to the church and the general public.

Current Distinctive Characteristics

As much as PCs still retain what may be considered an other-worldly kind of spirituality, they have, with time, also embraced a this-worldly spirituality. This is due to the development of a spirituality that not only focuses on eschatological glory ("This world is not our home; we are just passing through"), but also balances that with existential questions and an emphasis on engaging with the affairs of this world. This emphasis retains the idea that the kingdom of God is present in the world and not something that is still to come. According to this worldview, it is possible to experience eschatological glory on the earth and, therefore, Christians should be in the forefront of promoting kingdom values, having an understanding already of what heaven is like. In support of this, Pastor Eddie Chansa states, "The kingdom of God is not the future but is now."[25] Similarly, Bishop Eddie Mulenga argues, "We the Pentecostals are trying to rise up to be relevant and, yes, there is a shift, and this is why we are rising up to build schools, orphanages, and hospitals and engaging in politics."[26]

The prosperity gospel's popularity grew in Zambia in the early 1990s with the influence of North American televangelists. During interviews with a number of the Zambian preachers that preached prosperity on television at that time, they agreed they had been influenced by North American prosperity teaching. However, they said that their understanding has been altered, leading them to take a less aggressive approach, because some of the ideas underpinning the prosperity gospel were not practical within the Zambian context.[27] Based on the questionnaire survey carried out in Lusaka, Zambia, in 2012, 70 percent agreed with the statement, "God grants material prosperity to all believers who have enough faith." By contrast, 50.2 percent agreed with the statement "God does not always give wealth to believers who have faith," and 38.1 percent disagreed with this. What was apparent during this research was that an adaptation had taken place of the teaching of the prosperity gospel.

Two trends were identified as emerging within this gospel. One trend follows a move from a magical approach to attaining wealth to a cultivation of entrepreneurship. Following this is a move from a focus on personal enrichment to altruistic behavior. These trends are linked to how people participate and contribute to the economics of the country, which also remains within the confines of the definition of politics given in the introduction.

While the PC movement continues to have a tremendous influence on Zambia's religious culture, civil society, and the general public, the opposite is also true—for example, the adoption of some PC beliefs and practices within mainline churches. Similarly, the PC movement has been impacted by mainline churches and other civic organizations. This is because they have been open to ecumenical links with mainline churches and to networking with other civic organizations in their quest to gain knowledge, skills, and expertise in their target areas. This is demonstrated mainly in the issues of politics and HIV/AIDS from 2001–2013.

In addition, key events and individuals who were born-again Christians participated in matters of civic concern—in this case, politics and political processes (having come from an apolitical stance, focused on soul craft, in their past history). With regard to civic engagement, Anderson states:

> Pentecostals have not always felt comfortable with relating to the wider society, but this is something that is gradually changing. They have been accused of a spirituality that withdraws from worldly issues like politics and the struggle for liberation and justice and of proclaiming a gospel that spiritualizes or individualizes social issues.[28]

(This accusation is, however, based on a definition of the political—focused on state craft—that they might not accept.) Nevertheless, an example that fits Anderson's claim can be seen in the way that Zambia's poor economy was blamed on the works of the devil, rather than on the poor performance of government officials and widespread corruption.

During the last decade of the twentieth century, Zambia was ruled by a president who once belonged to a mainline church but became Pentecostal. In addition to the many national and political reforms introduced, he also ensured that Christianity was promoted. According to Okite, "He opened the country up to the gospel and brought it from the fringes to the centre of Zambia public affairs."[29] The declaration of Zambia as a Christian nation in 1991 was a key event during the Chiluba era. Noble as it may have appeared, it became a yardstick by which the Christian government's performance was measured. Despite the negative press that accompanied Chiluba's government due to widespread corruption and embezzlement of funds by government leaders,[30] the PC movement continued to flourish, contributing not only to the religious presence but also to the reshaping of the religious culture in Zambia.

Chiluba, aware of the growing corruption scandals in the country, stated, "What the people need is the word of the Lord, then there shall be no corruption."[31] In relation to PCs' civic engagement, Olsen speaks of a "lack of consistency in their actions and rather serving as watchdogs in promoting justice on a variety of topics," as opposed to mainline churches.[32] Similarly, David Martin, based on his analysis of John Burdick's observations of Pentecostals in Brazil, speaks of their minimal presence in social movements, despite the fact that their faith encourages "empowerment and participation in such."[33] In a country like Zambia, where PC leaders have been known to speak with a fragmented voice at the cost of direct and open challenges to government, it may not be appropriate to be too cynical, since many PC pastors may not have had the level of backing and authority enjoyed by clergy from other mainline churches. Therefore, PCs have tended to focus on issues of morality rather than more challenging national and global problems like poor public health and education, corruption, and human rights violations. They have also been known to champion prayer and "religious imperatives such as brotherhood, love, caring, peacefulness and forgiveness as compatible" with other forms of civic engagement.[34] Though the spiritualization of social ills and injustices still exists, and will for some time, a gradual shift from this mind-set has continued to develop in Zambia, more so since the Chiluba era. Chalwe, the current principal of Trans-Africa Theological College, a PAOGZ Bible college, attributes this to born-again Christians who now see the lack of sociopolitical involvement as disobedience to God. He recommends that the involvement in sociopolitical tasks should continue to inform the church's work in Zambia, especially among born-again churches.[35] Chalwe also acknowledges this shift to the "social dimension being added to the PC evangelistic thrust," as a catalyst for further civic engagement.[36]

Conclusion

This chapter has endeavored to examine the historical and theological developments of PC Christianity in Zambia for the last seven decades. The analysis has involved an exploration of the history of PC Christianity in Zambia, the nature of their beliefs and practices, their influence on personal transformation, and their impact on civil and religious culture and national development. The picture of PC Christianity in the twenty-first century in Zambia is different from that of the twentieth century. The difference lies in the fact that having previously eschewed sociopolitical engagement in favor of prayer and evangelism, the late twentieth and early twenty-first centuries have seen PCs move to a more positive and engaged attitude. Though it may appear that PCs have adopted nonpolitical identities over the last decade, this is far from the case. Even those that choose not to engage directly in politics do so informally through prayer initiatives, as shown.

Miller and Yamamori argue that "as opposed to a Social Gospel tradition espoused by mainline churches, the Pentecostal and

Charismatic movement has sought a more balanced approach that encompasses evangelism and social action by emulating Jesus' ministry."[37] They attribute this to what they call a maturing of Pentecostalism from being otherworldly to a this-worldly force that has contributed to the reshaping of Christianity across the globe.

Having examined the reality of social oppression, poverty, injustice, war, and different forms of discrimination faced by many societies in the global south, Dhan Prakash suggests that Christians need to continue to ask themselves about their responsibility in responding to social evils. People have sometimes accused the church of doing little, and the PC churches have borne the brunt of much of that criticism.[38]

Inasmuch as Zambia remains constitutionally a Christian nation, the new generation of PC leaders needs to ensure that they are not only aware of the issues affecting civil society but also develop enough confidence to rise up and challenge matters at the core of their communities. PC churches need to engage with those that ask the state difficult questions that those on the margins cannot ask due to their place in society. Unfortunately, the exercise of their prophetic voice is one area which remains underdeveloped. Their seemingly weakened prophetic and fragmented voice as a movement and those characteristics that encourage and impede civic engagement are among the issues identified as detrimental to their cause. More than ever, they need to be in the forefront, spearheading programs of national interest that benefit the community, as well as training their members to be those that are aware and are proactive to act on issues. With regard to political affairs, I would also like to propose that PC churches create a tangible theology that can guide their civic engagement, because without this, divisions will continue to arise between those who are pro-government and those who are not. While this would be easier to implement for Pentecostal churches that are more institutionalized, like the PAOGZ, Pentecostal Holiness, Church of God, and Assemblies of God, such theologies may be difficult to enact due to the various strands of Pentecostalism as well as the newer (constant appearing of) Pentecostal churches that are not institutionalized.

Chapter 12

The Rural Narratives of a Zimbabwean-Based Religious Movement and the Shaping of African Pentecostal Spirituality

Kudzai Biri

Many studies have focused on the interaction between Christianity and African traditional religion. Most of these studies also capture the adversarial stance of the born-again Christians toward the traditional religion and culture. While these insights are useful, I have instead described African traditional religions as a "silent but echoing voice" among Pentecostals in Zimbabwe[1] and urge there is need for periodization in our engagement with the interaction between African traditional religions and Christianity. As my work has focused on the influence of African traditional religions in healing techniques, prophecy, and the status that is accorded to the founders, I will in this study attempt a deeper engagement between African traditional religions and especially Zimbabwean Pentecostalism. I pay attention to how Ezekiel Guti, the "founder" of one of the oldest, largest, and most influential Zimbabwean Pentecostal denominations—Zimbabwe Assemblies of God Africa (ZAOGA)—has negotiated with the traditional religion and culture in a rural setting to present what he believes to be biblical truths to his church. Although David Maxwell argues that ZAOGA was founded by a group of youths from the Apostolic Faith Mission of which Guti was a part and that he later stood out to lead the group as a Charismatic evangelist,[2] the church's official *History of ZAOGA* emphasizes the rural experiences of Guti's divine call and his leading role in forming the church in Bindura. I argue in this chapter that the rural narratives function in ZAOGA to highlight God's plan for the black race before the intrusion of missionaries into the heartland of Africa.

Guti is regarded as spiritual father by the Evangelical Fellowship of Zimbabwe, the umbrella body of Pentecostals and Evangelicals, and he has greatly influenced Pentecostal beliefs and practices through his powerful and charismatic movement. In this chapter, I argue also that a hallmark of ZAOGA and African Pentecostalism is their resonance with traditional religion and culture. In particular, Pentecostals in postcolonial Zimbabwe have drawn, both consciously and perhaps unintentionally, from traditional cosmologies and rural narratives in their liturgies. This is partly a result of postures that have increasingly been critical of the West and all that is associated with the West in a state wracked by sociopolitical and economic collapse. I unravel how the rural narratives are merged with the biblical message to authenticate the leadership of Guti so that tradition and the Bible have become important in Pentecostal interpretations of their lived realities. All these have shaped Pentecostal spirituality in Zimbabwe and beyond.[3]

Methodologically, this study derives primarily from participant observation. The researcher has enjoyed an advantage of being a church member and, at some point, a leader in the church. Further, I have used material from ZAOGA archives, sermonic discourses, and other published material. I have analyzed these materials together to establish the significance of Guti's rural narratives and how they have shaped Pentecostal spirituality. Before we begin, I examine the influence of the Shona traditional religion and culture in ZAOGA's naming system.[4]

The naming system in ZAOGA is very important. I establish the patterns of continuity from the indigenous religion and culture. First, the achievements of ZAOGA have been renarrated by the movement as occurring solely under Guti's leadership so that he emerges in his role as a traditional "chief" or "big man" who exudes knowledge and wisdom. Second, urban developments in the formation of the movement have been marginalized in favor of rural narratives of claimed divine encounters. Development of the latter has culminated in a unique brand of African Pentecostalism featuring rural sensibilities and orientation. While many properties in ZAOGA are named after Ezekiel Guti, this study focuses selectively on a few of these names.

Handinawangu: From Family Politics to Universalism

At birth, Guti was named Handinawangu. Guti's father was a polygamist. In the family context, as in most African families grappling with effects of polygamy, the father of Guti could have been communicating a message to his wives, who vied for his attention. *Handinawangu* means "I do not have my own," and in that context Guti's father might have been sending the message that he loved all the wives. The naming system among Africans is important, not only emerging from but also speaking into lived realities. This is most likely to have been the meaning of *Handinawangu* in such a setting.

However, this name has been reinterpreted in ZAOGA's theological history of the church to mean that Guti was chosen by God to lead because he loves all the people and carries people's burdens, especially through intercession. Guti's *History of ZAOGA*, among other sources, makes reference to his prayer in 1957, when he interceded for the continent of Africa to be saved and to be spared from judgement by God because the Bible had not yet been preached to many people and God's miracles had not yet been performed.[5] That is why he is often referred to as "father" and "African Apostle" by many Pentecostals. Also, ZAOGA has become popularly known as "*baba*'s church" (father's church) or *kwababa* by outsiders.[6] Guti's name thus mediates the divine commission to lead Africa. According to Guti, his name Ezekiel was also given by God and adopted later in his ministry (he does not mention the year) because his mission was to "make the dry bones in Africa live" (cf. Ezek. 37) through preaching the gospel of Jesus.

Apart from Guti's name, Grange Christian School in Harare was also built by ZAOGA. The blocks of the school are named after the places that are said to be important in the history of the church. These are predominantly rural areas and include Mutema Ngaone, Guti's rural home in Chipinge; Vumba, a place in Manicaland province where Guti comes from; and Bindura, the mythical birthplace of ZAOGA. It is therefore important to analyze why these places are significant to the history of the movement.

Mutema Ngaone: God Remembers the Black Race

The first narrative of Guti's encounter with the divine in Mutema Ngaone village, where he comes from, is significant. The English translation of *Mutema Ngaone* means "Let the black person see." This has been interpreted theologically in the *History of ZAOGA* to mean, first, spiritual sight. Africa needed salvation and the gospel of Jesus Christ, so Guti is understood to have been commissioned to lead the black people of Africa to "see," repent, and be saved. Second, the meaning of the name is understood within the context of colonialism, whereby the blacks suffered racism and were marginalized and oppressed. Therefore, because of experiences with colonialism, Africans have tended to internalize their own racial inferiority even as they have elevated the white race. Africans are therefore challenged by Guti to appreciate the black skin, African culture, and the purpose of God in Africa. Thus, Guti and his wife Eunor always emphasize that "whites are just but the skin."[7]

These are recurring themes in Pentecostal theologies in Africa, as they tap into political discourses and emphasize the need to empower the black race, elevate Mother Africa, and denounce white racial superiority.[8] Thus, Ngaone is an epitome of "enlightenment" for blacks and has become a pilgrimage center. The significance of the pilgrimage to Ngaone is twofold. First, it deletes from memory ZAOGA's cofounders, as the establishment of ZAOGA is tied to Ngaone and not to Salisbury, where Guti and other youths originally broke away from the Apostolic Faith Mission to start a prayer band.[9] Second, on a broader spectrum, Ngaone represents the reality of God's love for the black race because Africans had encounters with the divine there first, before the white missionaries came and preached the gospel to them. Such a narrative is consistent with the claim of leading African theologians that missionaries did not bring God to Africa but that God brought the missionaries to Africa.[10] Guti writes, "I met God before I met a preacher."[11]

The claimed divine encounters in Ngaone have popularized Ngaone. Guti recalls having had an encounter with angels in the bush, and he was told to "fear not and sin not."[12] The "fear not and sin not" voice was accompanied by a vision of many stars. Guti was told that he would have many children.[13] "Fear not and sin not" is a recurring theme in ZAOGA sermons and testimonies, apart from inscriptions on church and individual vehicles, regalia, stickers, and posters. The statement has become a trademark in Zimbabwean Pentecostalism, which, apart from emphasizing the need to shun evil, serves to highlight the uniqueness and distinctiveness of the Pentecostal message over and against other forms of Christianity. Pentecostals seek to demonstrate that they embody a true, authentic form of African Christian spirituality through divine encounters, sense of mission, and obedience to God.

Because of the claims of divine visitations by Guti and how these claims have influenced theology in Pentecostalism, Guti embodies multiple titles, including "African Apostle" and "father." The theme of fatherhood can be traced from the Bible, but it is important to note that Guti as father transcends the biblical boundaries of the term. Among the Shona people, *mutana* (elder) is significant, as it refers to elders (males) who have vast knowledge of society's ideals and values. When people call Guti *father*, there are two connotations. First, he is spiritual father, as it is common in the Pentecostal fraternity. Second, Guti is perceived as a custodian of the morality of the community, due to his age and wisdom that is associated with seniority, and this includes the preservation of whatever is valuable from the traditional rural community, of which many ZAOGA members are a part, and assimilation with their newfound Christian and Pentecostal commitments. When Guti implores his followers not to imitate Western values that are degrading and destroying the moral fabric of African way of life, he is seen as representing authentic African Pentecostal spirituality, which calls for the total health and well-being of the Africans.

The Ngaone narrative affirms Guti as an admirer and defender of Shona traditional religious morality, in which God revealed Himself to the Africans apart from and at least prior to the arrival of the gospel of Jesus. Guti emphasizes Christian morality and at the same time is interested in the traditional values that are consistent with the biblical teachings. In one of his books, Guti appraises Shona religion and culture and appraises the revelations of God to the ancestors through sacred forests, birds, and animals.[14] This book is significant because Guti theologizes from Shona indigenous spirituality, and this has subsequently raised the profile of Shona traditional religions over and against Western moral values. Most Pentecostal churches in Zimbabwe have been influenced by Guti's teachings, and they join hands with other African leaders, such as Mensa Otabil of Ghana, in lifting up African indigenous values and morality and elevating Mother Africa and the black race.[15] Like the Apostle Paul, Guti commends his followers to a life of moral integrity, and it is claims such as "fear not and sin not," preached by angels to Guti and not by Western missionaries, that shape the church's theology of obedience and purity. In other words, the Bible came later to reinforce a message of purity that had been delivered earlier by an angel. Such a narrative shapes ZAOGA contemporary identity, defines its historical reputation, and influences its direction amidst a dynamic and fragmenting Pentecostal field. But most importantly, it recovers the role of Africans as agents of the spread of the gospel that was often downplayed by the narratives of Western missionaries.

Before moving on, we need to briefly address Achunike's point that one of the leading errors in Pentecostalism is making founders appear like living saints.[16] The official story that Guti obeyed God from the beginning, combined with his public and vehement condemnations of sin, has evolved, practically, into a myth that he lives a sinless life. Critics of Guti counter that he divorced and married another wife, which they construe as adultery. Guti himself has rejected this charge,[17] but he has also admitted publicly, in his sermons, how he erred in the ministry as a young pastor.

Regardless of Guti's personal sanctity, his followers are now mythically decorating their leader. Through such (mis)representations, ZAOGA perpetuates a personality that is distracting, as it distorts reality. However, these developments ought to be understood within the matrix of African and Zimbabwean politics, in which the church attempts to minimize other possible claims to leadership of the movement.

Vumba and Bindura: Mountains of Divine Encounters

Related to Ngaone are two important places of pilgrimage among Pentecostals: Vumba and Bindura. Guti stayed in Vumba before coming to Salisbury (Harare) and often retreated to the mountain to pray. In his solitude, he had several divine encounters where he received commands from angelic visitations, including power to heal the sick.[18] Guti further claims that in the manner of Abraham, he was commanded to leave Highfield (a suburb in Harare) and to go to Bindura to mark the birth of the church in a despised place.[19] Vumba and Bindura are important areas of pilgrimage in ZAOGA and among other Pentecostals, especially for big events. The Vumba and Bindura mountains are depicted as places of spiritual nourishment for Guti. The ZAOGA cathedral has been built at the foot of the mountain, and the cathedral has become a center for Pentecostal conferences and workshops. It is claimed that ZAOGA was born under a gum tree at the foot of the mountain, where miracles took place. There is a cave at the mountaintop in Bindura, where the church claims Guti had divine encounters with angels and Jesus and many miracles are believed to have happened. The site is open for many people, even from other churches outside the Pentecostal fraternity, and has become a popular pilgrimage center.

It is important to note that Guti accepts the traditional notion of the sacrality of mountainous areas and caves. Guti writes that the ministry began when he was commanded by God to go to the mountain of Bindura, where he prayed in a cave shortly after his prayer for Africa.[20] Traditionally, mountains and caves are sacred places where elders go to perform traditional rituals and the community gets spiritual nourishment through the cordial relations that are maintained between the living and the "living" dead.[21] Pentecostals have resacralized the mountains and the caves to convey meaning from the perspective of their new faith. Places of encounter with guardian spirits of the land have been resacralized and have become places of encounter with the angels, Jesus, and the Holy Spirit, as evidenced by many testimonies. Zimbabwe Ezekiel Guti University is in Bindura, and the choice of the site is associated with the important history of the movement as enshrined in the life of Guti.

The Hospital: Physical Healing and Spiritual Deliverance

"Fear not and sin not," the refrain used pervasively in ZAOGA services (see above), also marks deliverance sessions in this and many other Zimbabwean Pentecostal churches. While these deliverance sessions are part and parcel of most services, ZAOGA also runs deliverance sessions at the church's hospital in Waterfalls. Mbuya Dorcas Hospital is ZAOGA-owned and operated and named after Guti's deceased mother, as it is important among the Shona people to remember deceased ancestors and their veneration is sometimes achieved through naming after an ancestor. The deliverance center has moved from Baines Avenue in the city center of Harare and is currently operating at the hospital premises in Waterfalls.

ZAOGA leadership is intentional about conducting deliverance sessions at the hospital. A ZAOGA evangelist justified this by pointing out that it is a response to the realization that Western medicine has certain limitations when it comes to addressing the full scope of life's vicissitudes.[22] Gordon Chavunduka points out that despite the introduction of Christianity, Western education, and scientific medicine, these have not addressed Zimbabwean ills, which are, in turn, believed to be caused by evil spirits.[23] Deliverance is both spiritual and physical, especially because of the belief in witches and witchcraft activities. People have to be delivered from the powers of darkness that militate against progress in their lives. Deliverance at the hospital thus symbolizes the need for both spiritual and physical healing in order to enjoy the Christian life.

Yet deliverance and healing (both facilitated by the hospital) do not minimize the need for hard work and other kinds of obedient human responses to God. Thus does ZAOGA insist on the abilities of God even through national and economic crises. In fact, Guti indicates that God told him to return from America because "money is in Zimbabwe,"[24] and the church has regularly offered moral support to believers and empowered them during the crisis.[25] In 2015, as the economy of Zimbabwe continued to go downhill, Guti urged his followers "not to live in the economy of Zimbabwe but of God."[26] Followers in Canada and Australia are also urged to live above the economy of their nations. As the father of many Pentecostal leaders, Guti has been motivated by the continued crisis to give more sermons emphasizing God's provision in difficult situations, although some of the sermons are not intelligible, especially if they insist on prosperity amidst economic crisis. Many Pentecostal leaders in Zimbabwe have embraced what Guti teaches and have presented Guti's sermons in their churches. Thus the insistence that God blesses during the crisis is now common in Pentecostal churches, such as the New Covenant

Church led by Tudor and Chichi Bismark and the Power, Healing, and Deliverance Ministries of Walter Magaya. In spite of the economic crisis that Zimbabwe has undergone, Pentecostal leaders insist that people should continue to work hard so that they prosper.

Yet it ought to be admitted that sometimes the pressure on followers to get deliverance in order to prosper does not make sense. In the wake of closure of companies and factories, civil servants going for months without salaries, and the economy almost grounded, any insistence that God blesses people during difficult economic times is inappropriate. On the one hand, nothing is impossible with God, and God is not bound by the economic situation but operates above human incapabilities; on the other hand, it is morally improper to talk only about blessings during hard times without coming alongside people during these situations. In fact, the Pentecostal insistence that God blesses and prospers His children in crisis moments might even be understood as serving a specific agenda to finance the ever-expanding Pentecostal denominations and ministries that finance the lavish lifestyles of leaders. There is, therefore, need of an in-depth critique of the significance of these rural narratives and all that is associated with them.

Significance of the Rural Narratives: Embodiment of the African Indigenous Spirituality

Arguably, African Pentecostal churches are unique in their diagnoses of life's ailments that do not ignore African traditional perspectives and then in their proposal of solutions that combine Christian beliefs and practices and medical science and technology. Perhaps this is one of the major reasons for Pentecostal growth in spite of negative public criticisms. What is significant is that such practices unfold in ZAOGA from the rural narratives of divine encounters that in Ngaone and later in America, God told Guti that he and his followers will prosper. My overarching point here, however, is what anthropologist Birgit Meyer has argued: that Pentecostals have emphasized a complete break from the past.[27] In the light of the naming system that captures the significant events and developments from the traditional religion and culture, such a thesis needs to be nuanced. I suggest that ZAOGA's theology that frames Guti's experiences in rural areas exemplifies the remodeling, revitalizing, and resacralizing of traditional religion and culture. This has exerted a lot of influence on newer Pentecostal churches, like the United Families International led by Emmanuel and Ruth Makandiwa and Heartfelt Ministries International led by Chipo and Tavonga Wutabwashe. Members of these churches have followed suit by emphasizing the rural narratives or divine encounters of their founders. Such approaches are increasingly widespread as many African Pentecostal leaders seek to disassociate themselves from so-called Western theologies and embrace a Pan-African stance as they increasingly interact with the wider culture.

In part for these reasons, I agree with Gerrie ter Haar, an astute observer of African Pentecostalism, who notes that although Pentecostalism has roots in North America, African Pentecostalism has developed separately.[28] My own work identifies the creativity of African men and women in ZAOGA to construct a counterthesis to the notion that African Pentecostals are mere recipients of televangelists from the West. This chapter shows how different narratives have been harnessed and adapted to authenticate the leaders as men and women of God. Rather than writing off their past, African Pentecostals have creatively woven their rural experiences into their theological narratives. While some traditional beliefs and practices are demonized and, in that sense, represent their complete break from the past, in other respects they have attempted to redeem their heritage and held tight to the faith and identity of their forefathers and mothers. In ZAOGA, the interpretation of Guti's names and names of places in the rural Chipinge district are fitting examples of such reclamation.

That the traditional names are read with Christian lenses shows that God, and not the white missionaries, has plans for Africa and Africans. This has given birth to what I understand as *religious nationalism*, not only in Zimbabwe but elsewhere in Africa, that has tapped into political discourses as we witness increased "religionisation of politics and politicisation of religion."[29] African religious leaders network and espouse national ideologies of God's purpose for Africa and Africans based on their claimed divine encounters, particularly in the rural areas. This is significant, first, because it loosens the connections and links with overseas white churches and thereby subtly, if not explicitly, undermines the idea that churches in Africa are mere extensions or recipients of overseas churches. This might be one of the reasons why ZAOGA and most African Pentecostal churches have established headquarters in their countries, particularly in the birthplace of the founders, in order to reconstruct their religious history. The past is retrieved as a rich tradition in which God had revealed Himself to the chosen men and women, and this ushered in the new dispensation before the encounter with the Western missionaries preached the gospel of Jesus to them.

Second, the significance of these rural narratives ought to be understood against the backdrop of the history of colonialism and subjugation of the black race on the African continent. The emergence of African Pentecostal theology has both emphasized the importance of the black race and the divine plan for Africa and negated the superiority of the white race. Guti has condemned the begging mentality among Africans, and he insists on the need for black empowerment.[30] Kalu has observed how Pentecostals engage in politics through intercessory prayers and the elevation of Mother Africa as a blessed continent in spite of the woes that are troubling her.[31]

Guti embodies multiple titles, roles, and statuses. He is an African statesman. The prayer for Africa in 1957 confirms this role accorded to him. The significance is in that secluded place in the mountains. The growing prominence of Mother Africa and African-oriented discourses on Africa and advocacy of the cherished way of life in the rural areas reveal both the potency of the traditional and religious heritage and the nostalgia that drives the anti-white and anti-Western sentiment.

Ecumenism: Reinventing Indigenous Spiritualities

I would further argue that religious nationalism manifested in such discourses is a revitalized form of communalism in indigenous societies that has been regarded as *ecumenism* in modern terms. Perhaps ironically, in terms of what Pentecostal ecumenists have intended with their projects, emphasis on the ecumenical orientation of Pentecostalism has facilitated openness to and then recovery of rural narratives. While interdenominational fellowships have become common, emphasizing the need to partner with each other, especially through the Evangelical Fellowship of Zimbabwe, there are many paradoxes that run within the Pentecostal fraternity. Competition has always characterized ministries and denominations, and one of the major ways in which Pentecostals market their religious movements is by "selling" their founders and denominations. This evangelistic, or "growth," strategy has exposed the contestation and disunity among Pentecostals based on doctrines of the churches and ministries and, most importantly, on the backgrounds of the founder. The crucial questions that appear to have shaped membership in denominations in Zimbabwe are: What is the background of the founder, in terms of the divine call, and what does the founder offer to his people? Zimbabwe has witnessed the rise and fall of many Pentecostal prophets who claimed to perform miracles that included miracle money, miracle shoes, miracle babies, the lengthening of male sexual organs, changing people's height, and many other miracles.[32]

This is the context in which this chapter has documented the increased revivalism and emphasis of Guti's rural narratives in all ZAOGA church services and events to present him as an authentic leader over and against other Pentecostal prophets that are now, implicitly or explicitly, condemned in the public domain. As a result, Guti becomes an uncontested hero and ZAOGA emerges as a personality cult.[33] Guti's image transcends the boundaries of Zimbabwe, as he is embraced also as a spiritual father of many Pentecostals around the world, including the late Myles Munroe, of the Bahamas, who often attended ZAOGA leaders' Deeper Life Conferences as a motivational speaker, even as "luminaries such as the Ghanaian Mensa Otabil and the Jamaican Kissley Fletcher have paid tribute to the movement's leader Ezekiel Guti hailing him as 'father' and pioneer of an entire generation of churches."[34] Thus, ZAOGA regalia on Guti's ninety-first birthday celebrations in 2014 were printed with the words "The world's greatest father turns 91."[35] This has set the pace for newer Pentecostal churches.

I have pointed out elsewhere that the title "African Apostle" had been given to John G. Lake of the Apostolic Faith Mission.[36] But in defiance of that historical development in the expansion of Pentecostalism from North America into southern Africa, ZAOGA presents Guti as an authentic African apostle.[37] The quest to universalize the leader is manifest. This universalization of Guti emanates from the vision that Guti claimed to have seen many stars while he was still young in his rural village and was told that he would lead many people to heaven. He also encourages his followers to pray to God and say, "God of Ezekiel because Israelites called the God of Abraham."[38] Thus, he sees himself as the Abraham of today for his ZAOGA followers and many others who acknowledge his divine call and leadership. This marks the distinctiveness of ZAOGA as one of the leading Pentecostal movements. The movement's influential theology is anchored in the rural narratives of the founder and has impacted the entire Pentecostal fraternity.

Conclusion

I have pointed out that ZAOGA has a denominational theology that is based on the experiences of the founder. The rural claims of divine encounters by Guti suffuse ZAOGA theology. This has been facilitated by printed regalia, the theological history book, and the naming system. All these ways help to glorify ZAOGA leadership and to perpetuate the rural narratives and the resultant ideologies in order to strengthen the movement, especially in a highly contestable climate, where churches vie for clientele. Most important is the influence of the narratives beyond ZAOGA borders to inform other Pentecostal denominations and ministries and even non-Pentecostal churches. This has been facilitated by the gravity of the reading, interpretation, and affirmation of these narratives and places, thus appealing to the social, political, and economic situation and needs of Zimbabweans and other Africans.

Chapter 13

"Thus Far the Lord Has Brought Us!": Histories and Theologies of Southeast African Pentecostalisms

Chammah J. Kaunda

The origin of Pentecostalism in southeast Africa dates back to the end of nineteenth century if its definition includes some of the African-initiated Pentecostal-type churches (also known as African Initiated Churches, or AICs) that began in those countries at that time. The approach in this chapter favors a broader definition that includes AICs—because of the Pentecostal-type spirituality that they exhibit (see below)—classical Pentecostal churches, and neo-Pentecostal groups. African-initiated, Pentecostal-type churches include the Zionists and Apostolic movements, while classical Pentecostalism includes the Assemblies of God, the Apostolic Faith Mission, and the Full Gospel Church, among other groups. Toward the end of the twentieth century, southeast Africa also experienced an influx of neo-Pentecostal churches, which have found fertile ground for growth, especially among the marginalized communities.[1] These neo-Pentecostals include the Universal Church of the Kingdom of God, among other networks. In the rest of this chapter, unless qualified otherwise, I will use the term *Pentecostal* and its cognates as inclusive of these three streams.

Scholars attribute the growth of these various Pentecostalisms in Africa across the last century to various factors, much of which applies to the southeast African context too. First, the movements utilize flexible theologies that enable them to easily secure their credentials in beliefs and practices of the hosting cultures.[2] Due to this cultural flexibility, Pentecostalism in southeast Africa has mutated to acquire distinctive features when compared with Pentecostalism in other parts of the world, including other parts of Africa.

Second, from their inception in the African context, Pentecostal movements have taken experience as a legitimate and basic source of Christian life and formation. As a result, Pentecostalism has sought to address core problems of southeastern Africa, such as poverty, sickness, unemployment, witchcraft, and demon possession. This approach has resonated with African thought systems that take experience as a foundation for knowledge.

Third, Pentecostal movements presume the activities of the Holy Spirit in the world,[3] and this also resonates with African metaphysics. One might argue that in this sense, the African worldview has functioned as *praeparatio evangelica* for Pentecostalism. The movement emphasizes the new experience of the supernatural power and empowerment of the Holy Spirit in the realm of the miraculous, divine healing, exorcism, prophecy, and lifestyle. This also resembles the southeast African traditions in which the Spirit is conceived as the pervasive life force in all reality.[4]

Very little has been written on the history and theology of Pentecostalism in southeast Africa. Therefore, this chapter cannot give a full picture of the history of this complex movement but attempts a sketch of Pentecostalism in this part of the continent. The first section develops a more general missiological model for reflecting on the way Pentecostal history has evolved in southeast

Africa, especially as it pertains to the import of African Initiated Churches for thinking about Pentecostal history and theology. The next part traces the introduction of Pentecostalism in Mozambique and Madagascar following the proposed historiographical framework. Finally, I outline some contours of Pentecostal theology in this region of Africa.

Negotiating the "Single Origin" of Pentecostalism in Southeast Africa: A Marginal Perspective

The current interest in Pentecostal historiography and its criticism of white origins can be traced from Pentecostal historians such as Walter Hollenweger and his students, who, though concerned with the Azusa Street origin in 1906, resisted situating Pentecostal historiography with white middle-class North Americans.[5] Stressing instead the black origins of some Pentecostal movements signaled a paradigm shift in historiography from an elitist-centeredness to where people on the margins become the primary agents and subjects of their historical experiences.

The trend is consistent with the emergence of historiography from the underside of history, rather than from the dominant perspective of the powerful and the rich. This so-called "history from below" applied in our context, gives the voice to African founders who contributed to the emergence and spread of Pentecostalism independent of the North American Azusa Street experience. It is therefore now more difficult to talk about a single origin for the movement, not least for southeastern African Pentecostalism. In saying that "neither a creed, an institution nor a place is the beginning of Pentecostalism,"[6] Michael Bergunder believes that the movement—*movements*, more precisely—have been intrinsically global from the beginning and that locating or specifying their origins to a single place or country undermines the distinctiveness that sets them apart from other Christian traditions. This is not to ignore the significance of Azusa Street as an important, if not central, node in the network of early modern Pentecostal missions, but it does underscore the point that revivals in various regions of the world led to emergence of this "very contextual phenomenon" across the globe.[7]

Allan Anderson, an important voice on Pentecostalism in Africa, provides a more inclusive approach for understanding the origins of the movement without undermining the local contexts and giving due recognition to the many historical narratives of emergence.[8] According to Anderson, Pentecostal revivals took place in various places, including North America, before the event at Azusa Street in 1906, and there were also many revivals around the same time or even after, all independent of the Azusa Street experience. Anderson believes in the multiplicity of origins—what he calls "multiple or many Jerusalems"[9]—from which various distinctive Pentecostalisms originated. However, the majority of Pentecostal missionaries who went out to spread the message in other parts of the world came from or were linked with Azusa. What could have been the reason for this? Perhaps this was in part because of economic factors.

I believe that African revivalists at this stage were not economically ready to undertake missionary activities across their own continent, much less around the world. Yet several indigenous revivalists were already recognized as prophets in various places in southeast Africa. Though they never categorized themselves as Pentecostals, the early scholars who have studied them discovered an inherent resemblance with the wider family of Pentecostalism.[10] Ogbu Kalu, an African scholar who studied the history of Pentecostalism in Africa extensively, unswervingly held that African Pentecostalism was of African origins.[11] Although it must certainly be granted that not all Pentecostalism originated in Africa, nevertheless this chapter proceeds from the assumption that there are African-founded expressions of the movement that developed spontaneously, without missionary assistance from outside. Such a view is central to the decision adopted in this chapter to define *Pentecostalism* broadly, as including not only Western missionary-established Pentecostal churches but also African-initiated groups that have exhibited Pentecostal- and Charismatic-type spirituality predating the arrival of classical Pentecostalism.

History of Pentecostalism in Southeast Africa

This section aims at locating the historical roots of Pentecostal movements in the two southeast African countries, Mozambique and Madagascar.

Pentecostalism in Mozambique: a struggle for self-establishment

There is a growing presence of Pentecostalism in Mozambique in its various manifestations. In the 2007 census, the African-initiated, Pentecostal-type churches were the third-largest religious tradition, attracting 16 percent of the total population.[12] The same census results indicated that the Evangelical/Pentecostal Christianity churches, counted together for the first time as a single distinctive category, were the fourth-largest religious group in Mozambique, representing 11 percent of the total population.[13] Whereas statistics are political and not reliable, to a certain extent they still give a picture of the influence Pentecostalism is exerting in Mozambique. Thus, it is important to understand the history of Pentecostalism in Mozambique in its three streams.

The first category of Pentecostalism in Mozambique is the African-initiated Pentecostal-type. These were the earliest form of

Pentecostal expressions in Mozambique. Some of these churches were introduced during the colonial period by the Mozambican migrant miners returning from South Africa and Zimbabwe mines.[14] Patrick Harries speaks of the indigenous revival that took place in Mozambique around 1884. He believes that this was "an indigenous version of the Pentecostalism that Sundkler would later classify as 'Zionism'; and in this sense, it was one of the first independent Church movements in Southern Africa."[15] This spiritual movement, like Pentecostal churches since, emphasized the power of the Holy Spirit, especially manifested through practices of miracles, healing, prophecy, exorcism, and glossolalia. The first churches were planted in Mozambique as early as 1907, but the first official African-initiated Pentecostal-type was *Igreja Luz Episcopal*, established in 1918 by Muti Sikobele, one of the two ordained Mozambican preachers in the Methodist Church.[16] The distinctiveness of *Igreja Luz Episcopal* was its appropriation of African culture and worldview as a substratum for the relevance of Christian faith in Mozambique. The early leaders sought to allow the traditional worldview to influence Christian outlook and practice.

The liberal political climate of the Portuguese in the First Republic from 1910 to 1926 seems to have provided a safe environment for the establishment of these churches. However, during the Second Republic (1933–1974), the Portuguese authority perceived the African-initiated, Pentecostal-type emphasis on the Africanization of the Christian faith as a political threat.[17] Even in the postcolonial era, religious repression continued with the ruling government (Frelimo). Unfortunately, the independence in 1975 did not bring about religious freedom—in fact, much to the contrary. Despite the constitutional guarantee of freedom of religion, the ruling government condemned and persecuted religions. Thus, Pentecostalism in its African-initiated type, such as Zionist and Apostolic churches, and also classical expressions, such the Assemblies of God, Apostolic Faith Mission, and the Full Gospel Church of God, remained marginal throughout the 1970s and much of the 1980s.[18]

There was not much Pentecostal missionary activity until the beginning of the 1990s, shortly after the end of civil war. Linda van de Kamp, a cultural anthropologist who has done extensive research on the development of Brazilian Pentecostalism in Mozambique, writes that "the end of the war also marked the end of the socialist era and the start of the democratization and liberalization of the economic and political domains, including a relaxing of regulations concerning religious expression."[19] Hence, during the early 1990s, the African-initiated, Pentecostal-type churches began to grow and became one of the largest Christian groups in Mozambique.[20] They attracted large numbers of young people from both the rural and suburban areas, such as Maputo. The largest African-initiated Pentecostal-type is Zion Christian Church of Mozambique, which also has the highest number of adherents. One of its congregations in the Maputo area has the largest building, inaugurated in 1991.[21] By 1998, this congregation had approximately two thousand members. In the other eleven parishes in and around Maputo, the membership is estimated at ten thousand. There are also a few Apostolic churches, such as *Velha Apostolica de África em Mocambique* (Old Apostolic Church of Africa in Mozambique) that have spread throughout Mozambique, with congregations in almost every province. In the Maputo area *Velha Apostolica de África em Mocambique* has about ten thousand members and numerous congregations in most of the suburbs.[22]

Mozambique was also one of the first African countries to receive classical Pentecostal missionary activities, which began in

1911, when the Assemblies of God was established.[23] The largest classical Pentecostal church in Mozambique, also known as the Evangelical Assemblies of God of Mozambique, has its origins in the South African Assemblies of God and the work of Austin and Ingrid Chawner, in partnership with the Portuguese Assemblies of God and Mozambican local preachers, such as Laurentino Mulungo.[24] Today there is a fellowship of approximately three thousand churches and one million members. Maputo is home to the largest Evangelical Assembly of God congregation in Mozambique, with a membership of about forty-five thousand.[25]

Another classical Pentecostal presence is the Church of God that began in 1931 through the activities of Pentecostal missionaries from Portugal (which had colonized the country in the sixteenth century). Later, in 1951, this group of Pentecostals associated itself with the broader Church of God following the merger of the Church of God (Cleveland, Tennessee) from the United States and South Africa's Full Gospel Church. As the nation grew more stable in the 1990s, the Church of God was energized, leadership strengthened, and new churches were planted. Bill George reports that in 2010, the membership was 10,327 in 117 churches and nine missions.[26] The classical Pentecostal churches have grown, albeit more gradually, even as those with connections abroad have maintained their historical and theological expressions with their Western Pentecostal counterparts and at the same time tried to establish their indigenous credentials within the southeast African context.

Another prominent classical Pentecostal movement in Mozambique is Iris Global (previously Iris Ministries), a Christian NGO with administrative offices in Redding, California, USA.[27] Iris Global was started in 1995 by American Assemblies of God missionaries Heidi and Rolland Baker. In less than ten years, its network grew from two churches and children's homes to more "than 10,000, including some 2,000 churches among the Makua people of northern Mozambique."[28] Currently, the organization feeds over 10,000 children a day, including various members of different communities, including another 4,000 families in Malawi. It has established five Bible schools, three primary schools, and a school of missions. Iris Global seeks to build international bridges among the churches within its network that is spread around the world.

Neo-Pentecostal churches are also present in Mozambique. Scholars have highlighted the introduction and expansion of neo-Pentecostalism in Mozambique, especially in its post-socialist period (since the early 1990s).[29] There are two conspicuous streams of neo-Pentecostalism in Mozambique.

First, there are many South African and Zimbabwean neo-Pentecostal missionaries who have entered Mozambique to preach the gospel. James Pfeiffer gives a concise historical overview of the spread of neo-Pentecostalism in Mozambique in the aftermath of civil war in the early 1990s.[30] He observes that South African and Zimbabwean Pentecostals already had large followings and were eagerly looking for opportunities to spread their message to other parts of southern Africa, and with the opening of borders, Mozambique was seen as ripe for harvesting souls for the kingdom of God. Among such churches were the Zimbabwe Assemblies of God Africa under Bishop Ezekiel Guti.

The second prominent neo-Pentecostal group that arrived in Mozambique in the early 1990s came from Brazil.[31] The most visible is the *Igreja Universal do Reino de Deus* (Universal Church of the Kingdom of God, also known as the Universal Church), which started in Maputo in 1992. As of 2011, the Universal Church had approximately two hundred fifty uniformly built church structures around Mozambique, with about one hundred of these scattered in every neighborhood in Maputo.[32] The other Brazilian Pentecostal churches are *Igreja Pentecostal Deus É Amor* (the Pentecostal Church God Is Love, known as God Is Love), also one of the earliest from Brazil, and the *Igreja Mundial do Poder de Deus* (the World Church of the Power of God), which arrived a bit later.

Van de Kamp observes that regardless of some differences, Brazilian Pentecostalism largely shares neo-Pentecostal characteristics, such as a special orientation to prosperity gospel and spiritual warfare.[33] These churches are an urban phenomenon and attract large numbers of successful and upwardly mobile individuals. Their evangelistic strategy is generally militant, with particular focus on demonization of Mozambican traditional cultural beliefs and practices.[34] They urge their Mozambican members to "distance themselves from 'African culture' and 'evil spirits'" as means for acquisition of prosperity.[35] Arguably, these churches are uncritically exporting Brazilian culture to Mozambique as a Christian culture. Brazilian pastors believe God has sent them to save Mozambicans from *macumba*, a derogatory term used to denounce the religions of African slaves in Brazil as religions of witchcraft or black magic. The African slaves in Brazil did not abandon their African religious tradition; rather, they continued to practice them as Afro-Brazilian cults. Therefore, the Brazilian pastor-missionaries perceive Africa as the heartland of all evil: "It is this evil that they have come to Africa to fight."[36]

To bring this section to a close, Pentecostalism across this spectrum of expressions—from African-initiated to classical to neo-Pentecostal—has gained national prominence and become one of the most significant manifestations of Christianity in Mozambique.

Pentecostalism in Madagascar: *Fifohazana* (Wake Up!)

The history of Pentecostalism in Madagascar is similar to that of Mozambique. Madagascar is a large island in the Indian Ocean off the southeastern coast of Africa. In the two decades following independence from France in 1960, the country was under a harsh Marxist government that resulted in sociopolitical and ethnic unrest until the beginning of a structural adjustment program in 1988. It was also around this time when Pentecostalism started experiencing unprecedented expansion.

But we must begin with the African-initiated, Pentecostal-type movements that have been present in Madagascar from the later 1800s. The first manifestations of these groups on this island nation also derived from a revival movement. In Madagascar, these indigenous revivals were called *Fifohazana*, "awakening" or "revival," a term that is of Malagasy origin. As in Mozambique, the revivals emerged independently of any Western missionary movement or mainline Christian influence.[37] Hence, these did not follow along the lines of mainline or mission-founded churches but started and existed parallel to or alongside mainline Christianity. These versions of African-initiated, Pentecostal-type churches thus developed spontaneously within Madagascar not only with no associations or links to Western Pentecostalism, but also as, in fact, despised, ostracized, and hereticized sects by both mainline and Western Pentecostal churches when they later arrived. This observation has been made elsewhere by scholars such as J. Kwabena Asamoah-Gyadu, who notes that the Pentecostal-type spirituality that was expressed by many indigenous prophet figures in the early stages was "sometimes scandalously perceived by church authority as belonging to the 'occult.'"[38] Yet this did not deter these so-called prophets from expressing their spirituality in an African way. As with the Mozambican case, these initial indigenous Pentecostal-type movements in Madagascar emphasized a communal spirituality and an indigenous apprehension of the Holy Spirit through healing and exorcism, prophecy, and speaking in tongues.

Scholars have dated the first *Fifohazana*, called "Disciples of the Lord," back to 1894 to a movement started by Rainisoalambo, an obscure traditionalist healer-turned-revivalist prophet.[39] The movement was at least in part a response to socioeconomic and political hardship resulting from heavy taxation imposed on the peasants by the traditional Malagasy leadership in its effort to resist French colonial ambitions. However, the Madagascans were overpowered between 1894 and 1896, and the island was declared a French colony.[40] Yet in this context, *Fifohazana* reclaimed the cultural values of Malagasy. For instance, although Western missionaries had minimized the religious authority and political role of women in society, the *Fifohazana* women exerted both ecclesial and social influence.[41] From these humble beginnings, and through the process of Africanization of the Christian faith, the movement has grown into many forms and expressions, some with links to the original revival movements, with others developing out of interfaces with mainline and other churches. Arguably, the later classical and neo-Pentecostal arrivals have not been as impactful as the *Fifohazana* movements in Madagascar.

Classical Pentecostal churches in Madagascar include the *Assembles de Dieu* (Assemblies of God), which was started in 1968 by George Burki, who was sent by the Assemblies of God in France.[42] From another perspective, this specific church emerged from a schism of the former *Fiangonana Protestanta* Malagasy (French Reformed Church) and a mission of the Swedish Free

Mission. But the church only began to grow in the 1990s in partnership with the Assemblies of God USA and other French missionaries, as well as with local Malagasy preachers. As of 2001, there were 115 Assemblies of God congregations with 10,000 total members and 21,000 affiliates in Madagascar.[43] Even slightly earlier, the United Pentecostal Church was established by the Denzil and Frieda Richardson family from North America between 1969 and 1970.[44] In 2015, the United Pentecostal Church in Madagascar had over 75,000 members claimed for 900 congregations and 600 pastors.[45] Another classical Pentecostal network of churches is the Apostolic Church of Madagascar, founded in 1968 by priest Benjamin Diedericks.[46] As of 1995, there were 123 congregations in Madagascar with 14,000 members and 25,000 affiliates.[47] These classical Pentecostal churches have retained strong links with North American and South African Pentecostalism and, perhaps for these reasons, are still struggling to express their spirituality in distinctively Madagascan terms.

Neo-Pentecostalism has also gradually accelerated and intensified subsequent to the period of structural adjustment in Madagascar, especially since the 1990s.[48] *Jesosy Mamonjy* (Jesus Saves) is a neo-Pentecostal church that began as a rural phenomenon and became active in urban centers only by 1999. It now has a stadium-sized church structure in the Malagasy capital, Antananarivo, which belongs to the largest-reported congregation in Madagascar.[49] Other large neo-Pentecostal churches on the island are the Rhema Family Church of Madagascar that started in 1991, with roots in Pastor Ray McCauley's South African Rhema Bible Church in Johannesburg, and the *Pentecotiste Afaka* (Pentecostalism Saves).[50] The expansion of these churches has been precipitated by the critical roles of deliverance ministry and healing, which are well documented by scholars.[51] The success of these facets of Pentecostal spirituality in Madagascar cannot be overlooked, and their popularity has raised concerns within the mainline churches, which are increasingly worried about losing their members. In addition, some neo-Pentecostal churches, such as Christ Embassy Madagascar, have roots in Nigerian neo-Pentecostalism, with their emphases on spiritual warfare and the gospel of prosperity as *the* underlying Pentecostal experience. These specific expressions of Pentecostalism have also been threatening to the mainline churches because they have provided a therapeutic space for those experiencing traumas of social disruption and economic hardship in the Madagascan context.[52]

Contours for Pentecostal Theologies in Southeast Africa

As historiographically framed and outlined above in the first two sections, Pentecostalism in southeast Africa is constituted both by Western mission-related churches and African-initiated-type movements.[53] This section on theological reflections thus follows what I have called the *marginalized perspective* of African traditions central to the African-initiated Pentecostal movements. I will suggest that the way forward for southeast African Pentecostal theology is to build on the foundations laid by African traditional spirituality.

Before outlining some of the contours of Pentecostal theologies in this region, it is important to note that there is a growing literature on Pentecostal theology in Africa.[54] What is it, precisely, that can be observed, described, and qualified as Pentecostal theology in this continent? Clearly, African Pentecostal Christians are beginning to reflect on and articulate their theological beliefs. The intention in what follows is not to repeat what has been generally observed and described. Rather, for reasons to be indicated, our purpose is to deduce some theological features of the movements that were initiated by African revivalist prophets, especially in the southeastern African region.

As shown above, some Pentecostal churches, particularly those initiated by Africans, have gained prominence in southeast Africa because they function with an indivisible cosmology that is both simple and complex, one that embraces the world as a totality. Such cosmological assumptions address African challenges within the paradigm of the primal imagination by making room for, if not also inviting, theologies of liberation, theologies of gender justice and equality, theologies of transformation, theologies of empowerment, and theologies of holistic spiritual ities, all of which are informed by African religio-cultural philosophy and wisdom. While the attitude of the early Christian missionaries in Africa was to reject African traditional ways of perceiving and responding to reality, the early African-initiated revivalist movements in Mozambique and Madagascar, such as *Fifohazana*, embraced the African traditional worldview. They drew parallels between biblical perceptions of reality and those of the African cultures that empowered and facilitated the process of Africanization of Christian faith.[55] There are many theological themes that might be identified as central to Pentecostalism in southeast Africa, but for the purpose of this chapter I suggest two overarching hermeneutical points of departure for understanding the African Pentecostal theological imagination.

Theologies of life

In order to appreciate Pentecostalism in southeast Africa, it is important to understand the worldview undergirding African-initiated Christian beliefs and practices as based on the quest for the fullness of life.[56] In this system, religions have a social and functional purpose. Rather than being oriented first and foremost toward a spiritual Supreme Being, religions are instruments, vehicles, and "moral traditions of abundant life."[57] This primary purpose of religion appears to have been marginalized through the clash of African traditions and Western missionary Christianity.

The concept of life establishes both the context and the content of African religio-theological imagination. Africanists have argued that life is an all-inclusive and central symbol for making sense of the African worldview.[58] In African thought, "right" understandings of the notion of life bring with them cardinal principles, such as transformation, justice, hospitality, dignity, empowerment, human rights, exorcism, etc., whereas the by-products of any "wrong" understanding lead to destructive behaviors and actions. Right actions promote life and oppose selfishness, greediness, individualism, exploitation, corruption, etc. These commitments and values are presumed by many Africans, including those in Pentecostal churches in the southeastern African context.

Vincent Mulago defines these values as focused on the "whole life, individual inasmuch as it is received by each being which exists, and communal or collective inasmuch as each being draws from a common source of life."[59] God is not only the ultimate Source, but also the Life itself that permeates and animates all reality. God is Life, the inescapable One who pervades all existence. There is an indivisibility of creation life and God. Life is what God is in Himself. It is what God has in common with all creation. By sharing life with creation, God shares His own being and essence. Life does not exist in God; it is the nature of God, an attribute of God. This means that life can never be a personal possession, as no one owns life, but all creation participates in the divinity and the being of God. Elsewhere, I have argued for the oneness of God and creation—the God who is one with creation without losing Godself as the One who is above and transcends creation.[60] There is a tension here, in that "God is above" and cannot be equated with creation, but simultaneously God is also in creation and apparent in and through creation. Such views inform the African Pentecostal understanding of the interconnectedness or oneness of reality, held together by God. It is the basis for the African view of all existence as sacred. Life is a cohesive social entity and the basis of critical solidarity. On the one hand, there is awareness that life has been distorted and that religious movements have been struggling against the forces that inhibit life. On the other hand, the resurgence of life-centered theologies across the African content has also inspired and invigorated African Pentecostal thinking about the Holy Spirit of life as a starting point for doing theology.

Southeast African Pentecostals, understood according to the broad and inclusive definition of this chapter, have also presumed this distinctively African way of thinking that prioritizes the promotion of life as the purpose and foundation of Christian belief and practice. It is not what human beings do to God that is most important but what they do to one another and the rest of creation, which as such is inevitably done also unto God. Therefore, "Life as a starting point and abiding context of hermeneutics is not only important; it is a reality that imposes itself."[61] Southeast African Pentecostals have always believed that encountering God has implications for and applications to their life situations, even if at least classical Pentecostals and many neo-Pentecostals have not always utilized this specifically African frame of reference in their religious thinking. Yet from this perspective, the biblical accounts can also be seen as narratives of people struggling to understand, first, the meaning of life within their cultural context and, second, how that life continues to flourish in the midst of tension, anti-life forces, and contradictions in relation to the ultimate Life and Source—God.

Theologies of the Spirit: African pneumatology

The pervasiveness of pneumatology in southeast African Pentecostalism can thus be seen to be part and parcel of the African traditional understanding of life. The realms of the spiritual and the material or physical are interwoven in one fabric called life. There is therefore an undeniable indivisibility between these dimensions of reality. In many African societies, the word for *Spirit* means "wind" or "breath" and is perceived as life immanent in all things.[62] As argued above, the life force is that which an individual receives from God and has in common with God and which gives being and life, strength and power, that harmonizes a person with other human beings, other creatures, and the cosmos.[63] In African thought, there is no distinction between the Spirit and God: God as the Spirit is Life who animates the cosmos. The whole creation is a web of life woven together and filled by life, which is the divine Spirit. The Spirit who is experienced in daily concrete realities is the one who enables realization of the fullness of life. The Spirit of God is encountered more concretely through other human beings who embody the divine Spirit. That is why the theologies of African Pentecostals are embedded in and derivative from the concrete realities of the people within their contexts. The Spirit of God within them empowers them to engage with daily contradictions and overcome hostile spiritual forces directed against them and also enables their enjoyment of life as it should be experienced in the world. This pneumatological concept of power in the African worldview carries with it the ability, dignity, and capacity to resist all forms of dehumanization, exploitation, and oppression, whether physical or spiritual. The divine Spirit immanent in the created order also brings about the ability of individuals within their communities to understand themselves and their place in the local and cosmic environments.

This perspective imbues southeast African Pentecostalism, urging its members and adherents beyond a merely spiritualized and privatized pneumatology (and concomitant otherworldly soteriology) toward an interpersonal, social, environmental, and cosmic pneumatology, one that encompasses fully a "materio-spiritual" way of life. As such, the Holy Spirit is understood as the transforming power of God that repels all anti-life forces. The traditional "African quest for power thus becomes fertile ground for a Christian pneumatology incarnated in Africa. The omnipotence of God is revealed through the Holy Spirit."[64] The Spirit is a Spirit of liberation who gives believers power, delivers them from evil spirits, and emancipates humanity from life-denying forces that threaten their well-being and sociopolitical and economic progress. Thus, many African Pentecostals seek to build an inclusive community through the power of the Holy Spirit, who empowers them to incarnate God's love in the presence of the marginalized and suffering. This comforting Spirit is manifest through the ministry of healing and the visitation of and caring for the elderly and the sick.

Relatedly, the Spirit also, in effect, fights on behalf of believers, and this is seen in their ongoing Spirit-empowered spiritual warfare. The Pentecostals believe that believers are involved in a daily struggle against principalities and powers that can be defeated only by and through the empowerment of the Holy Spirit. The pastors thus engage in spiritual warfare prayers on behalf of their members, and some even conduct exorcisms so that people can be freed from perceived demonic bondages and live victorious lives.

Conclusion

This chapter suggests that Pentecostalism in Mozambique and Madagascar is the fruit of both indigenous and missionary initiatives. Over the last century, these movements have managed gradually to reconfigure the way of being church and doing ministry in southeast Africa. They present themselves as providing new forms of thinking, speaking, acting, and doing ministry that affirm the full humanity of African people while providing a bridge for dialogue between African traditional cultures and contemporary global Christian and Evangelical currents. Although there is a growing literature on African Pentecostalism in Africa, much more work is needed to understand how the movement has unfolded and continues to grow, specifically in the southeastern region of the continent; and, given the size of Africa and the variety of African cultural expressions—not to mention the multiplicity of Pentecostal types of Christianity—much more research is also needed in order to understand the nature, the character, and the emerging theologies of Pentecostal spirituality in its diverse African-initiated, classical, and neo-Pentecostal forms as we move further into the twenty-first century.

Chapter 14

Rising to the Challenge: Pentecostalism in Angola, Botswana, and Namibia

Trad Nogueira-Godsey

THE GENERAL TRAJECTORIES of Pentecostalism throughout southwestern Africa are quite similar to each other and consistent with renewal movements in other sub-Saharan African (SSA) nations. Because of this, and because of the fact that their numbers are slightly less impressive, many researchers of African Pentecostal Christianity choose to focus on other SSA nations. However, though the trajectories may be similar, the nature and essence of Pentecostalism is unique to each context. There are several factors contributing to the composition of these various "faces" of Pentecostalism in Angola, Botswana, and Namibia, some of which will be discussed in this paper.

While research into Pentecostalism in SSA nations has provided a great deal of understanding and nuance to the movement, the limitations inherent to any single study have often led to a more general approach to the study of African Pentecostalism. This is not to say that findings from research into African Pentecostalism generally or specifically in other African nations (such as Ghana, South Africa, or Zimbabwe, among others) cannot be applied to similar movements originating from or imported to Angola, Botswana, and Namibia, respectively. On the contrary, we see many of the same mechanisms at work in the nations in focus here, as we do elsewhere in SSA nations. For example, Joel Robbins's and Rijk van Dijk's assertions about anthropological approaches to understanding conversion to Pentecostalism find resonance with researchers studying the phenomenon throughout the region.[1] Likewise, Allan Anderson's work on Pentecostalism in South Africa is a useful starting point to understand African Pentecostalism more generally and does not require "unlearning" much studying the movement further north.[2]

Moreover, the distinctions that can be made among Pentecostals in the nations under focus here are inextricably tied to the respective sociopolitical histories and contemporary contexts. Approaching Pentecostalism in the framework of these contrasting sociopolitical environments gives a twofold perspective of Pentecostalism that both illuminates the elasticity and durability of Pentecostal spirituality while pointing to important factors that have had a hand in shaping the global movement to accommodate locally experienced realities. The fact that many aspects of Pentecostalism can be recognized across these three nations, despite the disparity in political stability, languages spoken, historical origins of Pentecostalism in each respective country, and the influences of various colonial powers, points to the cohesive essence of Pentecostalism and its formidability in overcoming all manner of obstacles in its path. At the same time, the unique influences of these and other factors cannot be ignored at those points in which Pentecostalism in southwestern Africa take on exceptional, or even peculiar, characteristics.

African Independent Churches

Any discussion on African Pentecostal-Charismatic Christianity must pay respect to the classification of African Independent

Churches (AICs) as included or excluded in this amorphous category. This has become a contentious issue in scholarship but perhaps even more contentious among believers on the ground. However, it is not as simple as including or excluding AICs from the breadth of African Pentecostalism. Many, but not all, have historical roots in Pentecostal mission churches, and many, but not all, share common practices with Pentecostal churches, such as miraculous healing and demon exorcism. For the purposes of this paper, I have refrained from drawing clear lines to demarcate where Pentecostalism ends and African Independent Christianity begins. While the "gray area" that currently exists in scholarship between these two branches of Christianity poses problems for researchers on either or both subjects, it is important to recognize the fluid and porous edges between them in order to simultaneously pay respect to the various (and sometimes contradictory) boundaries that the believers themselves erect and the undeniably shared characteristics identified by scholars. In this paper, I use the terms *Pentecostal* and *Pentecostalism* not so much as identifying markers but rather as descriptive terms to denote various affinities that are commonly understood to be associated with the movement in Africa. Therefore, this paper focuses on African Pentecostalism with the understanding that not all groups discussed would self-identify as such.

However, even here one must be careful not to group these affinities in ways that favor predominantly North American and European Pentecostal characteristics. Pentecostals have always drawn on various traditions (both Christian and non-Christian) to produce an eclectic spirituality, irrespective of geographic location. The same is no less true for Pentecostals in Angola, Botswana, and Namibia. Therefore, just because we may identify a particular characteristic as distinctly African does not necessarily make such a characteristic any less Pentecostal.

These eclectic spiritualities in the African context are often given their own classification as African Christianity or African Independent Christianity and are sometimes treated as something wholly other than Christianity in Africa, or even Pentecostalism in Africa. This classification is sometimes used to distinguish between that which was imported and that which came into being indigenously. Of course, the lines here are fuzzy because all Christianities are imports to southern Africa in the most basic sense. More to the point, however, African Independent Christianity arose *in response to* colonialism and its religion, and in this sense the differentiation is warranted. Nonetheless, such distinctions draw attention to boundaries created by colonial powers and often do more to reinforce the dichotomies of power and oppression while simultaneously ignoring, particularly in the case of Pentecostalism, the eclectic composition of faith that can be found the world over. We therefore must be careful when we make such distinctions based on the qualitative aspects of African Pentecostalism and Pentecostalism in Africa.

This is not to say that Pentecostalism should be used as a catchall term, but rather I merely intend to illustrate that the appropriation of non-Christian rituals into Pentecostalism is not only an African phenomenon (for example, Candomblé rituals in the Universal Church of the Kingdom of God in Brazil and Angola) and that to isolate African Christianity as something wholly other because of such integrations creates a barrier along colonial lines that does not necessarily exist for Pentecostals in other parts of the world that have similar histories of adopting local/indigenous aspects of worship and ritual. Therefore, the inclusion of African traditional rituals and practices does not preclude such rituals from being viewed as Pentecostal in this study.

Externalities

Traditionally, Pentecostalism in the West has been understood by scholars as a product of, or response to, modernity and all its trappings. As such, Pentecostalism is seen as having a close, but not always cozy, relationship with social change. This holds true, to some degree, with the history of Pentecostalism in Africa, which cannot be extrapolated from the context of colonization and exploitation. Below, I will briefly discuss these historical contexts and the earliest arrival of Pentecostalism in Angola, Botswana, and Namibia, respectively.

Angola

Throughout the early period of Portuguese occupation, the main interest in Angola was to supply the slave trade to the Americas, with little attention given to building up society in Angola. Consequently, Portugal struggled to administrate the colony and eventually was forced to give up control over the region due to mounting turmoil at home. In 1975, a *coup d'etat* occurred in Portugal known as the Carnation Revolution, or *Revolução dos Cravos* in Portuguese. The military government agreed to give all remaining Portuguese colonies independence, including Angola. This sparked contests among the many political parties, all of which had their own armed wings. These confrontations became bloody quickly and led to a civil war among the many groups competing for control over the nation. The civil war lasted, with some interruptions, until 2002, when many of the political parties began to dismantle their armies.

Angolans inherited the religion of their occupiers, Roman Catholicism, and to this day roughly half of Angolans identify as Catholic. The remaining half of the population adheres to various mainline Protestant groups (including Pentecostal), AICs, and African Traditional Religions (ATRs). Few Angolans, by comparison with Botswana and Namibia, are exclusive followers of African Traditional Religions, though elements of ATRs are prominent in AICs. Portugal's religious influence in the country in recent years has dissipated and been replaced by missionaries of Brazilian origin. As such, Pentecostalism has seen significant growth, particularly through the Brazilian *Igreja Universal do Reino de Deus*, or Universal Church of the Kingdom of God (UCKG). The church has its roots as a Charismatic Brazilian church (established in 1977) that has integrated various indigenous rituals into the practice of Christianity. Many of these rituals have historical ties to African Traditional Religions, brought to Brazil through the slave trade and ensconced into the religious landscape through various spiritualist movements, such as Candomblé. This has created the unusual situation of Brazilian missionaries coming to Angola to proselytize a Christianity that has elements of African religion sewn into it. Paul Freston has called the UCKG's success in SSA nations a prime example of the "transnationalization of Third World evangelical religion."[3]

Botswana

When Robert Moffat and his team of missionaries from the London Missionary Society arrived in what is today Botswana in 1824, they discovered that Tswana religion was deeply ingrained into every facet of Tswana life. Without a founder, sacred text, or clear sense of origins, Tswana faith was indispensably part of the Tswana understanding of the world and naturally composed the fabric of Tswana society. Tswana religion had no creeds or doctrines that must be taught but rather represented life itself and was lived rather than practiced as such.

Despite the chief characteristics of a belief in a supreme and omnipotent deity, *Modimo*, belief in ancestral mediators, and in lesser deities, Europeans refused to recognize Tswana systems of belief as a religion and were blind to its strong monotheistic aspects. Christian missionaries belittled their beliefs as mere witchcraft and were adamantly opposed to Tswana rituals and beliefs being integrated into the Christianity they sought to impose. However, it was not always clear which practices and beliefs held by Batswana[4] were, in fact, religious, as the boundary between sacred and profane was not always pronounced. This led many European observers to the conclusion that Batswana had no belief in God or that their God was of little consequence. As James Amanze has pointed out, "This, of course, was a misconception for God has always been real to the African people as they experience his power in the world in all aspects of their lives."[5]

Unsurprisingly, this condescension did not make the missionaries' activities any easier. However, the missionaries themselves were already associated with military conquest and subjugation, an association that they were not always ready to distance themselves from. Amanze elaborates:

> It is interesting to note that quite often when Christianity came to Africa it was like a military expedition. The early missionaries looked upon themselves as engaged in a mortal battle against Satan. This Satan was disguised and active through the network of false African religious values, traditions and practices. Their eradication symbolized the fall of Satan and the victory of Christ over the powers of the devil and the coming into being of the light of salvation.[6]

This approach to mission and ministry caused many conflicts between Christians and the Batswana, with the former on a mission to eradicate evil from Tswana culture and the latter facing an onslaught against life as they knew it.

Not long after Pentecostalism emerged in the United States did missionaries, full of zeal to take this gospel to all corners of the earth, arrive in South Africa, and from there to Botswana. Amanze recognizes the Reverend Buller Moukangoe and his wife as the first Pentecostal missionaries (from the Pentecostal Holiness Church) to Botswana, who entered the country from Mafeking (today Mafikeng, South Africa) and ministered itinerantly from village to village, praying for the sick. Several churches were established and incorporated into the Transvaal Conference of Pentecostal Holiness churches. When Botswana achieved independence in 1966, a separate conference was established eight years later called the Annual Conference of Botswana. At this time, there were 24 congregations and 903 members registered with the Pentecostal Holiness conference. Other Pentecostal missions to Botswana during the same period include the Church of God of Prophecy (registered in Botswana in 1973) and the Holiness Union Church, a Swedish Pentecostal organization brought to Botswana by the missionary Berth Axkle in 1972.[7]

Namibia

Similar to Botswana, the first Christians to bring the gospel to Namibia were missionaries from the Cape Colony in what is today South Africa. The London Missionary Society arrived in 1805 and began ministering and building infrastructure. They constructed the town of Bethanie in 1811 and built a church there that still stands today. However, religious influence in the region came more from German Lutheran missionaries after Germany established its protectorate there, known as German South-West Africa. Finnish missionaries also successfully established Lutheran missions of their own in the region beginning in 1870.

The discovery of diamonds in the region attracted thousands of German settlers in the early years of the twentieth century. However, the German colony was placed under South Africa's rule (which was a member of the British Commonwealth) after Germany's defeat in World War I. While South-West Africa, as it was known, was not officially incorporated into South Africa, it was represented by a white minority South African Parliament and was generally considered to be the "fifth province." Because of this, the story of Pentecostalism in Namibia cannot be easily separated from that of South Africa, meaning that much of the early work done by Pentecostals in Namibia was done by those who were disciples of the ministry of John G. Lake in the early twentieth century.[8]

Due to the imposition of apartheid practices and the harsh treatment of indigenous peoples, Namibians struggled for independence in much the same way that South Africans struggled for freedom from apartheid. This struggle culminated in a long and arduous transition from South African rule to administration of the territory by the United Nations to independence on March 21, 1990.

Geopolitics

It may be argued that the geopolitical scene plays a much larger role when considering the state and trajectory of Pentecostalism on the African continent. This has to do with the size and nature of renewal movements as well as the pressing social issues that governments seem to lack interest in or are unable to adequately address. As Pentecostalism grows, so do expectations about the scope of its ability to contribute to social welfare and to build up civil society.

These expectations are all the more compounded by the desperation created by ineffective governments and corrupt politicians. This is a common theme among countries in southern and West Africa, where Pentecostalism is growing most rapidly, though the details and nuances are significant and worth a look here.

Angola

Situated on the southwestern African coast, Angola has a unique colonial legacy that has, until recently, been characterized by long periods of war and infighting. Poverty remains the biggest threat to Angolan life, which has been exasperated by deep-seated corruption.

The Angolan Civil War has had an enormous impact on all aspects of Angolan life. Almost the entire white Portuguese population fled Angola after independence and left the country without a stable and working infrastructure. Refugees remain reluctant to return to Angola to begin rebuilding life there for many reasons, not least of which is the presence of thousands of landmines littered throughout the countryside.

Since independence, Angola has had only two acting heads of state. President Augustinho Neto served as Angola's first president, reigning from 1975 until his death in 1979. As the leader of the Popular Movement for the Liberation of Angola (MPLA), which had close ties with Marxist-Leninist ideology, Neto received support from the Soviet Union and other Communist sympathizers. He was succeeded by Jose Eduardo dos Santos, who continues to serve as president to this day.

Angola's government is generally regarded as one of the most corrupt regimes in Africa, and, despite announcements that he would step down, President dos Santos has remained the face of the MPLA and the Angolan government. After taking power, dos Santos's wealth began to grow immensely, as did that of his immediate family. After various anticorruption measures were instituted requiring that the president have no financial interests in large corporations, dos Santos transferred the majority of his assets to his daughter, Isabel, who is now one of the richest women in Africa. Even still, dos Santos's government has been horribly inefficient with managing revenue from various investments, particularly the large sums of revenue derived from the exportation of oil. The population, however, is left to suffer in the poverty left behind by war. Survival itself is not an easy feat, with the average life expectancy for males in Angola just above thirty-seven years, the second lowest in Africa.

Botswana

Botswana is the third least densely populated country in Africa. Landlocked Lesotho, a nation bordered on all sides by the Republic of South Africa, has a slightly larger population than Botswana, despite being almost twenty times smaller in area. Even though Christians compose roughly the same percentage of the population in both Botswana and Ghana, the major difference in overall population size (Ghana has over twelve times the population of Botswana) is certainly one of the factors influencing the disproportionate interest in Ghanian Christianity by the scholarly community.

The Botswana Democratic Party has won every presidential election since independence in 1966. Despite this de facto one-party system (though other political parties are gaining ground), Botswana has an impressively stable government, which has also held free and open elections on schedule since independence. The current president, Ian Khama, took office in 2008 and is the second-born son of Botswana's first president, Seretse Khama, who was a prominent leader in the struggle for independence.

President Khama comes from a royal lineage; he is the great-grandson of Khama III, king of the Bamangwato people that successfully transferred their leadership to the democratic setting after independence. The former commander of Botswana's defense force, President Ian Khama is portrayed as one who does not stand on ceremony and one who takes decisive action. Though critics have warned against his authoritarian tendencies, Khama is generally seen to be responsible for Botswana's remarkable economic growth and political stability.

Ian Khama identifies as a Christian and has the support of various Christian organizations in the country, including the Botswana Council of Churches. He has used his faith to justify his attempts to reduce the consumption of alcohol in his country, which he made a priority in his inaugural address, saying, "Abuse of alcohol is one of the ills that we have to address as a nation."[9] By and large, however, not much has been made of Khama's personal spirituality, though he is recognized as the descendent of Khama III, who converted to Christianity and was baptized by the Lutheran Church through the London Missionary Society. Khama III is often credited with transforming Botswana into a de facto Christian nation through his personal commitment to faith and breaking with African traditions that were believed to be un-Christian, such as polygamy.

Namibia

The earliest inhabitants of modern-day Namibia were the nomadic San, Damara, and Namaqua peoples, but these were later joined by various groups of Bantu tribes during the Bantu expansion of the fourteenth century. Large swaths of desert kept the population relatively sparse, though the discovery of diamonds and other precious metals did attract Europeans and led to the creation of a thriving mining industry. Much like Botswana, Namibia remains sparsely populated and has relative economic, political, and social stability. However, the very dry climate and the poor quality of soil has historically made agriculture a small and toilsome enterprise.

Namibia's first president, Sam Nujoma, is a practicing Lutheran who attended a Finnish missionary school in his youth. Religious ideology featured little in Nujoma's presidency and public life, though Nujoma has been outspoken against homosexuality, even calling for the arrest, deportation, and imprisonment of homosexuals in 2001.[10] Nujoma's prime minister, Hage Geingob, ascended to the presidency in 2015 as Namibia's third president after the two terms served by former president Hifikepunye Pohamba. All three of Namibia's ruling presidents have come from the SWAPO (South West Africa People's Organization) political party and were immensely popular when elected to office.

Namibia is unique among the three nations under focus here because of the relatively large population of white settlers, composed mostly of people from English, Dutch (Afrikaner), and German descent. As a territory administered by South Africa, Namibia was ruled by a white minority and implemented the system of apartheid to keep black and colored populations from obtaining wealth, political power, and education. Tensions among the races remain high, and religious groups are among those that have contributed to both easing this tension (through encouraging multiracialism in worship) and increasing this tension (through maintaining implicit racial boundaries in church).

Contemporary Religious Landscape

Unlike some other African countries, Angola, Botswana, and Namibia share an overwhelming Christian majority, and one does not expect this to change in the near future. Rather, the major changes that can be anticipated with regard to the religious landscape are intra-Christian, with major shifts already being seen away from the denominational heritages of the former colonizers and toward various renewal movements. Yet despite these broad commonalities, a closer look reveals significant distinctions among these nations.

Angola

Religion in Angola continues to reach new levels of vitality following peace from civil war in 2002. As Ruy Llera Blanes has pointed out, "Religion (especially Christianity) now has a central role in Angolan society which would have been inconceivable just a few years before the end of the war."[11] In addition to war, the MPLA, which was the contested ruling party, suppressed many forms of religion, inspired by Marxist-Leninist ideological stances against religion.

As stated earlier, Catholics comprise roughly half of the religious landscape in Angola, with other Christian groups making up the majority of the rest. There are two African Christian groups of no small consequence operating in the country that differ from other AICs: the Tokoist Church and the Kimbanguists. These two groups are often referred to as syncretic, even when other African Christianities are not, due to the relatively recent formation and the deification of its respective founders. Both groups are named after their founders, Simão Toko and Simon Kimbangu, respectively. While the two groups have little connection between them (Kimbanguism is an export from the former Belgian Congo, with over five million followers, whereas the Tokoist Church was founded by an Angolan mission student after a prophetic experience while in Leopoldville, today known as Kinshasa), both founders came from the Baptist tradition, and both groups hold on to many Baptist elements of worship. The Tokoists are now a transnational movement self-identified as the Angolan Christian Church.

Todd Johnson's survey "The Global Demographics of the Pentecostal and Charismatic Renewal" distinguishes between three waves of Pentecostalism, or, as he calls it, "The Renewal."[12] They are Pentecostal, Charismatic, and neo-Charismatic. Those that Johnson refers to as *Pentecostal* refer only to the older, more established Pentecostal churches, such as the Assemblies of God. *Charismatic* refers to members of non-Pentecostal churches that have experienced baptism in the Holy Spirit and the accompanying gifts. The term *neo-Charismatic*, for Johnson, refers to the numerous independent churches and organizations that have no direct ties with Pentecostalism but share many of the traits often attributed to Spirit-filled believers.

Angola, according to Johnson, is a country with significantly higher numbers of Pentecostals than Charismatics or neo-Charismatics,[13] though it is unclear if one of Angola's most populous churches, the Brazilian-based Universal Church of the Kingdom of God (UCKG), is classified as neo-Charismatic or Pentecostal. While the UCKG fits more closely with Johnson's description of neo-Charismatics, it is heavily dependent upon Brazilian missionaries and support, which exemplifies an organizational model that Johnson claims is more closely affiliated with the Pentecostals. Or, just as likely, Johnson does not consider the UCKG to be part of the Pentecostal/renewal movement spectrum at all.

Paul Freston places the UCKG somewhere between classifications of Pentecostalism and African Independent Christianity.[14] While the UCKG makes wide use of ritualistic and symbolic objects, they condemn some practices that are, in some cases, tolerated by AICs, such as polygyny and so-called witchcraft. The success of the UCKG in Angola is all the more remarkable, considering the church-planting model used by UCKG leadership, which seeks to maintain centralized control in Brazil and frequently utilizes Brazilian pastors and missionaries in the running of churches abroad. While this model is not unique to the UCKG, the success of this model in Angola is astounding, considering the long and fervent nationalistic spirit cultivated by such groups as the MLPA. Freston notes that this model may be an obstacle to further growth of the UCKG in sub-Saharan Africa, but there are many other factors that give the UCKG an advantage over other religious movements. Perhaps most importantly, the UCKG is a church born from the third world and is no stranger to the adversities people face in impoverished locations. "Globally speaking, the [UCKG] is almost exclusively a phenomenon of *Christian poverty*. Where Christians are not poor, or the poor are not Christian, it fares badly," says Freston.[15]

Botswana

Botswana is among the most Christianized nations in southern Africa, with most estimates hovering around 70 percent Christian of the two million Batswana in the country. With such a sparsely populated nation, it is no surprise that African Traditional Religions have held a particularly strong following even after the introduction of Christianity. In the last twenty years, however, there has been a rapid decline in the number of adherents of ATRs and a significant increase in Batswana claiming Christianity as their identifying faith. Though the factors pushing this shift in religious makeup are difficult to pin down, the numbers suggest that Pentecostal churches and AICs are largely responsible for drawing Batswana away from ATRs. In 2003, there were seventy-five registered Pentecostal churches in Botswana, a figure that excludes AICs. Fidelis Nkomazana supposes that Pentecostalism is growing more rapidly than the AICs and is poised to become the dominant faith in the near future.[16] He also notes that Pentecostalism is particularly popular among immigrants to Botswana from other parts of Africa.

Namibia

In the years following independence, Namibia's religious landscape had shifted to include much larger numbers of Evangelical Christians, as well as Charismatic and Pentecostal Christians. In 1990, it was estimated that only 2.5 percent of the population was Pentecostal. In the years to come, however, many Pentecostal missionaries would establish themselves within Namibian borders and Pentecostals would expand their public presence through various media outlets.[17] In the media, religious broadcasting produced by the Namibian Broadcasting Corporation consisted of Evangelical and Pentecostal programming for all languages, except Afrikaans, which was still dominated by Dutch Reformed Christian programming.[18] All the while, Namibia boasted the highest percentage of Christians of any African country, with 90 percent of the population identifying with some form of the Christian faith (the majority of which were Lutheran). Pentecostal Churches in Namibia (both black and multiracial churches) were generally opposed to the apartheid system that was imposed on them by South Africa, though, according to Nico Horn, most opted out of joining the liberation struggle.[19]

Concomitantly with, and usually as, Pentecostal itinerant evangelists in Namibia are prosperity-theology preachers. The relationship between Pentecostal and Charismatic Christianity and prosperity theology is an uneasy one, not so much theologically as politically. Most Pentecostal churches would support some form or some aspects of prosperity theology, however diluted or secondary it may be. At the same time, almost all prosperity teachers in Namibia integrate Pentecostal and Charismatic spirituality and worship into their ministry. This overlap naturally causes confusion and often results in Pentecostalism becoming synonymous with prosperity teachings, which is even more polarizing than Pentecostal spirituality itself.

It should be noted that while prosperity teachings all over the world carry varying degrees of influence from American evangelists, either directly or indirectly, Namibian prosperity churches and rallies more closely resemble those that have come out of Nigeria. Evangelists such as David Oyedepo, Matthew Ashimolowo, and Yinka Yusuf have amassed great influence in SSA nations (and indeed abroad as well), and their influence is palpable in Namibian prosperity teachings. Nigerian prosperity theology teachings have been described as having a more African worldview, one that shuns asceticism and seeks abundance in all areas of one's life.[20] This further distinguishes the Word of Faith movement from prosperity evangelists in Namibia, as the former was introduced via South Africa as early as the 1940s and the latter the result of more recent Nigerian evangelization.[21]

Basilius Kasera has noted that the "father" of prosperity theology in Namibia is Haruna B. Goroh, a Nigerian evangelist and head of the Namibian-based Greater Love Ministries. Goroh arrived in Namibia claiming to have been sent by God and set up his ministry, which became increasingly focused on prosperity teachings. He was responsible for introducing many Namibians to various prosperity theology celebrities, such as Matthew Ashimolowo and Myles Munroe, among others, through the national conference Goroh began hosting, Faith Conventions. According to Kasera,

"These conferences mainly focused on issues related to financial breakthroughs, healings, discovering one's hidden potential and personal success."[22]

It has been postulated that Pentecostalism has achieved more success recently than other Christian denominations in Africa due to certain common affinities between Pentecostal spirituality and African Traditional Religious beliefs and practices, such as spiritual warfare, demon possession, and some gifts of the Spirit. Yet, as Kasera points out, the focus on abundance and wealth that is found in various forms of the prosperity gospel resonates with Africans on a deeper level, one that is consistent with traditional folklore and speaks to Africans' principal concerns of escaping poverty.[23]

Crossroads: Prosperity and HIV/AIDS

While Pentecostalism appears to be winning the race to gather adherents among other Christian denominations, among Pentecostals it appears that prosperity-gospel adherents are in the front of the pack. Generally, those ministries built foundationally on prosperity theology tend to be larger, have bigger budgets, and be more proficient with various media technologies. Naturally, these all contribute to greater penetration into the everyday lives of their followers and increase their visibility on the national and, indeed, the world stage.

In Amos Yong's typology of prosperity theology, he elucidates the various biblical sources for theological arguments employed.[24] The argument for prosperity is straightforward: biblical verses are used to paint a picture in which prosperity is God's intention for all Christians. Jesus's work among the poor and sick is illustrative of where many people begin their journey with Christ but not where they are expected to be perpetually. Yong goes on to elaborate on several other perspectives and possibilities regarding prosperity in the Christian gospel, but it is this argument for prosperity that is most prevalent in SSA nations and that which is usurping Pentecostalism more broadly on the continent.

Pentecostalism must be careful to differentiate itself from prosperity teachings more clearly, much like Protestants differentiate between Reformed and Arminian theologies. However, in Africa, this is not an easy task. The big budgets and extensive networks of prosperity-oriented ministries have dwarfed those Charismatic and Pentecostal churches that may have other feelings on prosperity. On the other hand, the success of these large ministries is heavily dependent upon the charismatic personalities that sit at the helm. In the United States, we have seen since the 1970s the devastating results one person's scandal or impropriety can have on enormous ministries. Therefore, while these prosperity-oriented ministries are indeed impressive and expansive, their dependence upon a single public figure or family points to a particular kind of fragility not shared by organizations of independent Pentecostal groups, especially those that are actively participating in Pentecostal networks and organizations.

Still, it is not clear that Pentecostals want to be differentiated from the theology of prosperity or what the actual economic and social consequences are of such a theology. Yong and others have suggested that the residual effects of belief in a prosperity theology may be a more positive attitude and a more committed work ethic, which could likely lead to the betterment of one's finances, though an ascetic lifestyle is generally not a prominent feature among prosperity-gospel leaders. On the contrary, many scholars have noted that rather than the spirit of capitalism, Pentecostal prosperity followers are being filled with the spirit of consumerism. Regardless, we are seeing increased diversity in perspective and approach with regard to the prosperity gospel, which Yong acknowledges: "The prosperity gospel should be recognized as not being all of one stripe, with the possibility that various aspects of its reception and performance may have positive economic outcomes."[25]

Another major concern for the countries in focus here is the ongoing HIV/AIDS pandemic. Botswana has the second-highest percentage of people aged fifteen to forty-nine living with HIV/AIDS in Africa, at 23.4 percent. Namibia also has an extremely high prevalence rate, at 13.4 percent.[26] Generally, Pentecostalism has been seen, along with some other Christian groups, as a hindrance in the fight against HIV/AIDS. It should be noted, however, that there are numerous faith-based organizations and churches that are actively involved in outreach to aid and support victims of HIV/AIDS. In Botswana, the Pentecostal churches have taken the lead in looking after children that have been orphaned by AIDS.

Still, there are some serious concerns regarding the Pentecostal approach to HIV/AIDS prevention and awareness. Many Christians from all over the world have discouraged the promotion of condom usage, believing that such an endorsement is an endorsement for premarital sex or infidelity. However, this has been changing in Africa, with some organizations (such as the Catholic Church in Namibia) becoming more ambiguous about their stance on condom usage and others (such as the Evangelical Lutheran Church in Namibia) adopting condom usage as a viable, though not preferred, means of preventing HIV infection. This has been called the ABCD strategy, where *A* stands for *abstinence*, *B* stands for *be faithful*, *C* stands for *condom*, and *D* stands for *death*. The *D* is added to justify the inclusion of *C*, meaning that if the choice is between contracting HIV (which is still a death sentence in many parts of Africa) or wearing a condom during sex, then the condom is the preferred choice.[27]

However, Pentecostals in SSA nations are among the most adamant and vocal opposers of condom usage and have even launched campaigns to urge people to stop using condoms. In Nicole Rigillo's research on condom usage in Namibia, she found that Pentecostal leaders seek "to convince Namibians that condoms are much less effective than popularly believed, mainly through the presentation of scientific data that calls condom efficacy into question."[28] Interestingly, the Pentecostal onslaught against condom usage is framed in scientific terms (the content of which is misinformed and/or falsified) rather than in religious terms and is disseminated through multiple media outlets and political channels. In an interview with Rigillo, a Namibian Pentecostal pastor explained:

> We're against condoms because 15% don't work…15% of condoms worldwide are not effective. And actually we've got statistics from Kenya, Cameroon, and some other countries: the more condoms that were sold, the higher HIV rate, the less condoms sold, the less HIV. We have thirty nine [*sic*] international scientists and investigators…look at the articles.[29]

It is not entirely clear the motivations behind framing their opposition in such terms. In some cases, these statistics can point to conspiratorial thinking, either geopolitical or spiritual. It may be the case that many Pentecostal leaders are simply misinformed regarding the efficacy of condoms, or maybe this is thought to be the most effective strategy to convince the public to shun condoms altogether.

Another factor fueling the Pentecostal disdain for condom usage is a strong belief in miraculous healing. Some leaders go so far as to claim that they have special HIV healing powers. But even where such claims are not made, there is nonetheless a belief in God's ability to cure any disease and His will for all believers to be healthy and whole. For many Pentecostals, it therefore becomes not only a matter of having faith in oneself to be disciplined and abstain from sex, but also a matter of having faith that God can protect you from disease or subsequently heal you from it.

Pentecostal leaders risk further alienation by spreading rumors, misinformation, and conspiracy theories. Pentecostal leaders should rather carefully consider their opposition to condom usage in the context of AIDS and decide if such opposition is warranted, and, if so, on what grounds their battle should be fought.

A promising development and potential model for Pentecostal organizations working in the context of HIV/AIDS comes from Botswana, where faculty from Pennsylvania State University and Botswana University collaborated with Christ-Citadel International Church (a branch of the nondenominational Pentecostal church based in Accra and founded by Anthony Appiah in 1978) from 2009 to 2011 to better understand the role and efficacy of Pentecostal approaches to HIV/AIDS, vis-à-vis church youths. The resulting conclusions from this research suggested that a combination of religious and secular approaches would best equip Pentecostal youths to protect themselves from contracting the virus and promote empathy and compassion for those living with the disease. This is representative of recent trends of research in public health that are increasingly incorporating faith perspectives and resources into analyses and recommendations.

Conclusion

Research into Pentecostalism in Africa is demonstrating its impressive and ever-expanding presence in public life. Increasingly, Pentecostals in southwestern Africa are tackling pressing social concerns and looking for faith-based responses to issues such as poverty, corruption, and public health, among others. This has increased the responsibilities and expectations of the Pentecostal church in these nations. In this process, Pentecostals are becoming more aware and better equipped to effectively deal with these social issues, though the tendency to spiritualize social issues sometimes serves as an obstacle to effecting change. Inevitably, the future of Pentecostalism in southwestern Africa will be closely tied to its ability to address the needs of the impoverished, oppressed, and diseased. To this end, Pentecostalism can benefit from increased and closer ties not only with other Pentecostal and mainline churches, but also with other religious organizations and secular groups to share this burden.

Chapter 15

The Rise of the Megachurches in South Africa

Maria Frahm-Arp

THE FOCUS OF this chapter is primarily on four different mega-style Pentecostal Charismatic churches in South Africa: His People, Grace Bible Church, Rhema Bible Church, and the Universal Church of the Kingdom of God. The Pentecostal movement grew out of the Holiness movement in America that recognized the gifts of the Holy Spirit. Many people date the beginning of the spread of the movement to the Azusa Street revival under William J. Seymour in 1906.[1] In 1908, the first missionaries of the movement came to South Africa. The fruit of their work resulted in the first wave of Pentecostal churches that included the Apostolic Faith Mission and Assemblies of God.[2] During the 1950s and 1960s, a second wave of Pentecostalism emerged that was deeply influenced by the Charismatic movement that swept through the mainline churches. In South Africa, Vineyard churches quickly grew into a popular independent Charismatic church. Amongst the mainline churches, St. Charles Catholic Church in Victory Park in Johannesburg was a leading light in the Charismatic movement during the 1970s and '80s. Those in the Charismatic movement advocated being filled with the Holy Spirit through laying on of hands but argued that speaking in tongues was not the only way in which an infilling of the Holy Spirit could be recognized.[3] Once baptized in the Spirit, believers could manifest any number of spiritual gifts, including prophecy, healings, speaking in tongues, interpreting tongues, and preaching.

Also during the late 1970s, a third wave of Pentecostalism began to emerge that was influenced by both the Charismatic and the Evangelical movements (the latter made popular by evangelists like Billy Graham). This new wave was marked by a wealth-and-health message in which everyone who believed and was filled with the Holy Spirit should expect to achieve material success and physical blessings in this life. This type of Christianity began to spread its message through various media, including US televangelists like Jimmy Swaggart, Kenneth Hagin, and Jim Bakker, who became superstars in some Christian circles. Quentin Schultze has described televanglistic programs as "a combination of self-help philosophy, variety show, personal soap opera and charismatic worship."[4]

In this chapter, I will look specifically at four different churches that are part of this third wave of Pentecostal Charismatic churches (PCCs). The research for this chapter is drawn primarily on my own research done over the last fourteen years. In 2001, I began by mapping the different PCCs in the Johannesburg area. This was followed by in-depth ethnographic research with His People and Grace Bible Church during 2003–2004. Much of my findings for this research are published in *Professional Women in Pentecostal Charismatic Churches in South Africa*.[5] Following this first extensive engagement with the churches, I have done subsequent ethnographic research in both churches during 2010 and 2014. Many of the interviews conducted in 2010 and 2014 were follow-up interviews with members I had met before. My research into Rhema was done during a series of three-month sessions between 2011 and 2014. During this time, I had in-depth, open-ended interviews with twenty members of both the Soweto and Randburg Rhema churches. The discussion in this chapter draws on this research and begins with the earliest of the mega Pentecostal Charismatic churches, Rhema Bible Church, and then looks at three very different types of PCCs that in 2014 were amongst the largest megachurches in South Africa. These should be understood amidst many other types of PCCs in South Africa, like the Apostolic Faith Mission, Assemblies of God, and thousands of smaller churches established throughout the country.[6]

Rhema Bible Church

Ray McCauley[7] began Rhema Bible Church in his parents' Johannesburg home in 1978 after returning to South Africa from the United States. He preached that those who accepted Jesus as their personal Lord and Savior were born again and must also be baptized in the Spirit. This was mostly evidenced by speaking in tongues but also by other gifts of the Spirit. Those born again and filled with the Spirit were also expected to enjoy material blessings and prosperity. His church services focused on praise and worship, lengthy sermons that encouraged people to commit their lives to God, and prayer for the things they needed. Each service ended with an altar call in which people could dedicate their lives to Christ anew. At all his services, people were encouraged to give money generously to the work of the church. By giving generously, people were expressing their faith in God, who would in turn bless them. McCauley quickly began to attract a growing congregation around himself, and within a short time Rhema Bible Church was born. From the beginning, preaching from the Word (the Bible) was a central aspect of Ray's ministry, and he encouraged all his members to be part of home cells (groups of believers who met regularly in each other's homes and studied the Bible together). The ever-growing groups of people who came to Rhema were almost all white South Africans.

As the church continued to grow during the 1980s, its members showed very little interest in the politics of South Africa. Many of them felt that Christianity should be separate from politics, and they were attracted to Rhema because, unlike many mainline churches, this congregation purported to have an apolitical message. Members of Rhema did not see Christianity as an exclusively white religion, and a group set up a new church in Soweto in the early 1980s that quickly attracted just over one hundred members. As the political tensions increased and the country was held in a state of emergency, the white Rhema missionaries had to give up their work in Soweto and handed the church over to a young man named Mosa Sono, who had been involved in some biblical studies at Rhema Church. This fledgling community in Soweto would go on to form the core members who started Grace Bible Church, which we will examine in more detail below. Although the move out of Soweto restricted Rhema's ministry amongst black South Africans, their church in the wealthy northern suburbs of Johannesburg continued to flourish. By the end of the 1980s, the face of South African politics and the elite status of its white citizens was beginning to crumble.

The early 1990s saw the emergence of a variety of political and religious meetings that demanded the end of apartheid and tried to find a peaceful solution to this process. In November 1990, the leaders of the South African Council of Churches gathered together 230 delegates from eighty churches and forty Christian organizations in Rustenburg. At this meeting, the delegates drew up the Rustenburg Declaration that denounced apartheid as sinful and unchristian. Ray McCauley was one of the church leaders to admit that apartheid was not a godly institution and that it should be condemned by Christians.

Since the end of apartheid, Rhema Bible Church has continued to grow in numbers and has planted various churches in previously black townships. The political involvement of the church has undergone a remarkable change, as Ray McCauley and his church have moved into the center of the political arena. In 2009, as president of the African National Congress (ANC), Jacob Zuma invited Ray McCauley to head the National Interfaith Leadership Council (NILC), in which the dominant voice was Pentecostal-Charismatic and Evangelical Christianity. Not long after this, in the months leading up to the 2009 elections, McCauley, in turn, invited Zuma to Rhema to preach to his congregation, thus politically supporting Zuma's bid for presidency. This move of PCCs into the political arena came at a time when Christianity had again begun to play a role in the country's political debate.[8]

During the years of the Mbeki government, Christianity was considered part of the colonial past and unsuitable in a secular democracy that valued modernity and progress. Rhema was not the only PCC church to begin to play a far more active role in the political and public space in the years after Mbeki's government. Grace Bible Church, which began as a church plant from Rhema, started engaging in the political life of the country during the early 2000s, when it played a key role in a campaign focused on the moral regeneration of the police force.

Grace Bible Church

In 1983, a small group of white South African missionaries from Rhema who had begun a new church in Soweto decided that, given the implications of the state of emergency, it was too dangerous for them to work in the black townships of Soweto on the outskirts of Johannesburg. The fledgling church had just over a hundred members when the white leadership pulled out and gave the church over to a young man—Mosa Sono—who wanted to become a pastor and had done some courses through Rhema Bible School. After the white leaders left, the congregation shrunk, and those left tried to replicate everything they had learned from Rhema. Pastor Mathola,[9] in an interview, explained that things really began to change when they started to meet the needs of the people in Soweto and began to preach a message that was relevant to them. Soon the congregation was so big that they had to move to a school for services on Sunday, and some years later they moved to the Jubavu Homemakers Fairground, where they could accommodate over one thousand people under the tin-roof shelter. But this "building" was very hot in summer and cold in winter because it had no walls. By 2002, the church had been able to raise enough money from the congregation and secure a loan from a bank in order to purchase a piece of land in Pimville Soweto, where they built their church to accommodate over forty-five hundred people at one service. By 2014, the Grace Bible Church complex in Soweto had expanded to include the main church building, a smaller chapel, a bookstore, administrative offices, and teaching facilities for computer literacy and other community-development projects. Pastor Sono was referred to as "Bishop" because he had become the head of over twenty-three Grace Bible Churches throughout South Africa and numerous small satellite churches. Grace Bible Church had its own television program, *Xihlovo*. They had an active media team, the Grace Bible News Team, which streams services, inspirational sermons, and podcasts on various social media platforms and YouTube.

Over the fourteen years, between 2000 and 2014, during which I did research into Grace Bible Church, a key theme of the church has been on prosperity and life purpose. Prosperity theology essentially claims that Christians are meant to experience the blessings of God in this world through material wealth, good health, and a happy family life. Christians are able to access these blessings by living a good Christian life; giving generously to their church, in terms of money and their time; and faithfully attending church services and Bible study groups. These blessings are only possible if the person has been born again, has undergone a physical and spiritual baptism, and has committed his or her life to Christ. Wealth is regarded as a key marker of spiritual blessing, and consumer goods, like designer handbags, luxury cars, and smart clothes, are all recoded to denote the spiritual blessing of the individual. The nuclear family has also been recoded to symbolize modern Christianity as a form of spiritual blessing. Bishop Sono and his family epitomize the ideal nuclear family of two parents living in the same home with their two or three children.

Diarmaid MacCulloch,[10] in his history of Christianity, argues that the nineteenth-century parsonage was held up as the ideal Victorian family, where the mother taught her daughters good manners, how to be thrifty, and how to run an efficient household. The father taught his sons and daughters to read, and the home was always filled with interesting conversation. It was a home that did not feature the extended family and where the nuclear family was nurtured. In much the same way, the pastors of PCCs offer the contemporary congregations a model of the twenty-first-century nuclear family. The nuclear family, as idealized in these churches, is a space in which priority is given to the education of children, a pension plan, and medical aid for the family. Financial ties and demands of the extended family are kept to a minimum. This family ideally lives in the suburbs, and their children go to good "previous white schools" (schools that had been exclusively for white children under apartheid). Both parents have cars, and the home is filled with the latest technology. It is a space in which individuals are able to develop their own interests and pursue their own dreams and goals. In most instances, both parents work. For many women, the ideal is to be a stay-at-home mom, which, according to the theology of this church, is the ideal role for women so that they can provide a nurturing environment for their husband and children.[11] Pastor Sono and his family appear to live up to this ideal, and he actively encourages husbands and fathers to honor their families and be good providers.

To provide for a family, men and women need to earn a living. Over the years, Pastor Sono has consistently preached a message of purpose theology and prosperity theology. He encourages Christians to understand that God has given each person a life purpose. No life is without purpose or meaning. In the context of high unemployment, many unwanted pregnancies, and violent petty crimes, the lives of individual people often seemed to have little value in South Africa. Pastor Sono actively preaches against this and inspires his congregation to realize what their life purpose is. It might be to be a teacher or an investment banker; to do something that pays well; or to do something like home-based care of an AIDS patient, for which they are paid nothing or very little. The focus here is not on material wealth as a marker of spiritual blessing but of every life being valuable, meaningful, and purposeful.

Grace Bible Church also sees its ministry in South Africa as transforming the leadership of the country and working toward ethical and moral principles guiding the decision-making process of those in leadership. To implement this mission, the church became increasingly involved in political and public debates in the country. In 2001–2002, the church was deeply involved in a moral-regeneration project amongst the Gauteng police force.

During the 2000s, the church regularly asked political officials, mainly from the ANC, to address their congregations on important political public holidays, like Freedom Day and Heritage Day. In the buildup to the 2014 elections, Grace invited speakers from the ANC leadership and Floyd Shevambu[12] from the Economic Freedom Fighters to address the Sunday congregations. Cell leaders in the church, in an interview, explained that these political figures were given a platform by the church so that the congregation was informed about its political choices and so that Christians would be elected into key political positions.[13] These leaders maintained that the people chosen by God would be elected into office because the people of God were praying for them and against any forces of evil.

The power of evil and prayers for healing from the influence of bad witchcraft, ancestral spirits, and bad *muti* (herbal medicines and potions made by *sangomas*, which are believed to cause misfortune in the lives of other people) are other key aspects in the theology of churches like Grace Bible Church. Many members of Grace read the books of prominent televangelists T. D. Jakes (from the United States) and T. B. Joshua (from Nigeria), and some I interviewed were hoping to be able to go to Nigeria to be prophesied over by Joshua. In the theology of this church, the world is understood as a place in which good and evil spirits are always at work and in which Christians continually need to fight against the powers of evil that cause illness, poverty, and broken relationships. Members of Grace believe that through powerful prayers in prayer groups, at church on Sundays, and in their home cell meetings, people can be filled with the Holy Spirit and exorcise their demons. Grace Bible Church teaches its members that ancestor veneration is not godly and that they must fight against the evil forces of ancestors, witchcraft, and Satan. The church, like many other PCCs, encourages its members to make a break with their extended families who practice ancestor veneration.[14] Research has shown that across Africa, PCCs often help people to find a new way of negotiating the demands of modernization and urbanization and the culture of individualism that goes with that.

His People Christian Ministries

His People Church, founded in 1988 by Paul Daniels on the campus of the University of Cape Town, is another PCC that focuses on helping individuals thrive in the modern capitalist economy. The vision of Daniels and his followers has been to transform the world by having committed Christians in positions of leadership. In order to do this, the ministry was initially focused on university campuses throughout South Africa because they believed that by influencing the thinking of the leaders of tomorrow, they would be able to change the world into a place governed by Christian principles. By the late 1990s, there were His People churches all over Africa, in the United Kingdom, in Australia, and in various parts of North America. In South Africa, churches were established in Cape Town, Johannesburg, Port Elizabeth, Grahamstown, Pretoria, Durban, and Kimberley.[15]

In Johannesburg, His People Ministries began in the early 1990s, and by 2014, they had churches on the University of Witwatersrand, the University of Johannesburg Kingsway, and the Soweto campuses. They also had five other churches in the Gauteng area. Like Grace Bible Church and Rhema, they offered a number of church services on Sundays and encouraged all members to be a part of a home-cell or Bible study group. It is in these groups that all three churches encourage members to create a community where people support each other. Pastors in these megachurches, which have over ten thousand people coming to their services on any given

Sunday, are unable to minister directly to individuals. The role of the head pastors is normally to preach at the Sunday services and to minister to the needs of the other pastors giving direction and vision to the church. In all three churches, most of the ministry to people is done through church counselors, cell leaders, and prayer-group members who pray for the needs of people. For both His People and Grace Bible Church, the common New Testament injunction to "equip the saints (believers) for ministry" extends to giving people training in the skills they need in order to become leaders in the workplace.

On and off the church campuses, His People runs a variety of different workshops, seminars, conferences, and courses aimed at helping young people develop so that they have the skills needed to become leaders in their chosen careers. Grace Bible Church offers a similar array of courses. In these workshops, members learn how to budget their money so that they are able to tithe every month and also meet their financial commitments. People learn negotiation skills, time management skills, how to develop a personal brand, and how to begin or manage a small business. Research done in 2003–2004 showed that for many members of these churches, the most valuable part of their church life was linked to these social-skills-development courses.[16] Sermons were another important space in which people learned how to become successful in the world of work.

Grace Bible, His People, and Rhema Church all gave sermons that explained a passage of Scripture and showed how the Bible offered Christians guidance on how to deal with the world in which they were currently living. These sermons often sounded like motivational speeches and were delivered in the language of the business world, encouraging people to have goals, develop their own personal mission statements, and cultivate the tools to negotiate difficult situations at work.

In these churches, success in the workplace and in life more generally is due not only to skills training and good time management alone. Each of these churches also actively teaches and encourages people to pray for their own success and to fight against any forces of evil that might be holding them back. Leaders at His People and Grace Bible Church emphasize that it is through a combination of hard work, moral living, personal discipline, tithing 10 percent of their earnings, and prayers against the forces of evil that a Christian is able to succeed. These churches speak out strongly against an attitude in which all life experiences of difficulty, poverty, and illness are immediately linked to evil forces. For Bishop Sono, it was important that people who were living in the townships and unemployed did not give up on their dreams and did not deflect responsibility by blaming their misfortunes on the powers of Satan or on witchcraft. He continuously encouraged people to find their destiny and pursue every avenue to find success and not blame the so-called "spirit of poverty" for their misfortune.

While the discourse of witchcraft and the fight against evil spirits has been a part of the theology and daily life of members at Rhema, His People, and Grace Bible Church, it is not the central message. Their message centers on the belief that each person will only achieve salvation when they are born again and commit their lives to Christ. Once a believer is born again, they are filled with the Holy Spirit (spiritual baptism) and express their faith through adult water baptism. As born-again Christians, they believe they are filled with the Holy Spirit and protected from the forces of Satan to a large extent. The job of Christians is to live a life of victory over death and evil.

But this message has not attracted everyone, and many people in South Africa do not experience a life filled with purpose, blessings, health, and wealth. South African statistics show that in 2014, roughly 24 percent of the population was unemployed.[17] This figure does not include people who have part-time or seasonal work or are underemployed, often working as petty roadside traders.

Universal Church of the Kingdom of God

A PCC that gives a very different answer to the continued misfortune, illness, poverty, joblessness, and broken relationships that so many people live in is the Universal Church of the Kingdom of God (UCKG), which maintains that all people are continually under attack from Satan and that all misfortune can be explained by this attack. This church insists that the only way to combat spiritual attacks is through prayer. Overcoming the devil through powerful or strong prayers is at the heart of the teaching and practice of the UCKG.

In this theology, the central concept that has been developed is not a relationship with Jesus Christ or an emotional feeling of being filled with the Holy Spirit. Rather, it is based on a detailed cosmology of evil spirits, demons, and angels who are in continual warfare over the souls and fortunes of believers. Only through the power of the Holy Spirit can evil be exorcised and the blessings of God experienced. When good things are taken away or blessings do not materialize even though believers have prayed fervently, attended services daily, and given all they own to the church, then the problem is due to the work of evil spirits. In the South African context, this includes the work of *sangomas* and *iyangas*, who work bad witchcraft with *muti* on the lives of believers. Such misfortune is overcome only by prayers and tithes.

In her detailed study of the UCKG in Durban, Ilana Van Wyk[18] argues that this church is simultaneously a local and global church. It is global because there are hundreds of UCKG churches throughout Latin America, Africa, and Asia. It is so successful because it works within the context, language, and beliefs of the local spirits in each region and local understandings of misfortune. In the Durban context, the cosmology of evil was understood in the terms of the people living in the region, while in the Gauteng area, the specific demons and witchcraft practices that the churches rallied against were specific to that area.

This church was started in Rio de Janeiro, Brazil, in 1977 by a group of five young men from working-class Catholic families.[19] Edir Macedo soon emerged as their leader, as he and his friends preached to and healed people in the streets of the city. Macedo, who had little theological training, began to preach a prosperity gospel based on a spiritual war against the Afro-Brazilian religions. He maintained that poverty, illness, misfortune, and broken relationships were due to the work of the devil and that Christians needed to be exorcised of their demons through "strong" prayers.

In 1992, a group of missionaries was sent from Brazil to South Africa and tried to establish a church in Bez Valley in Johannesburg. This area had a high number of Portuguese-speaking people, and it was hoped that, as the Brazilian missionary pastors were all Portuguese, the language would not be a barrier. The white Portuguese-speaking community did not join the new church, but the black community who worked in the area did. Soon the church moved to a rented space in downtown Johannesburg, and in the first week the numbers had doubled to four hundred people. A few months later, the church opened a second branch at the Victoria Street market in Durban. Subsequently, the church has established branches in all major cities in South Africa and in many townships and some rural areas.[20]

While this church has grown rapidly, attracting huge numbers of people to its daily services, the South African Council of Churches and the Evangelical Alliance in South Africa launched an investigation into UCKG in 2000. Both organizations accused the church of occult behavior and asked the Human Rights Commission to investigate the church further.[21] The commission refused to comment on the occult behavior but disclosed that the UCKG did exploit the poor financially and performed "rituals that amount to forms of psychological conditioning."[22] After a legal battle between the Human Rights Commission and the UCKG, the commission retracted its statement.[23] Since then, the UCKG has been investigated by a number of journalists who have drawn primarily on the accounts of ex-members and ex-pastors. In 2009, six ex-pastors of the church accused it of being a money-making scam in which only the Brazilian elite of the church were benefiting. They told of the difficult circumstances under which they lived in small flats and one-bedroom apartments while they ministered, and they explained how the leadership moved them every few months to a different church so that they could not form any emotional ties with the congregation. The pastors were all paid meager wages, and when they left the church or were thrown out of the church, they were given a severance package of a few thousand rands.[24]

In September 2010, the UCKG held a rally called "All Answers," and sixty thousand people came to Durban and filled the Curries Fountain stadium. Similar rallies were held in Johannesburg, Cape Town, Bloemfontein, Lenasia, Thokoza, Qwaqwa, Randfontein, Rustenburg, and Pietermaritzburg.[25] These rallies were high points in the church's year and attracted thousands of people.

During the course of a normal week, any UCKG church attracted several thousand people to its daily services. An example of this was the Smith Street UCKG in Durban. Van Wyk reports in her book that during 2004–2012, this congregation had five daily services, held at 6:00 a.m., 7:30 a.m., noon, 17:30 p.m., and 19:30 p.m. Pastors led the prayers at each of these services. Every day, they focused on a different prayer theme, whether praying for wealth, against bad family relationships, for a job, for romantic love, or for healing. At each service, the congregation was told that in order to achieve their desired blessings, they must give generously to the church. Rallies were held regularly at the church in which people publicly pledged how much they would give to the church. These pledges started at 50,000 rand and went down to 300 rand; anything less was not accepted. The pastors told people not to pay school fees or mortgages and not to buy groceries or medicines. If they were being held back by misfortune, they should give their government pension grants (780 rand) or childcare grants (180 rand) to the church. By showing God and Satan their commitment, the powers of evil holding them back would be overcome, and then they would have all the money they needed.

In her study of the Durban UKCG, Van Wyk found that many people who attended these services had problems with their families, who were against their participation in the church because the church demanded extraordinary amounts of money from members. Van Wyk writes, "Pastor Vladimir, for instance, often said that people who used their tithes to pay their children's school fees would see their children fail."[26] Several of the people she interviewed tried to keep their involvement with the church secret from their families. This type of Christianity did not argue that fostering good family relationships or being an ideal nuclear family was up to the behavior of individuals. Rather, it maintained that bad family relationships were due to the work of the devil and that once the evil and witchcraft holding them was overcome, believers would begin to enjoy a happy family life. While others may argue that it was the very teaching of the UCKG that was causing family problems and poverty for those who went to this church, this was not how the church's adherents understood their world. Rather, they believed evil forces caused their misfortune and that if that was overcome, they would be blessed.

Overview of the Theology and Practices of PCCs

The preceding section has shown that the types of PCCs that have flourished in South Africa between 1994 and 2014 have varied in style and theology. In the following, we will compare these different churches according to themes of leadership and community, symbolic codes, worship, family, and political engagement.

Leadership and community

While some churches, like Rhema and Grace Bible Church, were centered around a key leader, a "cult of the leader" was not central to the identity or functioning of the UCKG and His People. His People tried hard to create a sense of community amongst members and purposefully created multiple smaller (in comparison to other PCC churches) congregations. These churches used social media and small cell groups as methods through which people could develop social ties with other believers and offer each other support. On the other extreme, the UCKG actively avoided the formation of any sense of community or unity amongst members. The leadership changed regularly so that no emotional bonds could be nurtured between the congregation and its leaders. Most people that attended these churches had no idea about the lives of their leaders and often did not know their pastors' full names.

In the UCKG model of church, those who frequented services generally did not regard themselves as members of the UCKG but rather as people who were just attending some services in order to break the demonic forces that were holding them back in life. Based on a theology of evil forces and the power of prayer, the UCKG did not create any form of social care or outreach programs or any type of life-skills training. Once the power of evil was broken and while it was kept away, people would automatically find jobs, be able to buy houses, and fall in love; therefore, skills training was not important.

Grace Bible Church and His People worked on a different principle. They believed that God wanted to bless all believers with a good life in this world. To make this happen, Christians needed to commit their lives to God, tithe regularly as much as they could, pray earnestly, and develop their skills through workshops, conferences, and courses offered by the church. Their future blessings were dependent on both God's blessing and their own efforts.

Symbolic codes

Among churches like Rhema, Grace, and His People, it was particularly important to show one was blessed by God. In these churches, consumer goods were recoded to symbolize spiritual blessing. On the one hand, these churches advocated a puritan lifestyle—in other words, people worked hard and spent their money on "good things," like designer clothes and expensive cars, which were recoded to be signs of blessing, but not on "bad things," like pornography, gambling, prostitution, or excessive amounts of alcohol. On the other hand, these churches nevertheless practiced a consumer type of puritanism, in which aspects of modern life, like private school fees, insurance policies, and overseas travel were all considered godly or indicators of blessing. In these churches, wearing designer clothes and expensive shoes to church were important expressions through which members could signify their spiritual status to each other. This type of Pentecostalism embraced capitalism and the consumption of goods that underpins it.

While the UCKG saw consumer products as things that could be purchased when one was in a state of victory over evil, the symbols that they were primarily concerned with at services were very different. UCKG churches used a plethora of different symbolic objects to combat evil. Most popular were holy oils, water blessed by pastors, and sashes or cords tied around the waist underneath clothes so that they were in direct contact with the skin. At different services, these objects were brought out of the "preparation room" by assistants, prayed over by the pastors, and then handed out to people at the service. These largely unseen objects were believed to have strong spiritual powers, which people use to combat evil and witchcraft.

None of these churches featured crucifixes, crosses, statues of saints, or depictions of the life of Christ. Little in their decor distinguished them symbolically from secular halls or conference venues.

Worship

While the theology of these churches varied, they all used worship and the testimonies of believers as key ways to promulgate their theology. In each church, there were more women than men, and at Rhema, His People, and Grace, women were made pastors but never leaders of a church or senior pastors in the church unless they were married to senior pastors in the church. At UCKG, women were not allowed to be pastors; they served only as assistants within the church. Services and the message of sermons were based on how the Holy Spirit led and inspired the leadership of the church, rather than following any formal liturgical calendar. In all the churches, to different degrees, praying against misfortune and for the blessings of God was given priority. At each service, there was a time dedicated to prayer in which the congregation prayed for healing, for an infilling of the Holy Spirit, and against any forces of evil that might be blocking God's blessings on them. Blessings were not just for the people individually but also for larger public organizations, like politics, good management of municipalities, medical care, schools, and education.

Family

Since 1994, there has been a dramatic migration of people into urban areas like Gauteng. Due to HIV/AIDS, poverty, and social mobility, the structure and meaning of the family has changed over the last twenty years, and the idea of family has come to mean the nuclear family, headed by a husband with a wife and two or three children all living in the same geographic space. This ideal is exemplified powerfully by PCC pastors. With their theology of prosperity, these pastors have spread a message of investment in the individual and his or her immediate family, a break with the larger family, and generous financial support to their churches so that God will bless them and their nuclear family with material wealth in this life.

Political engagement

His People, Grace Bible Church, and Rhema all encouraged their members to pray that God would bless these institutions with good, moral leaders and tried to equip their members to engage with all spheres of public life so that Christians are leaders in politics, business, and social care. Each of these churches was engaged in the 2009 and 2014 presidential elections. In the case of

His People, its congregations debated the merits of different political parties and leaders on social media leading up to the 2014 election.[27] Rhema, through Ray McCauley's involvement, strongly supported the ANC and Zuma's election, while Grace gave both the ANC and the Economic Freedom Fighters a platform in their Sunday services. All three churches actively reminded members to vote and sent out a variety of tweets, Facebook posts, and e-mail reminders. The UCKG, in contrast, did not in any way publicly encourage voting, nor did it invite political figures to preach. In its theology, political involvement would be regarded as unimportant. What was important was that people gave "strong prayers" against the power of Satan and witchcraft, which always manipulated politics. They should pray that the witchcraft that kept people like Zuma in power was broken. This power of healing through prayer and the form of Christianity that negotiates the world of African ancestors and witchcraft through the Holy Spirit, who brings healing and liberation to people, is also found at the heart of many African Independent Churches.

Conclusion

Over the last thirty years, a variety of very different PCCs have risen in popularity in South Africa. Through the millions of members these churches attract, they are beginning to influence the social, economic, and political fabric of post-apartheid South Africa, but in very different ways. In this chapter, the different theologies and practices of four of the most popular PCCs in South Africa have been explored, and it has become clear that the category of PCCs in South Africa is not a uniform or unified collection of churches. Grace Bible Church and Rhema have both taken on important roles within the political arena of South Africa. Rhema is positioned firmly behind the Zuma government, with its head pastor, Ray McCauley, holding an important advisory position as head of the National Interfaith Leadership Council. Grace Bible Church encourages its members to be politically informed and involved but does not support one particular party. The other two churches in the study placed less importance on political involvement. His People, Grace Bible Church, and Rhema all aim to change the world, or at least the social milieu of South Africa, by equipping their members with social and business skills so that they are able to become leaders in their fields of work, thereby bringing Christian values into the workplace. While these three churches avoid preaching about witchcraft, the UCKG holds witchcraft and the fight against evil powers as its central focus. Hundreds of thousands of people flock to these UCKG churches daily to be delivered from the powers of evil, which they believe are holding them captive in poverty, loveless relationships, and ill health. In this style of PCC, the focus is far less on equipping believers with social and practical skills to improve their life chances and much more on helping to free them from the forces of evil that are believed to be holding them back.

What these churches all have in common is a strong belief in the power and gifts of the Holy Spirit to conquer evil; the belief that through fervent prayers and self-sacrifice (usually of money), believers will be blessed with "the good life" from God; and a belief in leaders whose charismatic preaching enthuses members to remain committed to the "gospel" they present.

Part IV
Select Theological Themes

Chapter 16

"Nativizing" the Gospel: Pentecostalism and Theology in Africa

Joseph Quayesi-Amakye

THIS CHAPTER WILL suggest that African Pentecostalism is fertile soil for the contextualization of Christian theology in Africa. That Pentecostalism continues to contribute to the African theological definition must not be ignored. The search for a theology that responds adequately to the African religious and cultural expectations has been an ongoing enterprise for the last century. Although the journey may be traced to the Edinburgh Conference of 1910, the debate for contextualizing the gospel in Africa has continued. For instance, Harry Sawyerr, a leading Sierra Leonean theologian, observed that "in spite of the difficulties inherent in the term African, there is a strong case for a *Theologia Africana* which will seek to interpret Christ to the African in such a way that he feels at home in his new faith."[1] It is clear that Sawyerr visualized an African theology that did not depart from basic biblical teachings in order to avert the situation of theologizing to satisfy the whims and caprices of theologians.

I will approach this essay as a descriptive, discursive, and analytical task by looking first at the proposal by African theologians for Africanizing the gospel for the African context. At the time the debate on nativizing the gospel started, Pentecostalism was still a nascent movement. Today it has become the representative face of Christianity in Africa, so my second task would be to examine Pentecostal versions of "nativizing" the gospel. I end by exploring Pentecostal achievements in this regard and drawing some conclusions.

Africanizing the Good News

The late Ghanaian theologian Kwame Bediako called for a Christianity that faithfully engages the African traditional religious context with the truth claims of Christ but that does not necessarily condemn everything African as evil.[2] But is there a case for an African Christian theology? If there is, how is it to be and how must it be approached? Generally, proponents of African Christian theology maintain that such must result in a Christianity that impels African converts to a genuine and sincere engagement between who, what, and how they are with the demands of Christ's gospel. In this way, they can faithfully and confidently call themselves true followers of Christ while at the same time maintaining their authentic African identity. In other words, contextualization must not mean shedding off everything African but rather appropriately synthesizing the Bible and traditional religion and culture.

Bediako thinks that vernacularization of Scripture is one sure way of contextualizing the gospel for Africans.[3] With the Pentecost experience of Acts 2 as his departure point, he emphasizes the marvel of receiving the Christian faith in the vernacular. Vernacularization eases the appropriation of Christ in a more definitive way to the African socially, psychologically, and theologically. Like Pentecost, vernacularization comes with surprises when Africans experience the Christian God as a universal God of all. In Bediako's thought, part of the miracle of Pentecost was the revelation that God enables the gospel, that is, the "wonders of God," to be apprehended in different tongues.

Vernacularization of Scripture results in the fusion of horizon as recipients engage the Scripture with their contextual experiences and questions. This underpinned the success of the African Independent Church (AIC) movement in dealing with the myriad of spiritual and etiological questions posed by Africans.[4] It is important to state that a number of affirmative actions that Bediako identifies with the AICs, such as the adaptation of the African communal solidarity in the ecclesiastical sphere, are not peculiar to them. Indeed, African Pentecostals have developed elaborate solidarity systems that cater to the needs of the faithful. This is equally true of the Africanization of Christian worship. Like the AICs, African Pentecostals take advantage of the rich primal psycho-religious resources to launch a localized Christian life and worship toward Africans and thus succeed in presenting Christianity to Africans in their own terms and categories.[5] In this way, Christ ceases to be an alien and stranger to Africans and rather becomes their host in their cultural context.

Rightly, Bediako rationalizes early Western missionaries' intolerance of Christian patronage of traditional worship and practices. Such a missiological approach was necessary for ensuring that converts gave their undivided loyalty to Christ as their new Lord. Generally, African Pentecostals will not begrudge the missionaries on this, since vernacularization does not mean syncretizing Christianity. That scholars like Bediako underline vernacularization as an effective evangelizing tool clearly signifies that African Christians have begun to appreciate the need to contextualize Christianity in the African way.[6]

Emmanuel Martey, another Ghanaian theologian, traces the origin of the term *Africanization* to early-twentieth-century

African nationalism, a political rather than religious phenomenon.[7] According to him, the concept took ecclesiastical meaning in the 1950s and 1960s when both Catholic and Protestant Christianity reevaluated the traditional North Atlantic Christian theology from an African perspective. It was felt, however, that this quest should not be characterized by

> an uncritical acceptance of the theology developed in the West, and an equally uncritical rejection of anything different from it, (since such attitudes) are both signs of theological immaturity and intellectual irresponsibility in Christian obedience to the Gospel within the context of a given, concrete, social situation.[8]

Martey then notes that as a theological reality, Africanization has assumed various nuances, ranging from "stepping-stone" theory to adaptation, incarnation, and indigenization by both Catholic and Protestant theologians. Within African Catholicism, beset with papal frustration, have emerged such expressions like *adaptation*, *accommodation*, *indigenization*, *translation*, *incarnation*, *localization*, *inculturation*, *interculturation*, and *inter alia*, most of which have been used interchangeably.

African Catholics shifted from adaptation to incarnation due to the former's characteristic Western prefabrication and imposition as well as its superficiality. However, Pope Paul VI disapproved incarnationalism despite its Christological and biblical basis by labeling it "dangerous" among all "diversified" theologies while maintaining that "the content of the faith is either Catholic or it is not" and urging the African bishops to adopt "a better expression of faith."[9] The pope's disapproval may be viewed as ecclesiastical gerontocracy that sought to muffle African Catholics and perpetuate Rome's grip on the African Church.

Meanwhile, among African Anglophone Protestants, "indigenization" was adopted, although later the All African Conference of Churches lost interest in it. Inculturation, with its undertones of African liberation, cropped up during a Pan-African Conference of Third World Theologians held in Accra, Ghana, in 1977, which for the first time brought together both Protestant and Catholic theologians and Francophone and Anglophone African theologians. This term, which has sociological and anthropological derivatives and now was conceptualized theologically, was popularized by the Jesuit superior general, Father Pedro Arrupe, in 1978.[10]

Inculturation appropriates Christ's incarnation as paradigmatic for Christian theology. For example, Peter Kwasi Sarpong, a Ghanaian Catholic bishop emeritus, wonders how the church could ever progress without inculturation and argues that, theologically, "the Incarnation of the Son of God is the principle and model of inculturation of Christianity."[11] He also feels convinced that "inculturation is an end in itself"; otherwise, if seen as a means, one will be tempted to do things that are not acceptable.[12] For Sarpong, then, *inculturation* means "contextual theology." He is nonetheless quick to condemn the infringement of people's rights by practitioners of African Traditional Religions (ATRs) and calls for a purifying of the African culture.[13] Despite the divergent reactions to it, inculturation came to be accepted as embracing all of Christian life and thinking that involves conceptualization, symbolism, innovation, and creativity.

Martey also analyzes the different contours or trends in African theology. For example, in the early 1970s, Charles Nyamiti differentiated between the "speculative school," with its philosophical emphasis; the "social and biblical school," with its pragmatic biblical approach; and the liberationist "militant school"; while Ngendu Mushete distinguished between a "theology of adaptation" and "critical theology."[14] At least partially in response, Martey suggests four sources for defining African theology as:

1. The Bible, Christian tradition, and theological heritage
2. African traditional religion, culture, and philosophy
3. African anthropology and other social sciences
4. African independent churches[15]

The Bible, Martey indicates, is the normative source for further theological inquiry, religious experience, and celebration of God. The importance of Christian tradition, on the other hand, is because it is the bridgehead between the Christian past and the present. For African theologians, the stress on Christian heritage is significant for the fact that it was shaped by Africans like Origen, Cyprian, Tertullian, Clement of Alexandria, Athanasius, and, above all, Augustine. Despite the "invasion" of Christianity and Islam, ATR still holds sway in Africa simply because both its cosmology and philosophy have never been on the decline and it is, therefore, a *conditio sine qua non* in the theological discourse.

Martey advocates for a Christology that takes the religio-cultural, sociopolitical, and economic contexts of the African seriously in response to the liberative need of the African person. Such Christology not only provides a framework within which the oppressed of Africa can conceptualize the person of Christ but will also respond correctly to the wrong arguments that Christ is foreign in Africa or that His very essence is incompatible with autochthonous religious conceptions that even elude Africans.

Martey further asserts that while accepting the liberative approach to Christology, most African feminists reject the cultural approach because they see African traditional culture included in the contemporary structures of oppression. Central to the reflection of African female theologians is the contention that the gender disparities in societies are culturally conditioned. Thus, the experience of women in patriarchal societies and male-dominated churches is not one of equal partnership but of a master/servant relationship. It is not surprising, therefore, that (African) feminist theologians make women's experience the point of departure for Christology. Thus, Mercy Amba Oduyoye argues that feminism aims at realizing full humanity as God intended for all humans and calls for all to get interested in liberating humanity from dichotomized and hierarchical attitudes and tendencies.[16]

From the foregoing, we will ask: How should African theology present Jesus Christ to the African? Martey offers a twofold answer. First, African theology must meet the African at the sociopolitical level of poverty, racism, sexism, classism, colonialism, neocolonialism, imperialism, injustice, political dictatorship and repression, imprisonment without trial, rampant *coup d'etats*, hunger, drought, incurable diseases, and all that dehumanizes the African personality.[17] Second, it must meet the African at the religio-cultural level by offering a pneumatological supplement to the soteriological interests of the liberationist approach, and that means a search for an image of Christ that can answer Africans' question of the nature of the *absent* but yet *present* Christ willing and ready to promote the African humanity.

An important source Martey proposes is the place of African anthropology and the social sciences in the construction of a relevant African theology. The African understanding of the human being reveals the intrinsic and extrinsic values Africans attach to being human. The human being is the center of creation, and the African view about brotherhood and sisterhood encompasses all humanity without genetic, ethnic, racial, class, religious, or gender boundaries.

Pentecostal "Nativizing" Efforts

In the past, non-Pentecostal Ghanaian Christians classified Pentecostals together with the *Sunsum Söre,* the Ghanaian local brand of the African Initiated Churches (AICs). Pentecostals vehemently repudiate this categorization since they generally deem the AICs to be syncretic in their Christian practices. Being syncretic, the AICs are alleged to inappropriately mix the Christian faith with ATR, resulting in questionable beliefs and practices, such as the pacification of deities, ghosts, animal sacrifices, necromancy, spiritism, and ritualism, among others. Nonetheless, Martey's suggestion that the AICs are important sources for theological enterprise in Africa today still applies to Pentecostalism. In the main, however, Pentecostalism offers a more authentic contextualization of African Christianity than the AICs because of its unapologetic commitment to biblical inerrancy and finality of authority. This makes it important for constructing a new and relevant theology for Africans today.

African Pentecostals have begun to respond (perhaps unconsciously) to Martey's four-tier sources of an authentic African theology for African peoples. First, unlike the AICs, African Pentecostals can be described as Biblicists who jealously guard against the adulteration of the Scriptures. In Ghana and Nigeria, for example, it is not uncommon to hear a Pentecostal pastor deliberately stressing that his or her sermon is an unadulterated word of God. Whether, indeed, their sermons are pure word is not the issue here. It is common knowledge that many of them lack exegetical skills in the use of the Bible; nonetheless, by stating that their sermons are the pure word of God, we can infer their commitment to biblical orthodoxy.

Like the AICs, African Pentecostals are responding to African feminist queries on patriarchal chauvinism by creating ministerial spaces for women. Thus, Philomena Njeri Mwaura draws attention to the significant roles African Pentecostal women play in the Christianization of the continent.[18] As far as she is concerned, the enterprising efforts of these African "Spirit-filled women as agents of religious innovation" is commendable.[19] Indeed, like the AICs, Pentecostal churches are physiological and psychological spaces of women's liberation and communal solidarity. She describes the charismatic innovations at church planting of several African women, from East to West Africa. In Kenya, there is, for instance, Margaret Wangare, whose religious experiences culminated in faith healing and revivalism that began in 1974. Dorcas Olaniyi founded the Agbala Daniel Church in 1979 in Nigeria after several religious experiences interpreted as signs of her call to ministry.

Significantly, some African male Pentecostals have encouraged ministerial gender equality. Typical is the late Nigerian archbishop Benson Andrew Idahosa, whose All Nations for Christ Bible Training Institute in Benin City admitted and trained females for ministry. Some of the Pentecostal women pastors have been consecrated bishops, such as the Malawian bishop Mercy Yami, who in 1994 teamed up with Pastor Lumwira to establish Blessed Hope Church. It is also significant to note that in several places in Africa, Pentecostal women are on the forefront of healing camps. This is particularly common in Ghana, where prayer centers often are led by Pentecostal women. Good examples are Abura Edumfa Bethlehem Prayer Revival Centre that was founded and led by the late Aunty Grace Mensah, a very powerful and popular prophetess. Others include deaconess Mrs. Georgina Grant Essilfie at

Abowinmu, near Anyan Denkyira, among many others. While these women do not approach the African liberation agenda politically, their pneumatic approach eventually results in providing spiritual, psychological, and even political hope to clients. Indeed, as with all cases of prophetic ministries, patrons of these women prayer centers include politicians in search of spiritual protection and assurances of victory.

African Pentecostals have awakened to their civic obligations to their countries. In the past, they were apathetic to social concerns, leaving all the sociopolitical critique to the ministers of the mainline churches. Today, however, a number of them have plunged themselves into public spheres to help the state create a meaningful life for citizens.[20] They now set up schools, establish health facilities, and engage in political debates. When Pentecostals carry out these social projects, it is because of their belief in the value of the *imago Dei* of the African person that must be respected and helped to live unsaddled by avoidable evils. Of course, some Pentecostal leaders suffer public outcries because of their perceived partisanship, particularly with unpopular governments. In Ghana, for example, the opposition parties do not spare Opoku Onyinah, chairman of Ghana's leading Pentecostal church, the Church of Pentecost, in their attack against the National Peace Council that they perceive to be "in bed" with the ruling National Democratic Congress government. The chairman of the council is the Most Reverend Emmanuel Asante-Antwi, a Methodist minister.

Onyinah, it must be stated, represents a new breed of African Pentecostal leadership that seeks to contextual Christianity in ways unknown to Pentecostals.[21] He advocates and actually organizes conferences that discuss the compatibility of the Christian faith with traditional leadership or monarchy. While such a task may not be viable, given the religious nature of traditional monarchy, nonetheless his attempt must be recognized as a real subversion of the Pentecostal status quo and demands commendation from all. Meanwhile, long before Onyinah's civic advocacy, some Pentecostals in South Africa had taken keen interest in the civic life of their society. Pastors like Frank Chikane and Christiaan de Wet adopted revolutionary stands for dismantling Apartheid.[22]

Perhaps despite their appeal to pneumatic experiences, some Pentecostals do not appear to have matured politically. Indeed, some have become politicians although their Christian impact is yet to be felt. Some others have been disgraced and brought their Christian confession to disrepute. This was the case that we see in Rijk van Dijk's examination of the political culture of Malawi during the era of Kamuzu Banda. Van Dijk demonstrates that it was the youth that, with their revivalist Pentecostal politicking, helped in the democratization process of the country.[23] Similarly, in Paul Gifford's book *African Christianity: Its Public Role*, we see how some African Pentecostals kowtow to political pressures and manipulations.[24] Indeed, Zambian president Frederick Chiluba went down in history as one of the most corrupt African leaders of all time, and yet he was a tongues-speaking Christian.[25]

It is also important to state that the Pentecostal contextualization of the gospel in Africa has not been without problems, especially in the area of prophecy. Suspicion and cynicism surrounding the prophetic movement abounds in many quarters. Those who have worked extensively on this phenomenon in Ghana can say that much of what goes on in the name of Pentecostal prophetism is spurious and un-Christian. Thus the contributors to *Prophets, Profits, and the Bible in Zimbabwe* have raised pointed queries about the validity of the commercialization and occultic nature of prophetism in Zimbabwean society carried out in the ambit of Pentecostalism.[26]

Pentecostal Success in "Nativizing" the Gospel

Today, much of African Christianity is becoming Pentecostalized. It should be said that the Pentecostalization of the older churches must not be seen as an unworthy encroachment onto alien spheres. Indeed, objective analysis of the Pentecostal movement will reveal that it benefited from the older churches enormously. First, for example, it was the missionaries of the older churches whose foresight introduced literacy to Ghana. In order to carry out their evangelistic mission, the missionaries started schools to teach Gold Coasters (now Ghanaians) to read and write. Second, some actually reduced the native languages in their diverse dialects into writing and thereby translated the Bible into those languages, making it easy and possible for African Christians and scholars to read and understand the Bible in their own languages. Consequently, God's Word came home to African converts. It is this vernacularization project of the Western missionaries that laid the biblical foundation that the Pentecostals later cashed in on to run their own race.

Third, as a corollary of the foregoing, it is important to point out that the early converts and leaders of the Pentecostal movement came mostly from the mainline churches. Indeed, Anim's Faith Tabernacle Church that metamorphosed into the Apostolic Faith Church, the Apostolic Church, and finally the Christ Apostolic Church, benefited greatly from membership in the Presbyterian Church. In fact, it was Anim's exposure to the Christian faith in the Presbyterian Church that ignited in him a search for greater light of Christian reality. So we can say that while the historic churches later drew spiritual strength and inspiration from the

Pentecostals, the latter had earlier benefited from them. Thus, both reaped from what the other had labored, one laying scriptural foundation and the other providing the spiritual insight and experience, a religious symbiosis at its best.

Perhaps it will be wrong to overlook the contribution of the AICs to the work of Pentecostalism. Before the Pentecostals arrived, the AICs had watered the religious soil by subverting the traditional status quo that espoused and projected the traditional deities and vital forces as the sources and means of spiritual succor to the African. It was the AICs that first challenged the religious mind of Africans and made them revise their views about the Christian God as one more capable to deal with their existential fears and needs. For example, Harris's simple gospel message laid a great stress on the Bible's divine inspiration and ever-abiding relevance.[27] His monotheistic zeal made him to condemn cultic objects, such as amulets and charms, of the idolatrous old religion of his audience and produced in him an intense hatred for witchcraft.[28]

So it was that when the Pentecostals appeared, they had no difficulty in building and improving upon the AIC heritage of spirituality and translatability of the gospel via cultural idioms (supernaturalism of indigenous cosmology, songs, music, dances, spirit possession/baptism and empowerment, healing and exorcism, power encounters, etc.) to present the gospel to their receptor cultures. It is true that Pentecostals found AIC contextualization of the gospel problematic. This is because their practices and theology posited a form of Christianity that Pentecostals considered syncretistic and unacceptable. Hence, they would not associate with the AICs as belonging to the same spiritual fold.

The success of Pentecostalism does not lie only in its ability to "nativize" the gospel to Africans through the vernacularization of sermons, liturgies, and practices, among others. Showing awareness of the needs and aspirations of Africans from the spiritual perspective, Pentecostals employ appropriate methods, such as healing, exorcism/deliverance, power evangelism, and so forth. This traditional approach to Christian evangelization has continued for a very long time. But Christianity is contextual, and so from time to time practitioners must be resourceful in uncovering fresh ways of responding to current needs and aspirations of converts. This is where the neo-Pentecostal gospel of prosperity came in to supply impetus to the Pentecostal effort at translating the gospel to Africans.

We may say neo-Pentecostalism emerged in response to the heady socioeconomic and political challenges that bedeviled the African continent from the late 1970s to the 1990s. In their effort to find religious solutions, the actors looked for and expanded their networking with external, notably American, brands of Pentecostalism. In the process, they exposed themselves to and mimicked their Western mentors, often via audiovisual media, the gospel of prosperity, liturgy, and ecclesiology. The combined effect of this state of affairs was the production of a hybrid and alien ecclesiological culture that used and promoted an Africanized American English as a sermonizing tool and created a tasty, sophisticated church setting unlike the traditional type. Can we say that such cultural repackaging is unnecessary and an unsafe way to approach inculturation?

Against the backdrop that the media has become crucial to our postmodern globalized world, it is needed for the survival of the Christian faith in its multicultural environment. In fact, it is an important route for reaching a

> youthful audience who are already enmeshed, wired in the electronic culture and bored with the equally-packaged

> institutional religion. Religion and popular culture must be enmeshed to attract the youths, just as mainline churches experiment with new liturgies and music.[29]

Consequently, the theology of African neo-Pentecostal preachers has been influenced by and identified to re-echo the North American prosperity theology with the Nigerian "demonology gospel." For example, Onyinah posits that from the late 1980s to early 1990s, a kind of "gospel" that taught that demons could repress, suppress, and oppress human beings, including Spirit-filled Christians, filtered into Ghanaian Pentecostalism. This new "gospel," which attributed the causality of all evil to the activities of evil spirits, was promoted by Western Pentecostal preachers, such as Derek Prince, and Nigerian preachers, such as Emeka Nwakpa, a lawyer turned preacher.[30] The basic response of this gospel is that God has met all the needs of believers and that this can be appropriated through positive confession of faith and application of right spiritual formulas.[31] It appears many contemporary Charismatic ministries have shifted their approach to prosperity to what is now common in the so-called New Prophetic Churches, where the prophetic gift is critical in experiencing prosperity of life.

As may be expected, the popularization of the Christian gospel via the entrepreneurial skills of youth would result in the development of a brand of Christianity that appealed especially to the emerging, growing, and adventurous youthful population with a taste for exotic lifestyles. New forms of Christian music, like gospel rap music, and art, hitherto considered worldly, have found their way into the Pentecostal church to "turn the youth on to Jesus." Thus, by successfully whetting the appetite of their followers, it was natural that the protagonists should tie overseas travels to their interpretation of prosperity. This internationalizing vision and program is thought to be successful through the use of television and radio preaching.

This psychological repackaging has undergone diverse transformations leading to enormous appropriation of modern social media platforms and also the display of iconic founders on church billboards. How have the older Pentecostals responded to this development? They have had to go along with the neo-Pentecostal innovative leadership in crafting a new ecclesiological image and culture. Leaders such as Opoku Onyinah have shown awareness of the importance of taking serious the impact of emerging cultures on the postmodern human being. Onyinah argues that the disciple of Christ today must interpret contemporary lifestyles and cultures in response to the changing trends. He sermonized that the early church

> wouldn't understand the internet, television, things that we have now they wouldn't have understood them at that time…the thing that has come is new so [we] will have to let the Holy Spirit guide [us] so that [we] can interpret the new thing that has come through the old thing.[32]

The popularization and constancy of prophetism in Africa's religious climate may be due to the fact that in several parts of Africa, many Christians and non-Christians are curious about their existential concerns, such as wealth, health, business, progress, education, marriage, promotion, foreign travels, and so on. Therefore, they explore sources of vital forces to change their destinies for the better. As society is fast changing and becoming more and more "Christianized" and "civilized," curious minds resort to Christian mystics to elicit particularized data. Yet because of their particular *modus operandi*, contemporary Pentecostal prophetism has elicited suspicions and doubts among followers, both Christians and non-Christians.

A cursory observation of their fund-raising activities reveals shrewd fiscal policies that outsiders consider devious and encourage unconventional Christian wealth accumulation. Some of them have begun to offer lotto numbers to clients. This is true in Zimbabwe, as it is in Ghana and other parts of the continent, giving vent to the belief that "those who trade with God never lose."[33] Thus, the prophets have developed such entrepreneurial skills that enable them to stimulate financial giving in their patrons. The atmosphere in which this prophetic monetization operates is the general Pentecostal imaging of Jesus Christ as the all-powerful one who saves people from their troubles, including poverty. It may be incorrect, however, to bracket all prophets as false. There are perhaps some who are godly and genuinely motivated by the love of God to win souls for Him. The false prophets parade themselves as prophets, since to them the quickest way to make money is to be a prophet and to prophesy to people, especially women.

Conclusion

The African Christian quest for an authentic Christianity has engaged the attention of many African theologians. Several proposals and attempts have been made in the older churches to make Christianity a true African religion. Scholars like Bediako have seen in the AICs the desired paradigm for the fulfillment of this religious quest. I have tried to suggest that in this age and time, it is rather the Pentecostals who offer the resources for the realization of this African Christian theological dream.

Chapter 17

The Spirit and the African Spiritual World

Allan Heaton Anderson

There are many scholarly studies about Pentecostalism in different regions worldwide, but what has not been explored thoroughly is what may be considered a principal reason for its popularity. This is the extent to which Pentecostalism, through its experience of the Spirit, often unconsciously taps into popular religious and cultural beliefs and draws from these sources while also using a biblical rationale for its practices. This article explains the popularity of this form of Christianity from this perspective. In sub-Saharan Africa, where I spent forty-three years, Pentecostalism has become one of the most prominent forms of Christianity, permeating every historic denomination and independent church. It has not only contributed to the reshaping of the nature of Christianity itself, but also left an indelible mark on popular religion and culture throughout the continent. The ordinary adherents of Pentecostalism and the independent churches known as "churches of the Spirit" are usually on the cutting edge of encounters with the dynamic popular religion that has existed for generations and still permeates African societies, albeit in interaction with a constantly changing context with globalizing tendencies. Christianity on the whole and Pentecostalism in particular are both affected by and affect religious beliefs in many fundamental ways, including the beliefs of members of older churches.

The African Pentecostal encounters in the spiritual world have many parallels in other continents where a holistic, spiritual world is central to human experience and beliefs. This article will consider how important ideas of popular Pentecostalism relate to the continuing prevalence of a pervasive spiritual world. This world of ancestors, evil spirits, hobgoblins, and demonic forces is believed to be responsible for all manner of events—including misfortune, illness, poverty, and a host of social problems. In its encounter with this spirit world, Pentecostalism offers solutions to these problems through its emphasis on the power of the Spirit and the exercise of spiritual gifts. Does this mean that Pentecostals are otherworldly and unconcerned with the larger structural, social, and political issues that are behind continental misfortunes? This question is important, because the African spiritual world, in popular religious parlance, is also related to the prevalence of poverty and disease throughout this continent. In this popular understanding, poverty and disease are not primarily social or physical problems, but behind them is the world of spirits, witchcraft, and manipulating evil forces that need to be encountered and dealt with. As in popular religion, so in much of Pentecostalism, a religion that does not promise deliverance from evil or promote health and prosperity is a dysfunctional religion. This is why the so-called prosperity gospel has flooded this, the economically poorest continent. This chapter will shed light on processes of religious change in other parts of the world where similar popular beliefs prevail. While there are significant differences, the similarities of these beliefs provide a compelling explanation for the popularity of Pentecostalism.

I grew up in Zimbabwe and Zambia, the son of Salvationist missionaries who lived and worked in rural areas. I moved to

South Africa to attend a Bible college in 1971 and was based there until moving to England in 1995. As a result, I have been exposed to African Christianity and religious practices for much of my life, and I worked with Pentecostals in ministry in six southern African countries. My assumptions are influenced by my years of immersion in southern Africa and the Pentecostalism I describe. The concept of the Spirit occupies an important place in Charismatic Christianity in Africa, whether it be the beliefs of Pentecostal, new Charismatic, or older African Independent Spirit churches. In some parts of Africa, these churches constitute up to 40 percent of the total population--a significant fact with enormous implications, not only for understanding religion in Africa, but also for understanding the relationship between religion and society. Theologians of the past have claimed that the Spirit is emphasized almost to the exclusion of other Christian doctrines, resulting in an impoverished theology. Whatever the merits or demerits of this argument, religious historians, social scientists, and theologians are beginning to take this phenomenon seriously. I have subsequently been exposed to various studies that have further motivated me to return to this one. Because the spiritual world is such a central concept in many popular religious beliefs elsewhere, serious attention must be given it.

Although my present context is infused with Western rationalism, culture, and education and my perspective influenced by over two decades of working in a British university, I have an abiding interest in Africa, its peoples, and their cultural heritage. My paternal ancestors of at least seven generations lived and died in southern Africa. I identify with the long struggles of Africans for freedom, progress, and success. I have been actively involved with African churches for a great deal of my life. My years in southern Africa have given me a wealth of experience, and research here and in other parts of Africa have exposed me to scholarship on African Christianity. One of the most influential people in my early academic career, Marthinus L. (Inus) Daneel, was my supervisor for my masters' and doctoral degrees from 1985–1992. His extensive writings constantly strove to purge the study of African Christianity in general and Zimbabwean independent churches in particular from ill-informed presuppositions. His influence was reflected in my earlier publications but in particular my first book *Moya: The Holy Spirit in an African Context*, which dealt with a subject that forms the foundation for this study.[1] Daneel has done substantially more research and writing on African Independent Churches than anyone I know.[2] Although some of his publications are more than four decades old, his pursuit of accuracy in the field of independent churches in Zimbabwe, where he grew up as a missionary kid (as I did), have been a constant source of inspiration. My approach also tries to be sensitive and sympathetic while avoiding idealization. Nevertheless, the concept of the Spirit and the spiritual world in Africa is an important factor explaining the continuing growth of Pentecostalism and its impact on transforming Christianity worldwide.[3]

Terminology and Presuppositions

When dealing with Pentecostalism, and African Pentecostalism in particular, the problem of terminology arises. I do not need to enter into this debating arena extensively because it has been covered elsewhere, but it is necessary at the outset to briefly define terms to minimize confusion.[4] Most contemporary scholars take *Pentecostalism* as a broad, generic term to apply to a bewildering variety of different churches and movements.[5] Walter Hollenweger, one of the earliest authorities on global Pentecostalism, referred to South African Zionist churches as "independent African

Pentecostal churches," a description that is not universally accepted.[6] Nevertheless, those churches with an emphasis on the Holy Spirit and spiritual, supernatural gifts should be distinguished from other independent churches, like "Ethiopian" or "African" churches.[7] So *Spirit churches* describes those independent churches that have an emphasis on prophetic revelation and healing, as they cannot always be described as Pentecostal without further qualification. But this is a broad term. These churches sometimes have historical links with the healing and Pentecostal movements of the United States, imported to Africa in the early years of this century but led by African leaders. One example was the Zion movement of John Alexander Dowie, with headquarters in Zion City, north of Chicago. This movement had links with the thousands of Zion churches in southern Africa and the Faith Tabernacle in Philadelphia that was also connected with the emergence of the first Pentecostal churches in West Africa. These non-Pentecostal American movements were completely transformed by African leaders, both through secessions and through the influence of Pentecostalism.

There are also many independent churches in Africa without connections to churches founded by Western missionaries that may be called either *Pentecostal* or *Charismatic*. They tend to be closer to Western Pentecostalism in character and practice than to the Spirit churches, but the lines between these various churches today are blurred. In evaluating Pentecostalism in the majority world, however, one must always resist the temptation to consider Western (particularly American) forms of Pentecostalism as the benchmark by which all other movements are to be measured. One might venture to say that most churches in Africa, whether independent or connected with Western Christianity, have developed an African character that has many parallels to independent

Spirit churches, mainly because they all emphasize the working of the Spirit in an African context.

Presuppositions and assumptions are common weaknesses, and we all have them. For example, some of the earliest writings on African Independent Churches in southern Africa half a century ago were filled with these assumptions. In his revealingly titled *Post-Christianity in Africa*, South African Dutch Reformed writer G. C. Oosthuizen considered that "the great difficulty" Christianity faced in Africa was "the misunderstanding of the Holy Spirit." He wrote that this was "not due only to the African's strange sense of the supernatural world, but also because of his [*sic*] essentially suprarational and suprahistorical disposition."[8] There is an implicit admission that he did not understand "strange... suprarational and suprahistorical" spirituality because this did not fit nicely into the European philosophical categories he was accustomed to. Indeed, this is the challenge facing many Western observers of majority-world Christianity. Anglican bishop and former missionary in Africa John V. Taylor rightly observed in his classic on African spirituality, *The Primal Vision*, that the Christianity exported to Africa was a "too-cerebral religion... the white man's religion... a classroom religion."[9] In contrast, African religions were essentially "spiritual" religions, by which Africans were essentially united with their holistic environment of spiritual and natural forces.[10] Taylor warned that in trying to understand African religious symbolism, Western observers should be careful not to be "too precisely analytical, for that would transpose the imagery back into European symbols and destroy its meaning."[11] This observation applies to most things non-Western. In our increasingly globalizing world, it is too easy to assume that what we are most familiar with is the grid with which to interpret the less familiar or strange. The global and the local, however, often collide. Before we can comprehensively understand anything outside this interpretative grid, we should attempt to detach ourselves from the Western tendency to have dualistic presuppositions that separate secular from sacred, religious or spiritual. When referring to the supernatural world and the "suprarational and suprahistorical disposition" of Africans, or a spiritual religion, then something is usually being described beyond what is included within: natural, rational, historical, secular, and so on. This is rarely done outside the Western world, except when there needs to be an orientation to a Western audience or readership. People throughout the world would much rather emphasize that things belong to each other and that there are common elements in things and events. Taylor has wonderfully described this religious world as the "primal vision" with a certain "sense of cosmic oneness":

> Fundamentally all things share the same nature, and the same interaction one upon another…a hierarchy of power but not of being, for all are one, all are here, all are now.…No distinction can be made between sacred and secular, between natural and supernatural, for Nature, [Humanity] and the Unseen are inseparably involved in one another in a total community.[12]

In fact, the religious world of much of humanity is holistic; everything is at the same time given spiritual and secular meaning without being dichotomized or separated. Some of the theological evaluations concerning interpretations of spirit/Spirit and Christian theology suffer from a tendency toward "investigating and systematising things or experiences by means of dispassionate analytical probing."[13] In particular, because of the propensity of Western observers to filter ecstatic religious phenomena through their own cultural and theological grids, they often do not fully understand the thought world behind these beliefs and practices. Long ago, Nigerian scholar Bolaji Idowu made the apt remark that "those who seek to communicate and inculcate the Gospel in Africa" have an important assignment "of understanding Africa and appreciating the fact that they must learn to address Africans as Africans."[14] In considering Pentecostalism outside the Western world (where at least three-quarters of its adherents live) and its ideas about the Spirit and the spiritual world, we should make every effort to give this world the understanding and respect it deserves.

The Central Role of the Spirit

Pentecostal and Charismatic Christians interpret ideas of the Spirit in the light of both a holistic religious world and the Bible and that their focus on the Spirit and the spiritual world is one of the central reasons for their growth. Hollenweger wrote that the basis of early Pentecostalism was "the presence of the living God, the reality of the Holy Spirit, which people looked forward to receiving in conversion, sanctification, the baptism of the Spirit and the gifts of the Spirit."[15] For most Pentecostals today, this central experience involves a belief in the imminence of God and the power of God's Spirit and is realized through prayer, worship, and gifts of the Spirit. In turn, this empowerment is regarded as bestowing the ability to evangelize the whole world, which is one of the reasons for their rapid growth. Pentecostals are "missionary" by nature.[16] Their spiritual experience is the heart of their theology. One of the foremost scholars of modern religion, Harvey Cox, is an important observer of this. He writes that the rapid spread of Pentecostalism was because of its "heady and spontaneous spirituality."[17] It touched people emotionally, and its emphasis on experience was spread through testimony and personal contact. Cox suggests two underlying factors for any religion to grow: "It must be able to include and transform at least certain elements of pre-existing religions which still retain a strong grip on the cultural subconscious" and "It must also equip people to live in rapidly changing societies"; he sees these two "key ingredients" in Pentecostalism, which help "people recover vital elements in their culture that are threatened by modernization."[18]

Some Pentecostals are uncomfortable with this analysis, and because of their belief that they are solidly biblical, they resist the idea that there are any pre-Christian religious practices in their rituals. Indeed, they oppose such practices as divination and shamanism. There is certainly no conscious syncretism in Pentecostalism, if *syncretism* means "to distort Christian beliefs." But because a spiritual world pervades social consciousness worldwide and underlies all religious expressions, Pentecostalism acknowledges and addresses needs arising from that spiritual world. It might be better to consider Pentecostalism as a culturally contextual form of Christianity interacting with and confronting the spiritual world. Both continuity and discontinuity with the old religion are kept in creative tension. In Africa and elsewhere, there is also the phenomenon of mass urbanization. Independent, Pentecostal, and Charismatic churches have provided places of spiritual security and personal community for people unsettled by rapid social changes. In the holistic religious world of most non-Western societies, all that exists is a present, material-spiritual, or holistic unity, and in this religious world the spirit (or the Spirit) pervades everything. In Pentecostalism, the all-encompassing Spirit is involved in every aspect of both individual and community life. This is particularly evident in the person of the prophetic or Charismatic leader, who is preeminently a man or woman of the Spirit. Canadian theologian Gary Badcock writes of the role of the Spirit in African Christianity being closely related to the "theme of wholeness, in terms of the perception and realization of the vitalist principle that ultimately binds the whole of society and world together, in the normal expectation of healing and visions, in the simple celebration of life."[19]

Action and expression are probably more important than theoretical reflection for most people. Religion is especially something that you do rather than something you articulate. The emphasis on the Spirit expressed in active participation in Pentecostalism gave Christianity vibrancy and relevance. God intervening in human affairs was possible in visible ways. The rationalistic and "objective" etic scholarship of social scientists sometimes obscures how the often seemingly strange and unnerving manifestations in Pentecostalism reflect both the dynamic nature of Christianity and the religious thought world of the participants. Pentecostalism itself usually gives credit to the Spirit for everything that takes place in its practices and various manifestations. The Spirit causes people to receive or be baptized in the Spirit, prophesy, speak in tongues, heal, exorcize demons, have visions and dreams, live holy lives—and, generally, the Spirit directs the life and worship of these believers. African participants in Pentecostal churches see their practices as manifestations of the presence of the Spirit. The fact that no-less-unusual manifestations were recorded in biblical times means that these manifestations are accepted as responses to the working of the Spirit among ordinary people. Sometimes there may be play-acting and manipulation—but Africa does not have a monopoly on religious charlatans. Christianity as a whole has had its share of those leaders who use religious sanctions to manipulate, deceive, and enforce their will.

The difficulty with some approaches to religion is a dualistic rationalizing that does not always or adequately understand a holistic religious world uniting physical and spiritual and personal and social, for there is a presumed interpenetrating of both. Contextual theologies are often articulated within the parameters of Western theology. This often creates a vacuum because it does not adequately address felt needs. The grassroots beliefs and practices of majority-world Pentecostals become a theology from the underside and an "ordinary theology," but a theology spoken and practiced rather than written about. Pentecostal churches have made possible a dialogue between holistic religious worlds and Christianity at an existential level. This has largely been more effective than indigenous theologies, which have often tended to be justifications for the continuation of pre-Christian religions. Both the Bible and human experience in most of the world often transcend and defy explanations and rationalizations. When Christianity is entangled in this materialistic and rationalistic web, it becomes less meaningful for most people. As Badcock observes, "The tendency of the Western institutional churches toward a more rationally definable ecclesial life ordered through ministerial office, the Word, and the sacraments tends to be regarded as culturally alien and religiously undesirable" in many other contexts.[20]

Africa is illustrative of this tension, where, historically, people regarded Western missionaries with their logical presentations of religion as out of touch with the real, holistic world that they experienced. Their deepest felt needs were not addressed and their questions remained unanswered. Because the real implications of the questions arising from the African religious world were not fully engaged with, the full significance of Christianity was often missed. In contrast, Pentecostalism was motivated by a desire to meet physical, emotional, and spiritual needs, offering solutions to life's problems and ways to cope in a threatening and hostile world. Their pastors, prophets, bishops, and evangelists proclaimed that the God who saves the soul also heals the body and is a good God, interested in providing answers to human fears and insecurities, accepting people as having genuine problems, and trying conscientiously to find solutions. They proclaimed that a God who forgives sin is also concerned about poverty, sickness, barrenness, oppression by evil spirits, and liberation from all forms of human affliction and bondage. This message made Pentecostalism attractive to people in these contexts. The insight of African and other societies that life is a totality, that there can be no ultimate separation between sacred and secular, and that religion must be brought to bear on all human problems is their great contribution to the West, a faith that might even revive the religious consciousness of the West in the face of increasing secularization.[21]

Pentecostal Spiritualities

In most religions worldwide, and especially in Africa, almost everything is invested with religious meaning and there is no clear-cut division between spiritual and secular. This spirituality is often pragmatic, practical, and this-worldly rather than esoteric, reflective, and otherworldly, as one finds in some Western forms of Christian spirituality. *Spirituality* may be defined simply as "that pertaining to and describing the spiritual or religious experience of people and all that is affected by or affects it." The operative word in this definition is *experience*. Spirituality can be described as people's awareness and lived experience of God. Examples of this understanding are found in the religious traditions of Christian and Jewish mysticism and Islamic Sufism—but it also includes Pentecostalism, with its accompanying ecstatic manifestations of the Spirit. In recent years, partly through the influence of postmodern thought, there has been a greater acknowledgement of the importance of the role of experience in understanding reality, and even theology begins to recognize that experience is an authentic source of divine revelation. To return to the observations of Harvey Cox, he sees the rapid growth of Pentecostalism throughout the world as a resurgence of "primal spirituality" with three dimensions: (1) *primal speech*, found in glossolalia (speaking in tongues), "another voice, a language of the heart"; (2) *primal piety*, found in the resurgence of "trance, vision, healing, dreams, dance, and other archetypal religious expressions"; and (3) *primal hope*, which he describes as "pentecostalism's millennial outlook…that a radical new age is about to dawn." Cox describes speaking in tongues as responding to "an ecstasy deficit" in the contemporary world and is "an ecstatic experience, one in which the cognitive grids and perceptual barriers that normally prevent people from opening themselves to deeper insights and exultant feelings, are suspended." He suggests that this is a type of "primary speech" by which people can "safely become as little children, at least temporarily." It is also "breaking through the limitations of human language" and the means by which humans can speak to God. Pentecostalism is thus "closer to the most sublime forms of mysticism than are the more respectable denominations that sometimes look down on it." Tongues as a form of "ecstatic utterance" are, for Cox, another example of what links the religions together.[22]

A major reason for the attraction of Pentecostalism for people oriented to popular African religiosity is a sympathetic and serious approach by its preachers to African life and culture, to fears and uncertainties, and to the religious world of spirits, magic, and witchcraft. The Pentecostal and Spirit churches, with their firm commitment to a cohesive community and their offer of full participation, provide substantial responses to universal human needs. Scholars who have discussed theories for the growth of Pentecostalism have sometimes overlooked the obvious: that Pentecostalism is fundamentally a religious (or spiritual) movement with religious reasons for its burgeoning strength. Chinese American Pentecostal theologian Amos Yong writes of the importance of a holistic understanding of human religiosity and that the Pentecostal and Charismatic experience "demands interpretation of the experiential dimension of spirituality over and against an emphasis on textuality in religious life."[23] Pentecostal spiritualities reflect the conviction that God is experienced as real through the Spirit, and this is expressed in liturgies that are primarily oral, narrative, and participatory. The Spirit invades all of human life. The popularity of Pentecostalism in the majority world can also partly be attributed to a particularly *contextual* spirituality. Pentecostalism purports to provide for much more than the spiritual problems of life. The important role given to divine healing and exorcism, the particular emphasis on the power of the Spirit, but also the comprehensive community projects and significant involvement in political and civic organizations and trade unions represent a vigorous spirituality offering help to human problems. This spirituality is a holistic approach to Christianity that connects more adequately to popular (and sometimes ancient) religious worlds than other Christian traditions have done. In some respects, this was also more meaningful than the so-called traditional religions had become. Furthermore, throughout the world, Pentecostalism has been more relevant because it has continued some pre-Christian religious expressions and ritual symbols and invested them with new meanings. This might be controversial, but Christianity as a whole has been in both a continuous and discontinuous relationship with other religions for two millennia.

Amos Yong points out that Pentecostals in the majority world, especially those who are part of Christian minorities, are in constant interaction with other religions. He writes that the experiences of the Spirit common to Pentecostals and Charismatics demonstrate "indubitable similarities across the religious traditions of the world." This opens up the way for a constructive Pentecostal theology of religions that explores "how the Spirit is present and active in other religious traditions."[24] Yong demonstrates that Pentecostal spirituality is a useful starting point for understanding other religions. The great attraction of Pentecostal spirituality is that it claims to provide answers to existential problems throughout the world. In their encounter with other religions, Pentecostals have themselves been challenged and enriched in the content of their proclamation, which, without the encounter, would have been impoverished and foreign. Pentecostalism offers solutions for these problems through the indwelling Spirit; they accept them as real problems, conscientiously attempt to provide explanations for them, and expect something to happen to resolve the problems through faith in God. In addition, pre-Christian beliefs and practices have been transformed in many Pentecostal churches so that Christianity is presented as an attractive and spiritual alternative.

The subject of contextualization is one that has engaged scholars of religion for many years. Contextualization not only takes into account cultural values, but also tries to make Christianity relevant to the current situation of social change and new economic, cultural, and political contexts. It may be argued that often Pentecostalism attempts to do this and that its success has had a profound effect on older churches. Until recently, Pentecostals did not talk about their spirituality, as it was not part of their religious vocabulary. But Pentecostal spirituality has become recognized as a distinctive form of Christian spirituality that can be described through its various activities and rites.[25] Steven Land describes this as

> the dimension of praise, worship, adoration and prayer to God...[and] the abiding, decisive, directing motives and dispositions which characterize Pentecostals...this depth of conviction and passion...is a steadfast longing for the Lord and the salvation of the lost...a continuous, joyous exclamation of the inbreaking presence and soon to be consummated kingdom of God.[26]

This "passion for the kingdom" is the way Land describes Pentecostal spirituality, centered in the Pentecostal experience of the "lived reality by the eschatological, missionary community, expressed by prayer and integrated by apocalyptic affections."[27] This might still be too esoteric a description of Pentecostal spiritualities, however. Daniel Albrecht's *Rites in the Spirit* approaches the subject through the lens of rituals observed in three Californian churches. Although his descriptions of spirituality might not be appropriate for many other parts of the world, his methodology is relevant, for this spirituality is best expressed in the actions of Pentecostal and Charismatic people at worship, ceremony, and prayer. Comparing Pentecostals and Charismatics in North America, Albrecht finds "a fundamental common belief in the imminent activity of God's Spirit" and that the "fundamental goal of the Pentecostal service" is "experiencing or encountering God."[28] For him, this is the essence of Pentecostal spirituality.

A common Pentecostal spirituality, however, probably cannot be defended because of the diversity of Pentecostalism throughout the world. It is more accurate to say that there are different Pentecostal spiritualities. But even when scholars describe a singular Pentecostal spirituality as the experience of God through the Spirit, this transcends cultural boundaries and provides a genuine and flexible encounter with God that is meaningful in its different cultural expressions. Whatever else they might show, these studies indicate that Pentecostal spiritualities are centered on the experience of the Spirit that pervades the whole person; makes Jesus Christ more real and relevant to daily life; and inspires testimony, praise, unknown tongues, prophecies, healings, dancing, clapping, joyful singing, and many other expressions that characterize Pentecostalism worldwide. These spiritualities are expressed in liturgies that often take on the characteristics of the host culture and are not unaffected by older religious traditions that have permeated that culture. This makes a comparative and contextual study of Pentecostal spiritualities, or Pentecostal experiences of the Spirit in different parts of the world, absolutely essential.

In this discussion of the important role and nature of Pentecostal spiritualities, it is important to remember what has always been a central part of Pentecostal understanding of the purpose and work of the Spirit, which is to honor Jesus Christ. From the beginning, Pentecostals have declared their faith in strong Christological terms. Their "full gospel" was declared in the words "Jesus Christ the Saviour, Sanctifier, Healer, Baptizer, and Soon Coming King."[29] This is proclaimed in the storefront churches, village churches, halls, tents, stadiums, and on street corners. For the vast majority of Pentecostals and Charismatics the world over, the presence of Christ as Lord is the focus of their worship and central theme of their proclamation. Like other Evangelicals, Pentecostals are primarily Christocentric. They declare that Christ is the one who, by His Spirit, transforms the lives of Christians in a "born again" experience and makes them useful in this world in the service of God and humanity. We can only fully understand Pentecostalism's emphasis on the Spirit and spiritualities in this light.

Chapter 18

Charismatic Renewal and Roman Catholicism in Africa: Challenges and Prospects of Pentecostalism

Donatus Pius Ukpong

THE CATHOLIC CHARISMATIC Renewal is one of the ecclesial movements in the Roman Catholic Church in Africa. As a renewal movement closely connected to modern Pentecostalism, it has witnessed various phases of development. There are differing opinions about the opportunities and challenges it presents to the Catholic Church.[1] How the Pentecostal movements have been assessed in Catholic theology has affected how Catholics in Africa have responded to the nascent Catholic Charismatic Renewal. Therefore, many African bishops were concerned about its development in the continent and relied upon the assistance of the International Catholic Charismatic Renewal Service to guide them in providing oversight for the movement in Africa.[2] This chapter studies the genesis of the Catholic Charismatic Renewal in Nigeria as a model of its development in Africa and observes how the Catholic Charismatic Renewal has contributed to the proclamation of Christian and Catholic faith and satisfied the yearning for Pentecostal experience by Roman Catholics in Africa.

Origins and Development in Africa

In order to situate the Catholic Charismatic Renewal in Africa, I briefly examine the origins of the global Catholic Charismatic Renewal. The Vatican II Council (1963–1965) was convoked for the purpose of renewing the mission of the Church in contemporary culture.[3] The outburst of the Catholic Charismatic Renewal in 1967 has been understood by some as a legacy of the council. The Catholic Charismatic Renewal emerged from a university community and was interwoven with enlightened intellectualism and a quest for experiential spirituality.[4]

From the perspective of the Vatican II Council, the Catholic Charismatic Renewal is considered as a providential demonstration of charismatic gifts for the edification of the Church and a fruition of the prayer for a renewing power of the Holy Spirit in individuals and communities. Léon-Joseph Suenens was a pioneering Catholic theologian who observed that "Protestant Pentecostals might be able to contribute to the renewal of the Catholic Church."[5] He was referring to how the Catholic Charismatic Renewal had adopted Pentecostal spirituality as a model of ecclesial renewal.

The origins of the Catholic Charismatic Renewal in Africa is linked to the Charismatic phenomenon that emerged in the late 1960s in the United States and expanded to the Church in Africa in the 1970s.[6] The renewal served as a catalyst for the flourishing of African spirituality in the Roman Catholic Church. The engine of the Charismatic Renewal in Africa is what Harvey Cox describes as primal spirituality.[7] Such spirituality is fundamental for understanding the Catholic Charismatic Renewal on the continent.[8]

African Independent Churches (AICs) are the primal expressions of Pentecostal spirituality in Christian contexts. These churches set out to incorporate African religious experiences into Christianity, laying the foundation for the manifestation of dramatic charismatic gifts during Christian worship. To this end, "the African primal quest for the sacred and the transcendent: the quest for healing, well-being, material success and long life,"[9] are essential elements which made the charismatic experience appealing to many African Christians, including Catholics. Many African Catholics have known about and even had charismatic experiences from their contact with the indigenous or Africanized Christianity of the Aladura churches represented by the Cherubim and Seraphim Church, Celestial Church of Christ, and the like. These African Christians were enthused with the gifts of the Holy Spirit that could permeate human experience through healing and ecstatic manifestations.[10] The nascent Catholic Charismatic Renewal served as a catalyst, fanning into flame this consciousness among Catholics in Nigeria.

J. K. Olupona observes, "The origin of the charismatic movement in West Africa is very complex, and no single theory explains its rise and growth. We can locate the beginning of the charismatics in contemporary West African region from within and outside the continent."[11] This is true of the Catholic Charismatic Renewal in particular.

The origin of the Catholic Charismatic Renewal in Nigeria could serve as a model of its development in the Roman Catholic Church in the rest of Africa. From the happenings in the Aladura and Pentecostal communities, many Catholic priests began to reflect critically on what God may be telling the Church about the role of the Holy Spirit in real-life experiences, as the testimonies many Catholics gave from their encounter with these groups could not simply be swept under the carpet. To this end, "some priests were encouraged to go into prayer and healing ministries."[12]

Godwin Ikeobi was a recognized initiator of a Charismatic prayer group in Nigeria. According to Hilary Achunike:

> The Catholic Charismatic Renewal was actually started at Ibadan and Lagos where the expatriate priests lived and did their apostolate. Some expatriate priests who had been baptized in the Spirit while they were spending their summer holidays in the USA introduced the Catholic Charismatic Renewal to Nigeria in 1971.[13]

Through the instrumentality of these expatriate priests, mainly from the United States, many Charismatic prayer groups emerged in different parts of Africa in the early seventies, including one at the popular Obafemi Awolowo University in Ile-Ife. Official ecclesiastical encouragement was given to Catholic Charismatic Renewal in Nigeria when Francis Cardinal Arinze wrote, "I am in favour of Father MacNutt visiting Onitsha to conduct conferences on the charismatic renewal. I am ready to support any programme which will help towards deeper prayer and commitment to the apostolate of the Church."[14] Therefore, the Catholic Charismatic Renewal emerged in the Roman Catholic Church in Africa through the endorsement of the ministries of leading Charismatic priests in the United States who were welcomed to minister in the local churches in Africa. These ministries were powered by the involvement of lay, religious, and priests who facilitated the modern era of renewal on the continent. The renewal was initially welcomed as an antidote to the drifting of Catholics to the prayer meetings in Pentecostal and Charismatic congregations and to demonstrate that the Spirit was alive and active in the Roman Catholic Church even in a greater dimension.

With Francis MacNutt's visit to Nigeria in 1974, the renewal came to stay in the Roman Catholic Church in Africa. Its spread is attributable to the personal involvement and success of MacNutt with the local hierarchies. The impulses of Catholic Charismatic Renewal were judged to be in harmony with the perennial gospel values and spiritual expectations of Africans. From individual prayer-group meetings and the development of personal relationships with the Lord, the Catholic Charismatic Renewal metamorphosed into an ecclesial phenomenon, bringing hundreds of thousands of worshippers together in praise and worship. There were some negative reactions to the development of renewal in the Roman Catholic Church in Africa, but its spread was guided by the Malines Document prepared by Cardinal Léon-Joseph Suenens and distributed to the Roman Catholic bishops worldwide.[15] Following the directives of the document, priests were appointed to offer necessary leadership to the members, maintaining that the bishops were the first Charismatics in their dioceses. Thus, the Catholic Charismatic Renewal was approved by various Episcopal Conferences in Africa.[16] In spite of this approval, some practices and teachings of the Catholic Charismatic Renewal were scrutinized in order to distinguish them from traditional spirituality and practices of Pentecostal congregations.[17]

This led to the development of the Catholic Charismatic Renewal in Africa, and its growth has been phenomenal. In the 1970s, there were about two thousand Charismatics on the continent; by 1980, there were about one million; and by 2000, this number had increased to 8.7 million. Over the next thirty years, the number of Catholic renewalists is estimated to grow at the rate of 32.2 percent,[18] which implies that almost 35 percent of the Roman Catholics in Africa will be actively involved in the renewal by the year 2033.

Synopsis of the Catholic Charismatic Renewal and Pentecostalism

There are connections between the Catholic Charismatic Renewal and the Pentecostal movements. They are bound together fundamentally by the experience of the Holy Spirit in the life of believers, with or without the manifestation of speaking in tongues. An encounter with the Holy Spirit is the defining value of Pentecostalism. Thus, the Catholic Charismatic Renewal was initially known as Catholic Pentecostalism.[19]

I examine the relationship between the Catholic Charismatic Renewal and Pentecostalism from the perspective of MacNutt's visit to Nigeria. Hilary Achunike reported that MacNutt underlined the importance of his visit thus:

> The reason he (Fr. Ebben) gave me for this was because of the rapid growth of the Aladura or Independent African Churches in Nigeria and West Africa, and the fact that the Catholic Church was losing many members to them. Surveys have shown that in some areas in West Africa 60%–70% of Catholics were also attending Aladura Churches, which seemed to suit the African mentally more than the established Churches. He felt that the Charismatic Movement had much to offer such Catholics.[20]

From the reasons alluded to, there is a fundamentally favorable disposition toward Pentecostal and Charismatic experience among African Christians. This disposition found fertile expressions in Pentecostal communities. The Catholic Charismatic Renewal unlocks this disposition in the Catholic Church. It gives Catholics access to Pentecostal experiences within the boundaries of Catholicism.[21]

From a Pentecostal perspective, religious faith has a pragmatic goal: to enable experience of God's power amidst human vulnerability. *Pentecostalization* refers to the process of the wider church embracing Pentecostal spirituality as a means for achieving this goal in the Christian life.[22] Pentecostalism suggests that central to actualizing this goal is reception and experience of baptism in the Holy Spirit. The incorporation of such consciousness into Roman

Catholicism is at the heart of the Catholic Charismatic Renewal. This generates primal spiritualities (prophetic utterances, dreams, visions, healings, dances, exorcism, etc.) that heretofore were not adequately synthesized by the missionary churches on the continent. The Catholic Charismatic Renewal, therefore, gives new values to the rituals and traditions of the Church, harmonizing both with the emotional and intellectual dimensions of the faith.[23]

Contributions of the Catholic Charismatic Renewal

The Catholic Charismatic Renewal has made specific contributions to the development of Christian faith and enhancement of Catholicism in Africa. I discuss these under four headings.

Theological

The Catholic Charismatic Renewal adopted the basic elements of Charismatic theology related to the themes of healing, exorcism, and speaking in tongues. From a theological perspective, the renewal standardized such spiritual phenomena, engaging Africans' imagination on questions of demonic affliction, healing as divine intervention in human misery, and speaking in tongues as empowerment for effective Christian ministry. The renewal empowered Roman Catholics to confront Africans' worldview with Christian spirituality, making the mystery of the person and ministry of Jesus more relevant in the context of human suffering and deprivation. Through the renewal, theological insights of Pentecostalism are gaining acceptance in African Roman Catholic theology.

Ecclesiological

The Church is not simply a historical hierarchy with tested values and traditions, nor is it an impermeable fortress; it is a community empowered by the Holy Spirit for the worship of God and thereby not immune to the surprises of the Holy Spirit. The experience of the Spirit bridges the gap between the ordained (clergy) and nonordained (laity), empowering male and female together so that every member is respected and valued for gifts that edify the whole body. The Catholic Charismatic Renewal has contributed toward an ecclesiology of change and conversion, where the Holy Spirit unfolds the designs of God for men and women.[24]

The renewal's small church communities have revitalized the Church in Africa. They are dynamic expressions of the fullness of the Church in a vulnerable context, signs of how togetherness and solidarity provide mirrors of God's compassion for the world.[25] These communities are indispensable for en-ecclesiology, where the Church is seen primarily as "an environment where God encounters His children, irrespective of their age, sex and colour, pragmatically responding to their hopes and anxieties, and where they experience the compassion of the Father profoundly,"[26] thus becoming living stones in Christ.

Liturgical

The liturgy is the public act of worship of the universal church in its local contexts. It is a defining value of the church. The liturgy has universal structure as a means for the church to fulfill its goal of worshipping God in spirit and in truth. The liturgy defines when this is being done for all believers, irrespective of their personal whims and fancies.[27]

With the outburst of Catholic Charismatic Renewal and encounters with the Pentecostals, there are certain aspects of the liturgy that have been reawakened in the faithful. The liturgy is neither simply mechanically enacted nor reducible to the formal attitudes of persons; it is not simply unfolded according to rubrics fashioned and designed by the traditionalists of old, nor is it the magical supplier of benefits desired by religious enthusiasts. The liturgy is instead an encounter of the people with the living God.[28] It is the whole person's experience of the presence of God and the radiation of the joy of an intimate relationship with God, calling God Abba, Father. The Charismatic Renewal reveals that God is active in human affairs and operative when believers are gathered in worship.[29]

In Roman Catholicism, the heart of the liturgy is the Eucharistic celebration. Its rite has evolved along the centuries, from the apostolic experimentation in the New Testament era to the liturgical renewal of Vatican II Council. The goal of the Eucharist is the worship of the Father through the sacrifice of the Son (through Him, with Him, and in Him, to the almighty Father). This great doxology and the great Amen of the faithful remains the perennial value of Eucharistic celebration. The Catholic Charismatic Renewal often adds flavor or gusto to the Eucharistic celebration in Africa through its expressive and emotional dimension. The clapping of hands during worship is typical of the African style that the renewal has incorporated into the Church's worship.

The praise and intercessory dimensions of charismatic worship as prayers from the below of the Church during Eucharistic celebration promote soulful worship and enhance personal and active participation.[30] These minimize the mechanical and theatrical character of Eucharistic celebration that in more traditional Catholic experiences often alienate the worshippers from the liturgical goal. The adaptation of the prayer of the faithful during Eucharistic celebration to accommodate spontaneous prayers is a unique inspiration of the renewal that adds value to the Roman Catholic liturgy in Africa.[31]

Pastoral

The Catholic Charismatic Renewal reveals that primal spiritualities remain perennial in the religious consciousness of Africans.[32] Pastoral care should offer solutions to existential questions of human vulnerability. As presented in the New Testament, God intervenes in human affairs and brings succor to the afflicted. To this end, pastoral care is not simply sanctimonious quieting of a troubled soul but a demonstration of the power of God over evil.[33]

The Pentecostal and Charismatic movements have indicated that God still intervenes to restore harmony in the world. Prayer for healing, exorcism, and spiritual and material breakthroughs are essential ingredients of pastoral care, especially in a context of endemic poverty and economic disorientation underwritten by the ineptitude of political governance.[34] The Church cannot remain aloof to the cry, hopes, and anxieties of the faithful. For instance, a Charismatic prayer for healing is more appealing to human brokenness than simplistic and repetitive rituals. The Catholic Charismatic Renewal has demonstrated that primal spirituality is neither alien nor contradictory to the spirit of Catholicism. To this end, an aura of spiritual empowerment so central in Pentecostalism could make ministerial pastoral care more credible and effective in the Roman Catholic Church.

Challenges of the Catholic Charismatic Renewal

The modern Pentecostal revival as rooted in primal spiritualities has come to stay, and the face of Christianity will not be the same again. The Charismatic movements have challenged the presuppositions of the missionary churches and their evangelization processes in Africa. Rooted in Pentecostalism, the Catholic Charismatic

Renewal nevertheless poses challenges to Roman Catholicism in Africa. We will examine these under the following headings.

Theological

With the emergence of current religious movements within and outside Christianity, and with increasing awareness of the multicultural and pluralistic nature of contemporary societies, theological hegemony of any particular tradition belongs to the past. Theological plurality is fast becoming a virtue in the academy of today.[35] The Church as *mater et magister* watches over the *depositum fidei*. It is becoming challenging to define the contents of the faith for all Christians in all contexts of a pluralistic world.

Pentecostal and Charismatic spiritualities are leading the way in defining the experience of God in the here and now of various local contexts. Their focus is not simply the sustenance of universal orthodoxy but the projection of the power of God in the situations of believers.[36] Therefore, the Catholic Charismatic Renewal is concerned less about the soundness of Trinitarian doctrine or the intricacies of transubstantiation and more with what it means for Christians to worship a God who is in community and manifest with evidences or signs for believers who seek encounter of and union with Jesus, the Bread of Life.

Charismatic theologies are often locally rooted and seek to speak of God and interpret God from the actual experience of the worshippers. Such theologies manifest God in the midst of the people's struggle to define meaning, to interpret the challenges of life, and to have hope for the future.[37] Yet one major trend in this arena is the prosperity theology. Pentecostal and Charismatic movements in Africa (and elsewhere) attempt to give hope amidst the powerlessness of life today by presenting the Christian mystery as generative of wealth and health, not only in eternity but also in the present life. Such theologies are often judged to be infantile explanations of human existence, archaic and primitive ideas of God, a rash recourse to superstition, or an enthronement of supernaturalism. In spite of these negative judgments, these theological ideas are powering megachurches, and hundreds of thousands claim to experience the saving God. Such prosperity teachings are thus widespread in the African church, not least within the Roman Catholic Charismatic Renewal today.[38] The Catholic Church ought to learn from the popularity of these teachings but offer sound theological guidance and pastoral oversight for its vulnerable members.

Ecclesiological

The Catholic Charismatic Renewal has contributed toward the emergence of en-ecclesiology, which is a compelling vision of the Church as an encounter community where the *charismata* and sacraments coexist harmoniously.[39] The Church is intrinsically a Charismatic community where ecclesiastical authorities are derived from *munera Christi* for the promotion of the Kingdom's values.[40]

From a Charismatic perspective, the gifts of God are accessible to all believers, irrespective of their gender or place of birth. The Church should not exalt one gender over the other (male over female) nor extol one calling over the other (clergy over laity)[41] but value and appreciate the gifts and endowments of every member. There is a question of grounding the authority in the Church today: Is it simply based on the sacrament of ordination or on the charismatic gifting of persons? For instance, one may wonder, Who is exercising spiritual authority in Enugu Diocese of Nigeria? Is it Callistus Onaga, the diocesan bishop, or Ejike Mbaka, the fiercest Charismatic priest with a "cult followership"? Thus, from a Charismatic perspective, there is a difference between the man of God and the man of the Church, as renewalists more easily identify a Charismatic person as a man or woman of God than an ordained person who may be otherwise indistinguishable from the surrounding culture aside from his clerical collar.

Liturgical

The Pentecostal and Charismatic movements present basic challenges to the liturgical life of the Church. What is really appealing to God? What really gives honor to God, and when can the faithful worship God in spirit and in truth? There is a need to evolve a liturgy that gives assurance of worship and speaks to the whole person in the presence of God.[42]

The voluptuous nature of charismatic worship, the corporal expressiveness of dance, and the demonstrative, dramatic, and animated preaching of the Catholic Charismatic Renewal can alienate the movement from the liturgy of the historic Church that is often solemn and structured. As seminarians, we were taught that homily is the message of God to the community and that a preacher should not allow anything of himself to be felt and should avoid all forms of gesticulation. The challenge for liturgical renewal in Africa is to create a living symbiosis of solemnity and expressionism.[43] The Catholic Charismatic Renewal has the basic tools for bringing about this not only in Africa but also for the universal church.[44]

Pastoral

The Church adopts spiritual, educational, medical, and humanitarian initiatives for her pastoral care. These have strengthened the pastoral ministry of the Church in Africa. The Charismatic Renewal has challenged these traditional approaches, lifting up instead the spiritual dimension of pastoral care—for instance, visions, dreams, ecstatic prophetic utterances, etc. How can these charismatic manifestations be useful in caring for the faithful? Does God speak through ecstatic utterances today? Is there anything like spiritual diagnosis for the furtherance and sustenance of healthy life? What is the spiritual dimension of economics and politics?[45] Can charismatic endowments enhance engagement with political economy and promote wealth creation? Such questions are often answered affirmatively by Charismatics. The Catholic Charismatic Renewal foregrounds these challenges, thus compelling the Church in Africa to reevaluate her pastoral plan and strategy of evangelization.

Sociocultural

Religious faith is relevant for a vision of society and culture.[46] Pentecostal and Charismatic movements tend to emphasize the supernatural and obliterate human responsibility in society. This has implications for how the Church impacts the sociocultural dimensions. For a purposeful Christian engagement with the cultural and social realities in Africa, the Catholic Charismatic Renewal should attend to the gap they often posit between divine intervention and human responsibility with regard to the welfare of persons and communities. They may want to reconsider that it is not so much the tarrying nights and aggressive spiritual warfare practices that will meet the socioeconomic needs of the people as it is a purposive and reasonable engagement with social, economic, and political realities.

Prospects of the Catholic Charismatic Renewal

The question today is whether the springtime of the renewal is over or yet to arrive. The initial enthusiasm for the experience of the Holy Spirit, which was the hallmark of Catholic Charismatic Renewal, seems to be diminishing. What is the image of the

Church that speaks to and meets the fundamental religious expectations of African Catholics? Attempts to answer these questions can chart the prospects of the Catholic Charismatic Renewal for the Roman Catholic Church in Africa as we look ahead. Let me propose a few lines of inquiry.

Ecclesiogenesis and community renewal

In the message to the Eleventh National Conference of the Catholic Charismatic Renewal of Nigeria, Valerian M. Okeke, archbishop of Onitsha, writes, "I urge you to welcome and embrace an intense spiritual revival for the renewal of the face of the earth especially our country Nigeria...for the growth and edification of the Family of God—the Church and the society."[47] The role of the Spirit in bringing about the Church and renewing the human community is well documented in contemporary theology.

The Catholic Charismatic Renewal emphasizes the advent of Jesus as God's offer of divine love to humankind in the power of the Spirit.[48] The mysteries of Jesus's life, ministry, death and resurrection, and ultimate glorification make divine salvation present in human history through the Holy Spirit. Spiritual revival is therefore crucial for an ongoing appropriation of the events of Jesus. The impulses of Charismatic Renewal are essential for effective Christian witness in contemporary culture.[49]

Biblical engagement

The Catholic Charismatic Renewal could be described as a response to the prayers of the Vatican II Council in general and to a deeper and more profound engagement with the Word of God, *Verbum Dei*, in particular.[50] The Pentecostal movements in general have provoked new love for the Word of God and have demonstrated the perennial value of the Word of God for Christians of every culture and time. The communal studying, meditation, proclamation, and listening to the Word of God is the future of the Church.[51]

The Church has no authentic word for the salvation of the world outside the Word of God. To this end, theology that is not rooted in the Word of God is of disservice to the Church, and theology that is not manifested or authenticated in the everydayness of believers' lives by the power of the Spirit is an unincarnated theology. Therefore, vibrant biblical engagement is indispensable for the mission of the Church. The Catholic Charismatic Renewal has set a pace for an experiential and communal living of the Word of God and for engaging the biblical apostolate in the Roman Catholic Church. The future of the Church lies in the faithfulness to the Word of God.

Respect for African spirituality

The Roman Catholic Church in Africa is called to respond to the fundamental religious yearning of Africans. One of the peculiar religious values of Africans is the consciousness of the activity of the Spirit in the human world. God relates with human beings in all ramifications and nothing lies beyond the Spirit of God.[52]

The Catholic Charismatic Renewal rooted in Pentecostal theology often addresses the values of African spirituality, thereby offering road maps for Catholics who are desirous of spiritual uplifting and yearn for Christianity in power. It bears the prospects for the Church in Africa to meet the real hunger of the people for meaningful spiritual experience. This explains why many prayer groups in the Church lay emphasis on primal spiritualities. The Charismatic Renewal serves as the institutionalization of this consciousness in the Roman Catholic Church in Africa.

Conclusion

The Catholic Charismatic Renewal, from its humble beginnings among the lay university teachers and students in the United States, has spread to all parts of the universal church. From being considered as a *school of samba*, a South American popular dance common in Brazil, it has demonstrated itself to be a great force for the proclamation of the gospel in contemporary society. Its impact in the Roman Catholic Church in Africa is undeniable and indicative for future trends of being Church and Christian in the continent. Nevertheless, because of its origin in Pentecostal movements and the relative competitive nature of Christianity in Africa, the Catholic Charismatic Renewal is not completely embraced by both the lay and hierarchy in the continent. There are suspicions of the Charismatics, due to the awareness that the promises of the renewal are always in the Church and accessible to the faithful and dedicated seekers. Thus, the novelties of the Charismatic Renewal are seen as an invasion of Pentecostalism, generating confusion in the content and praxis of Christian faith in the Church. The challenges and opportunities the renewal offers the Church in Africa therefore cannot be overlooked. There is need for more theological, liturgical, pastoral, and cultural investigation of Pentecostalism for responsible, effective, and meaningful incorporation of its authentic religious and Christian values into the Roman Catholic Church in Africa. I, therefore, call on the ordained and nonordained members of the Church to encourage the Catholic Charismatic Renewal for effective renewal of ecclesial communities and societies today.

Chapter 19

Nigerian Pentecostalism and Islam: Toward a Pentecostalized Vision of Interreligious Coexistence Through *Ubuntu* Philosophy

Clifton Clarke

OVER THE PAST fifty years, the growth of Pentecostalism and Charismatic Christianity in sub-Saharan Africa has been simply astonishing.[1] Across major African cities, towering billboards—traditionally only used by Coca-Cola, Nestlé, or other large, multinational companies—now portray giant iconic figures of African megachurch leaders. As Allan Anderson observes, "Pentecostalism is big business in Africa."[2] What began as a fringe movement, springing up on university campuses across Africa, has now become the new face of African Christianity and possibly even global Christianity.

This newly founded platform given to African Pentecostal leaders—many of whom have the ear of the nation through their global media ministries—comes with a solemn responsibility. This was captured when one news reporter raised the microphone to a nationally known Pentecostal bishop after a suicide bomber killed scores of church attendees in northern Nigeria, and asked, "Bishop, do you believe all Muslims are going to hell?" Increasingly,

Pentecostals are asked to respond to pertinent issues in African public life. These issues range from views on politics to corruption to globalization to poverty to economic growth, just to name but a few. One of the urgent issues confronting African Pentecostals is how to coexist in spite of religious differences. Violent clashes along cultural and religious lines seemingly elevate Samuel Huntington's clash-of-civilizations theory to prophetic proportions. According to Ogbu Kalu, a major aspect of Pentecostal political theology is the lack of a viable theology of dialogue in an increasingly pluralistic public space.[3]

In this chapter, I seek to contribute to the African Pentecostal efforts in constructing a theology of religious dialogue. The essay provides the historical context of the acrimonious relationship between Christians and Muslims in Nigeria and then presents the African concept of *ubuntu* as a possible framework upon which a theology of interreligious coexistence and harmony may be premised. As the goal of this chapter is to contribute an African Pentecostal theology of interreligious dialogue, the focus is on developing a Christian, rather than Islamic, theology. We begin with a short discussion of Islam and Christianity in Nigeria and a look at the development of Nigerian Pentecostalism. We then turn to the concept of *ubuntu* as a possible construct for interreligious relations. Our concluding section suggests how *ubuntu* philosophy can assist Pentecostals in cooperative interfaith practice.

Nigeria: Islamic and Pentecostal Perspectives

Nigeria is the most populous country in all of Africa, with a formidable presence in the West African subregion. In the past few decades, Nigeria's forceful presence has been felt beyond the West African subregion. Whether it is in the area of religion, politics, media, business, entrepreneurship, art, or literature, tongue-tied announcers fumble over enigmatic Nigerian names as they appear on the global stage. Amidst this globalized cultural success story lies another picture closer to home. This is a story of a country ravaged by the torment of what Charles Selengut terms *sacred fury*.[4] The battle lines of this conflict have been drawn between Christianity and Islam, and the cost to national development and economic growth is incalculable. The relationship between these two global Abrahamic faiths goes as far back as the medieval times. It is a relationship that has had some measure of cordiality, but for the most part it has been one fraught with difficulties and acrimony.[5]

Christian-Muslim relations: causes of tension

There are multiple causes for the conflict between Christians and Muslims in Nigeria. According to Peter Clarke, the primary cause is the superior-inferior attitude of interaction manifest in the intent of each group to win more converts.[6] Islam presents itself as the final revelation and completion of previous prophetic messages, while Christianity claims to be a universal religion and the only way humanity can attain salvation.

Historically, specific events have exacerbated the tension. First, the application of Islamic law has been a major point of contention for Christians. The idea of no separation between Islam and the state is part of the Muslim ideal. Many normative Muslim scholars, such as Mawdudi, Hasan al-Banna, Sayyid Qutb, and his brother Muhammad Qutb, insist on no separation between Islam and the state. The efforts by Muslims to add the Sharia in the Nigeria Constitution in 1978, 1989, and 1991 had negative repercussions on Muslim-Christian relations. Other major events that strained the relationship between Muslims and Christians in Nigeria was the Maitatsine uprising in Kano and in other major cities in the North in 1982, 1984, and 1985. Although these were originally revolts by more conservative Muslims groups against the orthodox Muslims in the North, Christians also suffered much damage to property and lives, at times even more than Muslims. Third, the Nigerian federal government's attempt to gain full membership in the Organisation of Islamic Cooperation (OIC) in 1986 was seen as a back-door attempt to Islamize the country. The Christian student movement, along with other Christian bodies, was vocal in stating that membership in the OIC was synonymous with Islamization of the country and a contradiction of Nigeria's secular constitution and warned that this could lead to a religious war.[7]

Conversely, Muslims claim that Christianity is the cause of the conflict. Yushau Sodiqin outlines Muslim claims of Christian aggravation based upon the following four premises.[8] First, Christian missionaries target Muslims for conversion and do not recognize the legitimacy of Islam. Second, Christian schools before and after independence were used as a proselyting weapon to convert Muslims to Christianity. Third, Muslim students in institutions established by Christian missionaries were denied Islamic education and forced to attend and receive biblical instruction; this has had an adverse educational effect on Muslim students who were not sent to school because of fear of Christianization. Fourth, despite the fact that the Nigerian Constitution of 1979 makes it clear that students are free to choose in matters of religion and should not be forced to receive any religious knowledge against their will, the majority of Christian educational institutions prior to nationalization made it a policy to deny Islamic religious knowledge to Muslims attending their schools.[9]

These and a number of other factors have been the reasons why Islam and Christianity have clashed for many years. However, these clashes are accelerating to new heights with the rise of a more radical stream of Islam that is taking root in Nigeria, to which we briefly turn.

The rise of radical Islam in postcolonial northern Nigeria

These tensions are contributing factors to the brutal and violent outbreaks between Christians and Muslims. Since 1982, Christians and Muslims have been engaged in unprecedented violent conflicts in many parts of the country, especially northern Nigeria.[10] Northern Nigeria has been described by Marinus Iwuchukwu as the "axis and the center stage for the most destructive and outlandish expression of the fall out in that relationship."[11] The rise in the level of Islamic radicalization in northern Nigeria is partly due to increased Christian missionary efforts in that region, particularly from the Pentecostal and Charismatic brands of Christianity, as well as a deep-rooted desire to protect the Islamic legacy of the North from missionary incursion. In addition to this, there is a broader global Islamic agenda that has been on the rise in recent years. The success of the Islamic revolution of 1979, in which Ayatollah Khomeini brought down the Western-backed political administration of the shahs in Iran, also played a significant role. This was a major victory for Islamic militants and fundamentalism worldwide, and its impact was not lost on the northern Nigerian landscape as new radical Islamic groups emerged with the intent of making their mark.[12] The *Jama'atul Izalatul Bid'ah Wa'ikhamatul Sunnah* (Movement Against Negative Innovation), for instance, was highly critical of the Muslim status quo between the two existing brotherhoods, Tijaniyya and Qadiriyya, for being un-Islamic and heterodox, even as it perpetrated violence against Christians.

In more recent times, Christian-Muslim tensions have been aggravated by the violent attacks on Christians in northern and central Nigeria by Boko Haram. One of the shocking attacks was perpetrated against Christians on what is known as the Christmas Day bombing of St. Theresa's Catholic Church in Maddalla, Suleja City, Niger State. Reprisal attacks by Christians have also occurred in several places in northern Nigeria. Since 2009, Boko Haram has terrorized Christians, Muslims, clerics, traditional leaders, and politicians who have condemned the movement's methods.[13] Another deplorable shooting took place at an agricultural college in Yobe, where forty students were killed while sleeping. Although these are extreme examples of brutal killings by a suspect Muslim group, they point to the murderous depths people have sunk to in the name of religion. The kidnapping of innocent children, the burning of churches, and the massacre of innocent people is considered a price worth paying for the establishment of the Islamic state. Moderate Muslims insist that these radical groups are not Muslim; however, the groups themselves are clear that they are Muslim with a clear jihad mentality using violent resistance and armed struggle for the cause of Allah.

Pentecostalism in Nigeria

It is amidst this surge of Islamic revivalism that Nigerian Pentecostalism has exploded upon the religious scene with equal vigor and ambition for religious dominance as Islam. The crucial question Nigerian Pentecostals have had to contend with is: Will they coexist or continue to clash with their Muslim neighbors? I will focus my attention on Nigerian Pentecostalism, without rehearsing the historical trajectory of Christianity in Nigeria,[14] for two reasons. First, Nigerian Pentecostalism is experiencing a prolonged season of exponential growth and vibrancy, referred to earlier.[15] It is driven by bold dominion spirituality and theology that poses a direct challenge to Islam in Nigeria, particularly in northern Nigeria. Second, Nigerian Pentecostalism is in search of what Nimi Wariboko calls a "spiritual epistemology," by which he means knowledge from the invisible spiritual realm to guide its understanding and experience of the world.[16] In addition to this, I believe Nigerian Pentecostalism is also impelled by what Amos Yong calls a "pneumatological imagination," which envisions and engages the spiritual dimensions of human experience.[17] Last but not least, Ruth Marshall's recent study of Nigerian Pentecostalism focuses on how members are wrestling with what it means to be African Pentecostal Christians in the global context of the twenty-first century.[18]

A brief survey of the development of Nigerian Pentecostalism is in order. In his book *African Pentecostalism*, Ogbu Kalu delineates the development of African Pentecostalism in general and Nigerian Pentecostalism more particularly into three main periods.[19] The first was a period of separation from the African indigenous churches along with the hegemony of missionary churches. During this time, there was a distancing from the Aladura-type churches that carried the vestiges of traditional religion. This gave way to a more exuberant, youthful, born-again movement that placed great emphasis on holiness, sanctification, the gifts of the Spirit, and the immanent second coming of Christ. Students gathered in university cafeterias and dormitory rooms to pray and seek the baptism of the Holy Spirit.

The second period took place during the 1980s. During this period, there was a sharp increase in independent ministries and churches as the youthful exuberance of this Charismatic Renewal was frustrated by the historic mission churches as well as the classical Pentecostal groups. This took place at a time of massive economic downturn as the price of crude oil (the source of the economic boom of the 1970s) plummeted. At a time when the nation was feeling the weight amidst increase corruption and economic hardship, the new Pentecostal churches focused their message more on prosperity, healing, and deliverance from satanic powers.

The third period, from the 1990s to the present, shows Pentecostal churches emerging as the most important sources of religious and cultural creativity in Nigeria. Their popularity spread to all sections of the community, including the educated elite, successful businesspeople, the political class, and the armed forces, among others. I would argue that Nigerian Pentecostalism is entering into a fourth phase of "dignification" and stability wherein Nigerian Pentecostal leaders are increasingly called upon to show leadership on matters of social, economic, cultural, and political concerns.

Ubuntu: An African Vision of Humanness and Bridge to Pentecostal Theology

In this section, I would like to introduce the African philosophy and way of life called *ubuntu* (humanness) as a useful starting point for the development of a Nigerian Pentecostal practice of interreligious relations. Once again, the goal here is to contribute toward an African Pentecostal epistemology and realism that enhances public life and community building. I would like to use and expand on Dirk J. Louw's innovative thesis of *ubuntu* as a vision for interfaith relations, one that transcends absolutism without relapsing to relativism.[20] First, let us explore the usage of the *ubuntu* concept itself.

Ubuntu: "I am because we are"

Ubuntu is a Zulu African word that captures the spirit and philosophical foundation for African living. It is a unifying vision or worldview enshrined in the Zulu maxim *umuntu ngumuntu ngabantu*, meaning "a person is a person through other persons."

The essence of this African aphorism is the basic respect and compassion for others. It asserts our ability to coexist goes to the very core of our humanity. A definition proposed by Archbishop Desmond Tutu says:

> A person with Ubuntu is open and available to others, affirming of others, does not feel threatened that others are able and good, for he or she has a proper self-assurance that comes from knowing that he or she belongs in a greater whole and is diminished when others are humiliated or diminished, when others are tortured or oppressed.[21]

As an African philosophy, *ubuntu* is well summed up in Mbiti's words: "I am, because we are; and since we are, therefore I am."[22]

The philosophy that undergirds *ubuntu*, although popularized by South Africans such as Bishop Desmond Tutu in the post-apartheid era, is very much present in a West African context that is more pertinent to the Nigerian understanding of the *ubuntu* philosophy. *Ubuntu* is graphically depicted, for example, in the works of the father of African literature, Chinua Achebe.[23] In his novels, Achebe, a Nigerian author and poet, portrays African culture and traditions as deeply rooted in *ubuntu* philosophy. These books delineate the extent to which the Western varied outlook on ethical issues invariably altered the peaceful understanding and coexistence (*ubuntu*) enjoyed by the African people.[24]

For the Yoruba, the individual cannot be separated from the community and societal reality one is interlaced with.[25] For them, individualism has a limit; the purpose of individual existence is intricately connected with the purpose and health of communal and social existence, and hence individual existence cannot be reached without living within society.[26] Thus, Gyekye avers:

> For the Akan, religion is not seen as hindering the pursuit of one's interests in this world. . . . Akan humanism is the consequences not only of a belief in the existence of a supreme being and other supernatural entities but more importantly I think of the desire to utilize the munificence and powers of such entities for the promotion of human welfare and happiness.[27]

Much more could be said about African concepts of communalism,[28] but I maintain the use of the *ubuntu* terminology here because it has universal value and yet speaks to the Nigerian philosophical and cultural moorings with regard to interhuman relations. I will proceed by using Louw's essay on *ubuntu* to draw out how an African Pentecostal vision of humanness relates to the task of interreligious coexistence in a Nigerian context.

Louw elaborates on aspects of *ubuntu* for religious coexistence in the African context, each of which can be variously applied to or connected with Nigerian Pentecostalism. First, *ubuntu* affirms a respect for the "other" as a religious other. This attests, Louw argues, to the spiritual foundation of African societies.[29] The concept of *ubuntu* thus defines the individual in terms of his several relationships with others and stresses the importance of *ubuntu* as a religious concept. While the Zulu maxim *umuntu ngumuntu ngabantu*—"a person is a person through (other) person"—may have no ostensible religious connotations, in the African cultural context, it idiomatically carries the idea that the person one is to become by behaving humanely toward others is an ancestor worthy of respect or veneration.

Ubuntu as bridge to African Pentecostal theology

The first important bridge between *ubuntu* (as respect for the religious other) and African Pentecostal spirituality and practice is the robust communitarianism evident in African Pentecostalism's pneumatically driven Charismatic ecclesiology. The respect for others implicit within the concept of *ubuntu* can only be forged and nurtured within community. The importance of community within an African context cannot be overrated. Of course, traditionally, the African communal orientation tends to be based squarely on tribal loyalty. Yet the African metaphysical orientation demands that community be more than a physical face-to-faceness.[30] The existence and perpetuation of community depends on more than actual physical encounter; spiritual ties to the community always exist. It is here that the African Pentecostal pneumatic-ecclesial orientation makes a unique contribution to *ubuntu*. In ways reminiscent of the Apostle Paul's metaphoric depiction of the church as one body with many members (1 Cor. 12:12), African Pentecostalism brings people together not only physically but also under the unifying force of the Holy Spirit in Charismatic ecclesial relationship. Within this Charismatic community, unity in diversity is a biblical communal principle. The Apostle Paul's teaching referred to above notes:

> There are different kinds of gifts, but the same Spirit distributes them. There are different kinds of service, but the same Lord. There are different kinds of working, but in all of them and in everyone it is the same God at work.
>
> Now to each one the manifestation of the Spirit is given for the common good.
>
> —1 Corinthians 12:4–7, niv[31]

In the spirit of *ubuntu*, the African Pentecostal Charismatic community sees openness as a foundational principle.[32] The openness proposed here is two-pronged. One prong is directed toward God though the power of the Holy Spirit, and the other is directed toward others as vessels of the Holy Spirit, through whom the Spirit operates. There is therefore a vertical and horizontal dimension to the African Pentecostal ecclesial community. Members of this pneumatic community share in one power, yet because of the gift of the Spirit working uniquely through each person, this power allows each person an exercise of freedom. Asamoah-Gyadu observes that this "exercise of freedom" is most notably seen in the exercise of the gifts of the Spirit. He argues that the church has its being in the ecclesial Spirit, who is also the missionary Spirit. The spirit in the *koinonia* and empowered mission seeks to draw humanity into communion with God.[33]

This pneumatic community is by no means static but very much dynamic; it is in the process of being in the world. It is therefore capable of being open to newness that springs from within, as well as that which emerges from outside of the community. This dynamic pneumatic nature of African Pentecostalism, which opens up avenues for change and growth, is often overlooked or confused with the intransigence of Western fundamentalism.

Another important feature of the church as a fellowship of the Holy Spirit that bridges with *ubuntu* in the spirit of coexistence is that of its theological language. The language of this Charismatic ecclesial community speaks of love, fellowship, brotherhood, communion, the fatherhood of God, grace, righteousness, justice, sacrifice, and other biblical beliefs held dear by the faithful. It is the seriousness with which African Pentecostal believers uphold these truths that ultimately will serve as a corrective to any form of religious bigotry, intolerance, or violence. The healing and deliverance that emerges from the African Pentecostal ecclesial community also speaks to the spirit of *ubuntu*. As J. Kwabena Asamoah-Gyadu observes:

> Healing and deliverance is employed within African Pentecostal communities as a form of pastoral care. Its aim is the restoring of disturbed and sick persons to being a healthy member of the community of believers. Deliverance means more than exorcism, and the expulsion of evil spirits. It has to do with freeing people from "bondage" to sin and Satan.[34]

It is the bond of love and compassion that arises out of this pneumatic community that makes healing and wholeness a shared concern. The African Pentecostal ecclesial community is by no means a fully formed theological community. It therefore does not provide ready-made answers to the religious tension it is increasingly encountering. It does, however, I would argue, possess the theological and philosophical resources from which the *ubuntu* idea of respect for the religious other can be embraced and engaged.

A second important point of connection between *ubuntu* and African Pentecostal spirituality and practice pertains to the extremely important role that agreement or consensus plays within *ubuntu*. Without an interreligious agreement or consensus on criteria, the beliefs and practices of the religious other simply cannot be judged without violating them.[35] Consensus is an important value within African societies, in which decisions are traditionally made in consultation with community elders who represent the interest of the local constituents. Traditional African democracy operates in the form of lengthy discussions in the quest for consensus and agreement between parties.[36]

The idea of agreement is not a strange one for African Pentecostals either and could be creatively expanded to include dealing with people of other faiths. One area where agreement and consensus is expressed in African Pentecostalism that provides a possible inroad for furthering religious dialogue is "touching and agreeing."[37] African Pentecostals believe that much can be accomplished when people gather together and agree on a common course of action. This is evident in prayer meetings, where adherents are often seen holding hands and praying in concert.[38] During the annual "Twenty-One Days of Prayer" led by David Oyedepo, the founder of Living Faith Church Worldwide, also known as Winners Chapel, the congregation is drawn into corporate prayer with great emphasis on the power of agreement. During the prayer, the faithful grasp hands and bow heads as prayers are uttered with great fervor. Although the emphasis of this agreement is spiritual and the focus of consensus is religiously defined, there is a sense in which the focus on "outcomes"—i.e., healing, deliverance, reconciliation, victory, prosperity—could lend itself to cooperation with people from other religious faith traditions for the common good. It is not without significance that the agreement that is embarked upon is not simply on a human level but rather that all parties are in agreement with celestial powers beyond the human gaze. There is a strong sense that the desired outcome is theirs because it is decreed in heaven and awaits manifestation in the earthly realm.

My visit to the National Day of Prayer put on by Action Faith Chapel on July 1, 2015, was a fitting reminder of this. Thousands of believers gathered together to pray for the prosperity of the nation. The prayer leader directed adherents to Matthew 18:19, which says, "Again I say to you, that if two of you agree on earth about anything they ask, it will be done for them by My Father who is in heaven" (MEV). He then made reference to the Lord's Prayer, noting, "Thy Kingdom come on earth as it is in heaven." Following this, the people were led into a time of ecstatic prayers for the agreement of heaven to be manifested in time and space. In this type of corporate prayers of agreement, African Pentecostals enlarge *ubuntu* in three important ways. First, they are in agreement and cooperation with African ancestors, thus removing the necessity of libation prayers and other "non-Christian" ritual practices and replacing them with a Christian practice of praying in agreement with the biblical God, Yahweh. Second, the idea of praying for God's agenda and will to be manifested on earth challenges the perceptions that African Pentecostals operate purely on an otherworldly eschatology. For them, the victory is theirs first and foremost because it is God's. Third, the dynamic pneumatological emphasis in the prayers engages with the African universe more forcibly than the mere theoretic assent of a Christian vision of *ubuntu* put forward by Bishop Tutu and others.

Here I pause to pose a few questions for further reflection. Could an African Pentecostal reimaging of *ubuntu* be extended to the point in which victorious outcomes and breakthroughs include cooperating with people from different faith traditions? Could the *ubuntu* idea of "a person is a person through other persons" provide African Pentecostals with a fresh perspective on evangelism as based on communal and intercommunal harmony? Could an African Pentecostal reimaging of *ubuntu* open up new avenues for African Pentecostal pneumatology in which the Spirit is engaged in not only personal deliverance but also national and even cosmic deliverance? In this respect, African Pentecostals might have to go beyond their own sensibilities and religious comfort zones and agree with the Scripture, based on the scriptural idea that the wind of the Spirit blows where it pleases (John 3:8).

A third point of connection between *ubuntu* and African Pentecostalism I want to briefly highlight before moving on pertains to interreligious dialogue, or what Louw calls "mutual exposure,"[39] which epitomizes the conduct prescribed by *ubuntu*. In a similar manner, Jabu Sidane asserts, "Ubuntu inspires us to expose ourselves to others, to encounter the difference of their humanness so as to inform and enrich our own."[40] This highlights an issue important for both *ubuntu* and African Pentecostalism, namely religious experience. In spite of the degree of tension between Christianity and Islam, one cannot deny the level of mutual exposure they share. This is in part because religion in Africa is a private enterprise but is played out in the public space. An outcome of this mutual exposure is perhaps glimpsed though the enigmatic sect known as Chrislam.[41] The True Message of God Mission, also popularly known as Chrislam, refers to certain interfaith branches of Christianity and Islam that have fused the two religions together.[42] This sect is indicative of the degree of mutual exposure between Christianity and Islam in Nigeria. Contextually, African Pentecostalism in Nigeria has emerged in an environment of radical religious blending and sharing. Islam, Christianity, and traditional African religion have long existed alongside one another. Although this mutual exposure has not always led to conciliatory dialogue in the formal sense, dialogue has always ensued between Christians and Muslims informally, within the banality of everyday life. I will return to this theme below.

Performing *Ubuntu*: An African Pentecostal Practical Approach

In this final section, I want to further explore how an African Pentecostal reimaging of *ubuntu* might work in practice. We build on the preceding discussion.

Ubuntu as a call to prayer

If the *ubuntu* ethic emphasizes respect for others, how might this apply to African Pentecostal spirituality and practice in a multi-religious context? Let us revisit the violent attacks on Christians in northern and central Nigeria by Boko Haram and at the agricultural college in Yobe, referred to above. Unfortunately, the African

Christian response was a knee-jerk reprisal attack, a good proportion of participants being Pentecostals. Here the *ubuntu* ethic of respect for others was rendered helpless in the face of the insatiable desire for reprisal and revenge. This human instinct in Africa is most ugly in the face of tribalism and religious conflict. African Pentecostals are not innocent here, as its leaders, such as David Oyedepo, encourage the faithful to expect God to heap upon their enemies "unparalleled devastation."[43] There is no doubt that this reprisal and retaliatory expectation is a part and parcel of the African Pentecostal dominion theology, and that is also encouraged by a literal reading of the Bible.[44] I submit, however, that this dominion, warlike posture as a reaction to harrowing attacks must be countered otherwise, following, for instance, the response of groups like the Pentecostal Fellowship of Nigeria (PFN). PFN, in the face of escalating unrest both politically and religiously, have called for Christians across Nigeria and around the world to join in a yearlong 24/7 prayer for the healing and transformation of Nigeria.[45]

In this practical response to the crisis between Muslims and Christians by a Pentecostal group, *ubuntu* is expressed in at least three ways. First, it is seen in the charismatic fellowship of the Spirit, referred to above, through the corporate nature of the call to prayer. *Ubuntu* is expressed here as the quest for unity and harmony that transcends religious affiliation and sensibilities and seeks the well-being of the whole community. Prayer is one of the Christian ways to achieve harmony, even as its focus is to remove all that is bad from a community and restore what is good. Prayer, according to Laurenti Magesa and John Mbiti, also connects the visible and the invisible world and enhances mutual, interdependent relationships.[46] One prayer point listed on the PFN website states, "Ask God to cause peace, unity and love to manifest amongst all people of various religious backgrounds, tribes and ethnic groups."[47] An important focus of the PFN's "Year of Prayer for Nigeria" is the Lord's Prayer. Albert Haase summarizes the important *ubuntu* principle behind this PFN emphasis:

> The first word of the Lord's Prayer honors Ubuntu as a critical factor in spiritual formation. It confronts and challenges the belief that the Christian life is a quaint little individualistic affair between "me and Jesus." It also reveals one of the great illuminations in spiritual formation: all creatures, both rational and irrational, are brothers and sisters in Christ.[48]

Second, the PFN call for national prayers is the ultimate act of *ubuntu*, which is the command given by Jesus in Matthew 5:44: "Love your enemies, bless those who curse you, do good to those who hate you, and pray for those who spitefully use you and persecute you" (MEV). In this call for prayer, we see the enlarging of the African Pentecostal understanding of healing and wholeness. Antjie Krog, a well-known South African writer, puts the word *ubuntu* aside in her essay entitled "This Thing Called Reconciliation" and replaces it with *interconnectedness-towards-wholeness*. She explains *interconnectedness-towards-wholeness* as a

> mental and physical awareness that one can only "become" who one is, or could be, through the fullness of that which is around one—physical and metaphysical. Wholeness is thus not a passive state of nirvana, but a process of becoming in which everybody and everything is moving towards its fullest, building itself; one can only reach the fullest self though, through and with others, which include ancestors and universe.[49]

In many respects, the PFN call for national prayer in the face of national crisis is recognition of the interconnectedness that exists between all peoples, irrespective of tribe and religion. It is this interconnectedness that bears down on us through the command of Jesus in Matthew 22:39 to love our neighbors as ourselves. This call to love our enemies and to love our neighbors as ourselves implicitly calls for forgiveness, which is the third point. To forgive is to be healed of emotional, psychological, and physical sickness, which often leads to social, political, and physical ailments. This, of course, was the premise behind Desmond Tutu's theology of *ubuntu* that permeated the South African Truth and Reconciliation Commission. Tutu's well-cited quote runs:

> Forgiving and being reconciled to our enemies or our loved ones are not about pretending that things are other than they are. It is not about patting one another on the back and turning a blind eye to the wrong. True reconciliation exposes the awfulness, the abuse, the hurt, the truth. It could even sometimes make things worse. It is a risky undertaking, but in the end it is worthwhile, because in the end only an honest confrontation with reality can bring real healing. Superficial reconciliation can bring only superficial healing.[50]

The corporate call for prayer for the healing of the nations by PFN and the regular call to prayer by African Pentecostals all over Africa for the same reason, I would argue, provide important openings for a deeper discourse on the meaning and outworking of prayers for national healing and forgiveness. This call for national prayer for unity and healing is increasingly a popular feature of African Pentecostal services, particularly during the dawning of a new year and the precariousness of election seasons. The issue of Pentecostalism and reconciliation is an area that is in its infancy and most certainly in need of further exploration.[51]

An African Pentecostal enlargement of the *ubuntu* philosophy as reconciliation contributes three important Trinitarian insights.

First, African Pentecostals embrace the idea of one supreme God who is sovereign and under whom all things exist and to whom all prayers find their resting place. Second, prayer—understood by African Pentecostals as warfare—implies that healing and reconciliation can only be achieved through struggle. This struggle finds its ultimate victory through Jesus Christ. Third, African Pentecostals embrace the Holy Spirit as reconciler. It is the Holy Spirit—and not merely human effort—that causes things to come together.

Touching and agreeing: a call to unity in diversity

Above, we discussed the important role that agreement and consensus play in *ubuntu*. Here, I want to connect with the African Pentecostal practice of healing,[52] in which agreement and consensus also feature significantly. But how might the Pentecostal practice of healing contribute to interreligious dialogue in the spirit of *ubuntu*? During prayers, the African Pentecostal minister can often be heard saying, "Agree with me in prayer," or "Let us touch and agree." The idea here is that healing and deliverance begin with coming together and touching. I would like to suggest three practical ways that African Pentecostals could "touch and agree" to foster religious tolerance in ways that give integrity to their Christian witness.

First, I would suggest *touching and agreeing as intra-Christian resistance*. In some situations, African Pentecostals (and African Christians generally) have to be bold and confront the source of the tension between Muslims and Christians. In that case, Christians can touch and agree together as Christians against the common threat. Self-defense by nonviolent means is one of the duties and rights that all movements of justice and peace in our time support. In situations where Muslims refuse to practice justice with Christians, "touching and agreeing" is the language of resistance and a necessary form of engagement. Indeed, sometimes defending one's rights can result in unpleasant confrontation. This is the lowest form of dialogue, but it is sometimes necessary.

But, second, there is *touching and agreeing in the spirit of interreligious cooperation*. There are many interests Muslims and Christians have in common in the areas of economics, development, and social and moral progress. These concern not only government and religious leaders, but also individuals and private associations. One example where touching and agreeing transcends religious affiliation is the Women Without Walls movement in Jos, Nigeria. In the face of government inability to quell the murderous rampage of Boko Haram, Christian and Muslim women, realizing that both Muslims and Christians were victims of government inactivity and Boko Haram's brutal murders, mobilized hundreds of thousands of women and formed a resistance group against Boko Haram and addressed the Nigerian government's ineptitude in the face of terror.[53]

Other opportunities to touch and agree in common projects helps to foster healing and wholeness in community. In northern Nigeria from the mid-1990s onward, interreligious groups (some consisting of religious leaders, others of young people or women) were set up in an attempt to work toward peace. Hajiya Yusuf describes and evaluates a number of these efforts, particularly the successful Kaduna Peace Initiative.[54]

African Pentecostals have been slow to embrace this level of dialogue, though there are some encouraging signs in that direction. For instance, on October 18, 2004, a dialogue series titled "Pentecostalism in Public Life" was held in Lagos. The dialogue brought together Pentecostal and human rights leaders for frank and interactive discussions on issues of public accountability and governance, especially the question of how the moral influence of

Pentecostal churches can serve to improve the quality of governance in Nigeria. The Pentecostal-Civil Society Dialogue is facilitated by the Centre for Law and Social Action with support from the Nigeria Office of the Heinrich Böll Foundation.

Third, there is *touching and agreeing in the dialogue of life*. Here, I spring off the *ubuntu* ideal of dialogue and mutual exposure to connect further with the inherently dialogical nature of African Pentecostalism, seen through its preference for oral expression through such activities as prayer, prophecy, and symbolism.[55] In spite of the vicious, violent history between Christians and Muslims in Nigeria, dialogue is not an option and could be viewed, according to Akinade, as growing pains for this relatively young democracy.[56] The real issue is to develop the capacity to embrace differences and the "other." The "dialogue of life" is an example of interreligious dialogue that I believe is practical and contextual and builds upon the African Pentecostal orientation toward orality and lived experience. This is part and parcel of the daily encounter of Christians and Muslims in many parts of Nigeria.

Charles Amjad Ali provides a very useful critique of the epistemological presuppositions undergirding Western theologies of dialogue. One is the glorification of cognitive knowledge, based on Descartes's dictum "I think, therefore I am," with its emphasis on reason as the primary means of achieving a knowledge that claims to transcend particulars and achieve universality.[57] Another is liberal political theory, as well, which celebrates individual freedoms and choice over community rights and religious identity. All these factors have led to metalogue, or the

> search for a transcendent way beyond the particulars of the dialogue partners. Consequently, people's religious and cultural particularities have been sacrificed and theology has

> become divorced from its historical moorings. Such an approach reduces dialogue to "mentally constructed laboratories of objectivity."[58]

The dialogue between ordinary believers, harmonious and constructive sharing in the situations of daily contacts, is truly a more basic form of dialogue and is one that lays the foundation for more specialized encounters. Unlike Western approaches to dialogue, which tend to be highly text-centered, the "dialogue of life" takes into consideration other issues that are not considered in more theoretical approaches. Akinade argues such dialogue is not a contrived idea but the recognition of the interreligious conversations happening between Christians and Muslims on a daily basis:

> In many parts of southern Nigeria, there is a form of dialogue of life that operates on practical and day-to-day terms. Christians and Muslims live next to each other, mingle freely in all aspects of human endeavor, meeting in the market place and on the streets, in schools and other institutions. Both Christians and Muslims are awakened every morning by the strident voice of the muezzin from the minaret of the mosque, urging faithful believers that "it is better to pray than to sleep." Christians receive Christmas and Easter greeting cards from their Muslim friends, neighbors, and relatives. Muslims are present in churches for the baptism, wedding, or burial of relatives and friends. In this dialogue of life, Christians and Muslims are enriched by each other's experience and spirituality, and strengthened by certain features of the faith of the other.[59]

Thus, the "dialogue of life" points to the distinctive characteristics of Christian-Muslim relations in Africa, one that unfolds amidst the intimacies of family and communal life.

Conclusion

In this essay, I have attempted to bring together two opposing and significant growing movements in Nigeria: namely, Pentecostalism and Islamic revivalism. I have proposed using the African philosophy of *ubuntu* as an indigenous and wise counselor to inform how Pentecostalism might draw upon this ancient philosophical mooring to aid coexistence with Muslims. Although this is an academic construct that can be placed alongside others seeking to engage with pressing the issue of interreligious cooperation in Nigeria, my hope is that such conversation will begin to spark a broader conversation among the rank and file of African religious life.

Chapter 20

The Deregulation of Piety in the Context of Neoliberal Globalization: African Pentecostalisms in the Twenty-First Century

Asonzeh Ukah

> The spirit world, Muslim, Christian or traditional, lies at the heart of many African societies, a core belief in the power of spirits that can be harnessed by mediums. This belief partly explains Africans' lack of political and social agency.[1]

Unarguably, the most profound and widespread social transformations in Africa in the last century and a half have been religious in character. From a meager 18 percent of the African population who belonged to either Christianity or Islam in 1900, more than 80 percent of the 1.2 billion Africans today are either Christian or Muslim. Historically, no continent has been so transformed in so short a time. Religious conversion carries enormous social, political, and economic consequences, as religious faith interpenetrates other spheres of life. This is amply exemplified by the rapid spread and popular appeal of Pentecostalism, a strand of Christianity that emphasizes the embodiment of the power of the Holy Spirit in the daily life of the believer.

In the turmoil of the late twentieth and early twenty-first centuries, one socially visible phenomenon is the intense spiritual practices that anchor Africans as they navigate the turbulence of rapid socioeconomic and political changes. Dean Hamer argues that the instructions for the human sense of spirituality are wired in human DNA, and the popular appeal of Pentecostalism in Africa stands as a signpost of Africa's newly discovered "God gene."[2] Some scholars argue that Africans are "notoriously religious" such that there is no separation between the worlds of play and prayer, market and miracle.[3]

Scholars point to statistics about religious affiliation or conversion as evidence that Pentecostalism is the fastest-growing religion in Africa and from that conclude Africa is being Pentecostalized.[4] Early Pentecostal missionaries were determined to "claim Africa for Christ,"[5] and if the view of a Pentecostalized Africa holds, then Africa has become an integral part of "the heartland of world Christianity."[6] However, explaining this radical structural transformation has been a difficult and controversial task. Providential Pentecostal historiography and analyses point to "the practical expression of the work of the Holy Spirit."[7] As powerful and insightful as these articulations are, they represent a variant of the old, worn argument. But explaining African Pentecostal evanescence by appealing to the primal religiosity or to a special, and therefore singular, divine vocation for Africans and divine destiny of Africa not only is circular and an overgeneralization, but also attempts to explain the empirical (social transformation in Africa) by the meta-empirical (God). Though not discounting providential accounts that claim the success of Pentecostalism is because of the working of the Holy Spirit, yet "a variety of social factors also help to explain the explosion of Spirit-filled Christianity around the world and especially among the world's poor."[8] Hence, critical attention to the social, economic, and political contexts of Pentecostal practice and expansion adds strong explanatory force to understanding the varieties and characteristics of African Pentecostalisms. By examining the social, political, and economic characteristics of African Pentecostalisms, this chapter will contribute to ongoing debates about the social sources of religious transformation in Africa.

The appeal of Pentecostalism has coincided with the inexorable spread of neoliberal practices with an ethos of deregulation and accumulation, that Pentecostalism is both transforming the religio-social landscape of Africa and is being transformed into a political and economic ideology of practice. About 45 percent of Africans are Christians. The percentage of Christians who belong to the protean class of Pentecostal-Charismatic Christianity in Africa is estimated at about 31 percent[9] (up from 11 percent in 2004[10]), the largest in any continent in the world. This large cohort that continues to expand is of major consequence to the future of Africa. Aside from mineral resources flowing out of Africa, Spirit-filled Christianity is the only positive phenomenon attributed to the continent. If this is the case, it is important to search for the social causes and consequences of such burgeoning spirituality and why it has found traction in a continent both degraded and marginalized in the scheme of global events.

Pentecostal Self-Construction

The social facts about religious change in Africa are complex and ambivalent. The "success" and achievements of Pentecostalism are sometimes pointed out as part of the "Africa rising" narratives.[11] Pentecostal practice and discourses provide hope for many Africans; however, how this hope becomes a continental achievement or development is more difficult to delineate. As a continent,

Africa is vast and diverse, with more than three thousand ethnicities and distinct languages. Similarly, Pentecostal-Charismatic Christianity in Africa has produced a dizzying diversity that the use of the plural, *Pentecostalisms*, is warranted.[12] Important issues, therefore, in the discussion of African Pentecostalisms are those of definition, delineation, quantification, and characterization.

Of the four major divisions or traditions of global Christianity—the other three being Catholicism, Orthodoxy, and Protestantism—Pentecostalism is the youngest. Central to the self-understanding of Pentecostalism are the events narrated in the Acts of the Apostles, particularly chapter 2, where the Holy Spirit is described as descending on the fearful followers of Jesus Christ, imparting to them spiritual powers. Gifts of the Spirit emboldened them and allowed them to speak in strange tongues before huge crowds of people who came to Jerusalem to celebrate the feast of Pentecost. Pentecostal Christians are those who believe that the exercise of the gifts of the Holy Spirit as described in the letters of Paul is the distinguishing mark of true believers and followers of Jesus Christ. They are those "who expect to see God's miraculous power displayed on earth as part of normal, everyday experience."[13]

Yet internal divisions and a diversity of biblical interpretations mark Pentecostalism. In Africa, many church founders include *Pentecostal-Charismatic* and *International* or *Worldwide* as a part of the name of their organization, pointing to its global aspiration and interconnectedness as well as its emphasis on the Holy Spirit. The fluidity of the Pentecostal narrative provides the tool for the construction of a new self-empowered by the Holy Spirit. The Pentecostal spirituality, which revolves around the making of a new body and self through the infusion of the Holy Spirit, is an embodied and materialized way of connecting with God in order to exercise the gifts (Greek, *charismata*) of the Spirit. For many Charismatic Christians, the foundational experience and indicator of the presence of the Holy Spirit is the phenomenon of speaking in tongues. Furthermore, some believe that the born-again Christian is legally entitled to a set of gifts of the Holy Spirit, as enumerated by Paul: wisdom, knowledge, faith, healing, power to work miracles, prophecy, discernment, the ability to speak in many languages, and a similar ability to explain what is said in those languages (1 Cor. 12:7–10). Among many African Pentecostals, the gifts of the Spirit are marked by the trinity of healing (health), predicting the future (prophecy), and promoting success (prosperity). These practices come under the rubric of the miraculous. What sets Pentecostal Christians aside from other subgroups of Christians is the normalization of the miraculous as the default mode of Christian existence. Miracles testify to and certify a believer as properly believing. The miraculous is the way that God *ordinarily* interacts with the believer, through signs and wonders.

For African Pentecostal Christians, "You shall receive power" (Acts 1:8, MEV) is a central text in the construction and understanding of the Pentecostal self. Among other things, this power, some Pentecostal leaders have reiterated, is the ability to engage with mission but also, more fundamentally, the capacity to confront and even dominate the world. The first stirrings of the Pentecostal movement in Africa occurred under the conditions of existential angst and instability: the influenza epidemic of 1918 in Nigeria[14] or the sociopolitical and economic deprivation of the early 1900s in southern Africa.[15]

The second pivotal text in the making of a born-again self is "Ask, and it shall be given you" (Matt. 7:7, KJV). To be born again is to receive power to witness to the Holy Spirit as well as to ask for miracles of healing, wealth, and success. As Robert Mbe Akoko documents in the context of Cameroon, the appeal of Pentecostalism is in its promise to deliver on this command. Pentecostalism blossomed in Cameroon in the context of economic decline and a culture of lack, forcing people to resort to a do-it-yourself religion.[16] For the four and a half decades between 1970 and 2015, African Pentecostalism has made a complete transformation from an otherworldly, ascetic religion to a this-worldly, consumerist religion. If religion is the political economy of the sacred, Pentecostalism is then the political economy of the Holy Spirit.

The Neoliberal Turn in Africa: Deregulating the Spirit

In 2014, Pastor Danial Lesego of Rabboni Centre Ministries in Garankuwa, north of Pretoria, South Africa, caused his followers to consume grass growing within the premises of the church. For many weeks each Sunday, church members would literally scramble outside the church building to frantically consume as much grass as possible, as a demonstration of the power of the Holy Spirit residing in them. The pastor's point was to establish visually the ability of the Holy Spirit in the life of believers. He wanted the world to "see the body"; the body is the canvas upon which "the message through miracles, signs and wonders" are printed.[17] A more dramatic case happened in July 2015 when another South African pastor, Penuel Mnguni of End Times Disciples Ministries in Soshanguve, started feeding his congregation live snakes, lizards, and mice with the promise that it would taste like chocolate. For Mnguni, "A person with strong faith can eat anything," as a demonstration of the authority of the believer.[18] It is not coincidental that both Pentecostal leaders chose to demonstrate the political economy of the Holy Spirit through the consumption of items that are indeed edible but often only eaten during periods of scarcity, when people are on the brink of starvation. Some dismiss these local Pentecostal leaders as inconsequential or marginal to the mainstream Pentecostal discourse or practice, but that would amount to selective treatment of what counts for analysis and what does not. The emphasis on Pentecostalism as "an epistemological quest" for "things that are not seen"[19] underestimates the performative power of desiring the disgusting in the political economy of the Holy Spirit, as exemplified in the ministries of Lesego and his apprentice, Mnguni.

The euphoria that inaugurated the postcolonial African states in the 1960s was short-lived, as *coup d'états* and other social upheavals soon dissipated nationalist energies and stymied what was thought to be the era of African Renaissance.[20] The lost decades of the 1970s and 1980s ushered in stringent economic policies (called Structural Adjustment Programs, or SAP), designed by the Bretton Woods institutions and (viciously) foisted on one African state after another. The postcolonial moment soon turned into a neocolonial period when the African state was embroiled in a myriad of crises that vitiated it economically and politically, making it unable to provide goods and services to its citizens. With the withdrawal of state investment in social infrastructure, currency devaluation, and retrenchment of workers, citizens were left to their own devices to fend for themselves. Although there were some positive effects of SAP on African countries, "its tangible effects were devastating."[21] These included high unemployment rates, deregulation of the economy, privatization of state-owned corporations that provided essential services to the people, and commercialization of social amenities, which means that economic cost rather than social cost underpinned the provision of social goods and services. Commercialization manifested itself in the upward hike of tariffs and increased profits to shareholders or business owners. The mantra that "Government has no business in business" became pivotal to economic propaganda, which promised more efficiency and economic empowerment to the citizenry through increased competition in a free market (with minimal or complete absence of government intervention).[22] The focus on economic cost and profit rather than social cost and benefit changed the way the state related to its citizens.

Neoliberalism is a doctrine that emerged in the 1930s to encapsulate an advanced and rapacious form of Western capitalism, which espoused and promoted free-acting market forces, competition, and the attempt "to transform all spheres of human life in ways that render them amenable to economic calculation."[23] In the words of John Stuart Mill, neoliberalism references "the shaping influence of capitalism on modern life."[24] Business and profit generation are neoliberal imperatives that strengthen the hands of global corporations and hold them up as the definition of success, development, and human progress.

In the context of deregulation, intrusive neoliberal forces, ideology, and practice, which prioritize "the ideal of the independent individual agent" as a consumer,[25] became rampant in Africa. More importantly, it soon became the default mode of economic, political, and social practice. In contrast to the African indigenous philosophy of social relations as captured by *ubuntu*, which is humaneness towards the other or the view that the individual exists because of the community/others,[26] the individual is at the center of the neoliberal cosmos.

The decades of SAP not only deregulated the economic structures of relations in the African postcolony, they also, and more consequentially, deregulated social relationships and spiritual quest and practice. The "precarious contexts of deprivation and growing poverty rates"[27] was the backcloth against which new religious organizations, doctrines, practices, and lifestyles emerged to cushion the effects but also provided alternatives to a shrinking and fragile social and political ecosystem in Africa. The "context of radical economic and political insecurity... [created an] epistemological insecurity of life in the... [African] postcolony" that led to a transformation of how religion, particularly Pentecostalism, is done.[28] The megachurches of Africa were born out of this crucible, and those churches founded before this seismic shift quickly transformed in order to reposition themselves in an increasingly dense and competitive marketplace.

The social and ideological context of neoliberal forces foregrounded the expansion of Pentecostalism in Africa, including its doctrinal and ritual adaptation and economic practices. The doctrine that the individual should break free of the past as a condition of being born again also stresses that the born-again person should dissociate from his or her family. The freedom of being born again is partly the economic freedom of shirking (extended) family responsibilities and substituting the new community of faith for the filial family. In theory, the individual whose body is the locus of the operation and action of the Holy Spirit is believed to have a direct, unmediated access to the sacred. The deregulation of the Spirit decentered the sacred and its access points to believers, promoting individual interpretation of Scripture and (spiritual) experience. With no center and generally accepted organizational structure of authority, churches and ministries proliferated, each highlighting what the individual benefits from listening, seeing, and consuming the goods of religion. The liberated autonomous believer is the independent agent of the neoliberal ethos that is powerful and at the center of the market. For such a believer, attaining the divine is not through spiritual exercises but engagement with materialistic and worldly ends, such as consumerism and primitive accumulation.

J. Kwabena Asamoah-Gyadu captures the deregulation of the Holy Spirit when he writes:

> Literally anybody who *feels* called by God, possesses the necessary charisma, and can mobilize some material resources, can found a church. These independent reverend doctors, pastors, prophets, bishops, and archbishops...preach the word without theological accountability to any ecclesial institution or authority.[29]

Operating in the neoliberal, deregulated religious ecosystem, the individual, including the religious leader, is his or her own authority. This *laissez-faire* religious market promotes the rise of superstar religious entrepreneurs and Pentecostal empire-building driven by the priorities of the neoliberal practice such as dot the African Pentecostal landscape. The African Pentecostalism that is held up as the new face of global Pentecostal expansion has characteristics and practices drawn from its context of growth and consolidation, derived from the rubble of the Structural Adjustment era of the 1980s and 1990s in Africa.[30] In the twenty-first century, these features will imprint deeper onto Pentecostal self-understanding, institutions, and practices in Africa and beyond.

Liquid Spirituality: Typologizing and Characterizing African Pentecostalisms

In his critical analysis of the place of African Christianity in the transformation of Western societies, Jehu Hanciles points out the role of massive socioeconomic and political upheavals in dispersing Africans around the world, such as violence, epidemics, and economic downturn. Furthermore, he points to the role of globalization processes that marginalized Africa but "also facilitated the global spread of African forms of Christianity."[31] He ignores, however, the social consequences of these factors in the production of the type of African Christianity that is mainly Pentecostal in orientation. This section briefly discusses those social features, all the while insisting on the fluid or liquid character of African Pentecostalism. As Zygmunt Bauman makes clear in *Liquid Modernity*, the core feature of liquid is, among other chemical characteristics, its continuous alteration in shape when subjected to stress because of the loosely bound constituent molecules.[32] To the features of spiritual and experiential embodiment and intensity, it is important to add the socially significant liquid character of African Pentecostalism: its capacity to mutate at very short notice. African Pentecostalism is a liquid spirituality that assumes and responds to the social context of its practice, absorbing external influences, reworking indigenous cosmologies, and modifying its self-understanding and practice accordingly. In a similar sense, Jacobsen highlights Pentecostal nebulosity and claims that this is why it "has become the fastest-growing religion in the history of the world.... What also makes Pentecostal/charismatic Christianity popular is its lack of expense. It needs no cathedrals or icons, and it needs no highly trained clergy.... It offers so much for so little."[33]

Pentecostal liquidity complicates attempts at describing its social features or creating a typology of African Pentecostalisms. Using the paradigm of power and piety as an analytical tool and focusing on the rhetoric of belief/faith rather than practice, Matthews Ojo presents a typology of Pentecostal organizations in Nigeria, which he says "could be applied to other African contexts, provide[d] an analytical framework to make an in-depth enquiry and avoid generalization... has been found."[34] Ojo groups Pentecostal churches as follows: 1) faith seekers, 2) faith builders, 3) faith transformers, 4) reformists, 5) deliverance churches, and 6) modernists.[35] Like every typology, this is both helpful and problematic; for example, grouping Prophet T. B. Joshua and his The Synagogue, Church of All Nations as a modernist organization compounds the meaning of *modernity*. Many Pentecostal leaders in Africa distance themselves from T. B. Joshua precisely because they perceive him as the opposite of modern; as Paul Gifford points out, he trades on the gullibility of followers.[36] A more significant challenge to the above typology is that it omits the material, experiential, and embodied aspects of Pentecostalism:

> More than any other Christian tradition, Pentecostal/charismatic Christianity allows people who have been beaten down by the world to feel loved and empowered by God—and the emphasis on feeling is important. Pentecostal/charismatic Christians don't just believe in God; they claim to feel God's presence physically in their bodies.[37]

To omit the feeling part and to omit the economic angle will amount to omitting an important aspect of the Pentecostal self-construction and understanding.[38]

African Christians do not embrace Pentecostalism in search of faith;[39] they seek salvation, a technique of dealing with practical concerns. This is the point of David T. Ngong's argument "that the overall wellbeing of the people of the continent is what has contributed, and will continue to contribute, to the wellbeing of the faith on the continent" and that the central appeal of African Pentecostalism is that "many people seem to think that it enhances their vision of the good life."[40] According to Martin Riesebrodt, "Religions promise to ward off misfortune, to help cope with crisis, and to provide salvation. Religions are less about 'the holy' than about blessings, salvation, and protection from misfortune, as well as about the providers and mediators of salvation."[41] If religions are about the provision of goods of salvation, the mediators of these goods, and the institutional structures that have evolved through which these goods are produced, disseminated, and consumed, then accounting for the popularity and expansion of African Pentecostalism needs to pay critical attention to these structures of appeal.

An important feature of African Pentecostalism is that it is urban-based. Classical Pentecostal denominations were founded in the early twentieth century; however, the Charismatic movements of the 1970s started in the cities or within the campuses of tertiary institutions. Young, aspiring Pentecostal leaders usually move from the rural areas to city centers, where they polish their skills and imbibe a specific urban lifestyle consistent with their spiritual aspirations. Scholars often mention the urban character of African Pentecostalism but ignore the sociological consequences of urbanity. The city is important in the remaking of the African landscape and in the cultivation of the African mind, according to Western colonial and missionary narratives and practices. More importantly, the city is the storehouse of resources, a large concentration of populations, network structures, diverse skills, financial access, and technologies. For African Pentecostal Christians, the village is antithetical to the city; diseases, poverty, evil spirits, witches, and other malignant entities ravage it. Some Pentecostal churches, such as Living Faith Church Worldwide (Winners Chapel), closed down their parishes in rural and peri-urban areas all over Nigeria because they were not as financially profitable as the urban-based parishes. While 55 percent of the African population reside in rural areas, 95 percent of Pentecostal organizations are concentrated in cities because the city encapsulates the Pentecostal desire as much as the village represents its disgust.

From the urban character of this religion flows its embeddedness in the world of media technologies and culture. African Pentecostalism is a media-perceptive and rich religion. Leaders and organizations saturate the media with their presence through book and DVD/CD production, glitzy advertising (handbills, posters, billboards), satellite and Internet television/radio broadcasting, and social media. Multidimensional engagement with the media has enormous consequences for the production of spirituality and charisma, congregational life, and organizational reticulation. Through Pentecostal media production, African urban culture—visual and audible—has been transformed into a sacred gallery. The media facilitate the production of sacred sensational forms that imprint directly on the memory of both believers and nonbelievers alike.[42]

African Pentecostalism, particularly the independent churches (in contradistinction to classical Pentecostal churches, such as the Assemblies of God, Foursquare Gospel Church, the Apostolic Church, etc.), is entrepreneurial in practice. Churches are organized like religious firms, based on business principles and market logic and controlled by strong leaders who demand unflinching loyalty because they exercise unquestioned authority. Independent Pentecostal-Charismatic churches are controlled by charismatic figures who exercise absolute, unquestioning power and authority on matters of doctrine, administration, and financial control. This person, known variously as the founder, visioner, or chief missioner, decides what happens in the church and is not accountable to followers, state agencies, or any ecclesiastical structure. African Pentecostalism has morphed from a cottage industry controlled by or family firms headed by family members to transnational organizations (Pentecostal empires) with billions of dollars of untaxed/untaxable revenue. In line with the business model, African Pentecostal leaders of franchise churches, such as David Oyedepo, T. B. Joshua, Helen Ukpabio, and Ezekiel H. Guti, clearly identify themselves as chief executive officers of their organizations. Major Pentecostal organizations in Nigeria, Ghana, Zimbabwe, Kenya, and South Africa have become spiritual franchises, mass-producing religious goods and services and exchanging sacred bonds.[43] While others may still retain religious titles, such as bishop, pastor, or evangelist, their self-perception and their organizations are deeply intertwined in the marketing of salvation goods and services and the spirit of the neoliberal market. The Redeemed Christian Church of God (RCCG) is a prominent actor in the financial and real-estate markets in Nigeria.[44] Like Chris Oyakhilome's Christ Embassy, the RCCG is into charter flight business as well. Part of what accounts for the popularity of African Pentecostalism, particularly from the production side, is its entrepreneurial possibilities and the lack of state and ecclesiastical oversight and control. Although they employ a large number of people, African Pentecostal churches lack transparency, public accountability, and strong institutional structures to foment long-lasting social change. More importantly, they are yet to interrogate the neoliberal imperatives that drive their actions and doctrines.

The promise of miracles is important in the appeal of African Pentecostalism. The miraculous defines the legal right of the born-again believer's experience and daily life. Miracles are the Pentecostal credentials that substantiate belief and belonging. Four major shades of miracles are healing, deliverance, prophecy, and success or prosperity.[45] The promise of providing healing and deliverance (spiritual protection) connects African Pentecostalism with both the indigenous worldview and the core technologies of religion, as theorized by Riesebrodt.[46] The desire and search for miracles of healing, deliverance, prophecy, and prosperity have fashioned the Pentecostal market into more specialization of service providers or mediators of salvation. The four dominant specializations among mediators are 1) teachers, 2) healers, 3) deliverers, exorcists, and demonologists, and 4) prosperity providers or motivational actors.[47] Division of service is the motor of growth of African Pentecostalism. Specialization of the Pentecostal labor force ensures focus, deliberation, and efficiency in production but also secures a niche in a crowded spiritual market.[48] The segregation of the market is encouraged by the promotion of the believer as an autonomous consumer, a free agent who shops around from one spiritual producer to another in search of satisfying specific spiritual needs.

An important feature of African Pentecostalism that has not been highlighted sufficiently is its deep ambivalence about the family, gender, and same-sex relations. The spotlight placed on the individual as a consumer of salvation goods and the individual as the subject of salvation undermines the nature of the family as a unit. Salvation is personal, and not social, and so personal accumulation and consumption are Pentecostal virtues and a material sign of divine reward. Similarly, although Pentecostalism teaches that every believer has equal access to the sacred and sacral goods, in practice, gender roles are skewed against women and in favor of men. Authority and executive (decision-making) powers within organizations are vested in and exercised by men over women. Women, when they exercise authority, usually do so in areas like the choir or coordinating women's groups and other service sectors. In most African Pentecostal churches, if women are pastors and ritual leaders, they are mainly spouses of church owners who function in practice as Pentecostal first ladies cast in the mold of political first ladies. Pentecostalism challenges patriarchy but reinforces it in other respects.[49]

Perhaps the most controversial feature of African Pentecostalism is its unapologetic and vehement opposition of same-sex relationships and support for the criminalization of homosexuality raging all over sub-Saharan African states. From Nigeria to Ghana to Uganda to Kenya to Malawi to Zambia to Zimbabwe—all powerhouses of Pentecostal spirituality—anti-homosexual legislation and social opposition to sexual minorities have emerged from obscurity to ubiquity. This is remarkable, as it is the single issue that unites Pentecostal and Muslim communities. Indeed, this negative relationship between Pentecostalism and homosexuality is of enormous social and political consequence as gay rights' activism expands in the continent.[50]

Conclusion

The most visible and profound aspect of religious change in Africa is the upsurge of Pentecostalism as a social force that straddles cultural, economic, and political spheres. Africa in the twenty-first century is a continent of hope and promise, even as it is still the least-developed part of the world. Part of this hope is the promise that popular and public religion such as Pentecostalism offers for transformation. Pentecostal expansion coincided with neoliberal intrusion in Africa in the 1970s and 1980s engineered by the World Bank Group and the International Monetary Fund. Pentecostalism performs as the spiritual underbelly of neoliberal ideology and practice, encouraging aggressive competition, consumerism and accumulation, and a deregulated piety where anyone, in principle, can become a religious producer. As a liquid spirituality that emphasizes the power and effect of the Holy Spirit on the human body, Pentecostalism responds to the special circumstances of believers; it promises customized salvation goods to both the rich and the poor, politicians and traders alike. As a strong religion with a public and powerful ideology and a theory of practice, the expansion of African Pentecostalism will likely reflect on public policies, political realignments,[51] social accountability, and economic restructuring in many African states, particularly in light of continued socioeconomic and political distress occasioned by commodity price drops. Similarly, conservative interpretations of Scripture with respect to gender and sexual relations will be more pronounced in Africa and in the African diasporic religious communities. The expansion of African Pentecostalisms and its increased media presence have occasioned tension and conflicts in many African societies; the trend will only increase in the future, rather than abate, as more wealth controlled by a few Pentecostal elites will mean more public assertiveness, social visibility, and audibility. More importantly, the sacred economy and institutional architecture of African Pentecostalisms will continue to restrain its potential as a social force for long-term transformation of Africa.[52]

Chapter 21

Foreign on Own Home Front? Ruminations From an African-South African Pentecostal Biblical Scholar

Madipoane Masenya (ngwan'a Mphahlele)

"MAMA, WHEN YOU were my age," asked my nine-year-old son, "did my grandmother and grandfather teach you about the Bible?"

"No, my son," I said. "Your grandparents were not as keen as we are on these things. Though we did have family altars, we did not have regular Bible sessions."

He protested, "No, Mum, you have started these things on us just too early!"

While I marveled at what I thought was an unthankful comment from my son, in hindsight, I think I would have made the same comment, had I the boldness to ask my mom the same question. Why? My early introduction to the Christian religion was not only strenuous. It was boredom, to say the least. Apart from having to walk a long distance to church almost every Sunday, as a young girl I found the liturgies and, in particular, the delivery of sermons not appealing at all. If I had a choice not to go to (that particular) church, I would gladly have abstained. The observation that during my teen years I chose to attend a Pentecostal church to my parents' distaste reveals the kind of spiritual search that motivated me earlier on in life. As I was still under my parents' care, I decided to attend the two churches until I became independent.

An important question to be asked is: Within the colonized apartheid setting, one in which Christianity was mainly imposed on our forebears, was it by default or by divine design that I found myself in a Christian family? Given our royal roots, would it not have been naturally easy for the family to stay with the African traditions and customs and nothing more? In fact, the family chose to stay with both/and. Could it be that it was by divine design that I became the first in my family to make a Christian commitment, thus becoming a source of embarrassment to the family? Was it by divine design or by default that when I grew up, though I had planned to be a medical doctor, I ended up with a terminal degree not in medicine but in Bible? This happened despite the fact that within my high-school curriculum I studied mathematics, physics, and biology, culminating with a grade that qualified me to do a bachelor's degree in medical sciences. As I would begin my biblical studies journey, little did I know that the journey would resemble that of the Vashti character in the Hebrew Bible. Like Vashti, I would be at home yet on foreign ground.

Caged Inside Own Territory? A Gaze at Vashti

Vashti is portrayed as an insider to a powerful community under the Persian Empire. She is not an ordinary Persian community member, though. She is the Persian queen and therefore an upper-class woman. At face value, readers of her narrative might think that Vashti was a happy family member at home, within the empire. Not so, though. In order to see this, we might have to read between the lines, or beneath the surface, since, like many other female characters in the Hebrew Bible, her character is portrayed from the perspective of the male narrator of the story. Her visible role within this story of the Persian exile of the Jews is limited to the introductory chapter of the Book of Esther. However, for those commentators who choose to see the links between Vashti and Esther, her character is viewed as permeating the rest of the book.[1]

Traditionally, and also within Pentecostal interpretative circles, the Vashti character has been viewed in a negative light. I have had an opportunity on two different occasions to listen to sermons based on the two main female characters in the Book of Esther, both by Pentecostal pastors' wives. Vashti was cited by both as providing an example of a disobedient wife who had no respect for her husband or for God. Noteworthy was the emphasis put on the wifely loyalty toward a husband and not vice versa. In both cases, the preachers did not seem to be concerned about the logic behind the drunken husband's summons of his wife to appear before drunken men. It can be argued that Vashti's gender, rather than her courage and boldness, has worked against her throughout the history of the Book of Esther's interpretation.

But it is Vashti's "foreign" gender in a patriarchal context that sheds some light on her position as a stranger or outsider on her own home territory. Her resident-alien standing happens irrespective of her insider, royal, and socioeconomic status within the Persian community. Elsewhere I have argued:

> She is not treated as an independent character, but always delineated in relation to her husband.... As a matter of fact, Vashti never really appears as an independent character at all, except when she breaks the code of conduct by refusing to appear before the king, an act that culminates in her removal from the scene. Like an exile in a foreign country, Vashti cannot be allowed to possess her own will. She can

> only survive through being assimilated by patriarchy. Vashti is a stranger in what is supposed to be her own territory.[2]

Although presumably at home, given her ethnicity, queenly, and socioeconomic positions, Vashti's gender dictated that she would be foreign on her own territory, caged within her own ground. It is no wonder that, as a queen, she could be deposed at once by a drunken king. As a wife, she could be divorced unilaterally and quickly. Challenging power, particularly imperial and patriarchal power, can be costly. Silencing and removal are some of the consequences of the bold and defiant expression of power that patriarchy does not legitimate. Vashti is the one who bore the brunt of the preceding repercussions. Vashti's story mirrors mine some, if not to a greater extent. How so?

If I were to do some justice to the narrative of my status as a foreigner at home, I would begin with my journey as a girl child in a patriarchal African culture.[3] Within African cultures, like in many others, a woman's status is viewed as incomplete without a man as a marriage partner.[4] Within such settings, a girl child's status is like that of someone in transit; hence the Jamaican proverb "Marry your daughter when you can, your son when you please."[5] Also, within the broader South African political context, my race determined that the Lebowa homeland, one of the apartheid-constructed Bantustands, rather than South Africa, would be designated as my "home" (read: country). It was only with political independence in 1994 that I acquired South African citizenship. Yet my foreign status did not completely end with the establishment of the democratic state in 1994, although the elaboration of such is beyond the scope of this chapter. For now, suffice it to note that when in the early eighties I began my journey as a budding biblical-studies scholar, my exilic status on what was supposed to be my home front would not have been unexpected.

Navigating the Forest of Scientific Studies of the Bible at a Foreign Home Front

The preceding is intended to give readers some perspective on the ugly role played by one's skin pigmentation (read: race) in South Africa's apartheid past. The category of race determined the marginal status of blacks. The subjection of South Africa to the colonial-apartheid rule meant that those who were foreigners actually came to settle and make South Africa home while the indigenous peoples were made foreigners in what was supposed to be their own home front. In this context, the present xenophobic attacks on fellow Africans cannot make sense. Politically, South Africa was ruled by a white minority. It is on such a landscape of deprivation for some and plenty for others, basically on the basis of their race, that I happened to be the fortunate one among my siblings to be allowed to pursue higher education.

At what would later be designated a historically disadvantaged university, I chose biblical studies as one of my major subjects. The choice was "misguided" (was this by default or by divine design?) because in the naïveté of my Pentecostal upbringing, I thought that I was headed toward spiritual nurture and enrichment.[6] The faces of all the lecturers and faculty who taught me Bible and theology revealed how the apartheid regime, through its segregation policy, had successfully constructed the South African society racially. All of the academics were white and male:

> It is in this set-up, that I found myself totally lost. In my own "little" understanding, I thought I was "spiritually deprived" because of the critical approaches to Bible and Theology I

> consumed; "contextually empty" as the theology we were doing had basically nothing to do with my African context! It is in this context that we grappled with the biblical text—the emphasis was on the need for the knowledge of the original languages in order for one to be able to do "proper" exegesis. We were expected to know the *Sitz im Leben* of a particular text in order to be able to understand it within its historical context. However, we did not attempt to move our fingers an inch regarding the text's relevance for the modern reader's context. If the latter was considered, it would be spiritualised and many injustices on the ground would thus be left intact. We seldom, or rather, never addressed theological questions on African-South African issues such as the land question, unjust political systems, patriarchy et cetera. Instead, we would be referred to the works of European theological giants such as Rudolph Bultmann, Karl Barth, Dietrich Bonhoeffer and so forth, works which had nothing to do with the African context.[7]

Given the conservative nature of my academic (and church) upbringing, it occasions no wonder that later on in my scholarly endeavors, I would dislike and dread liberation theologies.

In retrospect, I cannot lament that I was introduced to critical approaches to the study of the Bible. I have gained much from exposure to such approaches, and I am further thankful I was (forcefully) introduced to the original languages of the Bible. I was taught, "You must not have faith in the Bible, but you must have faith in the God of the Bible."[8] I remain unsure about how such an exhortation would be received by Pentecostals, even today. The main criticism I had and still have with the Western and Eurocentric training I received is that my studies of the Bible appeared to be more preoccupied with theory, with little or no attention given to praxis. I am concerned here with praxis, not only in terms of leading a righteous life (as was and still is the main emphasis within many a Pentecostal context), but in terms of a faith that would lead to works that challenge racial oppression, patriarchy, xenophobia, and taking care of the poor, among others (cf. James 2).

What I also found and still find problematic as a Pentecostal biblical scholar is that such critical approaches to the Bible ended up making the Bible basically an object of intellectual scrutiny whose impact on the scholar's faith life would be ignored, if not denied. In such a context, it appears as though a biblical scholar is expected to park her or his faith at the doorstep of academia and be detached from the spiritual aspect of her or his identity. Also, a scholar's affirmation of the authority of the Bible as the Word of God is dismissed within such contexts. The application of one's critical faculties, the reveling in one's capacity to be rational, the keen desire to come out with a scientifically researched product, preferably detached from one's (spiritual) life, are all applauded and celebrated. As could be expected, the flag of so-called objectivity, one which favored a section of the global community, is held high within such circles. Brueggemann thus observes:

> The problem is that in the career of Western objectivity very few people were let into the room, which was peopled largely by white males of a certain class and perspective. Indeed it has been precisely the admission of others into the room that has made our treasured objectivity (and consequent hegemony) fragile and exposed.[9]

The past of the biblical text and the biblical text itself would be given (and, dare one say, is still given) all the attention at the expense of what the same texts could mean for present-day Bible readers. Particularly given the fact that in our African settings, the

Christian Bible was used both to conquer, colonize, and impoverish indigenous populations[10] and that it was used and continues to be used to perpetuate patriarchy and its subordination of women,[11] why did it not dawn on the producers and teachers of the offerings in Bible and theology not to use it to empower, enrich, and transform the lives of the marginalized? Given the harsh reality of gender-based violence in present-day South Africa, in the era of the pandemic of HIV/AIDS, a context with a huge gap between the haves and the have-nots, and one in which xenophobia has raised its ugly head, why are theologians and biblical scholars still choosing to leave contextual issues on the margins of their scholarship? What we do as biblical scholars perpetuates the kind of detached scholarship that produced us. Such scholarship theologizes as though the house was not on the fire, even if the flames were kindled by apartheid and all its atrocities. Yet the voices of those scholars who dared to challenge the apartheid status quo were hardly allowed to enter the discourse of academic biblical studies. From such a context of suppression and repression, it made sense, then, that one could not be exposed to the important works of black and liberation theologians such as Takatso Mofokeng, Simon Maimela, Frank Chikane, Archbishop Emeritus Desmond Tutu, and Itumeleng Mosala. With hindsight, one knows that if such works were to be exposed to many a black student, they would have led protests and perhaps instigated a revolution, thus upsetting the apartheid status quo. Yet such works could have contributed positively to the creation of balance between theory and praxis as well as objectivity and subjectivity by theologians and biblical scholars.

What could be regarded as a turning point in my academic life happened only in 1986, during my registration for a master's degree with the University of South Africa. My supervisor, professor J. J.

Burden, impressed on me the need to integrate the African context with my research in Old Testament studies. At first, I found his advice both strange and refreshing. The level of integration of the African context with my studies of the Bible became even more intensified when, in the early nineties, I began learning about issues pertaining to gender. Such perspectives were not introduced to me by my Pentecostal church or peers, nor by my studies as an undergraduate. It now dawned on me that it was not only my racial status that mattered but that other aspects of my foreign identity, such as gender, socioeconomic class, and culture had to be integrated into my studies of the Bible. Such integration would enable my scholarship not only to be more balanced; it would enable one to be at home and yet not feel foreign. Mine has not been an easy journey, though, neither in academia nor in the church.

One example of the struggles that I encountered on account of an "unconventional" scholarship can be cited. In my article "Invisible Exiles? An African-South African Woman's Reconfiguration of Exile in Jeremiah 21:1–10,"[12] I approached the text of Jeremiah nontraditionally. I argued that although South Africa had achieved political liberation, as a black woman who was still haunted by the legacies from our colonial-apartheid past, one who, like Vashti, was marked more by her gender, I was at home yet still in exile. Informed by the then South African context in which the exile narrative of the African National Congress members was deemed more important than that of others, I deconstructed such a notion. I argued that even within the text of Jeremiah, space is given to other exile narratives, like those of the Jews who were exiled in Egypt. I reasoned that the exhortation that there could be life in exile needed to be problematized. One of the peer reviewers of the article simply dismissed it by noting, "This article has a story to tell, but not in a scientific journal, in a magazine." I reckoned that the gatekeeper who conducted the preceding review needed to make sure that those biblical scholars who, like Vashti, chose to deviate from the status quo of historical-critical approaches to the Bible needed to be silenced and, if possible, barred from the guild of biblical scholarship.

From the preceding narrative of my initiation into the discipline of biblical studies, it is hopefully evident that my educational upbringing was not helpful in conscientizing me about my marginal status as constructed by those in power. On what is supposed to be one's academic home front—that is, on the terrain of biblical studies as one of the scientific disciplines—one could be at home but still experience alienation as a foreigner. I was at home as I was steeped in the traditions of the (Western) master, in terms of the trade of biblical studies. Yet I felt foreign because what I studied or researched did not always do justice to my African context. It is no wonder that later on I would argue as follows:

> Ours is a theological education characterized by one assuming the role of an insider in one context and that of an outsider in another context. One becomes an insider as one is being trained as a student, an insider to the theologies which are foreign to oneself, an insider as one trains African students in Western-oriented studies of the Bible, an insider as one does research. If the research conducted is not played according to the rules inside the game, it will not earn this "insider/outsider" accreditation to the Western academic status quo, which itself remains basically an outsider to the African status quo.[13]

Before I engage the challenges of navigating biblical scholarship as a person of faith, and particularly Pentecostal faith, I need to mention that the kind of detached training in biblical studies that I had received ironically paralleled what I encountered in my life journey as a Pentecostal African woman.

A Pentecostal Biblical Scholar in Bible-Conscious African Contexts?

At the beginning of the present essay, I noted that I was introduced to a Christian church at an early age of my life. I also remarked that at some point in my teen years, I joined a Pentecostal church. I ended up attending two different churches until I became independent. Earlier on in our marriage, we attended a mainline church. Our attendance of the latter church was short-lived, as we soon joined a Pentecostal church (at which we remain to the present). Although there is no space for exposition of the core teachings of Pentecostalism (and the predominantly Pentecostal readership of this chapter and book will not need such), suffice it to note the following commitments: that each believer should have a personal encounter with Jesus Christ. Jesus Christ is thus not only the Savior of the world out there; He becomes one's personal Savior.

An encounter with Jesus of necessity leads to a changed life; sin and its fleshly desires no longer have control over the lives of those who have been born of the Spirit. Each believer is supposed to undergo two kinds of baptism: water baptism and baptism through the Holy Spirit. Evidence of the latter baptism would be revealed in the recipient's speaking in tongues. The church—that is, the body of Christ—expects Jesus, the Head of the church, to return at an unexpected hour. Until then, not only should believers lead holy lives; they also have a responsibility to preach the gospel to the whole world with a view to the salvation of the lost. If I were to compare the kind of theology and biblical studies that I had received from my Pentecostal upbringing (in churches, conferences, meetings, etc.), what is lacking in the latter is the commitment to addressing societal concerns; challenging systemic evils, like the colonial-apartheid legacies of poverty and nonliteracy among the previously marginalized; engaging the social ills of patriarchy; and presenting HIV/AIDS-conscious sermons and Bible studies, among others. As noted, the emphasis is on the need to lead lives that are holy, even as believers' minds should be set on things that are above.[14] The godly aroma that ought to be manifested in the believers' active involvement in the lives of the poor and the oppressed, the HIV/AIDS and Ebola sufferers, the care for the widows and the orphans—none of these take center stage within our Pentecostal settings. Elsewhere I have argued, "Many women (and other marginalised people sitting in the church pews) are today being exhorted to focus on serious 'heavenly/spiritual' business. In the process, women are persuaded, through the use of the Bible, to call our own oppression, or violence done to our bodies in the name of a god, a 'worldly' matter that needs to be shunned."[15]

Such a detachment between biblical studies and the real issues confronting various people, including believers, in our contexts resembles the one referred to above in the narrative of my journey through academic biblical studies. How may believers understand the words of the eighth-century prophets as they came against the injustices that were perpetrated on the oppressed and the needy within their contexts? How may we understand the true meaning of fasting according to Deutero-Isaiah?

> Is not this the fast I have chosen: to loose the bonds of wickedness, to undo the heavy burdens, and to let the oppressed go free, and break every yoke? Is it not to divide your bread with the hungry and bring the poor who are outcasts into your house? When you see the naked, to cover him and not hide yourself from your own flesh?
>
> —Isaiah 58:6–7, MEV

How may a socially engaged biblical scholar fare within such a context? Could one be at home, in terms of her faith identity, without a feeling of foreignness?

What makes the journey of such scholars even more challenging is the kind of approach to the biblical text one would naturally use. Equipped with critical tools to engage the Bible, such a scholar who is also conscious of the leading of the Holy Spirit in his or her life will approach the text differently. Having background knowledge not only of the texts, but also of the Hebrew language in which the text of Esther 1 is cast, they will find it difficult to "park their brains" when male-identified readers of the Vashti story appropriate the narrative in a woman-unfriendly way. In the view of such a scholar, such traditional readings of biblical texts cannot deconstruct and challenge androcentric ideologies within the texts and the Bible readers' contexts. Such readings instead perpetuate patriarchy under the guise of God's Word. This dilemma is exacerbated by the fact that scholarly hermeneutics is viewed not only as dangerous but also as heretical in their ecclesial contexts, even as their believing or faith-filled approaches are unwelcome in the academy.

So, like Vashti, the scholar who chooses to be faithful to both her or his scholarly and faith identities bears the brunt of such hybridity through silencing or removal. A case in point might be cited here. At some point, I listened to one of the leading figures within a specific Pentecostal church argue, "For as long as I am in the leadership, feminine theologies cannot have a place in this denomination." Such comments were basically addressed probably as a protest about the inclusive language that a gender-identified attendee had used. Noteworthy is the fact that any deviation from the hermeneutic of the powerful, irrespective of whether it is Spirit-led or not, cannot be allowed to win the day.

What remains a challenging question is, for an outsider to the Pentecostal tradition, which hermeneutic should he or she adopt? Of significance for the present investigation is, how may a scholar fare who deliberately chooses to be faithful to both her faith and scholarly identities?

Conclusion

The easy way out for scholars in such settings is to succumb to the status quo, that is, to park their faith at the doorstep of academia and park their brains at the church's doorstep. For a committed believer and scholar, though, that might be easier said than done. Says an African Northern Sotho/Sepedi proverb, "*Serokolo se sennyane se ikoketša ka go nkga*" ("A small herb increases itself [its influence] by releasing a strong [offensive] odor").[16] In the midst of humiliation by the powerful, Vashti did not choose an easy path such as that of silence. No! She chose the path of resistance, choosing to retain her human dignity by refusing to appear before a drunken husband and his drunken buddies. Although her act of defiance did come with a price, its impact continued to be felt even after her removal. Two instances may be cited here. Before the king could decide to make an important decision about Vashti's replacement, her memories had to set in (Esther 2:1–2); then, Esther's act of defiance of appearing before the king without being summoned (Esther 5:1–3) suggests that the male narrator of women's stories was probably aware of female agency. While women paled in significance in the face of the monster that patriarchy was, they had the capacity to transform their situations for the better.

The pressure to keep quiet and not imitate the proverbial small herb was probably felt also by the prophet Jeremiah in his ruminations about his prophetic ministry:

> But if I say, "I will not make mention of Him Not speak any more in His name," then His word was in my heart as a burning fire shut up in my bones; and I was weary of forbearing it, and I could not endure it.
>
> —Jeremiah 20:9, MEV

Perhaps what is more urgent through it all is for scholars to pray for the spiritual ears to hear what the Spirit is saying to them as members of the churches and the academy and, more importantly, after hearing, to be empowered to act accordingly.

Notes

Introduction
"From Every Nation Under Heaven": Africa in World Pentecostalism

1. Allan Anderson, "Global Pentecostalism in the New Millennium," in Allan H. Anderson and Walter J. Hollenweger, eds., *Pentecostals After a Century: Global Perspectives on a Movement in Transition* (Sheffield: Sheffield Academic Press, 1999), 222.
2. Harvey Cox, *Fire From Heaven: Pentecostalism and the Reshaping of Spirituality in the Twenty-First Century* (De Capo, MA: Addison-Wesley, 1995), especially chapter 12.
3. Barrister Casely Hayford, as cited in Hans Debrunner, *A History of Christianity in Ghana* (Accra: Waterville Publishing House, 1967), 271.
4. Christian G. Baëta, *Prophetism in Ghana: A Study of Some Spiritual Churches* (London: SCM, 1962), 35–36.
5. Ogbu U. Kalu, *African Pentecostalism: An Introduction* (Oxford: Oxford University Press, 2008), 4.
6. For a representative study, see Frieder Ludwig and J. Kwabena Asamoah-Gyadu, eds., *African Christian Presence in the West* (Trenton, NJ, and Asmara, Eritrea: Africa World Press, 2011).
7. Jehu J. Hanciles, *Beyond Christendom: Globalization, African Migration, and the Transformation of the West* (Maryknoll, NY: Orbis Books, 2008), 325.
8. J. Kwabena Asamoah-Gyadu, *African Charismatics: Current Developments Within Independent Indigenous Pentecostalism in Ghana* (Leiden: E. J. Brill, 2005), 12.
9. Paul Gifford, *Ghana's New Christianity: Pentecostalism in a Globalizing African Economy* (Indianapolis, IN: Indiana University Press, 2004), 23–24.
10. Quoted in Ogbu U. Kalu, *African Pentecostalism: Global Discourses, Migrations, Exchanges, and Connections* (Trenton, NJ, and Asmara, Eritrea: Africa World Press, 2010), 24.

11. The significant authors include both insiders and outsiders—Allan Anderson, Ogbu Kalu, Ruth Marshall, Nimi Wariboko, Afe Adogame, Matthews Ojo, Asonzeh Ukah, Paul Gifford, and David Maxwell, together with a number of newer scholars in the field, all of whom have pointed to Pentecostalism as an important stream of Christianity in Africa.
12. John D. Y. Peel, foreword to Asonzeh Ukah, *A New Paradigm of Pentecostal Power: A Study of the Redeemed Christian Church of God in Nigeria* (Trenton, NJ: Africa World Press, 2008), xxi, xxiii.
13. Mensa Otabil, *Beyond the Rivers of Ethiopia: A Biblical Revelation on God's Purpose for the Black Race* (Accra: Altar Media, 2004), 8, 64.
14. See J. Kwabena Asamoah-Gyadu, *Contemporary Pentecostal Christianity: Interpretations From an African Context* (Oxford: Regnum, 2013), 5.
15. J. Kwabena Asamoah-Gyadu, *Sighs and Signs of the Spirit: Ghanaian Perspective on Pentecostalism and Renewal in Africa* (Oxford: Regnum International, 2015), chapter 3.
16. Kalu, *African Pentecostalism: An Introduction*, 22.
17. Baëta, *Prophetism in Ghana*, 1.
18. David Maxwell, *African Gifts of the Spirit: Pentecostalism and the Rise of a Zimbabwean Traditional Religious Movement* (Oxford: James Currey, 2006), 3; see also Kudzai Biri's chapter in this book.
19. Paul Gifford, *Christianity, Development, and Modernity in Africa* (London: Hurst and Co., 2015), 13.
20. Ibid., 20.
21. Abu Bako, *Establishing God's Altar Everywhere: Taking the High Places* (Accra: Logos-Rhema Foundation, 2004), 56.
22. Ibid., 153–54.
23. Charles Agyinasare, *Power in Prayer* (The Netherlands: His Printing Hoornaar, 2001), 125.
24. Craig S. Keener, *Miracles: The Credibility of the New Testament Accounts*, 2 vols. (Grand Rapids, MI: Baker Academic, 2011), 1.311.
25. J. Kwabena Asamoah-Gyadu, "Mediating Spiritual Power: African Christianity, Transnationalism, and the Media," in Afe Adogame and James V. Spickard, eds., *Religion Crossing Boundaries: Transnational Religious and Social Dynamics in Africa and the New African Diaspora* (Leiden: E. J. Brill, 2010), 87–103.

26. Frank D. Macchia, *Baptized in the Spirit: A Global Pentecostal Theology* (Grand Rapids, MI: Zondervan, 2006), 51.
27. Anaba Eastwood, *God's End-time Militia: Winning the War Within and Without*, rev. ed. (Accra: Design Solutions, 1997), 1.
28. Ibid.
29. Juan Sepúlveda, "Reflections on the Pentecostal Contribution to the Mission of the Church in Latin America," *Journal of Pentecostal Theology* 1 (1992): 100, 103.
30. Eastwood, *God's End-Time Militia*, 3, 5.
31. Allan Anderson, "Varieties, Taxonomies, and Definitions," in Allan Anderson et al., eds., *Studying Global Pentecostalism: Theories and Methods* (Berkeley, CA: University of California Press, 2010), 13.

Chapter 1
West African Pentecostalism: A Survey of Everyday Theology

1. See Amos Yong and Nimi Wariboko, eds., *Spiritual Presence and Spiritual Power: Pentecostal Readings of and Engagements With the Legacy of Paul Tillich* (Bloomington and Indianapolis, IN: Indiana University Press, 2015).
2. John Fiske, *Understanding Popular Culture*, 2nd ed. (London: Routledge, 2011), 22.
3. John Fiske, *Reading the Popular*, 2nd ed. (London: Routledge, 2011), 1.
4. Fiske, *Understanding Popular Culture*, 56.
5. Birgit Meyer, "Aesthetics of Persuasion: Global Christianity and Pentecostalism's Sensational Forms," *South Atlantic Quarterly* 109, no. 4 (2010): 742; italics in the original.
6. Annalisa Butticci, "Crazy World, Crazy Faith! Prayer, Power and Transformation in a Nigerian Prayer City," *Annual Review of Sociology of Religion* 4 (2013): 254.
7. Ibid., 256.
8. J. Kwabena Asamoah-Gyadu, *Contemporary Pentecostal Christianity: Interpretations From an African Context* (Oxford: Regnum, 2013), 33.
9. Fiske, *Reading the Popular*, 116.
10. Fiske, *Understanding Popular Culture*, 86, 88.

11. Jacques Rancière, *Dissensus: On Politics and Aesthetics*, ed. and trans. Steven Corcocan (London: Continuum, 2010).
12. Fiske, *Reading the Popular*, 13–16 and 27 inspired this paragraph.
13. Matthews Ojo, *The End-Time Army: Charismatic Movements in Modern Nigeria* (Trenton, NJ: Africa World Press, 2006), 89.
14. I have adapted the four modes of exchange as described by Kojin Karatani for my purposes here. See his *The Structure of World History: From Modes of Production to Modes of Exchange* (Durham: Duke University Press, 2014), 1–28.

Chapter 2
The New Face of African Christianity: David Oyedepo's Winners Chapel and the Pentecostal Message of Salvation

1. The Pew Forum on Religion and Public Life, "Spirit and Power: A Ten-Country Survey of Pentecostals" (Pew Research Centre, October 2006), 86, accessed February 17, 2016, http://www.pewforum.org/files/2006/10/pentecostals-08.pdf.
2. S. G. Williamson, *Akan Religion and the Christian Faith*, ed. Kwesi Dickson (Accra: Universities Press, 1965), 159, 164.
3. The major works on Wade Harris are Gordon M. Haliburton, "The Anglican Church in Ghana and Harris Movement in 1914," *The Bulletin of the Society of African Church History* 1 (1964): 101–106; and David A. Shank, "Prophet of Modern Times: The Thought of William Wade Harris, West African Precursor of the Reign of Christ" (PhD dissertation, University of Aberdeen, 1980).
4. Under Apostle Ayo Babalola's leadership in 1942, the Christ Apostolic Church came into existence; see E. K. Larbi, *Pentecostalism: The Eddies of Ghanaian Christianity*, Studies in African Pentecostal Christianity, no. 1 (Accra: Centre for Pentecostal and Charismatic Studies, 2001), 101, 111.
5. Ibid., 106.
6. See Dictionary of African Christian Biography, "Idahosa, Benson Andrew," accessed February 17, 2016, http://www.dacb.org/stories/nigeria/idahosa_bensona.html.
7. Nigeria may be regarded as the heartland of African Pentecostalism in that it appears all the ministers with global stature and leading

ministries have originated there. The key among them, besides Benson Idahosa mentioned above, include E. A. Adeboye, William Kumuyi, T. B. Joshua, Chris Oyakhilome, and D. O. Oyedepo. Some of the world's biggest Pentecostal churches were founded by Nigerians, including Sunday Adelaja's Embassy of God in Kiev, Ukraine, and Matthew Ashimolowo's Kingsway International Christian Centre in the United Kingdom.

8. J. Kwabena Asamoah-Gyadu, *Contemporary Pentecostal Christianity: Interpretations From an African Context* (Oxford: Regnum, 2013), 132.
9. Paul Gifford, *Christianity, Development, and Modernity in Africa* (London: Hurst and Co., 2015), 162; cf. 5–6, 17, 151. Gifford, in this book, makes other critical assertions about African Pentecostal Christianity; the present author plans a critique of the presuppositions and conclusions of Gifford in a different work.
10. Christ Apostolic Church Constitution, 1964, 9; quoted in Larbi, *Pentecostalism*, 148 (capitalization, here and elsewhere in this chapter, are original to the CAC's constitution).
11. Living Faith Church Worldwide International, *The Mandate* (Canaanland: Dominion Publishing House, 2012), 89, hereafter cited as *The Mandate*.
12. Scriptural references given parenthetically in the text are indicative of how many West African Pentecostals understand the basis of their faith.
13. Dag Heward-Mills, founder of the Lighthouse Chapel and the most successful church-planter among Ghana's neo-Pentecostal churches, has delineated seven steps. See Dag Heward-Mills, *The Greater Love of Jesus Christ* (Accra: Parchment, 2013), 29–32; Dag Heward-Mills, *How to Be Born Again and Avoid Hell* (Accra: Parchment, 2014).
14. Christ Apostolic Church Constitution, 12.
15. *The Mandate*, 150f.
16. Christ Apostolic Church Constitution, 12.
17. Oyedepo and the Winners Chapel have a more elaborate list, referred to as "mysteries" and "ordinances," which are considered the church's "Apostolic Doctrines." The following is the list of the institutionalized ordinances within the Winners Chapel: "Mystery of the Holy Communion," "The Mystery of the Anointing Oil," "The Mystery of the Blood

of Sprinkling," "The Mystery of Feet Washing," "The Mystery of the Prophetic Mantle," "The Ordinance of Water Baptism," and "The Ordinance of Marriage." The doctrine of the mystery of the blood of sprinkling is based on Hebrews 12:22–24, and the preparation is the same as that of the Holy Communion, except that the "mix should be lighter to avoid physical stains from the coloration of the liquid" (see *The Mandate*, 142–54).

18. Asamoah-Gyadu, *Contemporary Pentecostal Christianity*, 121–43.
19. We have evidence in Ghana where a businessman who thought his church wasn't doing enough evangelism donated several vans fitted with megaphones to the Church of Pentecost because their evangelistic zeal impressed him.
20. Dag Heward-Mills, *Tell Them: 120 Reasons Why You Should Be a Soul Winner* (Accra: Parchment, 2008).
21. David Oyedepo, "The Blessings of Spiritual Stewardship," recorded message, January 30, 2015.
22. See Larbi, *Pentecostalism*, 429; see also Elizabeth Dodd Tyson, "Neo-pentecostal Missiology" (PhD dissertation, University of Edinburgh, 1993).
23. David Oyedepo, *On Eagle's Wings: My First Thirty-Year Adventure in Ministry* (Canaanland: Dominion Publishing House, 2013), 14.
24. Ibid., 18.
25. David Oyedepo, *Signs and Wonders* (Canaanland: Dominion Publishing House, 2006), 23–25; cf. Oyedepo, *On Eagle's Wings*, 61–64; *The Mandate*, 451–53.
26. Oyedepo, *Signs and Wonders*, 23.
27. Ibid., 25–26.
28. *The Mandate*, 484.
29. Oyedepo, *On Eagle's Wings*, 69. The church's original, registered name is Living Faith Church. When Oyedepo moved from Kaduna in northern Nigeria to Lagos in 1989, the church, through a "heavenly vision," was renamed Winners Chapel (Ibid.; *The Mandate*, 485).
30. Oyedepo, *On Eagle's Wings*, 79.
31. Oyedepo, *Signs and Wonders*, 28f.
32. *The Mandate*, 460.

33. Though one can find numerous recordings of Oyedepo's messages on the subject matter, I find the DVD *Understanding the Mysteries of Financial Dominion*, recorded at the 2014 Supernatural Empowerment Summit, Accra, very helpful. It summarizes his reflections on the subject matter over the years. The numerous books by Oyedepo that corroborate his presentation at the summit include *Winning the War Against Poverty* (Canaanland: Dominion, 2006); *Walking in Dominion* (Canaanland: Dominion, 2006); and *Breaking Financial Hardship* (Canaanland: Dominion, 1995).
34. Gifford, *Christianity, Development, and Modernity in Africa*, 48.
35. David Oyedepo, *Mysteries of Financial Dominion*. Quotations and information in this and the next two paragraphs are drawn from this DVD; see also Oyedepo's *Breaking Financial Hardship* for other perspectives.
36. *The Mandate*, 159.
37. Ibid., 183.
38. Gifford, *Christianity, Development, and Modernity in Africa*, 34.
39. *The Mandate*, 158f.
40. Ibid., 159.
41. After the overthrow of Ghana's visionary first president, subsequent leaders failed to plan adequately to expand the sector in subsequent years as Ghana's population grew.
42. *The Mandate*, 66–67.
43. Ibid., 9.
44. It will be fascinating to study the missions strategy of Winners Chapel. Whereas some African Pentecostal denominations and churches seem to be local champions and less effective on the foreign field, Winners Chapel has demonstrated that it is effective both at home and elsewhere. Why are they flourishing when others are struggling?
45. *The Mandate*, 478.
46. I recommend for the reflection of all such "agnostic-pessimists" Ghanaian President and Pentecostal John Mahama's keynote address delivered at the sixth Oxford Africa Conference, May 22, 2015, speaking to the theme "A Continent on the Move: People, Politics, and Business Across Borders." He, *inter alia*, attempted to draw attention to some of the great things that are happening on the continent that the larger world

doesn't know. For a transcript of the address, see http://www.myjoyonline.com/politics/2015/May-22nd/live-updates-mahama-delivers-address-at-oxford-africa-conference-2015.php, accessed June 3, 2015.

47. Contained in remarks made by President John Mahama, the president of Ghana, on December 31, 2014, at Agyinasare's Watch Night service in Accra, available on DVD and MP3 recording (emphasis added).

Chapter 3
Indigenous Classical Pentecostalism: The Church of Pentecost in Ghana

1. Wonsuk Ma, Veli-Matti Karkkainen, and J. Kwabena Asamoah-Gyadu, eds., *Pentecostal Mission and Global Christianity* (Oxford: Regnum Books International, 2014), 1.
2. See J. Kwabena Asamoah-Gyadu, *African Charismatics: Current Developments Within Independent Indigenous Pentecostalism in Ghana* (Leiden: E. J. Brill, 2005).
3. Opoku Onyinah, *Pentecostal Exorcism: Witchcraft and Demonology in Ghana* (Dorchester: Deo Publishing, 2012), 88–104.
4. Asamoah-Gyadu, *African Charismatics*, 89.
5. E. K. Larbi, *Pentecostalism: The Eddies of Ghanaian Christianity* (Accra: Blessed Publications, 2001).
6. Hans W. Debrunner, *A History of Christianity in Ghana* (Accra: Waterville Publishing House, 1967), 327.
7. Christine Leonard, *A Giant in Ghana: Three Thousand Churches in Fifty Years—The Story of James McKeown and the Church of Pentecost* (Chichester, UK: New Wine Press, 1989), 100.
8. Jones Amanor, "Pentecostalism in Ghana: An African Reformation," *Cyberjournal for Pentecostal-Charismatic Research* 13 (April 2004), accessed February 17, 2016, http://pctii.org/cyberj/cyber13.html.
9. Larbi, *Pentecostalism*, 74.
10. Walter J. Hollenweger, *The Pentecostals* (London: SCM Press Ltd., 1972), 192.
11. Leonard, *A Giant in Ghana*, 138.
12. The Apostolic Church, *The Apostolic Church: Its Principles and Practices* (Bradford: Apostolic Publications, 1937), 35–44, 245–49.
13. Larbi, *Pentecostalism*, 124–25.

14. Ibid., 70.
15. Asamoah-Gyadu, *African Charismatics*, 89.
16. Allan Anderson, *To the Ends of the Earth: Pentecostalism and the Transformation of World Christianity* (Oxford: Oxford University Press, 2013), 249.
17. Ibid., 249–250.
18. Ibid.; see also Robert Menzies, *Empowered for Witness: The Spirit in Luke and Acts* (Sheffield: Sheffield Academic Press, 1994).
19. Russell S. Spittler, "Implicit Values in Pentecostal Missions," *Missiology: An International Review* 16, no. 4 (October 1988): 413.
20. Paul A. Pomerville, *Introduction to Missions: An Independent-Study Textbook* (Irving, TX: ICI University Press, 1987), 96, 100.
21. Africanist scholars like Paul Gifford, *African Christianity: Its Public Role* (London: Hurst & Company, 1998), 76, reasons sociologically that the growth of the Church of Pentecost (CoP) is due to a "lack of any education requirements, which enables anyone wanting to begin a church to do so on behalf of CoP," but this does not displace the theological reasons adduced above, even as his argument is inconclusive, because if such a requirement were to be the main factor of the growth of a church, then many churches would have seen growth similar to what the CoP is experiencing.
22. Gerrie ter Haar, *Halfway to Paradise: African Christians in Europe* (Cardiff: Cardiff Academic Press, 1998), 45.
23. Steven J. Land, *Pentecostal Spirituality: A Passion for the Kingdom* (Sheffield: Sheffield Academic Press, 1993), 96.
24. For example, see John Kildahl, *The Psychology of Speaking in Tongues* (New York: Harper & Row, 1972), 38–39, 54–55; and Mark J. Cartledge, "Interpreting Charismatic Experience: Hypnosis, Altered States of Consciousness, and the Holy Spirit?," *Journal of Pentecostal Theology* 13 (1998): 120.
25. Gary B. McGee, "Pentecostal Missiology: Moving Beyond Triumphalism to Face the Issues," *Pneuma* 16, no. 2 (Fall 1994): 279.
26. For example, see Cephas N. Omenyo, *Pentecost Outside Pentecostalism: A Study of the Development of Charismatic Renewal in the Mainline Churches in Ghana* (Zoetermeer, The Netherlands: Boekencentrum, 2002).

27. Wilbert R. Shenk, *Henry Venn: Missionary Statesman* (Maryknoll, NY: Orbis Books, 1983). R. Pierce Beaver, in his foreword to this book, rightly says that "the two men [Henry Venn and Rufus Anderson] are independently the authors of the 'Three-Self Formula'" (xii); see also the following pages for the development of the formula: 25–41, 109.
28. Leonard, *A Giant in Ghana*, 69.
29. Made up of all pastors of the church, Area Executive Committee members, chairmen of boards and committees, and ministry directors.
30. Kofi Abrefa Busia, *The Position of the Chief in Modern Asante* (London: Oxford University Press, 1951), 1–22, describes the political and military structures as centralized in the Akan states. The chief is the commander in chief of eight to thirteen (depending upon the Akan state) *asafo*, warrior companies and their divisional chiefs, and administers his territory with the help of these divisional chiefs. It is under the chief as the head that the Akan states formed a political unit or a nation. This structure is mirrored in the administration of the Church of Pentecost.
31. Walter J. Hollenweger, *Pentecostalism: Origins and Developments Worldwide* (Peabody, MA: Hendrickson, 1997), 298; Spittler, "Implicit Values," 416.
32. Gary B. McGee, "Pentecostals and their Various Strategies for Global Mission," in Murray A. Dempster, Byron D. Klaus, and Douglas Petersen, eds., *Called and Empowered: Global Mission in Pentecostal Perspective* (Peabody: Hendrickson, 1991), 212.
33. Leonard, *A Giant in Ghana*, 170–71.
34. Melvin L. Hodges, *The Indigenous Church* (Springfield, MO: Gospel Publishing House, 1953), 10, 133.
35. E. Kingsley Larbi, "Sustaining the Growth," in Opoku Onyinah, ed., *James McKeown Memorial Lectures: Fifty Years of the Church of Pentecost* (Accra: The Church of Pentecost, 2004), 143.
36. Paul Hiebert, *Anthropological Insights for Missionaries* (Grand Rapids, MI: Baker Book House, 1985), 196.
37. Leonard, *A Giant in Ghana*, 69; see also Opoku Onyinah, "The Man James McKeown," in Onyinah, *James McKeown Memorial Lectures*, 71.
38. She was an illiterate Ghanaian Christian woman, Christina Afua Gyan, commonly referred to as Afua Kuma, a native of the forest town of

Obo-Kwahu on the Kwahu mountain ridge in the eastern region of Ghana and a member of the Church of Pentecost. She was a peasant farmer and also practiced as a traditional midwife. She was the mother-in-law of one of the apostles of the Church of Pentecost. Even though her prayers and praises of Jesus are in her mother tongue, the Akan language, they have been translated into English by Fr. Jon Kirby to give the reader a good indication of their depth of Christian experience conveyed in the thought-forms and categories of the Akan worldview in her rural setting.

39. See Afua Kuma, *Jesus of the Deep Forest*, trans. J. Kirby (Accra, Ghana: Asempa Publishers, 1981); see also Kwame Bediako, *Christianity in Africa: The Renewal of a Non-Western Religion* (Edinburgh: Obis Books, 1995), 59–60; and Philip T. Laryea, "Mother Tongue Theology: Reflections on Image of Jesus in the Poetry of Afia Kuma," *Journal of African Christian Thought* 3, no. 1 (2000): 50–60.
40. Allan Anderson, *An Introduction to Pentecostalism* (Cambridge: Cambridge University Press, 2004), 117.
41. Eunice Johnson is one of the women in the CoP through whom a number of the church's local songs have been "received" (composed).
42. Nyansah Hayfron, *A Sound From Heaven: The Life and Singing Ministry of Mrs. Eunice Johnson of Ghana* (Accra, Ghana: Xchip Communications), 20–21.
43. Larbi, "Sustaining the Growth," 143.
44. J. Kwabena Asamoah-Gyadu, "Encountering Jesus in African Christianity: A Ghanaian Evangelical/Pentecostal Thought on Faith, Experience, and Hope in Christ," *HTS Teologiese Studies/Theological Studies* 62, no. 2 (2006): 373.
45. Walter J. Hollenweger, "After Twenty Years' Research on Pentecostalism," *International Review of Mission* 75, no. 297 (1985): 10–11.
46. Roswith I. H. Gerloff, "The Holy Spirit and the African Diaspora: Spiritual, Cultural, and Social Roots of Black Pentecostal Churches," *EPTA Bulletin* 14 (1995): 91.

Chapter 4
The Growth and Expansion of Pentecostalism in Francophone West Africa: The Assemblies of God of Burkina Faso

1. Elliot Skinner, *The Mossi of Burkina Faso: Chiefs, Politicians, and Soldiers* (Prospect Heights, IL: Waveland Press, 1989), 97.
2. A. A. Dim Delobsom Ouedraogo, *L'Empire du Mogho-Naba: Coutumes des Mossi de la Haute-Volta* [The empire of the Mogho-Naba: Customs of the Mossi of Upper Volta] (Paris: Editions Domat-Montchrestien, 1932), 203–4.
3. Cecil M. Robeck Jr., *Azusa Street Mission and Revival: The Birth of the Global Pentecostal Movement* (Nashville, TN: Thomas Nelson, 2006), 235.
4. "The Greatest Missionary Opportunity of the Century," *The Pentecostal Evangel*, October 10, 1920.
5. Harry M. Wright, "Revival Continues Among the Mossi," *The Pentecostal Evangel*, May 13, 1922.
6. Vinson Synan, *The Holiness-Pentecostal Tradition: Charismatic Movements in the Twentieth Century* (Grand Rapids, MI: W. B. Eerdmans, 1997), 142.
7. Lucille Booth-Clibborn, "Obedient Unto Death," *The Pentecostal Evangel*, January 2, 1926, 12.
8. William M. Faux, "With Christ, Which Is Far Better," *The Pentecostal Evangel*, February 21, 1942, 9.
9. While I was doing my doctoral studies, I was thinking of ways to remember these heroes of the faith. Even though they are unknown to the new generation of believers, they are worth remembering. I decided to restore the tomb markers of the missionaries and their children whose remains are resting in my country. I wanted to pay tribute to the missionaries who laid down their lives. As part of the Assemblies of God Church of Burkina Faso, we have a debt toward those who came and never returned home. The tombs have been rebuilt with headstones and tiles that will be permanent reminders of the sacrifices of these faithful servants of the Lord. Yes, we will remember. The sacrifice of all those who died inspired the Assemblies of God of Burkina Faso to develop a missions-minded church from its early beginning.

10. For further elaboration of mission strategies related to this and the next section, see chapter 4 of my "The Fire Is Still Burning: A Short History of the Assemblies of God of Burkina Faso" (PhD thesis, Regent University School of Divinity, 2011), 99–116.
11. Ibid., 84–85, where I discuss the issue of sickness and healing.
12. E. K. Larbi, *Pentecostalism: The Eddies of Ghanaian Christianity* (Accra: Blessed Publications, 2001).
13. Kouassi N'Guessan Emmanuel, *Ce Que j'ai vu, Entendu et Touché: Historique des Assemblées de Dieu de Côte d'Ivoire* [What I have seen, heard, and touched: A history of the Assemblies of God of Ivory Coast] (Abidjan: Presses Bibliques Africaines, 2009), 72.
14. Pierre-Joseph Laurent, "Transnationalisation and Local Transformations: The Example of the Assemblies of God of Burkina Faso," in Andre Corten and Ruth Marshall-Fratani, eds., *Between Babel and Pentecost: Transitional Pentecostalism in Africa and Latin America* (Bloomington, IN: Indiana University Press, 2001), 257.
15. Jean Baptiste Sawadogo, "Pentecostal Unity in Reaching West Africa: The Burkina Missionary Movement," in Arto Hämäläinen and Grant McClung, ed., *Together in One Mission: Pentecostal Cooperation in World Evangelization* (Cleveland, TN: Pathway Press, 2012), 211.
16. Philip Jenkins, *The Next Christendom: The Coming of Global Christianity* (Oxford: Oxford University Press, 2002), 2.
17. Elijah J. F. Kim, *The Rise of the Global South: The Decline of Western Christendom and the Rise of Majority World Christianity* (Eugene, OR: Wipf and Stock Publishers, 2012), xxiii.

Chapter 5
Pentecostalism in Cameroon and Nigeria's Cross-Border Pentecostal Influence

1. See Andres Caballero, "Pentecostal Churches Accused of Exploiting Cameroon's Poor," *NPR*, April 12, 2014, accessed February 17, 2016, http://www.npr.org/2014/04/12/302166602/revivalist-churches-accused-of-exploiting-cameroons-poor; see also Tapang Ivo Tanku, "Cameroon's President Orders Pentecostal Churches Closed," *CNN*, August 15, 2013, accessed February 17, 2016, www.cnn.com/2013/08/14/world/africa/cameroon-churches/.

2. The term *marketing strategies* is used here technically to describe the membership recruitment and retention techniques employed passionately by the Pentecostal churches in their evangelization drive and which have altogether contributed to the rapid spread of the movement in Cameroon. We realize that this is not how Pentecostals would describe their own evangelistic and missionary initiatives, but we use it only descriptively, without any pejorative connotations.
3. Pastor Victor Hill, district pastor of Winners Chapel, interview with author, Douala, Cameroon, March 30, 2015.
4. This church traces her origin to the 1904–1905 Welsh revival led by Evan Roberts; for details, see S. A. Fatokun, "A Pentecost From Wales to the 'Uttermost Parts of the World': A Reflection on the Gospel of Reconciliation and Its Impact on the Apostolic Church's Global Mission, 1916 to Date," *Swedish Missiological Themes* 96, no. 4 (2008): 395–416. Furthermore, the Apostolic Church Nigeria is a product of affiliation of the European mission with an indigenous Pentecostal group, "The Precious Stone Society," formerly affiliated with the Faith Tabernacle Congregation in Philadelphia in the United States; for details, see S. A. Fatokun, "The Apostolic Church Nigeria: The 'Metamorphosis' of an Indigenous-Prophetic Healing Movement Into a Classical Pentecostal Denomination," *Orita: Ibadan Journal of Religious Studies* 38 (2006): 49–70. See also G. Adegboyega, *Short History of the Apostolic Church in Nigeria* (Ibadan: Rosprint Industrial Press, 1978).
5. The Apostolic Church Cameroon—Group 18, Muyuka, "About TACC," accessed March 31, 2015, www.ourchurch.com/member/r/revokposin-tacc/index.php?p=1_3. Unless otherwise noted, here and below we have derived all information on the Apostolic Church Cameroon from this website in order to access the most updated information.
6. Pastor Gabriel Oladele Olutola, current national president of the Apostolic Church Nigeria and chairman, LAWNA territory, interview with author, March 31, 2015.
7. The Apostolic Church Cameroon, "Government of the Church by Apostles, Prophets, Evangelists, Pastors, Teachers, Elders, and Deacons," tenet 9; see The Apostolic Church Cameroon—Group 18, Muyuka, "Doctrines (What We Believe and Teach)." For details, see S. A. Fatokun, "The Fivefold Ministry in Ephesians 4:11 and the Concept of Divine Government in African Pentecostalism With Particular Reference

to the Apostolic Church Nigeria," *BETFA: Journal of the Ogbomosho Circle* 5 (2006): 115–25.

8. Victor Hill, interview.
9. The Assemblies of God is an American classical Pentecostal denomination founded in Nigeria through affiliation with an indigenous Pentecostal group, the Church of Jesus Christ. For details, see Francis C. Okeremgbo, "An Assessment of the Role of Augustus E. Wogu in the Founding and Consolidation of Assemblies of God in Nigeria, 1931–1974" (PhD thesis, University of Ibadan, Nigeria, 2014), 108–220.
10. Reverend Oganya, Assemblies of God pioneer missionary in Cameroon, interview with author, April, 2, 2015.
11. For details, see Harold Turner, *History of an African Independent Church: The Church of the Lord (Aladura)*, vol. 2 (Oxford: Clarendon Press, 1967); J. D. Y. Peel, *Aladura: A Religious Movement Among the Yoruba* (Oxford: Oxford University Press, 1968); and Wobo Sam, *A Life Course of Dr. J. O. Oshitelu* (Ogere, Nigeria: n.p., 1955).
12. For details, see J. O. Omoyajowo, *Cherubim and Seraphim Church: The History of an African Independent Church* (Lagos: Nork Publishers, 1982).
13. See J. O. Omoyajowo, "The Aladura Churches in Nigeria Since Independence," in Luke Fashole, ed., *Christianity in Independent Africa* (London: Rex Collins, 1978), 96–111; and Rosalind I. J. Hackett, "Thirty Years of Growth and Changes in a West African Independent Church: A Sociological Perspective," *Journal of Religion in Africa* 11, no. 3 (1980): 212–24.
14. For details, see Deji Ayegboyin and S. A. Ishola, *African Indigenous Churches* (Lagos: Greater Heights Publications, 1997).
15. Pastor Lawani of Deeper Life, interview with author, Douala, Cameroon, March 27, 2015; for further details on nomenclature of these churches, see Ayegboyin and Ishola, *African Indigenous Churches*, 11–20.
16. For details, see S. A. Fatokun, "Historical Sketch of Pentecostal Movements in Nigeria (With Emphasis on the South West)," *Cristianesimo Nella Storia* 28 (2007): 621.
17. Jide Akiode, former Redeemed Christian Church of God Cameroon mission pastor, interview with author, February 14, 2015.

18. News Express, "Redeemed Church Loses Big as Cameroonian President Shuts Branches, August 16, 2013, accessed February 17, 2016, http://www.newsexpressngr.com/news/detail.php?news=2541.
19. In an interview with Pastor Oyedotun, national administrative officer of the Gospel Faith Mission International, on April 6, 2015, he attributed the slow growth rate of the church in Cameroon to the secession of the founding missionary that gave the church some setbacks.
20. Victor Hill interview.
21. Pastors Lawani and Chike Onwansoanya, immediate past national overseer, Deeper Life, interview with author, Douala, Cameroon, March 27, 2015.
22. Tapang Ivo Tanku, "Cameroon's President Orders Pentecostal Churches Closed," CNN, August 14, 2013, accessed February 26, 2016, http://www.cnn.com/2013/08/14/world/africa/cameroon-churches/.
23. Victor Hill, interview.
24. See Andres Caballero, "Pentecostal Churches Accused of Exploiting Cameroon's Poor," NPR, April 12, 2014, accessed February 26, 2016, http://www.npr.org/2014/04/12/302166602/revivalist-churches-accused-of-exploiting-cameroons-poor.
25. As quoted in News Express, "Redeemed Church Loses Big as Cameroonian President Shuts Branches," August 16, 2013, accessed February 26, 2016, http://www.newsexpressngr.com/news/detail.php?news=2541.
26. See I. D. Ayegboyin and E. Nihinlola, "The Impact of Pentecostalism on Nigerian Baptist Convention," in *The Nigerian Baptist Convention in the Twenty-First Century* (Ibadan: Baptist Press, 1999), 58; cf. I. D. Ayegboyin and E. Nihinlola, "Pentecostalism and the Nigerian Baptist Convention Churches: The Way Forward," *Ogbomosho Journal of Theology* 13, no. 2 (2008): 218.
27. For details, see S. A. Fatokun, "The Blessing of Madness in Nigerian Pentecostalism," in Egbe Ifie, ed., *Papers in Honour of Tekena N. Tamuno Professor Emeritus at Seventy* (Ibadan: Oputoru Books, 2002), 109–18.
28. Tanku, "Cameroon's President Orders Pentecostal Churches Closed."
29. For details, see S. A. Fatokun, "A Critique of Warfare Prayers in African Pentecostalism," *Peace Studies and Practice* 1, no. 1 (June 2006): 18–38.

30. See www.bonnke.net/cfan/en.
31. Our interview with Pastor Victor Hill brought forth this comment: "Ministries here are not operating in love and unity; they are operating in competition and lack of trust."
32. Robert Mbe Akoko, "New Pentecostalism in the Wake of the Economic Crisis in Cameroon," *Nordic Journal of African Studies* 11, no. 3 (2002): 359–76; see also Robert Mbe Akoko, *"Ask and You Shall Be Given": Pentecostalism and the Economic Crisis in Cameroon* (Leiden: African Studies Centre, 2007).
33. See Benson Idahosa, "The Blessing of God Will Overtake You," *Redemption Faith Magazine* 5, no. 43 (1993); see also Godwin Onuoha and Chris Onuoha, eds., *Prosperity: What the Word of God Says About It* (Aba: Vincent International Publishers, 1996), 21.
34. David Oyedepo, *Breaking Financial Hardship* (Canaanland: Dominion, 1995), 7.
35. Chris Tunde Joda, "'Poverty or Prosperity': The Choice Is Yours," *Prosperity Now!* 2, no. 1 (January 1, 2001).
36. See Ruth Marshall-Fratani, "Mediating the Global and Local in Nigerian Pentecostalism," *Journal of Religions in Africa* 28, no. 3 (1998): 278–315.
37. E. B. Idowu, "Challenges of Witchcraft," *Orita* 4, no. 1 (June 1970): 3–16. Professor Idowu, in his reaction against C. K. Meek's opinion that witches and witchcraft do not exist but that belief in their existence is one of the most potent fears in the lives of most African people, categorically asserts that there are witches in Africa and that they are as real as murderers, poisoners, and other categories of evil workers, overt or surreptitious. He states further that to Africans, it is the supreme abomination, the most abhorrent yet unavoidable menace—a source of paralyzing, energy-sapping, soul-destroying fear.
38. A good example is the Rhema Christian Center of Pastor Warah Solomon at Bamenda, with about five thousand worshippers; for details, see Caballero, "Pentecostal Churches Accused of Exploiting Cameroon's Poor."
39. See Finis Dake, *God's Plan for Man* (Lawrenceville, GA: Bible Sales, 1997), 241.

40. See Tanku, "Cameroon's President Orders Pentecostal Churches Closed."
41. Ayegboyin and Ishola, *African Indigenous Churches*, 29.
42. See S. A. Fatokun, "Women and Leadership in Nigerian Pentecostal Churches," *Studia Historiae Ecclesiasticae* 32, no. 3 (Dec. 2006): 193–205.
43. I have done fieldwork research on this matter, the results of which have yet to be published.
44. See Douglas Petersen, "The Kingdom of God and the Hermeneutical Circle: Pentecostal Praxis in the Third World," in Murray A. Dempster, Byron D. Klaus, and Douglas Petersen, eds., *Called and Empowered: Global Mission in Pentecostal Perspective* (Peabody, MA: Hendrickson, 1991), 44–45.
45. For details, see Tomas Sundnes Dronen, *Pentecostalism, Globalization, and Islam in Northern Cameroon* (Leiden: Brill, 2013).
46. S. A. Fatokun, "Historical Sketch of Pentecostal Movements in Nigeria (With Emphasis on the South West)," *Cristianesimo Nella Storia* 28 (2007).
47. See I. D. Ayegboyin and E. Nihinlola, "The Impact of Pentecostalism on Nigerian Baptist Convention," in *The Nigerian Baptist Convention in the Twenty-First Century* (Ibadan: Baptist Press, 1999), 60.
48. Victor Hill, interview.
49. R. M. Anderson, "Pentecostal and Charismatic Christianity," in Mircea Eliade et al., eds., *The New Encyclopedia of Religion*, vol. 11 (New York: Macmillan, 1995), 229.

Chapter 6
"Blessed Be Egypt My People": The Neo-Charismatic Movement in Egypt

1. The regular capacity of the main hall of the CICC is nearly twenty-five hundred. During this three-day conference, the main hall was filled daily with more than three thousand people (hundreds were standing), in addition to the same number of people who were standing outside of the CICC and could not attend due to space restrictions.

2. *Mājālet al-Kīrāzā al-Qbtīā* [Coptic Evangelism Magazine], September 20, 1991; for all Arabic titles in this paper, the transliteration code of the Library of Congress is followed.
3. This classification follows the approach presented in Stanley M. Burgess and Eduard van der Maas, eds., *The New International Dictionary of Pentecostal and Charismatic Movements* (Grand Rapids, MI: Zondervan, 2002), xxi.
4. See the "Egypt" entry (unnamed) in Burgess and van der Maas, *New International Dictionary*, 84; nothing else is provided in this entry except these statistics.
5. Dan Sheffield, "Herbert E. Randall: A Canadian Holiness Missionary in Egypt and His Quest for More of the Holy Spirit," *Canadian Journal of Pentecostal-Charismatic Christianity* 2 (2011): 12.
6. For more details on Ralph C. Horner, see Laurence Croswell and Mark Croswell, *Lift Up a Standard: The Life and Legacy of Ralph C. Horner* (Indianapolis, IN: Wesleyan Publication House, 2012).
7. Sheffield, "Herbert E. Randall," 22–23.
8. Ibid., 15.
9. The Canadian and the Egyptian HMC merged with the Free Methodist Church in 1959. Today, the Egyptian HMC includes 105 congregations with more than 45,000 members. Daniel R. Sheffield, "Herbert Edward Randall," *Dictionary of African Christian Biography*, 2012, accessed January 1, 2014, http://www.dacb.org/stories/egypt/randall_herbert.html.
10. J. Booze, "Africa, North, and the Middle East (Survey)," in Burgess and van der Maas, *New International Dictionary*, 6.
11. Booze, "Africa," 8; and John Thomas Nichol, *The Pentecostals* (Plainfield, NJ: Logos International, 1971), 168.
12. Booze, "Africa," 8.
13. Allan Anderson, *Spreading Fires: The Missionary Nature of Early Pentecostalism* (Maryknoll, NY: Orbis Books, 2007), 152, 155. Eric Nelson Newberg, "The Pentecostal Mission in Palestine, 1906–1948: A Postcolonial Assessment of Pentecostal Zionism" (PhD thesis, Regent University, 2008), 186, 187, and 191, agrees with Anderson. A published version of Newberg's thesis is available as Eric Nelson Newberg, *The Pentecostal Mission in Palestine: The Legacy of Pentecostal Zionism* (Eugene, OR: Pickwick Publications, 2012).

14. Anderson, *Spreading Fires*, 152.
15. Ibid., 155.
16. Beth Baron, "Nile Mother: Lillian Trasher and the Orphans of Egypt," in Barbara Reeves-Ellington, Kathryn Kish Sklar, and Connie Anne Shemo, eds., *Competing Kingdoms: Women, Mission, Nation, and the American Protestant Empire, 1812–1960* (Durham, NC: Duke University Press, 2010), 240. For further readings on Lillian Trasher, see S. Shemeth, "Trasher, Lillian Hunt (1887–1961)," in Burgess and van der Maas, *New International Dictionary*, 1153.
17. Booze, "Africa," 7.
18. Sheffield, "Herbert Edward Randall." The online article shows that the number of churches of the Assemblies of God in Egypt is 130. However, in a personal correspondence with Pastor Yonathan Bolos, vice president of the Assemblies of God in Egypt, he confirmed that the accurate number in 2015 is 160.
19. For further details on the Catholic Charismatic Renewal in the West, see Peter Hocken, "The Catholic Charismatic Renewal," in Vinson Synan, ed., *The Century of the Holy Spirit 1901–2001* (Nashville, TN: Thomas Nelson, 2001), 209–32.
20. Adel Oncy and Sherif Kamal, "Khodām al-Khābār al-Sār: Lāā'īḥt al-Nīẓām al-'Asāsyā" [Good News' ministers: The basic system manual], unpublished manual (Cairo: 2014), 3.
21. See Vinson Synan, *The Holiness-Pentecostal Tradition: Charismatic Movements in the Twentieth Century* (Grand Rapids, MI: W. B. Eerdmans, 1997), 254–55.
22. Oncy, "Khodām al-Khābār al-Sār," 16.
23. Archbishop Maximus the First, founder of the Holy Synod of Saint Athanasius Congregation, interview with author, Cairo, Egypt, October 21, 2014. Peter Hocken ("The Catholic Charismatic Renewal," 211, 219), shows the centrality of Ann Arbor in the Catholic Charismatic Renewal in America.
24. Archbishop Maximus the First, interview.
25. Febe Armanios and Andrew Amstutz, "Emerging Christian Media in Egypt: Clerical Authority and the Visualization of Women in Coptic Video Films," *International Journal of Middle East Studies* 45 (2013): 517.

26. Synan, *The Century of the Holy Spirit*, 199.
27. Athanasius F. S. Emmert, "Charismatic Developments in the Eastern Orthodox Churches," in Russell Spittler, ed., *Perspectives on the New Pentecostalism* (Grand Rapids, MI: Baker, 1976), 40.
28. For more details on these two contemporary Coptic movements, see Omar H. Rahman, "Mass Exorcism in Cairo," *Vice*, accessed February 18, 2016, http://www.vice.com/gr/read/mass-exorcism-in-cairo; Jonathan Krohn, "Bizarre Christian Exorcisms Cast Out Muslim Devils," *Vocative*, November 26, 2013, accessed February 18, 2016, http://www.vocativ.com/culture/religion/bizarre-christian-exorcisms-cast-muslim-devils/; TBN.org, "As Conflict Continues in Syria, Egypt, TBN's Al-Horreya Network Brings a Message of Hope and Healing to the Middle East," September 20, 2013, accessed February 18, 2016, http://www.tbn.org/announcements/?nid=534; and Alkarma TV, *Live, With Father Makary Younan*, accessed February 18, 2016, http://www.alkarmatv.com/en/our-programs/father-makary-younan.
29. For more details on the Alpha course, see P. D. Hocken, "Alpha Course," in Burgess and van der Maas, *New International Dictionary*, 312. Also, for more details about Alpha course in Egypt, visit http://www.alphaegypt.org/.
30. Ayman Mounir, one of the cofounders of the movement in Egypt, interview with author, Heliopolis, Cairo, April 6, 2015.
31. George Aziz, founder of the Light of Life Ministry, interview with author, Heliopolis, Cairo, April 20, 2015; and Ghada Ghali, cofounder of The Way of Life Ministry, interview with author, Cairo, November 14, 2013.
32. See Father Daniel, *Wā Hūm Ghālābūh* [And they overcame him] (Cairo: G. C. Center, 1987); and Father Daniel, *Al-Fākh Īnkāsār* [The snare is broken] (Cairo: G. C. Center, 1988).
33. Shenouda III, "*Mā'ā 'Asīlāt al-Nās*" [With the people's question], *Mājālet al-Kīrāzā al-Qbtīā*, May 17, 1991, June 7, 1991, June 21, 1991, August 2, 1991, and August 16, 1991
34. *Mājālet al-Kīrāzā al-Qbtīā*, September 20, 1991.
35. For more details about Rivers of Life Canada, visit http://www.riversoflife.ca/rolar/.
36. Maher Fayez, interview with author, Shoubra, Cairo, April 14, 2015.

37. Maher Fayez, "*Al-Bāyān al-'Awāl l-ḥārākt al Kāroūz*" [The first statement of *Al-Kāroūz* movement], in Maher Fayez, *Al-'Ībādā bel-Māa' fī zamān Īstrātīgī* [Worship by water in a strategic season] (Cairo: *Al-Kāroūz* Movement, 2011), 112.
38. Carolyn Ramzy, "Repossessing the Land: A Spiritual Retreat With Maher Fayez," in Emma Dillon, Jocelyn R. Neal, and Bonnie C. Wade, eds., *AMS/SEM/SMT 2012 Annual Meetings Abstracts* (Brunswick, ME: AMS Inc., 2012), 30.
39. "Kīsāt Māx Mīshīl wā Rāḥīlūh mīn al-Urthūdhuksīyah" [The story of Max Michael and his departure from orthodoxy], accessed March 19, 201, http://st-takla.org/Coptic-Faith-Creed-Dogma/Max-Michel-the-new-Arius/The-Fake-Pope-Maximus-I-Maks-Mechel__01-Bishop-Bishoy-Who-is-he.html.
40. Archbishop Maximus the First, interview.
41. The Ugandan prayer movement is a Charismatic prayer movement that widely emerged in the late 1980s in Uganda and resulted in an official national declaration of the consecration of the Ugandan nation back to God on December 31, 1999. George Otis and Transform Nations Media and Sentinel Group, *Transformations II: The Glory Spreads* (Lynnwood, WA: Sentinel Group, 2001), DVD.
42. Michael Kimuli, *Al-Ṣalāh Al-f'ālah Al-moltahībah* [Effective fervent prayer] (Cairo: Dār Al-Nashr Al-Auskofīah, 2003), and John Mulinde, *Al-'āhd* [The covenant] (Minya, Egypt, 2002), recorded cassette, represent good examples of their teaching on prayer and spiritual warfare.
43. For more information about the International House of Prayer of Kansas City (IHOPKC), visit http://www.ihopkc.org/. Also, for more details about Mike Bickle, visit http://mikebickle.org/.
44. Moheb Milad, assistant pastor in KDEC, interview with author, Heliopolis, Cairo, April 9, 2015.
45. For more details about New Life Ministry, visit http://newlifeegypt.org.

Chapter 7
Kenyan Pentecostalism: An Epitome of Theological Shifts Within Pentecostal Christianity

1. Kavaya Phanuel, *Pentecostal Assemblies of God History* (Prayer of Mount House: Nairobi, 2003), 2.

2. Frederick B. Welbourne and Bethwell A. Ogot, *A Place to Feel at Home: A Study of Two Independent Churches in Western Kenya* (Nairobi: Oxford University Press, 1966), 73; Marian Keller, *Twenty Years in Africa, 1913–1933: Retrospect and Prospect* (Toronto: Full Gospel Publishing, 1933), 16–17; Otto Keller, "Keller Sends Canada Greetings," *The Pentecostal Testimony* 17, no. 11 (December 1936): 8, in the RC 1–12, series 15, Pentecostal Assembly of Canada archives. The PAOC archives has a section classified as "RC 1–09, Series 15, Kenya Records," with *RC* referring to Record Class. Audiovisual materials are classified as "SC5/RC 1–09, Series 15," while e-files on *The Pentecostal Testimony* from 1920–2001 are classified as "RC 1–12."
3. Keller, *Twenty Years in Africa*, 22–26.
4. Keller, "Keller Sends Canada Greetings," 8; George R. Upton, *Missionary Outreach of the Pentecostal of Canada* (Toronto: Pentecostal Assemblies of Canada, Missionary Dept., n.d.), 22–23, in RC 1–09, series 15, PAOC archives.
5. Keller, "Keller Sends Canada Greetings," 8.
6. D. J. Garrard, "Kenya," in Stanley M. Burgess and Eduard van der Maas, eds., *The New International Dictionary of Pentecostal and Charismatic Movements* (Grand Rapids, MI: Zondervan, 2002), 150–55; M. Ezekiel Kasiera, "The Development of Pentecostal Christianity in Western Kenya" (PhD thesis, Aberdeen University, 1984), 263.
7. Minutes of the second annual meeting of the Eastern District Council of the PAOC, held at Arnprior, August 27–31, 1923, in RC 1–09, series 15, PAOC archives.
8. Correspondence from Otto Keller to Walter McAlister, January 28, 1927, in RC 1–09, series 15; Otto and Marian Keller, "Echoes of Victory From Kenya," *The Pentecostal Testimony* 23, no. 14 (July 15, 1942): 10, in RC 1–12, PAOC archives.
9. Kasiera, "Development of Pentecostal Christianity," 488–89.
10. Ibid., 488–92.
11. Correspondence from John McBride to George Upton, May 26, 1960, in RC 1–09, series 15, PAOC archives.
12. Phanuel, *Pentecostal Assemblies of God History*, 19; Kasiera, "Development of Pentecostal Christianity," 465–66.

13. David B. Barrett, et al., *Kenya Churches Handbook: The Development of Kenyan Christianity, 1498–1973* (Kisumu: Evangel Publishing House, 1973), 25; Welbourne and Ogot, *A Place to Feel at Home*, 80–81. The place of meeting was called Nineveh, lending its name to the new church foundation.
14. Welbourne and Ogot (*A Place to Feel at Home*, 75–81) provide an analysis of Kivuli's background and his relationship with the Kellers; see also Zablon Nthamburi, *From Mission to Church: A Handbook of Christianity in East Africa* (Nairobi: Uzima Press, 1991), 17–18.
15. Agineta Lugangi Ndidi, interview with author, Nyang'ori, November 6, 2011.
16. Administrative report on "*Watu wa Roho*," "*Watu wa Mungu*," and "*Roho Maler*," from PC/NZA/2/1/140, Kenya National Archives (hereafter KNA). John Osogo claims that *Dini ya Roho* was founded in 1934 by both Alfayo Mango and Labi Obonyo. However, other sources credibly show an earlier beginning. John Osogo, *Life in Kenya in the Olden Days: The Baluyia* (Nairobi: Oxford University Press, 1965), 77.
17. Cynthia Hoehler-Fatton, *Women of Fire and Spirit: History, Faith, and Gender in Roho Religion in Western Kenya* (Oxford: Oxford University Press, 1996), 12–23.
18. Report on "*Watu wa Roho*," "*Watu wa Mungu*," and "*Roho Maler*"; see also Hoehler-Fatton, *Women of Fire and Spirit*, 26.
19. Report from the district commissioner to the provincial commissioner, Nyanza, dated August 27, 1942, in PC/NZA/2/1/140, KNA.
20. See more details on the beliefs and practices of this group as provided by the district commissioner, North Kavirondo; see also the report on the *Jo-Roho* by the district commissioner, Kericho, to the provincial commissioner, Nyanza, dated September 14, 1942, in PC/NZA/2/1/140, KNA.
21. Phanuel, *Pentecostal Assemblies of God History*, 11.
22. See http://www.eakenya.org.
23. For a further analysis on globalization and its effect on Pentecostalism in Kenya, see Susan Murimi, "The Changing Face of Pentecostalism in Kenya" (PhD thesis, Akrofi-Christaller Institute of Theology, Mission, and Culture, 2013), 186–96.
24. Ibid., 161–75.

25. Kevin Ward, "'*Tukutendereza Yesu*': The *Balokole* Revival in Uganda," in Nthamburi, *From Mission to Church*, 113–144; and George K. Mambo, "The Revival Fellowship (Brethren) in Kenya," in Barrett, *Kenya Churches Handbook*, 110–17.
26. See also Murimi, "The Changing Face of Pentecostalism in Kenya," 175–86.
27. Andrew F. Walls, "The American Dimension in the History of the Missionary Movement," in Joel A. Carpenter and Wilbert R. Shenk, eds., *Earthen Vessels: American Evangelicals and Foreign Missions, 1880–1980* (Grand Rapids, MI: W. B. Eerdmans, 1990), 8.
28. Correspondence from Otto Keller to Walter McAlister, January 28, 1927.
29. Marian and Otto Keller, "Sunday School Section," *The Pentecostal Testimony* 6, no. 5 (May 1927): 17, in RC 1–12, PAOC archives.
30. Marian and Otto Keller, "Kenya; News From Brother and Sister Keller in Africa," *The Pentecostal Testimony* 23, no. 1 (January 1, 1942): 13, in RC 1–12, PAOC archives.
31. Walter E. McAlister, "Do You Love the Lord's Appearing?," *The Pentecostal Testimony* 2, no. 2 (February 1922): 1, in RC 1–12, PAOC archives.
32. Ibid.
33. Otto C. Keller, "Kenya Colony, Africa," *The Pentecostal Testimony* 21, no. 11 (June 1, 1940): 8, in RC 1–12, PAOC archives.
34. John Kitts, "Send the Light," *The Pentecostal Testimony* (March 1, 1952): 12, in RC 1–12, PAOC archives.
35. SC5/RC 1–09, series 15, PAOC archives.
36. Charles Adenya, interview with author, Nairobi, April 28, 2013.
37. Correspondence from home office to Otto Keller, September 1, 1931, in RC 1–09, series 15, PAOC archives.
38. Correspondence from Otto Keller to J. W. Ford, April 6, 1934, in RC 1–09, series 15, PAOC archives.
39. Gorgo James, "Kumbukeni Kurudi Kwa Yesu" [Remember the return of Jesus], *Ushahidi wa Pentekote* 8 (Oktoba 1950), in RC 1–09, series 15, PAOC archives, translation mine.
40. Iris Scheel, "The Expulsive Love of Christ," *The Pentecostal Testimony* 41, no. 4 (April 1960): 9, in RC 1–12, PAOC archives.

41. Correspondence from Walter McAlister to Otto Keller, February 7, 1929, in RC 1–09, series 15, PAOC archives.
42. Correspondence from Otto Keller to Walter McAlister, February 7, 1929.
43. J. W. Skinner, *Plenteous Harvest of The Pentecostal Assemblies of Canada, Overseas Missions Department* (Toronto: Pentecostal Assemblies of Canada, Overseas Missions Department, 1965), 15–16, in RC 1–09, series 15, PAOC archives.
44. Naaman Bulimu, interview with author, November 6, 2011.
45. Simon Alovi, chairman of the PAG Church Council and Kariobangi district overseer, interview with author, March 28, 2013.
46. Murimi, "The Changing Face of Pentecostalism in Kenya," 287–91, 299–302.
47. On November 21, 2005, Kenya held a referendum on a proposed new constitution dubbed the "Wako draft," taking its name from the then attorney general, Amos Wako. Fifty-seven percent of the voters rejected the draft. The Pentecostals were on the fore in rejecting the draft because of its inclusion of the Kadhi courts. The Preliminary Report of the Committee of Experts on Constitutional Review (November 17, 2009), 12.
48. See Jesus Is Alive Ministries, "Bishop Margaret Wanjiru," accessed February 18, 2016, https://www.jiam.org/bishops-profile/.
49. Alovi, interview.
50. *Daily Nation*, April 10, 2013, 2.
51. Pentecostal Assemblies of God, Kenya Constitution (1988), 7.
52. See http://www.citam.org.
53. Kirk Kauffeldt, "The Cry of Sub-Saharan Africa," *The Pentecostal Testimony* 81, no. 10 (October 2000): 14, in RC 1–12, PAOC archives.
54. Paul Gifford, *African Christianity: Its Public Role* (London: Hurst & Company, 1998), 39.
55. Paul Gifford, *Christianity, Politics and Public Life in Kenya* (London: C. Hurst & Co. Ltd., 2009), 109–159.
56. Ibid., 161–62.
57. The programs were aired on Kiss TV in July 2013; a documentary on how pastors were using the media to extort money from unsuspecting

Kenyans, titled *A Pastor's Perspective on Tele-Extortionism: Miracles for Money?* aired on NTV Live on August 18, 2013.

58. Andrew Walls, "The Gospel as the Prisoner and Liberator of Culture," *Missionalia* 10, no. 3 (November 1982): 100.
59. Ibid.
60. Ibid., 101.
61. Kwame Bediako, "Scripture as the Hermeneutic of Culture and Tradition," *Journal of African Christian Thought* 4, no. 1 (June 2001): 2–11.

Chapter 8
Pentecostalism in Ethiopia: A Unique Case in Africa

1. Cf. Jörg Haustein and Emanuele Fantini, "Introduction: The Ethiopian Pentecostal Movement—History, Identity, and Current Socio Political Dynamics," *PentecoStudies* 12, no. 2 (2013): 150–61.
2. Some variation notwithstanding, it is impossible to clearly distinguish between Protestantism, Evangelicalism, and Pentecostal/Charismatic movements in many African countries. As the chapter will show, this is certainly the case in Ethiopia.
3. 3. See especially Tibebe Eshete, *The Evangelical Movement in Ethiopia: Resistance and Resilience* (Waco, TX: Baylor University Press, 2009); Jörg Haustein, *Writing Religious History: The Historiography of Ethiopian Pentecostalism*, Studies in the History of Christianity in the Non-Western World, vol. 17 (Wiesbaden: Harrassowitz, 2011); Jörg Haustein and Emanuele Fantini, eds., "Pentecostalism in Ethiopia," special issue of *PentecoStudies* 12, no. 2 (2013); Serge Dewel, *Mouvement Charismatique and Pentecôtisme En Éthiopie: Identité & Religion* [The Pentecostal and Charismatic movement in Ethiopia: Identity and religion] (Paris: L'Harmattan, 2014).
4. See Jörg Haustein, "The New Prime Minister's Faith: A Look at Oneness Pentecostalism in Ethiopia," *PentecoStudies* 12, no. 2 (2013): 183–204.
5. For details on this section, see especially Haustein, *Writing Religious History*; Eshete, *Evangelical Movement.*
6. See also Jörg Haustein, "Historical Epistemology and Pentecostal Origins: History and Historiography in Ethiopian Pentecostalism," *Pneuma* 35, no. 3 (2013): 345–65.

7. See Haustein, "The New Prime Minister's Faith."
8. See also Jörg Haustein, "Theorizing Pentecostal Historiography: Persecution and Historical Memory in Ethiopia," *PentecoStudies* 11, no. 2 (2012): 171–91.
9. See especially Jörg Haustein, "Embodying the Spirit(s): Pentecostal Demonology and Deliverance Discourse in Ethiopia," *Ethnos* 76, no. 4 (2011): 534–52.
10. For a comparative analysis of Orthodox, mainline Protestant, and Pentecostal Christianity during the Derg, see Jörg Haustein, "Navigating Political Revolutions: Ethiopia's Churches During and After the Mengistu Regime," in Klaus Koschorke, ed., *Falling Walls. The Year 1989/90 as a Turning Point in the History of World Christianity*, Studies in the History of Christianity in the Non-Western World, vol. 15 (Wiesbaden: Harrassowitz, 2009), 117–36.
11. Haustein and Fantini, "Introduction," 154.
12. For more information on this process in the Mekane Yesus Church, see Jörg Haustein, "Charismatic Renewal, Denominational Tradition, and the Transformation of Ethiopian Society," in Evangelisches Missionswerk Deutschland, ed., *Encounter Beyond Routine: Cultural Roots, Cultural Transition, Understanding of Faith, and Cooperation in Development* (Hamburg: EMW, 2011), 45–52, accessed February 19, 2016, http://www.emw-d.de/fix/files/doku_5_encounter-beyond-routine2011.pdf; for its origins in the larger Kale Heywet Church, see Tibebe Eshete, "The Early Charismatic Movement in the Ethiopian Kale Heywet Church," *PentecoStudies* 12, no. 2 (2013): 162–82.
13. There are few and rather minor churches that explicitly reject Pentecostal doctrines, but their leaders will occasionally admit in private that their youths seek or entertain certain Pentecostal practices nonetheless.
14. For one prominent example, see Lila W. Balisky, "Theology in Song: Ethiopia's Tesfaye Gabbiso," *Missiology* 25, no. 4 (1997): 447–56. Further research on Ethiopian gospel music is forthcoming by Hugo Ferran and Jan-Magne Steinhovden.
15. Mengistu Gobeze and Asamenu Kasa, የቤተክርስቲያን ታሪክ, ቁጥር ፪ [Church history, vol. 2] (Addis Ababa: Mehabir Qidusan, 2008), 166.
16. Esubalew Belete, የገሃነም ደጆች. ፕሮቴስታንታዊ ጂሀድ በኢትዮጵያዊነት - ተዋሕዶነት - ሳይ ሲፈፈም [Gates of hell: When the Protestant jihad against

Ethiopian-ness—Tewahedo—thrives] (Alexandria, VA: Artistic Printers, 2004).

17. Cf. Jörg Haustein and Terje Østebø, "EPRDF's Revolutionary Democracy and Religious Plurality: Islam and Christianity in Post-Derg Ethiopia," *Journal of Eastern African Studies* 5, no. 4 (2011): 758.
18. For all of the regional data, see the detailed census tables published at the Central Statistical Agency website, accessed March 17, 2016, http://www.csa.gov.et/index.php/2013-02-20-14-51-51/census-tables.
19. See also Tsega Endalew, "Protestant Mission Activities and Persecutions in Bahər Dar, 1968–1994: A Chronicle," in Verena Böll, Andreu Martínez d' Alòs-Moner, and Evgenia Sokolinskaia, eds., *Ethiopia and the Missions: Historical and Anthropological Insights* (Münster: Lit, 2005), 209–20.
20. Cf. Haustein, *Writing Religious History*, 219ff. For other instances of a continued persecution narrative, see Addise Amado, *Persecution in Ethiopia: Situation Analysis; Theological, Sociological, Economical, and Political Interpretations and Implications* (Addis Ababa: Voice of Martyrs Ethiopia, 2003).
21. Memher Getachew, ገድል ወይስ ገደል? [Saint or abyss?] (Addis Ababa, 2003); Merigeta Sereqe Berhan Sewongel, ጸሎት ዘሙታን:: ሙታን ስለሙታን ሲጸልዩ [Prayers to the dead: When the dead pray for the dead], 3rd ed. (Addis Ababa, 2004).
22. For details, see Jörg Haustein, "Die Pfingstlich/Charismatischen Bewegungen als aktuelle Herausforderung der Äthiopisch-Orthodoxen Kirche" [The Pentecostal/Charismatic movement as current challenge to the Ethiopian Orthodox Church], in Karl Pinggéra, ed., *Tradition und Wandel im Land der Königin von Saba: Ansichten aus und zu Äthiopien* [Tradition and change in the land of the Queen of Sheba: Insights from and into Ethiopia], Hofgeismarer Protokolle, no. 356 (Hofgeismar: Evangelische Akademie, 2011), 73–92.
23. Haustein, "Embodying the Spirit(s)."
24. Cf. Gary Ray Munson, "A Critical Hermeneutic Examination of the Dynamic of Identity Change in Christian Conversion Among Muslims in Ethiopia" (PhD thesis, University of South Africa, 2014), 321–28.
25. Dossier: "Chrislam በኢትዮጵያ?" [Chrislam in Ethiopia?], *Mathetes* (July 21, 2012). 10–21.

26. See Tamrat Layne, “Tamrat and Mulu’s Story,” accessed June 4, 2015, http://tamratlayne.com/story/.
27. His testimony was greeted with standing ovations in the largest Pentecostal church in Addis Ababa, cf. Haustein and Østebø, “EPRDF’s Revolutionary Democracy,” 764.
28. Cf. Haustein, “Navigating Political Revolutions.” Layne’s criticism against present church politics and schisms resonate with this as well: the persecuted church is seen as the pure church; see Haustein, “Theorizing Pentecostal Historiography.”
29. Cf. Emanuele Fantini, “Transgression and Acquiescence: The Moral Conflict of Pentecostals in Their Relationship With the Ethiopian State,” *PentecoStudies* 12, no. 2 (2013): 205–30.
30. See Haustein, “The New Prime Minister’s Faith,” 199ff.
31. See Dena Freeman, “Development and the Rural Entrepreneur: Pentecostals, NGOs, and the Market in the Gama Highlands, Ethiopia,” in Dena Freeman, ed., *Pentecostalism and Development: Churches, NGOs, and Social Change in Africa* (Basingstoke: Palgrave Macmillan, 2012), 159–80; and Freeman, “Pentecostalism in a Rural Context: Dynamics of Religion and Development in Southwest Ethiopia,” *PentecoStudies* 12, no. 2 (2013): 231–49.
32. Emanuele Fantini, “Go *Pente*! The Charismatic Renewal of the Evangelical Movement in Ethiopia,” in Gerard Prunier and Eloi Ficquet, eds., *Understanding Contemporary Ethiopia* (London: Hurst, 2015), 123–146; see also Emanuele Fantini, “Crafting Ethiopia’s Glorious Destiny: Pentecostalism and Economic Transformation Under a Developmental State,” *Archives de Sciences Sociales des Religions* 175 (fall 2016): forthcoming.
33. Fantini, “Crafting Ethiopia’s Glorious Destiny,” 17.

Chapter 9
Coming of Age: Pentecostalism and *Umunthu* in Malawi

1. In Chichewa (Malawi’s national vernacular), not unlike many other Malawian languages, *munthu* means “person.” Adding the prefix *u-* to make it *umunthu* transforms it to mean “personhood.” *Umunthu* is the same philosophy known as *ubuntu* in South Africa. It is a widespread African concept that describes a well-rounded philosophy of life and is known by many different vernacular names in different countries, but

the concept and the philosophy it stands for is always the same. It is known as *utu* in Swahili, *obonto* in Kiisi, *nunhu* in Shona, *bunhu* in Tsonga, *numunhu* in Shangaan, *botho* in Sotho, *uvumunu* in Kinga, etc. While there are some differences from country to country, the cultural contexts are similar enough to make possible some generalizations.

2. George Herbert Wilson, *The History of the Universities' Mission to Central Africa* (Freeport, NY: Books for Libraries Press, 1971), 4; see also Thomas Pakenham, *The Scramble for Africa, 1876–1912* (New York: Random House, 1991), 1.
3. For more on this history, see James Tengatenga, *The UMCA in Malawi: A History of the Anglican Church 1861–2010* (Zomba, Malawi: Kachere Series, 2010).
4. Oliver Ransford, *David Livingstone: The Dark Interior* (London: J. Murray, 1978), 159.
5. Ibid., 160.
6. Anglicanism in Malawi traces its history to the UMCA. See James Tengatenga, *Church, State, and Society: An Analysis of Anglican Ecclesiology*, Kachere Theses, no. 12 (Zomba, Malawi: Kachere Series, 2006); see also Tengatenga, *The UMCA in Malawi.*
7. The UMCA stayed at Magomero for two years before retreating to Zanzibar. They struggled with the two-pronged problem of malaria and the slave trade (as they were located on a slave route). They returned to Malawi in 1881 and settled down on Likoma Island on Lake Malawi in 1885. Soon, several other groups of missionaries started to appear. First, it was the Livingstonia Mission (of the Free Church of Scotland) that came to Malawi in 1875. Following Livingstonia, the Established Church of Scotland started the Blantyre Mission (named after David Livingstone's birthplace) in 1876. The Dutch Reformed Church Mission was the fourth mission to come to Malawi in 1888. The Roman Catholic missionaries arrived in Malawi in 1889. By 1891, Malawi—then called Nyasaland—was declared a protectorate of Britain to prevent the encroaching Portuguese from taking the territory, which could violate the agreements made at the Berlin Conference, where the boundaries of most African countries were drawn. See John McCracken, *Politics and Christianity in Malawi: The Impact of the Livingstonia Mission in the Northern Province*, Kachere Monographs, no. 8 (Zomba, Malawi: Kachere Series, 2008); see also Steven Paas, *The Faith Moves South:*

A History of the Church in Africa, Kachere Books, no. 27 (Zomba, Malawi: Kachere Series, 2006).

8. Ulf Strohbehn, *Pentecostalism in Malawi: A History of the Apostolic Faith Mission in Malawi, 1931–1994*, Kachere Theses, no. 8 (Zomba, Malawi: Kachere Series, 2005), 50.
9. They both expressed these views in telephone conversations, responding to my inquiry about the origins of Pentecostalism in Malawi.
10. Strohbehn, *Pentecostalism in Malawi,* 43.
11. Ibid., 44.
12. Chilembwe had been educated in the United States, where he got his ministry credentials. He returned to Malawi in 1900 to found the Providence Industrial Mission but later took arms against white farmers at Magomero. For more on this piece of Malawian history, see George Shepperson and Thomas Price, *Independent African: John Chilembwe and the Origins, Setting, and Significance of the Nyasaland Native Rising of 1915*, Edinburgh University Publications: History, Philosophy, and Economics, no. 8 (Edinburgh: Edinburgh University Press, 1958).
13. Many African independent churches emerged in the 1920s. These were generally spiritist churches led by a charismatic, anointed leader. The most popular of these is the Black Man's Church of God, led by Yesaya Mwase of the Tongaland. Such churches were suppressed during the colonial era. However, they paved the way for growth of the Charismatic and Pentecostal movement after independence.
14. Strohbehn, *Pentecostalism in Malawi,* 63–67. The Assemblies of God had been formally incorporated as a church in 1947. See Enson M. Lwesya, *Flames of Fire: The History of the Assemblies of God and Pentecostalism in Malawi* (Lilongwe: Assemblies of God Press, 2005).
15. See Harvey C. Kwiyani, *Sent Forth: African Missionary Work in the West* (Maryknoll, NY: Orbis, 2014), 62–67.
16. Kamuzu Banda was a Christian who had been sanctioned as a church elder in the Church of Central Africa Presybterian. He was also a dictator who did not allow any competition, even from church leaders.
17. See Rijk van Dijk, "Pentecostalism, Cultural Memory, and the State: Contested Representations of Time in Postcolonial Malawi," in Richard P. Werbner, ed., *Memory and the Postcolony: African Anthropology and*

the Critique of Power, Postcolonial Encounters (London: Zed Books, 1998), 155–81.

18. Klaus Fiedler, "The Charismatic and Pentecostal Movements in Malawi in Cultural Perspectives," *Religion in Malawi* 9 (1999): 27–38. Also see Rhodian G. Munyenyembe, *Christianity and Socio-Cultural Issues: The Charismatic Movement and Contextualization of the Gospel in Malawi*, Kachere Theses, no. 19 (Zomba, Malawi: Mzuni Press, 2011), 34.
19. See Allan Anderson, *Moya: The Holy Spirit in an African Context*, Manualia Didactica, no. 13 (Pretoria: University of South Africa, 1991).
20. Felix Nyika, "Apostleship Among Neo-Charismatics in Malawi" (PhD dissertation, Mzuzu University, 2015).
21. Richard A. van Dijk, "Young Puritan Preachers in Post-Independent Malawi," *Africa* 62, no. 2 (1992): 159–81.
22. These young prophets have also embraced the hierarchies of authority, with titles among them including minor prophet for the less-known ones to major or senior prophet for those leading megachurches.
23. Harvey J. Sindima, "Malawian Churches and the Struggle for Life and Personhood" (PhD dissertation, Princeton Theological Seminary, 1987).
24. John S. Mbiti, *African Religions and Philosophy* (Garden City, NY: Anchor Books, 1970).
25. John S. Mbiti, *Introduction to African Religion* (New York: Praeger, 1975).
26. Harvey J. Sindima, "Bondedness, *Moyo*, and *Umunthu* as the Elements of Achewa Spirituality: Organizing Logic and Principle of Life," *Ultimate Reality and Meaning* 14, no. 1 (1991): 5–20.
27. Harvey Sindima has suggested in a telephone conversation to me that there is a timely pneumatological renaissance in African theology taking place in these early decades of the twenty-first century. In addition to my thesis, Harvey C. Kwiyani, "Pneumatology, Mission, and African Christians in Multicultural Congregations in North America" (PhD dissertation, Luther Seminary, 2012), a few other significant monographs on African pneumatology have emerged since 2010, and these include David Tonghou Ngong, *The Holy Spirit and Salvation in African Christian Theology: Imagining a More Hopeful Future for Africa*, Bible and Theology in Africa, no. 8 (New York: Peter Lang, 2010), and Chigor Chike, *The Holy Spirit in African Christianity: An Empirical Study* (Milton Keynes: Paternoster, 2015).

28. Peter J. Paris, *The Spirituality of African Peoples: The Search for a Common Moral Discourse* (Minneapolis: Fortress Press, 1995).
29. M. L. Daneel, *Zionism and Faith-Healing in Rhodesia: Aspects of African Independent Churches* (Gravenhage, The Netherlands: Mouton, 1970).
30. Bengt Sundkler, *Bantu Prophets in South Africa* (London: Lutterworth Press, 1948).
31. Aylward Shorter, *Toward a Theology of Inculturation* (Maryknoll, NY: Orbis Books, 1989).
32. Gerrie ter Haar, *How God Became African: African Spirituality and Western Secular Thought* (Philadelphia, PA: University of Pennsylvania Press, 2009).
33. For instance, see Michael Welker, *God the Spirit* (Minneapolis, MN: Fortress Press, 1994), chapter 1.
34. The African understands, however, that these spirit-beings (including the Holy Spirit) have spiritual powers. See Harvey J. Sindima, *Africa's Agenda: The Legacy of Liberalism and Colonialism in the Crisis of African Values*, Contributions in Afro-American and African Studies, no. 176 (Westport, CT: Greenwood Press, 1995).
35. Contrary to those who have followed Platonic dualism, in which the body is prison to the soul and must be broken for the soul to be freed, Africans hold that the spirit is positively housed in the body and generally influences the individual's personality.

Chapter 10
Pentecostalism in Tanzania and Uganda: A Historical and Theological Perspective

1. Some newer groups and networks include the Pentecostal Assemblies of Canada, Full Gospel, Deliverance Church Uganda, Redeemed Church, Evangelical Fellowship of Uganda, Miracle Center Churches, National Fellowship of Born Again Pentecostal Churches, Christian Life Ministries, United Pentecostal Churches, Elim Pentecostal Evangelistic Fellowship of Uganda, and Born Again Faith Federation of Uganda.
2. Steven Dale Horsager Rasmussen, "Illness and Death Experiences in Northwestern Tanzania: An Investigation of Discourses, Practices, Beliefs, and Social Outcomes, Especially Related to Witchcraft, Used in a Critical Contextualization and Education Process With Pentecostal

Ministries" (PhD dissertation, Trinity International University, Deerfield, IL, 2009), 76.

3. W. B. Niwagila, *From the Catacomb of a Self-Governing Church: A Case Study of the African Initiative and the Participation of the Foreign Mission in the Mission History of Northwest Diocese of Evangelical Lutheran Church in Tanzania, 1890–1965* (Hamburg: Lottbek, 1991), 249.
4. Fredier Ludwig, *Questioning the Secular State: The Worldwide Resurgence of Religion in Politics* (London: C. Hurst and Company, 1996), 222.
5. For a study of Pentecostalism and holistic development in Uganda, see Ben Jones, "Pentecostalism, Development NGOs, and Meaning in Eastern Uganda," in Dena Freeman, ed., *Pentecostalism and Development: Churches, NGOs, and Social Change in Africa* (Basingstoke: Palgrave Macmillan, 2012), 181–202.
6. Allan Anderson, *An Introduction to Pentecostalism* (Cambridge: Cambridge University Press, 2004), 125–26.
7. Rev. Canon Francis Sender, diocesan secretary, Mara, and general secretary of the Mara Christian Association, interview with author, Mara, November 6, 2014, Mara.
8. T. O. Ranger, "Christian Independency in Tanzania," in David B. Barrett, ed., *African Initiatives in Religion* (Nairobi: East African Publishing House, 1971), 122.
9. Michael Jennings, *Surrogates of the States: NGOs, Development, and Ujamaa in Tanzania* (Bloomfield, CT: Kumarian Press, 2008), 65–66.
10. Ibid., 69–70.
11. Rev. Canon Sender, interview.
12. Frieder Ludwig, *Church and State in Tanzania: Aspects of Changing in Relationships, 1961–1994* (Boston: Brill, 1999), 184.
13. Rev. Canon Francis Sender, interview with author, Musoma, November 5, 2014.
14. To date, I see these elements are still very much alive in the churches that I had the privilege of visiting in November 2014, when I was in Tanzania on my research for this essay.
15. Bishop Hilikiah Omindo, interview with author, Musoma, November 5, 2014.

16. Simenon Jarle, "Religious Politics of Religious NGOs and the National Aid: The Norwegian Experience," *Forum for Development Studies* 1 (2006): 84.
17. David Maxwell, "The Durawall of Faith: Pentecostal Spirituality Liberation in Neo-Liberal Zimbabwe," *Journal of Religion in Africa* 35, no. 1 (2005): 28; see also David Maxwell, "Delivered From the Spirit of Poverty? Pentecostalism, Prosperity, and Development in Zimbabwe," *Journal of Religion in Africa* 28, no. 3 (1988): 351; and Dileger Hansjörg, "Healing the Wounds of Modernity: Salvation, Community, and Care in Neo-Pentecostal Church in Dar es Salaam, Tanzania," *Journal of Religion in Africa* 37, no. 1 (2006): 62.
18. Paul Gifford, "Complex Provenance of Some Elements of African Pentecostal Theology," in Andre Corten and Ruth Marshall-Fratani, eds., *Between Babel and Pentecost: Transitional Pentecostalism in Africa and Latin America* (Bloomington, IN: Indiana University Press, 2001), 62–79; Joel Robbins, "The Globalization of Pentecostal and Charismatics Christianity," *Annual Review of Anthropology* 33 (2004): 117–43.
19. Paul Gifford, *African Christianity: Its Public Role* (London: Hurst & Company, 1998), 328.
20. Samuel Zalanga, "Religion, Economic Change, and Cultural Development: The Contradictory Role of Christianity in Sub-Saharan Africa," *Journal of Third World Studies* 27, no. 1 (2010): 49.
21. Donald E. Miller and Testunao Yamamori, *Global Pentecostalism: The New Face of Christian Social Engagement* (Berkeley, CA: University of California Press, 2007), 162–65.
22. Gifford, *African Christianity*, 100.
23. President Apolo Milton Obote ruled Uganda a second time (1980–1985), commonly referred to as the Obote II regime. The first time was from 1962–1971.
24. Paddy Musana, *The Pentecostal Movement in Uganda* (unpublished manuscript), 63–65; I am grateful to Dr. Paddy for sharing his manuscript with me.
25. Kevin Ward and Emma Wild-Wood, eds., *The East African Revival: History and Legacies* (Farnham: Ashgate, 2012).
26. Musana, *The Pentecostal Movement in Uganda*, 65–66.
27. Ibid.

28. Gifford, *African Christianity*, 153.
29. Alfred Olwa, "Briefing: About Uganda and Its Churches," 10, unpublished paper presented at the opening of the jubilee celebration of the All Africa Conference of Churches, held at Gabba National Seminary, Uganda, May 26–June 9, 2013.
30. Pastor Fred Wantaate of Makerere Full Gospel, interview with author, Kampala, September 9, 2014.
31. Pastor Graham Sewanyana, Miracle Centre, interview with author, Mukono, August 15, 2014.
32. In 1996, justice Julia Semitunde was appointed chair of the Commission of Inquiry on Corruption in the Uganda police force and the Uganda Revenue Authority.
33. Quotations in this paragraph are from Pastor Gilead Mchaki, academic dean of Pentecostal Bible College, interview with author, Mwanza, November 5, 2014.
34. Bishop Tom Ibrahim Okello, Africa Pentecostals, interview with author, Lira, October 18, 2014.
35. Obadiah Eustace, tutor at Ngara Bible College, interview with author, Kagera, November 2, 2014, for this and the next two quotations in this paragraph.
36. Rev. Captain Sebukwekwe Narsis (PhD candidate), lecturer at Ngara Bible College, interview with author, Kagera, November 3. 2015.
37. Bishop Jacton Lugumira (DMin candidate), Luwero Diocese, interview with author, Bukoba, November 7, 2014, for quotations in this paragraph.
38. Pastor Lawrence Oseje (PhD candidate), Edinburgh University and lecturer at Uganda Christian University, interview with author, Mukono, May 23, 2014.
39. Bishop Martin Ogwal, Faith Mission, interview with author, Lira, October 17, 2014.

Chapter 11
Pentecostal and Charismatic Christianity in Zambia: Historical and Theological Developments and Civic Engagement

1. The term *Pentecostal* in Southern Africa also includes African Independent Churches (AICs) that are of a Zionist character with roots in

South Africa and Zimbabwe. Anderson refers to these as Pentecostal-type, "Spirit" or "prophet healing" AICs that use rituals and symbols of water and oil in their liturgy and healing services. For a more detailed study on African Initiated Churches, see the work of Allan Anderson, *Zion and Pentecost: The Spirituality and Experience of Pentecostal and Zionist/Apostolic Churches in South Africa* (Pretoria: University of South Africa Press, 2000), 37; *Bazalwane: African Pentecostals in South Africa* (Pretoria: University of South Africa Press, 1992); and *Moya: The Holy Spirit in an African Context*, Manualia Didactica, no. 13 (Pretoria: University of South Africa, 1991).

2. It is important to mention here that there were other African traditional religions that predated Pentecostalism; see John Mbiti, *Concepts of God in Africa* (London: SPCK, 1970); and John S. Mbiti, *Introduction to African Religion* (New York: Praeger, 1975).
3. Robert I. Rotberg, *Christian Missionaries and the Creation of Northern Rhodesia* (Princeton: Princeton University Press, 1965), 151–53.
4. Victor Chilenje, "The Origins and Development of the Church of God Central Africa Presbyterian (CCAP) in Zambia, 1882–2004" (PhD dissertation, University of Stellenbosch, 2007), 221.
5. In this case, these are churches that broke away from the mainline churches during what K. J. Phiri describes as the Pentecostalization of the Reformed Church in Zambia as well as other mainline churches; see Kelvin Jason Phiri, "African Pentecostal Spirituality: A Study of the Emerging African Pentecostal Churches in Zambia" (PhD dissertation, University of Pretoria, 2009), 22.
6. Allan Anderson, *An Introduction to Pentecostalism* (Cambridge: Cambridge University Press, 2004), 11; cf. Allan Anderson, *Spreading Fires: The Missionary Nature of Early Pentecostalism* (Maryknoll, NY: Orbis Books, 2007), 6; and Walter J. Hollenweger, *The Pentecostals* (London: SCM Press Ltd., 1972), 425.
7. Hollenweger, *The Pentecostals*, 13–14, 171.
8. Ibid., 266.
9. And how their engagement with the external dimension, in turn, affects their sacred/transcendental and internal dimensions; see André Droogers, "The Power Dimensions of the Christian Community: An Anthropological Model," *Religion* 33, no. 3 (July 2003): 263–80.

10. Bishop Mark Musonda, former presiding bishop of Apostolic Faith Mission in Zambia, interview with author, Lusaka, August 25, 2010. In 2006, Musonda was elected as international general secretary for Apostolic Faith Mission International and served until 2009.
11. Bishop Chrispine Zulu, interview with author, Lusaka, July 18, 2011. Zulu was then conference overseer of the Southern Conference and assistant national overseer of the Pentecostal Holiness Church in Zambia. For a detailed history of the PAOGZ, see Adrian Chalwe, "An Evaluation of the Mission History of the Pentecostal Assemblies of God Zambia" (PhD dissertation, North-West University, 2008).
12. Bishop Sky Banda, senior pastor of Maranatha Pentecostal Assembly of God Zambia in Kitwe, interview with author, Kitwe, August 6, 2010.
13. Bishop John Mambo, former overseer of the Church of God in Zambia, interview with author, Lusaka, July 20, 2011. Mambo served as overseer for nineteen years and was regional superintendent, overseeing nine countries, including East and Southern Africa. He is the founder of Chikondi Foundation, an orphanage for vulnerable children, including children of pastors who have died. After the Zambian independence, the Church of God in Zambia started experiencing problems with its links in South Africa and therefore decided to join the North American Church of God (Cleveland, Tennessee), according to Bishop Mambo.
14. Bishop Joel Imakando, senior pastor and founder of Bread of Life Church in Lusaka and part of the Evangelical Fellowship of Zambia's board of directors, interview with author, Lusaka, November 10, 2009.
15. Bishop Ndhlovu, founder of Bible Gospel Church in Africa, interview with author, Lusaka, August 24, 2011.
16. Bishop Harrison Sakala, chief bishop of PAOGZ, interview with author, Lusaka, August 9, 2011.
17. Rev. Steven Mwale, former general superintendent of PAOGZ, interview with author, Lusaka, November 10, 2009.
18. Ibid.
19. Robert Putnam, "Tuning In, Tuning Out: The Strange Disappearance of Social Capital in America," *Political Science and Politics* 28, no. 4 (1995): 665.
20. Paul Gifford, *African Christianity: Its Public Role* (London: Hurst & Company, 1998), 197–217.

21. Rev. Steven Mwale, interview. For further reading on the subject, see Harri Englund, ed., *Christianity and the Public Culture* (Athens, OH: Ohio University Press, 2001).
22. Ruth Prince, Philippe Denis, and Rijk Van Dijk, introduction to special issue, "Engaging Christianities: Negotiating HIV/AIDS, Health, and Social Relations in East and Southern Africa," *Africa Today* 56, no. 1 (2009): v.
23. Bishop Harrison Sakala, interview.
24. Bishop Edgar Ng'ambi, senior pastor of Praise Christian Centre and board member of the Evangelical Fellowship of Zambia, interview with author, Lusaka, August 18, 2011.
25. Pastor Eddie Chansa, senior pastor and founder of Lifeline Community Fellowship in Lusaka, interview with author, Lusaka, August 10, 2011.
26. Bishop Eddie Mulenga, senior pastor and founder of Liberty Christian Centre in Lusaka, interview with author, Lusaka, August 6, 2011.
27. Danny Pule, senior pastor of Dunamis Christian Centre, interview with author, Lusaka, August 17, 2011; Helmut Reutter, senior pastor of Gospel Outreach Fellowship, interview with author, Lusaka, August 10, 2010; George Mbulo, senior pastor of Capital Christian Centre, interview with author, Lusaka, August 10, 2011. Teachings on the prosperity gospel were introduced to Zambia in the 1960s, when Oral Roberts came to Zambia for a crusade. During that time, there was an increase in North American literature with authors writing on prosperity. However, this gospel became even more popular particularly in the 1990s. Its emphasis on the idea that God was not only interested in human spirituality but also in human health and finances, being physically healthy and financially wealthy became a pervasive teaching among many PC churches. What varied was the level of emphasis within different denominations. The idea of sowing a seed, or "seed faith," through the giving of tithes and offerings in faith was taught as what stirred God's blessings. To a greater extent, the coming of an American Christian channel, Trinity Broadcasting Network, in 1998 precipitated this theology, and the local preachers that were also aired on TBN reiterated the same message. Mainly, people were asked to sow their seeds to TBN Zambia in order for God to bless them and to help support the running of the network.

28. Anderson, *An Introduction to Pentecostalism*, 261. In response to this, I would argue that there were no politics in traditional Zambian society because people did not struggle for liberation and justice or for voting, as defined in the West or by the mainline churches. Given the spiritual-magico substratum of African politics, the use of the symbolic language of the devil might actually be political.
29. Odhiambo Okite, "Church Leaders Publicly Oppose Third Term for Christian President," *Christianity Today* 45, no. 6 (April 23, 2001): 26.
30. For example, Reverend M'membe, in a newspaper article, "felt the declaration was done to hoodwink the genuinely God-fearing citizen to win their support, and prey on majority Zambians' religious emotions"; see Masautso Phiri, "Ramifications of a Christian Nation," *The Post*, March 25, 1996, 5; and "Is Chiluba Really a Born Again?" *The Post*, March 26, 1996, 5.
31. Austin Cheyeka, "Concept of Zambia as a Christian Nation," *African Ecclesial Review* 44, no. 3–4 (2002): 170, quoting Chiluba on a *ZNBC* Television program, *This Is Your Day*, October 26, 1995.
32. Ted Olsen, "One Nation Under God," *Christianity Today*, February 4, 2004, 41.
33. David Martin, *Pentecostalism: The World Their Parish* (Malden: Blackwell Publishers, 2002), 89; see also John Burdick, *Looking to God in Brazil: The Progressive Catholic Church in Brazil's Religious Arena* (Berkeley, CA: University of California Press, 1993).
34. Martin, *Pentecostalism*, 89.
35. Chalwe, "An Evaluation of the Mission History of the Pentecostal Assemblies of God Zambia," 119.
36. Ibid., 40.
37. Donald E. Miller and Testunao Yamamori, *Global Pentecostalism: The New Face of Christian Social Engagement* (Berkeley, CA: University of California Press, 2007), 212.
38. Dhan Prakash, "Toward a Theology of Social Concern: A Pentecostal Perspective," *Asian Journal of Pentecostal Studies* 13, no. 1 (2010): 65.

Chapter 12
The Rural Narratives of a Zimbabwean-Based Religious Movement and the Shaping of African Pentecostal Spirituality

1. Kudzai Biri, "'The Silent Echoing Voice': Pentecostalism in Zimbabwe and the Quest for Power, Healing, and Miracles," *Studia Historiae Ecclesiasticae* 38 (2012): 37–55.
2. David Maxwell, *African Gifts of the Spirit: Pentecostalism and the Rise of a Zimbabwean Traditional Religious Movement* (Oxford: James Currey, 2006), 4.
3. The label *Zimbabwean Pentecostal spirituality* in my topic might spark debate, especially by those critics of Christianity, as happened when I presented a paper in 2011 that had "Zimbabwean Pentecostalism" as part of the title. Some critics argued that Christianity is not Zimbabwean. I maintain that label because Pentecostalism has become an identity of many Zimbabweans, which is thus my justification for applying the label in this study.
4. The Shona are the dominant ethnic group in Zimbabwe, and the group is comprise of people of different languages that include the Manyika, Karanga, Korekore, and Zezuru, among others.
5. See Ezekiel Guti, *History of ZAOGA, Forward in Faith: The Book of Remembrance—How It Began and Where It Is Going* (Harare: EGEA, 1999), 12–14.
6. The references identify ZAOGA with Guti, as there are tones of personalization of the church. The implications are that ZAOGA was founded by Guti, that the theology in ZAOGA is tied to the life and personhood of Guti, and that Guti leads the church.
7. Ezekiel Guti and his wife, Eunor, always denounce emulating Western cultural values and teach that most Western societies are immoral and that there is nothing that can be emulated from the white men. The white men are often portrayed as an example of the worst of moral decadence, especially in discourses of empowering the black race. On a related note, while Guti's wife serves as a role model for women alongside her husband, the couple also perpetuates traditional women's roles that in the HIV/AIDS-ridden African context promotes a message that in many cases keeps wives submissive to their husbands in oppressive ways; see my article "'The Perfect Shoe…': Zimbabwean Pentecostal

Women's Fellowships and the Discourse of Submission, an Overview and Critique in the Light of HIV and AIDS," *Journal of Gender and Religion in Africa* 20, no. 1 (2014): 35–50.

8. Ogbu Kalu, "The Third Response: Pentecostalism and the Reconstruction: Christian Experience in Africa from 1970–1995," *Studia Historiae Ecclesiasticae* 24, no. 2 (1998): 1–34.
9. See, for example, Kudzai Biri, "Pentecostalism, Migration, and the Shaping of Pentecostal Spirituality in Zimbabwe," *Journal of African Diaspora* 7 (2014): 139–64, where I have discussed at greater length the marginalization of other earlier leaders of ZAOGA and the narrative retelling emphasizing Guti's sole leadership. Here I mention only one more related matter. ZAOGA materials point to Guti's obedience to God and promote his empowering of the people through entrepreneurship programs called Talents. In recognition of Guti's leadership, ZAOGA has a song for the Talents, sung at big events, that glorifies Guti for obeying God in Ngaone and teaching the church to work hard and not to depend on the West for financial support. The song reiterates that "*Zvakatanga nababa Guti*" ("they were initiated by father Guti"). Yet this is a distortion of events, because the Talents initiative was started by one of the cofounders, Priscilla Ngoma, and even Eunor, the wife of Guti, recognized this during one of her sermons on the Talents. See also Kudzai Biri, "African Pentecostalism and Cultural Resilience: Zimbabwe Assemblies of God Africa" (DPhil thesis, Department of Religious Studies, Classics, and Philosophy, University of Zimbabwe, 2013), 151–58.
10. John S. Mbiti, *African Religions and Philosophy* (Garden City, NY: Anchor Books, 1970).
11. Guti, *History of ZAOGA*, 21.
12. Ibid., 23.
13. Ibid.
14. Ezekiel Guti, *Kuremekedzana Kunounza Hurnwari* [Respecting each other brings God's presence] (Harare, EGEA, 1997), 6–7.
15. Mensa Otabil is a Ghanaian Pentecostal leader who has a megachurch with ministry and influence parallel to Guti's in that context; for an overview discussion, see Rijk van Dijk, *Religious Fundamentalism in Southern Africa: The Case of Pentecostalism* (Copahagen: Centre for African Studies, 2000), 7–9.

16. Hillary Achunike, *Challenges of Pentecostalism* (Onitsha, Nigeria: Africana First Publishers, 2004).
17. Biri, "African Pentecostalism," 152.
18. Guti, *History of ZAOGA*, 32–34.
19. Ibid., 31.
20. Ibid.
21. For discussion, see David Maxwell, *Christians and Chiefs in Zimbabwe: A Social History of the Hwesa People, 1870s–1990s* (Edinburgh: Edinburgh University Press, 1999), 198–99.
22. Sermon by a ZAOGA pastor, November 2, 2013, Africa Multination for Christ College, Glen Norah, Harare.
23. Gordon Chavunduka, *Traditional Medicine and Christian Beliefs* (Harare: University of Zimbabwe Publications, 1994), 141.
24. Guti, *History of ZAOGA*, 47–48.
25. Maxwell, *African Gifts of the Spirit*, 202.
26. Sermon by a ZAOGA pastor at ZAOGA Grange International Christian Church, Harare, April 12, 2015.
27. Birgit Meyer, "'Make a Complete Break With the Past': Memory and Post-Colonial Modernity in Ghanaian Pentecostal Discourse," *Journal of Religion in Africa* 28, no. 3 (1998): 316–49.
28. Gerrie ter Haar, *Halfway to Paradise: African Christians in Europe* (Cardiff: Cardiff Academic Press, 1998).
29. Afe Adogame, "The Politicisation of Religion and Religionisation of Politics in Nigeria," in Chima J. Korieh and Ugo Nwokeji, eds., *Religion, History, and Politics in Nigeria: Essays in Honor of Ogbu U. Kalu* (Lanham, MD: University of America Press, 2005), 137–53.
30. Ezekiel Guti, *The Church and Political Responsibility and Resource Management: Preparation for the Next Generation, Pray for Africa to Become the United States of Africa* (Harare: EGEA, 1994), 44.
31. Kalu, "Third Response," 28.
32. See, for example, Ezra Chitando, Masiiwa Gunda, and Joachim Kügler, eds., *Prophets, Profits, and the Bible in Zimbabwe* (Bamberg, Germany: University of Bamberg Press, 2013).
33. Biri, "African Pentecostalism," 316.
34. Maxwell, *African Gifts of the Spirit*, 5.

35. These were the words written on ZAOGA regalia, posters, and stickers as they celebrated Guti's ninety-first birthday.
36. Biri, "African Pentecostalism," 152.
37. Gayle Erwin, *African Apostle* (Harare: EGEA, 1987), 89.
38. Guti, *History of ZAOGA*, 17.

Chapter 13
"Thus Far the Lord Has Brought Us!": Histories and Theologies of Southeast African Pentecostalisms

1. James Pfeiffer, "African Independent Churches in Mozambique: Healing the Afflictions of Inequality," *Medical Anthropology Quarterly* 16, no. 2 (2002): 176–99; Paul Gifford, "Some Recent Developments in African Christianity," *African Affairs* 93, no. 199 (1994): 513–34, reports similar trends of Pentecostal expansions across sub-Saharan Africa.
2. Paul Gifford, "The Primal Pentecostal Imagination: Variants, Origins, and Importance," *Suomen Antropologi: Journal of the Finnish Anthropological Society* 34, no. 2 (2009): 44–52; cf. Jörg Haustein, "Embodying the Spirit(s): Pentecostal Demonology and Deliverance Discourse in Ethiopia," *Ethnos* 76, no. 4 (2011): 534–52.
3. Leon Morris, *Spirit of the Living God* (London: InterVarsity Press, 1960), 66.
4. Michèle M. Sigg, "Carrying Living Water for the Healing of God's People: Women Leaders in the *Fifohazana* Revival and the Reformed Church in Madagascar," *Studies in World Christianity* 20, no. 1 (2014): 19–38; see also Allan Anderson, *Moya: The Holy Spirit in an African Context*, Manualia Didactica, no. 13 (Pretoria: University of South Africa, 1991).
5. Walter J. Hollenweger, *Pentecostalism: Origins and Developments Worldwide* (Peabody, MA: Hendrickson, 1997); Allan Anderson, "The Origins of Pentecostalism and Its Global Spread in the Early Twentieth Century," *Transformation* 22, no. 3 (2005): 175–85; Michael Bergunder, "The Cultural Turn," in Allan Anderson et al., eds., *Studying Global Pentecostalism: Theories and Methods* (Berkeley, CA: University of California Press, 2010), 51–73.
6. Michael Bergunder, "Constructing Pentecostalism: On Issues of Methodology and Representation," *The Journal of European Pentecostal Theological Association* 26, no. 2 (2007): 63.

7. Ibid., 70; for the argument about Azusa Street as a central node for early modern Pentecostal global missions, see Allan Anderson, *Spreading Fires: The Missionary Nature of Early Pentecostalism* (Maryknoll, NY: Orbis Books, 2007).
8. Allan Anderson, *An Introduction to Pentecostalism* (Cambridge: Cambridge University Press, 2004).
9. 9 Allan Anderson, "The Origins of Pentecostalism and Its Global Spread in the Early Twentieth Century," *Transformation* 22, no. 3 (2005): 181.
10. See, for example, Bengt G. M. Sundkler, *Bantu Prophets in South Africa*, 2nd ed. (Cambridge: James Clarke and Co., 1948).
11. Ogbu Kalu, *African Pentecostalism: An Introduction* (New York: Oxford University Press, 2008).
12. Surpassed only by Catholicism (23.8 percent) and Islam (17.8 percent); see Carolien Jacobs and Linda van de Kamp, "Christianity's Role in Dispute Resolution in Mozambique," *Social Sciences and Missions* 27 (2014): 198.
13. Ibid., 199.
14. Gerhard Seibert, "'But the Manifestation of the Spirit Is Given to Every Man to Profit Withal': Zion Churches in Mozambique Since the Early Twentieth Century," *Social Sciences and Missions* 17 (2005): 126; Pfeiffer, "African Independent Churches in Mozambique," 176; Ulla Alfredsson and Calisto Linha, "Where God Lives: An Introduction to a Study of the Independent Churches in Maputo, Mozambique," *Sociology of Education and Culture Research Reports* 20 (1998): 18.
15. Patrick Harries, "Christianity in Black and White: The Establishment of Protestant Churches in Southern Mozambique," *Lusotopie* (1998): 322.
16. Alfredsson and Linha, "Where God Lives," 18; cf. Alf Helgesson, "Church, State, and People in Mozambique: An Historical Study With Special Emphasis on Methodist Development in the Inhambane Region" (PhD dissertation, Uppsala University, 1994).
17. Seibert, "But the Manifestation of the Spirit," 128.
18. James Pfeiffer, "Commodity *Fetichismo*, the Holy Spirit, and the Turn to Pentecostal and African Independent Churches in Central Mozambique," *Culture, Medicine, and Psychiatry* 29 (2005): 256.

19. Linda van de Kamp and Rijk van Dijk, "Pentecostals Moving South-South: Brazilian and Ghanaian Transnationalism in Southern Africa," in Afe Adogame and James V. Spickard, eds., *Religion Crossing Boundaries: Transnational Religious and Social Dynamics in Africa and the New African Diaspora* (Leiden: E. J. Brill, 2010), 129.
20. Gerhard Seibert has particularly given concise analysis of the historical development of the African-initiated Pentecostal-type in Mozambique; see his "'But the Manifestation of the Spirit Is Given to Every Man to Profit Withal,'" 133.
21. Alfredsson and Linha, "Where God Lives," 20.
22. Ibid.
23. D. J. Garrard, "Mozambique," in Stanley M. Burgess and Eduard van der Maas, eds., *The New International Dictionary of Pentecostal and Charismatic Movements* (Grand Rapids, MI: Zondervan, 2002), 180.
24. Anderson, *An Introduction to Pentecostalism*, 121.
25. See Pentecostal Assemblies of Canada GlobalEd, "Brief History of the School," accessed June 29, 2015, http://paocglobaled.celect.org/mozambique-maputo.
26. Bill George, *Until All Have Heard: The Centennial History of Church of God World Missions* (Cleveland, TN: Pathway Press, 2010), 312.
27. Iris Global, "History," accessed July 3, 2015, http://www.irisglobal.org/about/history; see also Candy Gunther Brown, "Global Awakenings: Divine Healing Networks and Global Community in North America, Brazil, Mozambique, and Beyond," in Candy Gunther Brown, ed., *Global Pentecostal and Charismatic Healing* (Oxford: Oxford University, 2011), 353.
28. Iris Global, "History."
29. Besides what is mentioned in note 1 above, see also James Pfeiffer et al., "The Holy Spirit in the Household: Pentecostalism, Gender, and Neoliberalism in Mozambique," *American Anthropologist* 109, no. 4 (2007): 688–700; cf. Linda van de Kamp, "Converting the Spirit Spouse: The Violent Transformation of the Pentecostal Female Body in Maputo, Mozambique," *Ethnos* 75, no. 4 (2011): 510–33.
30. See especially the introductory section to James Pfeiffer, "Pentecostalism and AIDS Treatment in Mozambique: Creating New Approaches

to HIV Through Anti-Retroviral Therapy," *Global Public Health* 6, no. 82 (2011): 164.

31. See Paul Freston, "The Universal Church of the Kingdom of God: A Brazilian Church Finds Success in Southern Africa," *Journal of Religion in Africa* 35, no. 1 (2005): 33–65; Linda van de Kamp, "Public Counselling: Brazilian Pentecostal Intimate Performances Among Urban Women in Mozambique," *Culture, Health, and Sexuality* 15, sup. 4 (2013): 523–36.
32. See van de Kamp, "Converting the Spirit Spouse," 516; Jacobs and van de Kamp, "Christianity's Role in Dispute Resolution in Mozambique," 198–99.
33. Van de Kamp, "Converting the Spirit Spouse," 510.
34. Van de Kamp and van Dijk, "Pentecostals Moving South-South," 131; Jacobs and van de Kamp, "Christianity's Role in Dispute Resolution in Mozambique," 210.
35. Linda van de Kamp, "Afro-Brazilian Pentecostal Reformations of Relationships Across Two Generations of Mozambican Women," *Journal of Religion in Africa* 42 (2012): 441.
36. Linda van de Kamp, "South-South Transnational Spaces of Conquest: Afro-Brazilian Pentecostalism, *Feitiçaria*, and the Reproductive Domain in Urban Mozambique," *Exchange* 42 (2013): 347–48.
37. Karina Hestad-Skeie, "Mission Appropriation or Appropriating Mission: Negotiating Local and Global Christianity in Nineteenth- and Twentieth-Century Madagascar," in Hilde Nielssen, Inger Marie Okkenhaug, and Karina Hestad-Skeie, eds., *Protestant Missions and Local Encounters in the Nineteenth and Twentieth Centuries: Unto the Ends of the World* (Leiden: Brill, 2011), 159.
38. J. Kwabena Asamoah-Gyadu, "'Born of Water and the Spirit': Pentecostal/Charismatic Christianity in Africa," in Ogbu U. Kalu, ed., *African Christianity: An African Story* (Trenton: African World Press, 2007), 390.
39. Cf. Cynthia Holder Rich, "Spirit and Culture: Navigating Ecclesiological Minefields in Madagascar," *Journal of Theology for Southern Africa* 131 (2008): 58–71.
40. M. Esoavelomandroso, "Madagascar, 1880s–1930s: African Initiatives and Reaction to Colonial Conquest and Domination," in A. Adu

Boahen, ed., *Africa Under Colonial Domination, 1880–1935*, UNESCO General History of Africa, vol. 7: (Berkeley, CA: University of California Press, 1985), 221–48.

41. Cynthia Holder Rich, "Women Power and Authority in Madagascar," in Cynthia H. Rich, ed., *The Fifohazana: Madagascar's Indigenous Christian Movement* (Amherst: Cambria Press, 2008), 135–44.
42. "Malagasy, the Language of Madagascar," accessed March 17, 2016, http://www.wildmadagascar.org/people/malagasy.html.
43. WorldMap.org, "Madagascar: Christian Religion," accessed June 29, 2015, http://www.worldmap.org/country.php?ROG3=MA&QryHead=Christian%20Religion&QryFld=CP_Religion_Christian.
44. Bruce A. Howell, "Keep the Fire Burning!," as provided by Global Connection UPCI, accessed June 29, 2015, http://www.globalconnectionupci.com/preparation/Keep%20the%20Fires%20Burning.pdf.
45. Bernard Boutter, "Les pionniers du pentecôtisme à Madagascar (3): La famille Richardson" [The pioneers of Pentecostalism in Madagascar (3): The Richardson family], *Le Blog de Bernard Boutter*, June 3, 2015, accessed July 6, 2015, http://bboutter.blogspot.com/2015/06/les-pionniers-du-pentecotisme.html.
46. New Apostolic Church South East Africa, "NAC-SEA History, Part 3: 1970–2009," accessed November 13, 2014, http://www.nac-sea.org.za/storage/History%20Part%203.pdf.
47. WorldMap.org, "Madagascar: Christian Religion."
48. See Jennifer Cole, *Sex and Salvation: Imagining the Future in Madagascar* (Chicago: University of Chicago Press, 2010), 63.
49. Andrew Walsh, "Preserving Bodies, Saving Souls: Religious Incongruity in a Northern Malagasy Mining Town," *Journal of Religion in Africa* 32, no. 3 (2002): 369.
50. C. Raadimilahy and R. Andriamamphianina have given a concise summary of some main church traditions in Madagascar, including some neo-Pentecostals; see their "Lieux de Cultes Chrétiens, Musulmans, et Hindouistes a Antananarivo" [Christian, Muslim, and Hindu places of worship in Antananarivo], in Sophie Blanchy et al., eds., *Les Dieux au Service du Peuple: Itinéraires Religieux, Médiations, Syncrétisme à Madagascar* [The gods at the service of the people: Religious itineraries, mediations, syncretism in Madagascar] (Paris: Karthalac, 2006),

132. See also Jennifer Cole, "Women and Pentecostalism: Building New Urban Worlds in Madagascar," in Rajaonah V. Faranirina, ed., *Cultures Citadines dans l'Océan Indien Occidental (XVIII e XXIe Siècles): Pluralisme, Échanges, Inventivité* [Urban cultures in the Western Indian Ocean (XVIII–XXI centuries): Pluralism, exchange, creativity] (Paris: Karthala, 2011), 386.

51. Many essays in Rich, *The Fifohazana: Madagascar's Indigenous Christian Movement*, touch on these matters; see also Péri Rasolondraibe, "Healing Ministry in Madagascar," *Word and World* 4 (1989): 344–50.

52. Jennifer Cole examines the critical role Pentecostalism plays in providing recovery space for women with various sociopolitical traumas in Madagascar. She notes that many women have joined Pentecostalism in Madagascar because they see it as holistic therapeutic space. See Jennifer Cole, "The Love of Jesus Never Disappoints: Reconstituting Female Personhood in Urban Madagascar," *Journal of Religion in Africa* 42 (2012): 384–407.

53. J. Kwabena Asamoah-Gyadu, *African Charismatics: Current Developments Within Independent Indigenous Pentecostalism in Ghana* (Leiden: Brill, 2005); and Frieder Ludwig and J. Kwabena Asamoah-Gyadu, eds., *African Christian Presence in the West: New Immigrant Congregations and Transnational Networks in North America and Europe* (Trenton, NJ: Africa World Press, 2011).

54. For example, this is also noted by Kwabena Asamoah-Gyadu, "African Pentecostal/Charismatic Christianity: An Overview," *Lausanne World Pulse* (August 2006), accessed June 29, 2015, http://www.lausanneworldpulse.com/themedarticles-php/464/08-2006.

55. David J. Garrard, "African Pentecostalism," *Journal of Beliefs and Values* 30, no. 3 (2009): 231–44.

56. Harvey J. Sindima, *Africa's Agenda: The Legacy of Liberalism and Colonialism in the Crisis of African Values*, Contributions in Afro-American and African Studies, no. 176 (Westport, CT: Greenwood Press, 1995); Vincent Mulago, "Vital Participation," in Dickson Kwesi and Paul Ellingworth, eds., *Biblical Revelation and African Beliefs* (Maryknoll, NY: Orbis Books, 1969), 137–58.

57. As indicated in the subtitle of Laurenti Magesa, *African Religion: The Moral Traditions of Abundant Life* (Maryknoll, NY: Orbis Books, 1997).

58. Sindima, *Africa's Agenda*, 198.

59. Mulago, "Vital Participation," 138.
60. Chammah J. Kaunda, "Creation as a Dwelling Place of God: A Critical Analysis of an Africa Biocentric Theology in the Works of Gabriel M. Setiloane" (MTh thesis, University of KwaZulu-Natal, Pietermaritzburg, 2010), 59.
61. Teresa Okure, "First Was Life, Not the Book," in Teresa Okure, ed., *To Cast Upon the Earth: Bible and Mission Collaborating in Today's Multicultural Global Context* (Pietermaritzburg: Cluster, 2000), 209.
62. Gabriel M. Setiloane, *African Theology: An Introduction* (Braamfontein: Skotaville, 1986), 24–25.
63. Allan Anderson, "Stretching the Definitions? Pneumatology and 'Syncretism' in African Pentecostalism," *Journal of Pentecostal Theology* 10, no. 1 (2001): 103; Allan Anderson, "African Initiated Churches of the Spirit and Pneumatology," *Word and World* 23, no. 2 (2003): 178–86.
64. Anderson, "African Initiated Churches," 185.

Chapter 14
Rising to the Challenge: Pentecostalism in Angola, Botswana, and Namibia

1. See Joel Robbins, "Anthropology of Religion," in Allan Anderson et al., eds., *Studying Global Pentecostalism: Theories and Methods* (Berkeley, CA: University of California Press, 2010), 156–78; and Rijk van Dijk, "Time and Transcultural Technologies of the Self in the Ghanian Pentecostal Diaspora," in Andre Corten and Ruth Marshall-Fratani, eds., *Between Babel and Pentecost: Transitional Pentecostalism in Africa and Latin America* (Bloomington, IN: Indiana University Press, 2001), 216–34.
2. See, for example, Allan Anderson, *Bazalwane: African Pentecostals in South Africa* (Pretoria: University of South Africa Press, 1992).
3. Paul Freston, "The Universal Church of the Kingdom of God: A Brazilian Church Finds Success in Southern Africa," *Journal of Religion in Africa* 35, no. 1 (2005): 33.
4. The people of Botswana are collectively known as *Batswana*.
5. James Amanze, *African Christianity in Botswana* (Gabarone: Mambo Press, 1998), 5.
6. Ibid., 52–53.

7. Ibid., 48.
8. G. L. Buys and S. V. V. Nambala, *History of the Church in Namibia* (Windhoek, Namibia: Gamsberg Macmillan Publishers, 2003).
9. Seretse Khama Ian Khama, "Inauguration Address by His Excellency the President of the Republic of Botswana," October 20, 2009, accessed June 2, 2015, at http://www.gov.bw/en/News/Inauguration-address-by-His-Excellency-Lt-General-Ian-Khama/.
10. BBC News, "Gays 'Fearful' in Namibia," March 20, 2001, accessed April 25, 2015, http://news.bbc.co.uk/2/hi/africa/1231732.stm.
11. Ruy Llera Blanes, "Political and Religious Lines Redrawn in Post-War Angola," London School of Economics and Political Science, July 1, 2011, accessed April 25, 2015, http://blogs.lse.ac.uk/africaatlse/2011/07/01/political-and-religious-lines-redrawn-in-post-war-angola/.
12. Todd Johnson, "The Global Demographics of the Pentecostal and Charismatic Renewal," *Society* 46, no. 6 (2009): 479–86.
13. Ibid., 483.
14. Freston, "The Universal Church of the Kingdom of God."
15. Ibid., 62, emphasis in original.
16. Fidelis Nkomazana, "The Growth of Pentecostalism and Christian Umbrella Organisations in Botswana," *Studia Historiae Ecclesiasticae* 40, no. 1 (2014): 153–73.
17. Nico Horn, "Religious Freedom and Intimidation in a Secular State: The Namibia Experience," paper presented at the 2011 annual symposium of the International Center for Law and Religion Studies, Brigham Young University, 2, accessed July 9, 2015, http://iclrs.org/content/blurb/files/Horn%2020111002.pdf.
18. Ibid., 6–7.
19. Ibid., 4.
20. Basilius Kasera, "The Biblical and Theological Examination of Prosperity Theology and Its Impact Among the Poor in Namibia" (MA thesis, South African Theological Seminary, 2012).
21. Ibid., 45.
22. Ibid., 44.
23. Ibid., 45–47.

24. Amos Yong, "A Typology of Prosperity Theology: A Religious Economy of Global Renewal or a Renewal Economics," in Katherine Attanasi and Amos Yong, eds., *Pentecostalism and Prosperity: The Socio-Economics of the Global Charismatic Movement* (New York: Palgrave Macmillan, 2012), 15–32.
25. Ibid., 28.
26. Statistics were obtained from the international HIV and AIDS charity Avert, based in the United Kingdom; accessed May 25, 2015, at http://www.avert.org/professionals/hiv-around-world/sub-saharan-africa/overview.
27. Nicole Rigillo, "Broken Condoms, Corroded Trust: The Politics of HIV Prevention in Namibia" (MA thesis, Concordia University, Montreal, Canada, 2007).
28. Ibid., 69.
29. Ibid., 77.

Chapter 15
The Rise of the Megachurches in South Africa

1. Vinson Synan, *The Holiness-Pentecostal Tradition: Charismatic Movements in the Twentieth Century* (Grand Rapids, MI: W. B. Eerdmans, 1997).
2. Charles Peter Watt, "Assemblies of God: A Missiological Evaluation" (MA thesis: UNISA, 1991).
3. Meredith McGuire, *Pentecostal Catholics: Power, Charisma, and Order in a Religious Movement* (Philadelphia: Temple University Press, 1982).
4. Quentin Schultze, "The Great Transmission," in Harold B. Smith, ed., *Pentecostals From the Inside Out* (Wheaton, IL: Victor Books, 1990), 95.
5. Maria Frahm-Arp, *Professional Women in South African Pentecostal Charismatic Churches* (Leiden: Brill, 2010).
6. Maria Frahm-Arp, "Pentecostalism, Politics, and Social Media in South Africa," *Journal for the Study of Religion* 28, no. 1 (2015): 115–141.
7. For a more detailed analysis of Ray McCauley as a leader in one of South Africa's largest Pentecostal churches, see Allan Anderson, "New African Initiated Pentecostalism and Charismatics in South Africa," *Journal of Religion in Africa* 35, no. 1 (2005): 66–92.

8. Tracy Kuperus, "The Political Role and Democratic Contribution of Churches in Post-Apartheid South Africa," *Journal of Church and State* 53, no. 2 (2011): 278–306.
9. Pastor Themba Mathola, interview with author, Johannesburg, May 17, 2001.
10. Diarmaid MacCulloch, *A History of Christianity* (London: Penguin Press, 2010), 686.
11. Frahm-Arp, *Professional Women*, 209–42.
12. Floyd Shevambu was the deputy of the Economic Freedom Fighters in 2014.
13. Interview conducted in Johannesburg, May 28, 2014. The name of the interviewee is not given so that the members of the churches remain anonymous.
14. Birgit Meyer, "'Make a Complete Break With the Past': Memory and Post-Colonial Modernity in Ghanaian Pentecostal Discourse," *Journal of Religion in Africa* 28, no. 3 (1998): 316–49.
15. Paul Daniels, "His People Christian Ministries," in C. Peter Wagner, ed., *The New Apostolic Churches* (Ventura, CA: Regal Books, 1998), 227, 230.
16. Frahm-Arp, *Professional Women*, 151–76.
17. Statistics South Africa, "Quarterly Labour Force Survey: Quarter 4, 2014," February 10, 2015, accessed July 20, 2015, http://www.statssa.gov.za/publications/P0211/P02114thQuarter2014.pdf.
18. Ilana Van Wyk, *The Universal Church of the Kingdom of God in South Africa: A Church of Strangers* (Cambridge: Cambridge University Press, 2014).
19. Paul Freston, "The Universal Church of the Kingdom of God: A Brazilian Church Finds Success in Southern Africa," *Journal of Religion in Africa* 35, no. 1 (2005): 37.
20. Van Wyk, *The Universal Church*, 15–16.
21. Freston, "The Universal Church of the Kingdom of God," 53–54.
22. Anonymous, "Church Probe Reports 'Wrong,'" *The Mercury*, October 12, 2000.
23. Van Wyk, *The Universal Church*, 16.
24. Ibid., 16–18.

25. Ibid., 18.
26. Ibid., 182.
27. Frahm-Arp, "Pentecostalism, Politics, and Social Media."

Chapter 16
"Nativizing" the Gospel: Pentecostalism and Theology in Africa

1. Harry Sawyerr, "What Is African Theology," *African Theological Journal* 4 (1971): 24.
2. Kwame Bediako, "Scripture as the Hermeneutic of Culture and Tradition," *Journal of African Christian Thought* 4, no. 1 (June 2001): 2.
3. Kwame Bediako, *Christianity in Africa: The Renewal of a Non-Western Religion* (Edinburgh: Obis Books, 1995), chapter 4.
4. Joseph Quayesi-Amakye, "Prophetic Practices in Contemporary Pentecostalism in Ghana," *Canadian Journal of Pentecostal-Charismatic Christianity* 6 (2015): 43–69; "Prophetism in Ghana's New Prophetic Churches," *Journal of the European Pentecostal Theological Association* 35, no. 2 (2015): 162–73.
5. Joseph Quayesi-Amakye, "Christ, Evil, and Suffering in Ghanaian Christian Liturgy," *PentecoStudies* 14, no. 1 (2015): 9–41; "God in Ghanaian Pentecostal Songs," *Journal of Pentecostal Theology* 22 (2013): 131–51.
6. Bediako, *Christianity in Africa*, 104.
7. Emmanuel Martey, *African Theology: Inculturation and Liberation* (Maryknoll, NY: Orbis Books, 1993), 84–86.
8. From All African Churches Conference, *Africa in Transition: The Challenge and the Christian Response* (Geneva: WCC, 1962), 12, as cited in Martey, *African Theology*, 64.
9. Martey, *African Theology*, 66.
10. Ibid., 67–68.
11. Peter Kwasi Sarpong, *Dear Nana: Letters to My Ancestor* (Takoradi, Ghana: Franciscan Publications, 1998), 48.
12. Ibid., 48–49.
13. Ibid., 67.
14. See the references to Nyamiti and Mushete in Martey, *African Theology*, 69.

15. Ibid., 72.
16. Mercy Amba Oduyoye, "Feminism: A Pre-Condition for a Christian Anthropology," *African Theological Journal* 11, no. 3 (1982): 193–208.
17. Martey, *African Theology*, 84–86.
18. Philomena Njeri Mwaura, "Gender and Power in African Christianity: African Instituted Churches and Pentecostal Churches," in Ogbu U. Kalu, ed., *African Christianity: An African Story* (Trenton: African World Press, 2007), 359–88.
19. Ibid., 367.
20. I have discussed the Pentecostal-public interface in Africa in my book *Christology and Evil in Ghana: Towards a Pentecostal Public Theology*, Currents of Encounter, no. 49 (Amsterdam and New York: Editions Rodopi BV, 2013); see also my "Pentecostals and Contemporary Church-State Relations in Ghana," *Journal of Church and State* 57, no. 4 (2015): 640–57.
21. See Joseph Quayesi-Amakye, "Social Responsibility in the Christianised Akan Ethnic Culture of Ghana," *Studies in Interreligious Dialogue* 23, no. 2 (2013): 176–89.
22. Walter J. Hollenweger, *Pentecostalism: Origins and Developments Worldwide* (Peabody, MA: Hendrickson, 1997), 48–49.
23. Rijk van Dijk, "Pentecostalism, Gerontocratic Rule, and Democratisation in Malawi: The Changing Position of the Young in Political Culture," in Jeff Haynes, ed., *Religion, Globalisation, and Political Culture in the Third World* (London: Macmillan, and New York: St. Martin's Press, 1999), 164–85.
24. Paul Gifford, *African Christianity: Its Public Role* (London: Hurst & Company, 1998), 86.
25. Ibid., 181–244.
26. Ezra Chitando, Masiiwa Gunda, and Joachim Kügler, eds., *Prophets, Profits, and the Bible in Zimbabwe* (Bamberg, Germany: University of Bamberg Press, 2013).
27. David A. Shank, *Prophet Harris: 'The Black Elijah' of West Africa*, Studies of Religion in Africa, no. 10 (Leiden: E. J. Brill, 1994).
28. Kofi Asare Opoku, "A Brief History of Independent Church Movements in Ghana since 1862," in *The Rise of Independent Churches in Ghana* (Accra: Asempa Publishers, 1990), 16.

29. Ogbu U. Kalu, "The Big Man of the Big God: Fundamentalism, Media, and African Pentecostalism," chapter 6 in Ogbu U. Kalu, *African Pentecostalism: An Introduction* (Oxford: Oxford University Press, 2008), 108–9.
30. See Opoku Onyinah, "Deliverance as a Way of Confronting Witchcraft in Modern Africa: Ghana as a Case History," *Asian Journal of Pentecostal Studies* 5, no. 1 (2002): 116–22.
31. Gifford, "Some Recent Developments in African Christianity," 39.
32. Opoku Onyinah, "Entering Into God's Rest" (Pentmedia, 2012), CD series 9 and 10.
33. Asonzeh F. K. Ukah, "'Those Who Trade With God Never Lose': The Economics of Pentecostal Activism in Nigeria," in Toyin Falola, ed., *Christianity and Social Change in Africa: Essays in Honour of J. D. Y. Peel* (Durham, NC: Carolina Academic Press, 2005), 251–74.

Chapter 17
The Spirit and the African Spiritual World

1. Allan Anderson, *Moya: The Holy Spirit in an African Context*, Manualia Didactica, no. 13 (Pretoria: University of South Africa, 1991).
2. M. L. Daneel, *Old and New in Southern Shona Independent Churches*, vols. 1 and 2 (The Hague: Mouton, 1971–1974) and vol. 3 (Gweru, Zimbabwe: Mambo Press, 1988); *Quest for Belonging* (Gweru, Zimbabwe: Mambo Press, 1987); and *Fambidzano: Ecumenical Movement of Zimbabwean Independent Churches* (Gweru, Zimbabwe: Mambo Press, 1989).
3. Allan Anderson, *To the Ends of the Earth: Pentecostalism and the Transformation of World Christianity* (Oxford: Oxford University Press, 2013).
4. Allan Anderson, "Varieties, Taxonomies, and Definitions," in Allan Anderson et al., eds., *Studying Global Pentecostalism: Theories and Methods* (Berkeley, CA: University of California Press, 2010), 13–29.
5. Allan Anderson, *Zion and Pentecost: The Spirituality and Experience of Pentecostal and Zionist/Apostolic Churches in South Africa* (Pretoria: University of South Africa Press, 2000), 32–40.
6. Walter J. Hollenweger, *The Pentecostals* (London: SCM Press Ltd., 1972), 151.

7. Daneel, *Quest for Belonging*, 38; Allan H. Anderson, *African Reformation: African Initiated Christianity in the Twentieth Century* (Trenton, NJ: Africa World Press, 2001).
8. G. C. Oosthuizen, *Post-Christianity in Africa* (London: Hurst, 1968), 120.
9. John V. Taylor, *The Primal Vision: Christian Presence amid African Religion* (London: SCM, 1963), 21–22.
10. E. G. Parrinder, *African Traditional Religion* (London: Hutchinson, 1954), 24; Oosthuizen, *Post-Christianity*, 136.
11. Taylor, *The Primal Vision*, 59.
12. Ibid., 72.
13. F. A. J. Dierks, "Communication and World-View," *Missionalia* 11 (1983): 52.
14. E. Bolaji Idowu, "God," in Kwesi A. Dickson and Paul Ellingworth, eds., *Biblical Revelation and African Beliefs* (London: Lutterworth, 1969), 17.
15. Hollenweger, *The Pentecostals*, 505–6.
16. Allan Anderson, *Spreading Fires: The Missionary Nature of Early Pentecostalism* (Maryknoll, NY: Orbis Books, 2007).
17. Harvey Cox, *Fire From Heaven: Pentecostalism and the Reshaping of Spirituality in the Twenty-First Century* (De Capo, MA: Addison-Wesley, 1995), 71.
18. Ibid., 219–22, 224, and 228.
19. Gary D. Badcock, *Light of Truth and Fire of Love: A Theology of the Holy Spirit* (Grand Rapids, MI: W. B. Eerdmans, 1997), 140.
20. Ibid., 137.
21. Anderson, *Moya*, 100–4.
22. Cox, *Fire From Heaven*, 81–88, 91–92, 96.
23. Amos Yong, *Discerning the Spirit(s): A Pentecostal/Charismatic Contribution to Christian Theology of Religions* (Sheffield: Sheffield Academic Press, 2000), 134, 162, 319.
24. Amos Yong, "'Not Knowing Where the Wind Blows…': On Envisioning a Pentecostal-Charismatic Theology of Religions," *Journal of Pentecostal Theology* 14 (1999): 99–100.

25. Daniel E. Albrecht, *Rites in the Spirit: A Ritual Approach to Pentecostal/Charismatic Spirituality* (Sheffield: Sheffield Academic Press, 1999), 9, 14.
26. Steven J. Land, *Pentecostal Spirituality: A Passion for the Kingdom* (Sheffield: Sheffield Academic Press, 1993), 22–23.
27. Ibid., 218–19.
28. Albrecht, *Rites in the Spirit*, 39, 149, 238.
29. Anderson, *To the Ends of the Earth*, 145–47.

Chapter 18
Charismatic Renewal and Roman Catholicism in Africa: Challenges and Prospects of Pentecostalism

1. Peter Hocken, "The Catholic Charismatic Renewal," in Vinson Synan, ed., *The Century of the Holy Spirit 1901–2001* (Nashville, TN: Thomas Nelson, 2001), 218–30.
2. International Catholic Charismatic Renewal Services, "Statutes," article 5, accessed February 22, 2016, http://www.iccrs.org/_files/files/ICCRS-STATUTES_EnOFFICIAL.pdf.
3. Lode Wostyn, "Vatican II: A Momentous Event in the History of the Catholic Church," *MST Review* 16, no. 2 (2014): 58–86.
4. Hocken, "The Catholic Charismatic Renewal," 211–13. T. P. Thigpen, "Catholic Charismatic Renewal," in Stanley M. Burgess and Eduard van der Maas, eds., *The New International Dictionary of Pentecostal and Charismatic Movements* (Grand Rapids, MI: Zondervan, 2002), 460, writes, "Ralph Keifer, Patrick Bourgeois, and a few lay faculty at Duquesne University had been praying intensely for a return to the kind of vibrant Christian community they believed had characterized the first Christians."
5. Cited in Thigpen, "Catholic Charismatic Renewal," 466.
6. Taddeo Onoyima, *The Catholic Charismatic Movement and the Church*, 2nd ed. (Enugu: The Diocesan Catholic Secretariat, n.d.), 8–10.
7. Harvey Cox, *Fire From Heaven: Pentecostalism and the Reshaping of Spirituality in the Twenty-First Century* (De Capo, MA: Addison-Wesley, 1995), 81–119.
8. Donatus Ukpong, *Nigerian Pentecostalism: Case, Diagnosis, and Prescription* (Uyo: Fruities Publication, 2008), 35–56.

9. J. K. Olupona, "Africa, West (Survey)," in Burgess and van der Maas, *New International Dictionary*, 12.
10. Hilary Achunike, *Catholic Charismatic Movement in Igboland, 1970–1995* (Enugu: Fourth Dimension Publishing Company, 2009), 58.
11. Olupona, "Africa, West (Survey)," 15.
12. Achunike, *Catholic Charismatic Movement in Igboland*, 59.
13. Ibid., 60.
14. Archbishop Arinze's reply to Father Ebben's letter through Father Jagoe, August 12, 1974, cited by Achunike, *Catholic Charismatic Movement in Igboland*, 62.
15. The Malines Document was written in 1974 by group of Catholic theologians and lay ministers; the text is available at www.stucom.nl/document/0236uk.pdf.
16. The bishops called for a continuing study of the Catholic Charismatic Renewal and permitted priests to lead Charismatic prayer meetings. In Nigeria, the Catholic Bishops Conference issued two booklets: *Guidelines for the Catholic Charismatic Renewal of Nigeria, 1991*, and *Guidelines for the Healing Ministry in the Catholic Church in Nigeria, 1997.* These booklets indicate the official ecclesial approach to and evaluation of the Catholic Charismatic Renewal in the Catholic Church in Nigeria. See Achunike, *Catholic Charismatic Movement in Igboland*, 75.
17. Anthony Obinna, archbishop of Owerri, wrote in a letter dated July 20, 2012, "I love the Catholic Charismatic Renewal. I cherish the commitment and dynamism of the members. At the same time I remain critical and watchful of you and myself so that we may live and work in the spirit of Christ and His Church. For I am aware of aberrations and pride that have led many astray." See Catholic Charismatic Renewal of Nigeria, *Eleventh National Conference Ubulu-Uku 2012* (Enugu: Ebenezer Productions Ltd, 2012), 21.
18. David Barrett and Todd Johnson, "The Catholic Charismatic Renewal, 1959–2025," in Oreste Pesare, ed., *"Then Peter Stood Up…": Collection of the Popes' Addresses to the Catholic Charismatic Renewal From Its Origin to the Year 2000* (Nigeria: I. Loyola Books Centre and International Catholic Charismatic Renewal Services, 2000), 124.
19. Ukpong, *Nigeria Pentecostalism*, 4–8.
20. Achunike, *Catholic Charismatic Movement in Igboland*, 69.

21. Onoyima, *The Catholic Charismatic Movement and the Church*, 31–32.
22. Bob L. Johnson, "De-Constructing and Re-Constructing the Institutional Church: Towards the Theology of Spirit-Sensitive Change," *Journal of Pentecostal Theology* 23, no. 1 (2014): 122.
23. Achunike, *Catholic Charismatic Movement in Igboland*, 70–71.
24. Johnson, "De-Constructing and Re-Constructing," 128.
25. Donatus Ukpong, *The Phenomenology of Pentecostalism in Nigeria: A Theological and Ecclesiological Reflection* (Roma: Liveret, 2006), 105.
26. Ibid., 108.
27. Vatican II Council, *Constitution on the Sacred Liturgy Sacrasanctum Concilium*, 1963, §§5–13.
28. Ibid., §33.
29. Francis Sullivan, *Charisms and Charismatic Renewal: A Biblical and Theological Study* (Bangalore: Theological Publications in India, 2011), 48.
30. Donatus Ukpong, "African Root of Pentecostal Music: An Engine of Trans-Geographical Conversion Among Africans in Diaspora," in H. Anyanwu and Manasseh Udo, eds., *Religion and Culture: Understanding the Dynamism of Faith in Africa* (Beijing: Universal Academic Services, 2010), 140–42.
31. Donatus Ukpong, "Liturgical Prayer of the Faithful: A Theological Adaptation From a Pentecostal Perspective," *Pneuma* 33 (2013): 389–91.
32. Joseph Mulaa, "Rituals in the African Traditional Religions: The Cohesive Impact," *African Ecclesial Review* 56, no. 4 (2014): 345–75.
33. Ibid., 372.
34. Penelope Olive, "Models for Healing Prayer in Spiritual Direction: The Healing Ministry of Jesus, the Passion of Christ, the Consecration," *The Way* (2015): 16–26.
35. Thomas Fox, *Pentecost in Asia: A New Way of Being Church* (Maryknoll, NY: Orbis Books, 2002), 192.
36. William C. Turner Jr., "Pneumatology: Contributions From African American Christian Thought to the Pentecostal Theological Task," in Amos Yong and Estrelda Alexander, eds., *Afro-Pentecostalism: Black Pentecostal and Charismatic Christianity in History and Culture* (New York and London: New York University Press, 2011), 170.

37. Alan Schreck, *Rebuild My Church: God's Plan for Authentic Catholic Renewal* (Cincinnati, OH: St. Anthony Messenger Press, 2010), 184.
38. Dale T. Irvin, "Meeting Beyond These Shores: Black Pentecostalism, Black Theology, and the Global Context," in Yong and Alexander, *Afro-Pentecostalism*, 241.
39. Donatus Ukpong, "En-Ecclesiology: The Church as an Encounter Community in Nigeria," *Journal of Religious and Cultural Studies* 6, no. 1 (2008): 52–71.
40. Paul Steffen writes, "More and more Christians are finding the complicated and even bureaucratic organization of Western churches less and less meaningful for their own Christian life." Paul Steffen, "A New Way of Being Church: The Beginning and the Spread of Small Christian Communities and Bible-Sharing in Africa and Asia," *SEDOS Bulletin* 47, nos. 1 and 2 (2015): 18.
41. M. Gemma Victorino, "Pauline 'Variations' on the Theme 'Woman,'" *MST Review* 16, no. 2 (2014): 32–57.
42. Emmanuel Anagwo, "Christianity and African Culture: Integrating the Vision of Liturgical Inculturation," *African Ecclesial Review* 56, no. 4 (2014): 276–99.
43. Stephen Wilbricht writes, "Thus, culture is at the very theological heart of what liturgy is as an expression of the Church's universal faith; local culture gives the liturgy its 'flesh' in order to be accessible to the people's imagination." Stephen Wilbricht, "Anscar J. Chupungco, OSB: 'Adaptation' in Liturgy and in Life," *Worship* 89, no. 1 (2015): 52.
44. Ukpong, "Liturgical Prayer of the Faithful," 394.
45. Adrian Van Klinken, "Homosexuality, Politics, and Pentecostal Nationalism in Zambia," *Studies in World Christianity* 20, no. 3 (2014): 259–81.
46. Hilde Nielssen and Karina Hestad Skeie, "Christian Revivalism and Political Imagination in Madagascar," *Journal of Religion in Africa* 44, no. 2 (2014): 217.
47. Valerian M. Okeke, letter dated September 28, 2012, in Catholic Charismatic Renewal of Nigeria, *Eleventh National Conference Ubulu-Uku*, 19.
48. Steffen, "A New Way of Being Church," 18–20.
49. Schreck, *Rebuild My Church*, 222.
50. See again Wostyn, "Vatican II."

51. See also Scott Ellington, "Knowing God More or Less: Reading and Experiencing Exodus 33.11–23," *Journal of Pentecostal Theology* 23, no. 11 (2014): 20–28.
52. Diarmuid O'Murchu, "Spirituality: Daring New Horizons," *MST Review* 16, no. 1 (2014): 32–51.

Chapter 19
Nigerian Pentecostalism and Islam: Toward a Pentecostalized Vision of Interreligious Coexistence Through *Ubuntu* Philosophy

1. According to recent estimates, Pentecostals now represent 12 percent, or about 107 million, of Africa's population of nearly 890 million people; see Pew Research Center, "Spirit and Power: A Ten-Country Survey of Pentecostals," October 5, 2006, accessed March 19, 2015, http://www.pewforum.org/2006/10/05/spirit-and-power/.
2. Allan Anderson, *An Introduction to Pentecostalism* (Cambridge: Cambridge University Press, 2004), 103.
3. Ogbu U. Kalu, *African Pentecostalism: An Introduction* (Oxford: Oxford University Press, 2008), 225.
4. Charles Selengut, *Sacred Fury: Understanding Religious Violence* (Lanham, MD: Rowman & Littlefield Publishers, 2008).
5. Paul Gifford, in his book *New Crusaders*, presents both Pentecostalism and radical Islamic groups in Africa as fundamentalist, because of their seemingly absolutist theologies; see Gifford, *New Crusaders: Christianity and the New Right in Southern Africa* (London: Pluto, 1991).
6. Peter B. Clarke, *West Africa and Islam: A Study of Religious Development from the Eighth to the Twentieth Century* (London: Edward Arnold, 1982), 229.
7. Akintunde E. Akinade, *Christian Responses to Islam in Nigeria: A Contextual Study of Ambivalent Encounters* (New York: Palgrave Macmillan, 2014), 127.
8. Yushau Sodiq, "Muslim Christian Relations in Nigeria: Causes of Tensions," *Journal of Ecumenical Studies* 31, nos. 3 and 4 (1994): 279–306, especially 293–300.
9. For more on this issue, see Peter B. Clarke, *Islam in Modern Nigeria* (Munchen: Keiser, 1984), 180–92.

10. For a succinct outline of the clashes in recent years, see Amos Yong, *Hospitality and the Other: Pentecost, Christian Practices, and the Neighbor* (Maryknoll, NY: Orbis Books, 2008), 17–18.
11. Marinus Iwuchukwu, *Muslim-Christian Dialogue in Postcolonial Northern Nigeria* (New York: St. Martin's Press, 2013), 73.
12. Ibid., 74.
13. Akinade, *Christian Responses*, 58.
14. For a good overview of Nigerian Christianity, see Akintunde Akinade and David O. Ogungbile, eds., *Creativity and Change in Nigerian Christianity* (Lagos: Malthouse Press, 2010).
15. For a thorough historical account of the growth and development of Nigeria Pentecostalism, see Nimi Wariboko, *Nigerian Pentecostalism* (Rochester, NY: University of Rochester, 2014); and Ruth Marshall, *Political Spiritualties: The Pentecostal Revolution in Nigeria* (Chicago and London: University of Chicago Press, 2009).
16. Wariboko, *Nigerian Pentecostalism*, chapter 2.
17. Amos Yong, *Spirit-Word-Community: Theological Hermeneutics in Trinitarian Perspective* (Aldershot, UK: Ashgate, and Eugene, OR: Wipf & Stock, 2002), part 2.
18. Marshall, *Political Spiritualties.*
19. See Kalu, *African Pentecostalism*, chapter 1.
20. Dirk J. Louw, "*Ubuntu*: An African Assessment of the Religious Other," *South African Journal of Philosophy* 18, no. 4 (1999): 390–407.
21. Desmond Tutu, *No Future Without Forgiveness* (New York: Doubleday, 1999), 9.
22. Mbiti's summary of the African philosophy is sharply opposed to "I am; therefore, I exist" by Rene Descartes, the French philosopher who can be said to have summed up the Western philosophy; see John S. Mbiti, *African Religions and Philosophy* (Garden City, NY: Anchor Books, 1970), 108.
23. See Chinua Achebe, *Things Fall Apart* (New York: Fawcett Publications, 1958); Chinua Achebe, *No Longer at Ease* (New York: Fawcett Publications, 1960); Chinua Achebe, *There Was a Country* (New York: Penguin Group, 2012).
24. For more on Chinua Achebe and African humanism, see Emmanuel Edeh, "African Humanism in Achebe in Relation to the West," *Open*

Journal of Philosophy 5 (2015): 205–10, available at http://dx.doi.org/10.4236/ojpp.2015.53025.

25. A key effect of communal life is the deep sense of hospitality, which permeates African social relationship; see Chima J. Korieh and Ugo G. Nwokeji, *Religion, History, and Politics in Nigeria* (New York: University Press of America, 2005), 16.
26. Olusegun Gbadegesin, "Destiny, Personality, and the Ultimate Reality of Human Existence: A Yoruba Perspective," *Ultimate Reality and Meaning* 7, no. 3 (1984): 173–88.
27. Kwame Gyekye, *An Essay on African Philosophical Thought: The Akan Conceptual Scheme* (Philadelphia: Temple University Press, 1995), 144–45.
28. For further readings, see Kofi Asare Opoku, "Communalism and Community in African Heritage," *International Review of Mission* 316 (1990): 487–92; Peter Sarpong, "The Individual, Community, Health, and Medicine in African Traditional Religion: The Asante Model," *Bulletin of the Pontifical Council for Interreligious Dialogue* 84 (1993): 271–80; Julius Gathogo Mutugi, *The Truth About African Hospitality: Is There Hope for Africa?* (Mombasa: The Salt, 2001); and J. Teffo, *The Concept of Ubuntu as a Cohesive Moral Value* (Pretoria: Ubuntu School of Philosophy, 1994).
29. Louw, "*Ubuntu*," 390.
30. See A. Okechukwu Ogbonnaya, *On Communitarian Divinity: An African Interpretation of the Trinity* (Minneapolis: Paragon House, 1998), 10.
31. For an important discussion on African Pentecostal ecclesiology that also incorporates Pauline ecclesiology, see J. Kwabena Asamoah-Gyadu, *Contemporary Pentecostal Christianity: Interpretations From an African Context* (Oxford: Regnum Books, 2013), chapter 1.
32. Ibid., 9, argues that openness is and must be a criterion in defining both human and divine community.
33. Ibid., 61.
34. J. Kwabena Asamoah-Gyadu, *African Charismatics: Current Developments Within Independent Indigenous Pentecostalism in Ghana* (Leiden: E. J. Brill, 2005), 166.
35. Louw, "*Ubuntu*," 390.

36. The African traditional culture has, seemingly, an almost infinite capacity for the pursuit of consensus and reconciliation. Democracy in the African way does not simply boil down to majority rule since it operates in the form of discussions geared toward a consensus. This view is clearly captured by Jesse Mugambi when he says, "The traditional court would appreciate the views of every participant, and weigh the opinions of everyone irrespective of social status. Equally, decisions are reached through consensus, as there is no voting. Whenever there are 'irreconcilable differences,' decision is postponed until a consensus emerges." See Jesse Mugambi, *African Christian Theology: An Introduction* (Nairobi: Heinemann, 1989), 4.
37. This is taken from such biblical passages as Matthew 18:19, which says, "Again I say to you, that if two of you agree on earth about anything they ask, it will be done for them by My Father who is in heaven" (MEV).
38. For an informative discussion on prayers within an African Pentecostal context, see J. Kwabena Asamoah-Gyadu, *Contemporary Pentecostal Christianity: Interpretations From an African Context* (Oxford: Regnum Books, 2013), chapter 3.
39. Louw, "*Ubuntu*," 390.
40. Jabu Sidane, *Ubuntu and Nation Building* (Pretoria: Ubuntu School, 1994), 45.
41. See Mike Oppenheimer, *Chrislam: The Blending Together of Islam and Christianity* (Eureka, MT: Lighthouse Trails, 2013).
42. An example of Chrislam in Nigeria is the Ifeoluwa, which comprises about fifteen hundred adherents, predominantly in Lagos. As in other Chrislamic movements, its followers recognize both the Bible and the Quran as sacred texts and also practice "running deliverance," a distinctive practice of spiritual running likened to Joshua's army circling Jericho or the practice of pilgrims circumambulating a church for Palm Sunday, like Jews around the synagogue during Sukkot.
43. As cited by Paul Gifford, "Healing in African Pentecostalism: The 'Victorious Living' of David Oyedepo," in Candy Gunther Brown, ed., *Global Pentecostal and Charismatic Healing* (Oxford: Oxford University, 2011), 262.
44. The following are scriptural examples of God visiting the enemies of the people of God, which is adopted by African Pentecostals: Leviticus

26:18, Isaiah 13:11, Jeremiah 36:31, Ezekiel 3:17–18, Ezekiel 18:4, Ezekiel 18:20, and Zechariah 9.

45. Pray for Nigeria, "Call to Pray for Nigeria," accessed March 16, 2015, http://www.pray4nigeria.org/index.php?option=com_content&view=article&id=295&Itemid=255.
46. Laurenti Magesa, *African Religion: The Moral Traditions of Abundant Life* (Maryknoll, NY: Orbis Books, 1997), 197–98; John S. Mbiti, *African Religions and Philosophy* (Garden City, NY: Anchor Books, 1970), 61.
47. Pentecostal Fellowship of Nigeria, "Year of Prayer for Nigeria: Thirty-One Day Prayer Guide," 16, accessed February 22, 2016, http://www.pray4nigeria.org/images/PFN%20PRAYER%20GUIDE.pdf.
48. Albert Haase, *Living the Lord's Prayer* (Downers Grove, IL: InterVarsity Press, 2009), 38.
49. Antjie Krog, "This Thing Called Reconciliation . . . : Forgiveness as Part of an Interconnectedness-Towards-Wholeness," *South African Journal of Philosophy* 27, no. 4 (2008): 353.
50. Desmond Tutu, as quoted at Greater Good Science Center, "Truth and Reconciliation," September 1, 2004, accessed February 22, 2016, http://greatergood.berkeley.edu/article/item/truth_and_reconciliation.
51. For a useful contribution to this issue, see Martin Mittelstadt and Geoffrey Sutton, eds., *Forgiveness, Reconciliation, and Restoration: Multidisciplinary Studies From a Pentecostal Perspective* (Eugene, OR: Wipf and Stock, 2010); see also Allan Anderson, "The Holy Spirit, Healing, and Reconciliation Issues at Athens 2005," *International Review of Mission* 94, no. 374 (2005): 332–42.
52. Some useful sources on healing in Africa are Gunther Brown, *Global Pentecostal and Charismatic Healing*, part 3; J. Kwabena Asamoah-Gyadu, *African Charismatics: Current Developments Within Independent Indigenous Pentecostalism in Ghana* (Leiden: E. J. Brill, 2005), particularly chapter 6; and Clifton Clarke, *African Christology: Jesus in Post-Missionary African Christianity* (Eugene, OR: Wipf and Stock, 2011), chapter 7.
53. See http://wowwi.org for further information about this organization.
54. H. B. Yusuf, "Managing Muslim-Christian Conflicts in Northern Nigeria: A Case Study of Kaduna State," *Islam and Christian-Muslim Relations* 18, no. 2 (2007): 237–56, especially 252–55.

55. For more information on religious pluralism and symbolism, see my "Dialogue or Diatribe: Towards a Renewal Approach to Interreligious Conversation," in Clifton Clarke and Amos Yong, eds., *Global Renewal, Religious Pluralism, and the Great Commission: Towards a Renewal Theology of Mission and Interreligious Encounter* (Lexington, KY: Emth Press, 2011), chapter 1, especially pages 34–46.
56. Akinade, *Christian Responses*, 134.
57. Charles Amjad-Ali, "Theological and Historical Rationality Behind Christian-Muslim Relations," in J. P. Rajashekar and H. S. Wilson, eds., *Islam in Asia: Perspectives for Christian-Muslim Encounter* (Geneva: Lutheran World Federation, 1992), 14.
58. Ibid., 7–8.
59. Akintunde E. Akinade, "The Precarious Agenda: Christian-Muslim Relations in Contemporary Nigeria," lecture given at High Point University, High Point, North Carolina, summer 2002, accessed July 22, 2015, http://www.hartsem.edu/wp-content/uploads/Akinade.pdf.

Chapter 20
The Deregulation of Piety in the Context of Neoliberal Globalization: African Pentecostalisms in the Twenty-First Century

1. Richard Dowden, *Africa: Altered States, Ordinary Miracles* (London: Portobello Books, 2008), 3.
2. Dean Hamer, *The God Gene: How Faith Is Hardwired Into Our Genes* (New York: Anchor Books, 2004), 57.
3. John S. Mbiti, *African Religions and Philosophy* (Garden City, NY: Anchor Books, 1970), 1.
4. Ogbu U. Kalu, *African Pentecostalism: An Introduction* (Oxford: Oxford University Press, 2008), 3–12; Ogbu Kalu, "Who Is Afraid of the Holy Ghost? Presbyterians and Early Charismatic Movement in Nigeria, 1966–1975," in Afe Adogame, ed., *Who Is Afraid of the Holy Ghost? Pentecostalism and Globalization in Africa and Beyond* (Trenton, NJ: Africa World Press, 2011), 83–109; Ole Aleksander Østhassel, "Africa Pentecostalized? Understanding the African Appropriation of Pentecostalism in Light of African Perspectives" (MA thesis, MF Norwegian School of Theology, 2013), 89.

5. Allan Anderson, *Spreading Fires: The Missionary Nature of Early Pentecostalism* (Maryknoll, NY: Orbis Books, 2007), 151.
6. J. Kwabena Asamoah-Gyadu, *Contemporary Pentecostal Christianity: Interpretations From an African Context* (Oxford: Regnum Books, 2013), 1.
7. See, for example, Ogbu Kalu, *African Pentecostalism: An Introduction*, and Nimi Warioko, *Nigerian Pentecostalism* (Rochester, NY: University of Rochester Press, 2014).
8. Douglas Jacobsen, *The World's Christians: Who They Are, Where They Are, and How They Got There* (West Sussex, UK: Wiley-Blackwell, 2011), 50.
9. Ibid., 51.
10. Allan Anderson, *An Introduction to Pentecostalism* (Cambridge: Cambridge University Press, 2004), 103.
11. See the documentary film by James Ault, *African Christianity Rising: Christianity's Explosive Growth in Africa* (Worcester, PA: Vision Video, 2013).
12. In this discussion, *Pentecostalism(s)* is used interchangeably with *Charismatic Christianity* and will represent all the subsets, such as *neo-Pentecostal* and *neo-Charismatic Christians*.
13. Jacobsen, *The World's Christians*, 50.
14. Gbolahan Olukayode Akinsanya, "'You Shall Receive Power': The Establishment of the Pentecostal Movement in the Nigerian Context" (PhD dissertation, Drew University, 2000).
15. Allan Anderson, *Zion and Pentecost: The Spirituality and Experience of Pentecostal and Zionist/Apostolic Churches in South Africa* (Pretoria: University of South Africa Press, 2000), 4.
16. Robert Mbe Akoko, *"Ask and You Shall Be Given": Pentecostalism and the Economic Crisis in Cameroon* (Leiden: African Studies Centre, 2007), 1–7.
17. See Leonardo Blair, "South African Pastor Makes Members Eat Grass; Watch Him Command Demon Out of Woman's Stomach," Christian Post, January 9 2014, accessed December 24, 2015, http://www.christianpost.com/news/south-african-pastor-makes-members-eat-grass-watch-him-command-demon-out-of-womans-stomach-112320/.

18. Mpho Raborife, "South Africa: Pretoria Church Goes Viral Over Snake-Eating," News24, July 15, 2015, accessed December 17, 2015, http://allafrica.com/stories/201507151900.html.
19. Nimi Wariboko, *Nigerian Pentecostalism* (Rochester, NY: University of Rochester, 2014), 1.
20. Martin Meredith, *The State of Africa: A History of the Continent Since Independence*, rev. ed., (Johannesburg: Jonathan Ball Publishers, 2011), 687.
21. Toyin Falola and Matthew M. Heaton, *A History of Nigeria* (Cambridge: Cambridge University Press, 2008), 217.
22. A. Olalekan Dairo, "Privatization and Commercialization of Christian Message," in Akintunde Akinade and David O. Ogungbile, eds., *Creativity and Change in Nigerian Christianity* (Lagos: Malthouse Press, 2010), 192.
23. William Davies, "The Democratic Critique of Neo-Liberalism," *Renewal* 23, no. 3 (2015): 88.
24. Cited in Stuart Hall, "The Neoliberal Revolution," in Sally Davison and Katharine Harris, eds., *The Neo-Liberal Crisis* (London: Lawrence & Wishart Ltd., 2015), 13; see also Stuart Hall, Doreen Massey, and Michael Rustin, "After Neoliberalism: Analysing the Present," framing statement in Stuart Hall, Doreen Massey, and Michael Rustin, eds., *After Neoliberalism? The Kilburn Manifesto* (London: Lawrence & Wishart Ltd., 2015), 9–23.
25. Sasha Newell, "Pentecostal Witchcraft: Neoliberal Possession and Demonic Discourse in Ivoirian Pentecostal Churches," *Journal of Religion in Africa* 37 (2007): 463.
26. See Christian B. N. Gada, "The Historical Development of the Written Discourse on *Ubuntu*," *South African Journal of Philosophy* 30, no. 3 (2011): 303–29. Gada quotes a Nguni proverb that encapsulates the *ubuntu* philosophy: *umuntu ngumuntu ngabantu* (often translated as "A person is a person through other persons"). The Yoruba of West Africa have a similar saying, *Eniyan l'asoo mi*, which is translated as "The people are the center of my cosmos." See also Clifton Clarke's chapter in this volume.
27. Andreas Heuser, "Religio-Scapes of Prosperity Gospel: An Introduction," in Andreas Heuser, ed., *Pastures of Plenty: Tracing Religio-Scapes*

of Prosperity Gospel in Africa and Beyond (Frankfurt am Main: Peter Lang, 2015), 18.

28. Asonzeh Ukah, "Re-Imagining the Religious Fields: The Rhetoric of Nigerian Pentecostal Pastors in South Africa," in Magnus Echtler and Asonzeh Ukah, eds., *Bourdieu in Africa: Exploring the Dynamics of Religious Fields*, Studies of Religion in Africa, no. 44 (Leiden: Brill, 2016), 70–95.
29. J. Kwabena Asamoah-Gyadu, "Of Faith and Visual Alertness: The Message of 'Mediatized' Religion in an African Pentecostal Context," *Material Religion* 1, no. 3 (2006): 343, emphasis added.
30. Harvey Cox, *Fire From Heaven: Pentecostalism and the Reshaping of Spirituality in the Twenty-First Century* (De Capo, MA: Addison-Wesley, 1995), 243–62; Philip Jenkins, *The New Face of Christianity: Believing the Bible in the Global South* (Oxford: Oxford University Press, 2006), 92–93.
31. Jehu J. Hanciles, *Beyond Christendom: Globalization, African Migration, and the Transformation of the West* (Maryknoll, NY: Orbis Books, 2008), 129.
32. Zygmunt Bauman, *Liquid Modernity* (Cambridge: Polity Press, 2000), 1.
33. Jacobsen, *The World's Christians*, 50–51.
34. Matthews A. Ojo, *Of Saints and Sinners: Pentecostalism and the Paradox of Social Transformation in Northern Nigeria* (Ile-Ife, Nigeria: Obafeni Awolowo University Press, 2010), 27.
35. Ibid., 25–31. Ojo refines these six groups in his "Pentecostal and Charismatic Movements in Modern Africa," in Elias Kifon Bongmba, ed., *The Wiley-Blackwell Companion to African Religions* (New York: Blackwell Publishers, 2012), 304–5.
36. Paul Gifford, "Evangelical Christianity and Democracy in Africa: A Response," in Terence O. Ranger, ed., *Evangelical Christianity and Democracy in Africa* (Oxford: Oxford University Press, 2008), 227.
37. Jacobsen, *The World's Christians*, 50.
38. Paul Gifford, "Evangelical Christianity and Democracy in Africa," 227.
39. To claim African Pentecostals are "faith seekers" or "faith builders" is yet another version of Mbiti's "Africans are notoriously religious" trope.
40. David T. Ngong, "Christianity in Africa," Bongmba, ed., *The Wiley-Blackwell Companion to African Religions*, 208–9.

41. Martin Riesebrodt, *The Promise of Salvation: A Theory of Religion*, trans. Steven Rendall (Chicago: University of Chicago Press, 2010), xiii.
42. Birgit Meyer, *Sensational Movies: Video, Vision, and Christianity in Ghana* (Berkeley, CA: University of California Press, 2015).
43. Godwin Onuoha, "'Exit' and 'Inclusion': The Changing Paradigm of Pentecostal Expression in the Nigerian Public Space," in Irene Becci, Marian Burchardt, and José Casanova, eds., *Topographies of Faith: Religion in Urban Spaces* (Leiden: Brill, 2013), 218; David Morgan, *The Forge of Vision: A Visual History of Modern Christianity* (Berkeley, CA: University of California Press, 2015), 98–104; Masiiwa Ragies Gunda and Francis Machingura, "The 'Man of God,'" in Ezra Chitando, Masiiwa Gunda, and Joachim Kügler, eds., *Prophets, Profits, and the Bible in Zimbabwe* (Bamberg, Germany: University of Bamberg Press, 2013), 16.
44. Asonzeh Ukah, *A New Paradigm of Pentecostal Power: A Study of the Redeemed Christian Church of God in Nigeria* (Trenton, NJ: Africa World Press, 2008), 145–64; and Asonzeh Ukah, "God, Wealth, and the Spirit of Investment: Prosperity Pentecostalism in Africa," in Peter Smith and Sabine Dreher, eds., *Religious Activism in the Global Economy: Promoting, Reforming, or Resisting Neoliberal Globalization?* (London: Rowman & Littlefield International Publishers, 2016), 73–90.
45. It is possible to subsume all African Pentecostal churches into four headings of 1) teaching, 2) healing, 3) deliverance, and 4) prosperity/success. Of these, the least socially significant and visible is the first, teaching. Increasingly, belief is being relegated to the background; leaders and practitioners prioritize practice, performance, productivity, and deliverables.
46. See Riesebrodt, *The Promise of Salvation*.
47. There are more specializations, such as those religious leaders who claim to provide babies for those who are experiencing difficulty having babies. Others claim to provide spouses for those seeking them, and others divine the fore or supply prophecy.
48. Magnus Echtler and Asonzeh Ukah, "Introduction: Exploring the Dynamics of Religious Fields in Africa," in Echtler and Ukah, *Bourdieu in Africa*, 1–32. On the advantages of specialization of the labor force, see Adam Smith, *The Wealth of Nations* (1776; reprint, New York: Bantam Classic, 2003), 9.

49. Jane E. Soothill, *Gender, Social Change, and Spiritual Power: Charismatic Christianity in Ghana* (Leiden: Brill, 2007), 154–79.
50. Adriaan S. Van Klinken, *Transforming Masculinities in African Christianity: Gender Controversies in Times of AIDS* (Surrey: Ashgate Publishers, 2013), especially chapter 4; see also Asonzeh Ukah, "Sexual Bodies, Sacred Vessels: Pentecostal Discourses on Homosexuality in Nigeria," in Ezra Chitando and Adriaan van Klinken, eds., *Christianity and Controversies Over Homosexuality in Contemporary Africa* (Surrey: Ashgate Publishers, 2016), 21–37.
51. Many African Pentecostal leaders have aligned themselves with corrupt political actors—for example, in Zambia and Nigeria—to form an elite group of predators who use public resources for private gain and whose actions concentrate wealth in the hands of a few leaders. Their actions have reduced African Pentecostal ideals to "rhetorical devices to legitimate political hegemony, clerical indulgence, and antidemocratic governance structure... by ecclesiastical elites" (Wariboko, *Nigerian Pentecostalism*, 55).
52. So much more can be said here about the factors that restrain the effectiveness of African Pentecostalisms as a transformative ideology and practice. The focus on mystical sources of wealth and causality, the uncritical adoption of neoliberal market principles and practices, corporate-style religious empires built on the engine of profitmaking and charismatic personalities, personal conversion and personal empowerment/success, private accumulation, consumerism and endless schisms, and scandals and an absence of a quality-control system within the movement vitiate the transformative force of African Pentecostalisms. Samuel Zalanga and Amos Yong provide a similar list of five factors that attenuate the force of Pentecostal engagement with the capitalist empire in Africa; see their "What Empire? Which Multitude? Pentecostalism and Social Liberation in North America and Sub-Saharan Africa," in Bruce Ellis Benson and Peter Goodwin Heltzel, eds., *Evangelicals and Empire: Christian Alternatives to the Political Status Quo* (Grand Rapids, MI: Brazos Press, 2008), 237–51. See also Rosalind I. J. Hackett, "The Gospel of Prosperity in West Africa," in Richard H. Roberts, ed., *Religion and the Transformations of Capitalism* (New York: Routledge, 1995), 200–14; Dena Freeman, ed., *Pentecostalism and Development: Churches, NGOs, and Social Change in Africa*

(Basingstoke: Palgrave Macmillan, 2012); and Katherine Attanasi and Amos Yong, eds., *Pentecostalism and Prosperity: The Socio-Economics of the Global Charismatic Movement* (New York: Palgrave Macmillan, 2012).

Chapter 21
Foreign on Own Home Front? Ruminations From an African-South African Pentecostal Biblical Scholar

1. Timothy K. Beal, "Tracing Esther's Beginnings," in Athalya Brenner, ed., *A Feminist Companion to Esther, Judith, and Susana* (Sheffield: Sheffield Academic Press, 1995), 87–110; Michael V. Fox, *Character and Ideology in the Book of Esther* (Columbia: University of South Carolina, 1991).
2. Madipoane Masenya (ngwan'a Mphahlele), "Their Hermeneutics Was Strange! Ours Is a Necessity! Rereading Vashti as African-South African Women," in Caroline Vander Stichele and Todd Penner, eds., *Her Master's Tools? Feminist and Postcolonial Engagements of Historical-Critical Discourse* (Atlanta: SBL, 2005), 191; in the article cited in the footnote, as well as in this essay/chapter you are reading, I use the phrase "African-South African" to refer to the indigenous peoples of South Africa such as the Sothos, Ndebeles, Vendas, Tsongas, Xhosas and Zulus (I belong to the Northern Sotho ethnic group).
3. Madipoane Masenya (ngwan'a Mphahlele), "'. . . But You Shall Let Every Girl Live': Reading Exodus 1:1–2:10 the Bosadi (Womanhood) Way," *Old Testament Essays* 15 (2002): 99–112.
4. According to Oduyoye, "The language of marriage proverbs indicates that a wife only reflects the stage of the marriage and a man's competence as a husband. . . . *Society demands that she stays married, because a woman has no dignity outside marriage*"; Mercy A. Oduyoye, *Daughters of Anowa: African Women and Patriarchy* (Maryknoll, NY: Orbis, 1995), 68; emphasis added. Tapiwa Mapurunga points to the need for such an identity in the Zimbabwean context when she argues, "A woman's fertility and her marital status are the source of her social identity, and marriage provides women with economic and social support that would not be available to them if they were single"; Tapiwa Mapurunga, "'Tozeza Baba': Gender-Based Violence in Oliver Mtukudzi's Music," *Journal of Music Research in Africa* 9, no. 1 (2012): 63. The Northern

Sotho proverb "*Lebitla la mosadi ke bogadi*" ("A woman's grave belongs to her husband's home village") also points in the direction that, traditionally, each woman was expected to marry.

5. As quoted by Oduyoye, *Daughters of Anowa*, 67.
6. Such a concern for the spiritual upliftment of a believer by a university offering such as biblical studies would be revealed by the question I would later be asked by a fellow Christian believer: "Sister, as you continue to study the Bible in a more deeper way, are you not scared that the more you would know more about the Bible, the more the possibility of eventually losing your faith?" Already then, I knew what the friend was talking about even as, indeed, during my second year of studying biblical studies, I wondered whether I had not committed a grievous mistake!
7. Madipoane Masenya (ngwan'a Mphahlele), "Teaching Western-Oriented Old Testament Studies to African Students: An Exercise in Wisdom or in Folly?" *Old Testament Essays* 17, no. 3 (2004): 455–69.
8. An exhortation from professor J. J. Burden, my study leader for my doctoral program. The main argument behind such an exhortation was that if the Bible were to be elevated almost to the status of God, one would be in serious trouble, particularly in terms of one's faith in God if the Bible were to be severely criticized.
9. Walter Brueggemann, *The Bible and Post-Modern Imagination* (London: SCM, 1993), 8.
10. Musa W. Dube, *Postcolonial Feminist Interpretations of the Bible* (St. Louis, MO: Chalice, 2001).
11. Madipoane Masenya (ngwan'a Mphahlele), *How Worthy Is the Woman of Worth? Rereading Proverbs 31:10–31 in African-South Africa* (New York: Peter Lang, 2004).
12. Madipoane Masenya (ngwan'a Mphahlele), "Invisible Exiles? An African South African Woman's Reconfiguration of Exile in Jeremiah 21:1–10," *Old Testament Essays* 20, no. 3 (2007): 756–71.
13. Masenya, "Teaching Western-Oriented Old Testament Studies to African Students," 460.
14. In his study on the management of training of pastors in the colleges of the International Assemblies of God Church of South Africa, Malesela J. Masenya also cautions about the need to create a balance

when he argues, "Apart from ministry being a noble calling, there is a need for church leaders who will not be concerned with the spiritual development of members only, but also keen to help resolve the many challenges facing communities today." See Malesela J. Masenya, "Re-Envisioning Management Training of Pastors in the Colleges of the International Assemblies of God Church (IAG) of South Africa" (D.Ed. thesis, University of South Africa, 2014), 154.

15. Madipoane Masenya (ngwan'a Mphahlele), "For Better or Worse? The (Christian) Bible and Africana Women," *Old Testament Essays* 22, no. 1 (2009): 140; see also Sarojini Nadar, "On Being the Pentecostal Church: Pentecostal Women's Voices and Visions," in Isabel A. Phiri and Sarojini Nadar, eds., *On Being Church: African Women's Voices and Visions* (Geneva: World Council of Churches, 2005), 60–79.
16. For more on how the preceding proverb was used as a hermeneutical lens to read the Vashti character, refer to Madipoane Masenya (ngwan'a Mphahlele), "A Small Herb Increases Itself (Impact) by a Strong Odor: Reimagining Vashti in Esther 1 in an African-South African Context," *Old Testament Essays* 16, no. 2 (2003): 332–42.

Index

A

B

C

D

E

F

G

H

I

J

K

L

M

N

O

P

Q

R

S

T

W

X

Y

Z